Discrete Choice Methods with Simulation

Copy Chap 2-6 ✓

scan → Train2.pdf ✓

" 6

Copied 7-10 ✓

Scanned

his teaching and research.

Additional Praise for *Discrete Choice Methods with Simulation*

"Ken Train's book provides outstanding coverage of the most advanced elements of the estimation and usage of discrete choice models that require simulation to take account of randomness in the population under study. His writing is clear and understandable providing both the new and experienced reader with excellent insights into and understanding of all aspects of these new and increasingly important methods."
– Frank S. Koppelman, *Northwestern University*

"This is a masterful book, authored by one of the leading contributors to discrete choice methods and analysis. No other book covers this ground with such up-to-date detail in respect of theory and implementation. The chapters on simulation and recent developments such as mixed logit are most lucid. As a text or reference work this volume should have currency for a long time. It will appeal to the practitioner as much as to the specialist researcher who has been in this field for many years."
– David Hensher, *The University of Sydney*

"Simulation-based estimation is a major advance in econometrics and discrete choice modeling. The technique has revolutionized both classical and Bayesian analysis. Ken Train's many papers have made a large contribution to this literature. *Discrete Choice Methods with Simulation* collects these results in a comprehensive, up-to-date source, with chapters on behavioral foundations, theoretical and practical aspects of estimation and a variety of applications. This book is a thoroughly enjoyable blend of theory, analysis, and case studies; it is a complete reference for developers and practitioners."
– William Greene, *New York University*

Discrete Choice Methods with Simulation

Kenneth E. Train

University of California, Berkeley
and
National Economic Research Associates, Inc.

CAMBRIDGE UNIVERSITY PRESS
Cambridge, New York, Melbourne, Madrid, Cape Town, Singapore, São Paulo

Cambridge University Press
32 Avenue of the Americas, New York, NY 10013-2473, USA

www.cambridge.org
Information on this title: www.cambridge.org/9780521816960

First published 2003
Reprinted 2005, 2006, 2007

Printed in the United States of America

A catalog record for this publication is available from the British Library.

Library of Congress Cataloging in Publication Data

Train, Kenneth.
Discrete choice methods with simulation / Kenneth E. Train.
    p.   cm.
Includes bibliographical references and index.
ISBN 0-521-81696-3 – ISBN 0-521-01715-7 (pb.)
1. Decision making – Simulation methods.   2. Consumers' preferences –
Simulation methods.   I. Title.
HD30.23 .T725   2003
003′.56–dc21   2002071479

ISBN   978-0-521-81696-0 hardback
ISBN   978-0-521-01715-2 paperback

Contents

Truncated choice

Multiple hurdle

W 3-5

To
Daniel McFadden
and
in memory of
Kenneth Train, Sr.

1 Introduction

1.1 Motivation

When I wrote my first book, *Qualitative Choice Analysis*, in the mid-1980s, the field had reached a critical juncture. The breakthrough concepts that defined the field had been made. The basic models – mainly logit and nested logit – had been introduced, and the statistical and economic properties of these models had been derived. Applications had proven successful in many different areas, including transportation, energy, housing, and marketing – to name only a few.

The field is at a similar juncture today for a new generation of procedures. The first-generation models contained important limitations that inhibited their applicability and realism. These limitations were well recognized at the time, but ways to overcome them had not yet been discovered. Over the past twenty years, tremendous progress has been made, leading to what can only be called a sea change in the approach and methods of choice analysis. The early models have now been supplemented by a variety of more powerful and more flexible methods. The new concepts have arisen gradually, with researchers building on the work of others. However, in a sense, the change has been more like a quantum leap than a gradual progression. The way that researchers think about, specify, and estimate their models has changed. Importantly, a kind of consensus, or understanding, seems to have emerged about the new methodology. Among researchers working in the field, a definite sense of purpose and progress prevails.

My purpose in writing this new book is to bring these ideas together, in a form that exemplifies the unity of approach that I feel has emerged, and in a format that makes the methods accessible to a wide audience. The advances have mostly centered on simulation. Essentially, simulation is the researcher's response to the inability of computers to perform integration. Stated more precisely, simulation provides a numerical approximation to integrals, with different methods offering different properties and being applicable to different kinds of integrands.

Simulation allows estimation of otherwise intractable models. Practically any model can be estimated by some form of simulation. The researcher is therefore freed from previous constraints on model specification – constraints that reflected mathematical convenience rather than the economic reality of the situation. This new flexibility is a tremendous boon to research. It allows more realistic representation of the hugely varied choice situations that arise in the world. It enables the researcher to obtain more information from any given dataset and, in many cases, allows previously unapproachable issues to be addressed.

This flexibility places a new burden on the researcher. First, the methods themselves are more complicated than earlier ones and utilize many concepts and procedures that are not covered in standard econometrics courses. Understanding the various techniques – their advantages and limitations, and the relations among them – is important when choosing the appropriate method in any particular application and for developing new methods when none of the existing models seems right. The purpose of this book is to assist readers along this path.

Second, to implement a new method or a variant on an old method, the researcher needs to be able to program the procedure into computer software. This means that the researcher will often need to know how maximum likelihood and other estimation methods work from a computational perspective, how to code specific models, and how to take existing code and change it to represent variations in behavior. Some models, such as mixed logit and pure probit (in addition, of course, to standard logit), are available in commercially available statistical packages. In fact, code for these and other models, as well as manuals and sample data, are available (free) at my website http://elsa.berkeley.edu/~train. Whenever appropriate, researchers should use available codes rather than writing their own. However, the true value of the new approach to choice modeling is the ability to create tailor-made models. The computational and programming steps that are needed to implement a new model are usually not difficult. An important goal of the book is to teach these skills as an integral part of the exposition of the models themselves. I personally find programming to be extremely valuable pedagogically. The process of coding a model helps me to understand how exactly the model operates, the reasons and implications of its structure, what features constitute the essential elements that cannot be changed while maintaining the basic approach, and what features are arbitrary and can easily be changed. I imagine other people learn this way too.

1.2   Choice Probabilities and Integration

To focus ideas, I will now establish the conceptual basis for discrete choice models and show where integration comes into play. An agent (i.e., person, firm, decision maker) faces a choice, or a series of choices over time, among a set of options. For example, a customer chooses which of several competing products to buy; a firm decides which technology to use in production; a student chooses which answer to give on a multiple-choice test; a survey respondent chooses an integer between 1 and 5 on a Likert-scale question; a worker chooses whether to continue working each year or retire. Denote the outcome of the decision(s) in any given situation as y, indicating the chosen option or sequence of options. We assume for the purposes of this book that the outcome variable is discrete in that it takes a countable number of values. Many of the concepts that we describe are easily transferable to situations where the outcome variable is continuous. However, notation and terminology are different with continuous outcome variables than with discrete ones. Also, discrete choices generally reveal less information about the choice process than continuous-outcome choices, so that the econometrics of discrete choice is usually more challenging.

Our goal is to understand the behavioral process that leads to the agent's choice. We take a causal perspective. There are factors that collectively determine, or cause, the agent's choice. Some of these factors are observed by the researcher and some are not. The observed factors are labeled x, and the unobserved factors ε. The factors relate to the agent's choice through a function $y = h(x, \varepsilon)$. This function is called the behavioral process. It is deterministic in the sense that given x and ε, the choice of the agent is fully determined.

Since ε is not observed, the agent's choice is not deterministic and cannot be predicted exactly. Instead, the *probability* of any particular outcome is derived. The unobserved terms are considered random with density $f(\varepsilon)$. The probability that the agent chooses a particular outcome from the set of all possible outcomes is simply the probability that the unobserved factors are such that the behavioral process results in that outcome: $P(y \mid x) = \text{Prob}(\varepsilon \text{ s.t. } h(x, \varepsilon) = y)$.

We can express this probability in a more usable form. Define an indicator function $I[h(x, \varepsilon) = y]$ that takes the value of 1 when the statement in brackets is true and 0 when the statement is false. That is, $I[\cdot] = 1$ if the value of ε, combined with x, induces the agent to choose outcome y, and $I[\cdot] = 0$ if the value of ε, combined with x, induces the agent to choose some other outcome. Then the probability that the agent chooses outcome y is simply the expected value of this indicator function, where the expectation is over all possible values of the unobserved factors:

$$P(y \mid x) = \text{Prob}(I[h(x, \varepsilon) = y] = 1)$$

(1.1)
$$= \int I[h(x, \varepsilon) = y] f(\varepsilon) \, d\varepsilon.$$

Stated in this form, the probability is an integral – specifically an integral of an indicator for the outcome of the behavioral process over all possible values of the unobserved factors.

To calculate this probability, the integral must be evaluated. There are three possibilities.

1.2.1. Complete Closed-Form Expression

For certain specifications of h and f, the integral can be expressed in closed form. In these cases, the choice probability can be calculated exactly from the closed-form formula. For example, consider a binary logit model of whether or not a person takes a given action, such as buying a new product. The behavioral model is specified as follows. The person would obtain some net benefit, or utility, from taking the action. This utility, which can be either positive or negative, consists of a part that is observed by the researcher, $\beta'x$, where x is a vector of variables and β is a vector of parameters, and a part that is not observed, ε: $U = \beta'x + \varepsilon$. The person takes the action only if the utility is positive, that is, only if doing so provides a net benefit. The probability that the person takes the action, given what the researcher can observe, is therefore $P = \int I[\beta'x + \varepsilon > 0] f(\varepsilon) \, d\varepsilon$, where f is the density of ε. Assume that ε is distributed logistically, such that its density is $f(\varepsilon) = e^{-\varepsilon}/(1 + e^{-\varepsilon})^2$ with cumulative distribution $F(\varepsilon) = 1/(1 + e^{-\varepsilon})$. Then the probability of the person taking the action is

$$P = \int I[\beta'x + \varepsilon > 0] f(\varepsilon) \, d\varepsilon$$

$$= \int I[\varepsilon > -\beta'x] f(\varepsilon) \, d\varepsilon$$

$$= \int_{\varepsilon = -\beta'x}^{\infty} f(\varepsilon) \, d\varepsilon$$

$$= 1 - F(-\beta'x) = 1 - \frac{1}{1 + e^{\beta'x}}$$

$$= \frac{e^{\beta'x}}{1 + e^{\beta'x}}.$$

For any x, the probability can be calculated exactly as $P = \exp(\beta'x)/(1 + \exp(\beta'x))$.

Other models also have closed-form expressions for the probabilities. Multinomial logit (in Chapter 3), nested logit (Chapter 4), and ordered logit (Chapter 7) are prominent examples. The methods that I described in my first book and that served as the basis for the first wave of interest in discrete choice analysis relied almost exclusively on models with closed-form expressions for the choice probabilities. In general, however, the integral for probabilities cannot be expressed in closed form. More to the point, restrictions must be placed on the behavioral model h and the distribution of random terms f in order for the integral to take a closed form. These restrictions can make the models unrealistic for many situations.

1.2.2. Complete Simulation

Rather than solve the integral analytically, it can be approximated through simulation. Simulation is applicable in one form or another to practically any specification of h and f. Simulation relies on the fact that integration over a density is a form of averaging. Consider the integral $\bar{t} = \int t(\varepsilon)f(\varepsilon)\,d\varepsilon$, where $t(\varepsilon)$ is a statistic based on ε which has density $f(\varepsilon)$. This integral is the expected value of t over all possible values of ε. This average can be approximated in an intuitively straightforward way. Take numerous draws of ε from its distribution f, calculate $t(\varepsilon)$ for each draw, and average the results. This simulated average is an unbiased estimate of the true average. It approaches the true average as more and more draws are used in the simulation.

This concept of simulating an average is the basis for all simulation methods, at least all of those that we consider in this book. As given in equation (1.1), the probability of a particular outcome is an average of the indicator $I(\cdot)$ over all possible values of ε. The probability, when expressed in this form, can be simulated directly as follows:

1. Take a draw of ε from $f(\varepsilon)$. Label this draw ε^1, where the superscript denotes that it is the first draw.
2. Determine whether $h(x, \varepsilon^1) = y$ with this value of ε. If so, create $I^1 = 1$; otherwise set $I^1 = 0$.
3. Repeat steps 1 and 2 many times, for a total of R draws. The indicator for each draw is labeled I^r for $r = 1, \ldots, R$.
4. Calculate the average of the I^r's. This average is the simulated probability: $\check{P}(y \mid x) = \frac{1}{R}\sum_{r=1}^{R} I^r$. It is the proportion of times that the draws of the unobserved factors, when combined with the observed variables x, result in outcome y.

As we will see in the chapters to follow, this simulator, while easy to understand, has some unfortunate properties. Choice probabilities can often be expressed as averages of other statistics, rather than the average of an indicator function. The simulators based on these other statistics are calculated analogously, by taking draws from the density, calculating the statistic, and averaging the results. Probit (in Chapter 5) is the most prominent example of a model estimated by complete simulation. Various methods of simulating the probit probabilities have been developed based on averages of various statistics over various (related) densities.

1.2.3. Partial Simulation, Partial Closed Form

So far we have provided two polar extremes: either solve the integral analytically or simulate it. In many situations, it is possible to do some of both.

Suppose the random terms can be decomposed into two parts labeled ε_1 and ε_2. Let the joint density of ε_1 and ε_2 be $f(\varepsilon) = f(\varepsilon_1, \varepsilon_2)$. The joint density can be expressed as the product of a marginal and a conditional density: $f(\varepsilon_1, \varepsilon_2) = f(\varepsilon_2 \mid \varepsilon_1) \cdot f(\varepsilon_1)$. With this decomposition, the probability in equation (1.1) can be expressed as

$$P(y \mid x) = \int I[h(x, \varepsilon) = y] f(\varepsilon) \, d\varepsilon$$

$$= \int_{\varepsilon_1} \left[\int_{\varepsilon_2} I[h(x, \varepsilon_1, \varepsilon_2) = y] f(\varepsilon_2 \mid \varepsilon_1) \, d\varepsilon_2 \right] f(\varepsilon_1) \, d\varepsilon_1.$$

Now suppose that a closed form exists for the integral in large brackets. Label this formula $g(\varepsilon_1) \equiv \int_{\varepsilon_2} I[h(x, \varepsilon_1, \varepsilon_2) = y] f(\varepsilon_2 \mid \varepsilon_1) \, d\varepsilon_2$, which is conditional on the value of ε_1. The probability then becomes $P(y \mid x) = \int_{\varepsilon_1} g(\varepsilon_1) f(\varepsilon_1) \, d\varepsilon_1$. If a closed-form solution does not exist for this integral, then it is approximated through simulation. Note that it is simply the average of g over the marginal density of ε_1. The probability is simulated by taking draws from $f(\varepsilon_1)$, calculating $g(\varepsilon_1)$ for each draw, and averaging the results.

This procedure is called *convenient error partitioning* (Train, 1995). The integral over ε_2 given ε_1 is calculated exactly, while the integral over ε_1 is simulated. There are clear advantages to this approach over complete simulation. Analytic integrals are both more accurate and easier to calculate than simulated integrals. It is useful, therefore, when possible, to decompose the random terms so that some of them can be integrated analytically, even if the rest must be simulated. Mixed logit (in Chapter 6) is a prominent example of a model that uses this decomposition effectively. Other examples include Gourieroux and Monfort's (1993) binary probit model on panel data and Bhat's (1999) analysis of ordered responses.

1.3   Outline of Book

Discrete choice analysis consists of two interrelated tasks: specification of the behavioral model and estimation of the parameters of that model. Simulation plays a part in both tasks. Simulation allows the researcher to approximate the choice probabilities that arise in the behavioral model. As we have stated, the ability to use simulation frees the researcher to specify models without the constraint that the resulting probabilities must have a closed form. Simulation also enters the estimation task. The properties of an estimator, such as maximum likelihood, can change when simulated probabilities are used instead of the actual probabilities. Understanding these changes, and mitigating any ill effects, is important for a researcher. In some cases, such as with Bayesian procedures, the estimator itself is an integral over a density (as opposed to the choice probability being an integral). Simulation allows these estimators to be implemented even when the integral that defines the estimator does not take a closed form.

The book is organized around these two tasks. Part I describes behavioral models that have been proposed to describe the choice process. The chapters in this section move from the simplest model, logit, to progressively more general and consequently more complex models. A chapter is devoted to each of the following: logit, the family of generalized extreme value models (whose most prominent member is nested logit), probit, and mixed logit. This part of the book ends with a chapter titled "Variations on a Theme," which covers a variety of models that build upon the concepts in the previous chapters. The point of this chapter is more than simply to introduce various new models. The chapter illustrates the underlying concept of the book, namely, that researchers need not rely on the few common specifications that have been programmed into software but can design models that reflect the unique setting, data, and goals of their project, writing their own software and using simulation as needed.

Part II describes estimation of the behavioral models. Numerical maximization is covered first, since most estimation procedures involve maximization of some function, such as the log-likelihood function. We then describe procedures for taking draws from various kinds of densities, which are the basis for simulation. This chapter also describes different kinds of draws, including antithetic variants and quasi-random

sequences, that can provide greater simulation accuracy than independent random draws. We then turn to simulation-assisted estimation, look-
ing first at classical procedures, including maximum simulated likelihood, method of simulated moments, and method of simulated scores.
Finally, we examine Bayesian estimation procedures, which use simulation to approximate moments of the posterior distribution. The Bayesian
estimator can be interpreted from either a Bayesian or classical perspective and has the advantage of avoiding some of the numerical difficulties
associated with classical estimators. The power that simulation provides
when coupled with Bayesian procedures makes this chapter a fitting
finale for the book.

1.4   Topics Not Covered

I feel it is useful to say a few words about what the book does not cover.
There are several topics that could logically be included but are not.
One is the branch of empirical industrial organization that involves estimation of discrete choice models of consumer demand on market-level
data. Customer-level demand is specified by a discrete choice model,
such as logit or mixed logit. This formula for customer-level demand is
aggregated over consumers to obtain market-level demand functions that
relate prices to shares. Market equilibrium prices are determined as the
interaction of these demand functions with supply, based on marginal
costs and the game that the firms are assumed to play. Berry (1994)
and Berry *et al.* (1995) developed methods for estimating the demand
parameters when the customer-level model takes a flexible form such as
mixed logit. The procedure has been implemented in numerous markets
for differentiated goods, such as ready-to-eat cereals (Nevo, 2001).

I have decided not to cover these procedures, despite their importance
because doing so would involve introducing the literature on market-
level models, which we are not otherwise considering in this book. For
market demand, price is typically endogenous, determined by the interaction of demand and supply. The methods cited previously were
developed to deal with this endogeneity, which is probably *the* central
issue with market-level demand models. This issue does not automatically arise in customer-level models. Prices are not endogenous in the
traditional sense, since the demand of the customer does not usually
affect market price. Covering the topic is therefore not necessary for our
analysis of customers' choices.

It is important to note, however, that various forms of endogeneity
can indeed arise in customer-level models, even if the traditional type of

endogeneity does not. For example, suppose a desirable attribute of products is omitted from the analysis, perhaps because no measure of it exists. Price can be expected to be higher for products that have high levels of this attribute. Price therefore becomes correlated with the unobserved components of demand, even at the customer level: the unobserved part of demand is high (due to a high level of the omitted attribute) when the price is high. Estimation without regard to this correlation is inconsistent. The procedures cited above can be applied to customer-level models to correct for this type of endogeneity, even though they were originally developed for market-level data. For researchers who are concerned about the possibility of endogeneity in customer-level models, Petrin and Train (2002) provide a useful discussion and application of the methods.

A second area that this book does not cover is discrete–continuous models. These models arise when a regression equation for a continuous variable is related in any of several ways to a discrete choice. The most prominent situations are the following.

1. The continuous variable depends on a discrete explanatory variable that is determined endogenously with the dependent variable. For example, consider an analysis of the impact of job-training programs on wages. A regression equation is specified with wages as the dependent variable and a dummy variable for whether the person participated in a job-training program. The coefficient of the participation dummy indicates the impact of the program on wages. The situation is complicated, however, by the fact that participation is voluntary: people choose whether to participate in job-training programs. The decision to participate is at least partially determined by factors that also affect the person's wage, such as the innate drive, or "go-for-it" attitude, of the person. Estimation of the regression by ordinary least squares is biased in this situation, since the program-participation dummy is correlated with the errors in the wage equation.

2. A regression equation is estimated on a sample of observations that are selected on the basis of a discrete choice that is determined endogenously with the dependent variable. For example, a researcher might want to estimate the effect of weather on peak energy load (that is, consumption during the highest-demand hour of the day). Data on energy loads by time of day are available only for households that have chosen time-of-use rates. However, the households' choice of rate plan can be expected

to be related to their energy consumption, with customers who have high peak loads tending not to choose time-of-use rates, since those rates charge high prices in the peak. Estimation of the regression equation on this *self-selected* sample is biased unless the endogeneity of the sample is allowed for.

3. The continuous dependent variable is truncated. For example, consumption of goods by households is necessarily positive. Stated statistically, consumption is truncated below at zero, and for many goods (such as opera tickets) observed consumption is at this truncation point for a large share of the population. Estimation of the regression without regard to the truncation can cause bias.

The initial concepts regarding appropriate treatment of discrete–continuous models were developed by Heckman (1978, 1979) and Dubin and McFadden (1984). These early concepts are covered in my earlier book (Train, 1986, Chapter 5). Since then, the field has expanded tremendously. An adequate discussion of the issues and procedures would take a book in itself. Moreover, the field has not reached (at least in my view) the same type of juncture that discrete choice modeling has reached. Many fundamental concepts are still being hotly debated, and potentially valuable new procedures have been introduced so recently that there has not been an opportunity for researchers to test them in a variety of settings. The field is still expanding more than it is coalescing.

There are several ongoing directions of research in this area. The early procedures were highly dependent on distributional assumptions that are hard to verify. Researchers have been developing semi- and nonparametric procedures that are hopefully more robust. The special 1986 issue of the *Journal of Econometrics* provides a set of important articles on the topic. Papers by Lewbel and Linton (2002) and Levy (2001) describe more recent developments. Another important development concerns the representation of behavior in these settings. The relation between the discrete and continuous variables has been generalized beyond the fairly simple representation that the early methods assumed. For example, in the context of job training, it is likely that the impact of the training differs over people and that people choose to participate in the training program on the basis of the impact it will have on them. Stated in econometric terms: the coefficient of the participation dummy in the wage equation varies over people and affects the value of the dummy. The dummy is correlated with its own coefficient, as well as with the unobserved variables that enter the error of the regression.

A recent discussion of approaches to this issue is provided by Carneiro *et al.* (2001).

1.5   A Couple of Notes

Throughout the book, I refer to the researcher as "she" and the decision maker as "he." This usage, as well as being comparatively gender-neutral (or at least symmetrically noninclusive), allows both people to be referred to in the same paragraph without confusion.

Many colleagues have provided valuable comments and suggestions on earlier drafts of the book. I am very grateful for this help. I thank Greg Allenby, Moshe Ben-Akiva, Chandra Bhat, Denis Bolduc, David Brownstone, Siddhartha Chib, Jon Eisen-Hecht, Florian Heiss, David Hensher, Joe Herriges, Rich Johnson, Frank Koppelman, Jordan Louviere, Aviv Nevo, Juan de Dios Ortúzar, Ken Small, Joan Walker, Cliff Winston, Joachim Winter, and the students in my graduate econometrics course.

I welcome readers to contact me if you feel I have not covered material that you consider important, or if I have confused rather than clarified any of the material that I *do* cover. Hopefully, another edition of this book will someday materialize.

Part I

Behavioral Models

2 Properties of Discrete Choice Models

2.1 Overview

This chapter describes the features that are common to all discrete choice models. We start by discussing the choice set, which is the set of options that are available to the decision maker. We then define choice probabilities and derive them from utility-maximizing behavior. The most prominent types of discrete choice models, namely logit, generalized extreme value (GEV), probit, and mixed logit, are introduced and compared within the context of this general derivation. Utility, as a constructed measure of well-being, has no natural level or scale. This fact has important implications for the specification and normalization of discrete choice models, which we explore. We then show how individual-level models are aggregated to obtain market-level predictions, and how the models are used for forecasting over time.

2.2 The Choice Set

Discrete choice models describe decision makers' choices among alternatives. The decision makers can be people, households, firms, or any other decision-making unit, and the alternatives might represent competing products, courses of action, or any other options or items over which choices must be made. To fit within a discrete choice framework, the set of alternatives, called the *choice set*, needs to exhibit three characteristics. First, the alternatives must be *mutually exclusive* from the decision maker's perspective. Choosing one alternative necessarily implies not choosing any of the other alternatives. The decision maker chooses only one alternative from the choice set. Second, the choice set must be *exhaustive*, in that all possible alternatives are included. The decision maker necessarily chooses one of the alternatives. Third, the number of alternatives must be finite. The researcher can count the alternatives and eventually be finished counting.

The first and second criteria are not restrictive. Appropriate definition of alternatives can nearly always assure that the alternatives are mutually exclusive and the choice set is exhaustive. For example, suppose two alternatives labeled A and B are not mutually exclusive because the decision maker can choose both of the alternatives. The alternatives can be redefined to be "A only," "B only," and "both A and B," which are necessarily mutually exclusive. Similarly, a set of alternatives might not be exhaustive because the decision maker has the option of not choosing any of them. In this case, an extra alternative can be defined as "none of the other alternatives." The expanded choice set, consisting of the original alternatives plus this new one, is clearly exhaustive.

Often the researcher can satisfy these two conditions in several different ways. The appropriate specification of the choice set in these situations is governed largely by the goals of the research and the data that are available to the researcher. Consider households' choice among heating fuels, a topic which has been studied extensively in efforts to forecast energy use and to develop effective fuel-switching and energy conservation programs. The available fuels are usually natural gas, electricity, oil, and wood. These four alternatives, as listed, violate both mutual exclusivity and exhaustiveness. The alternatives are not mutually exclusive because a household can (and many do) have two types of heating, e.g., a natural gas central heater and electric room heaters, or a wood stove along with electric baseboard heating. And the set is not exhaustive because the household can have no heating (which, unfortunately, is not as rare as one might hope). The researcher can handle each of these issues in several ways. To obtain mutually exclusive alternatives, one approach is to list every possible combination of heating fuels as an alternative. The alternatives are then defined as: "electricity alone," "electricity and natural gas, but no other fuels," and so on. Another approach is to define the choice as the choice among fuels for the "primary" heating source. Under this procedure, the researcher develops a rule for determining which heating fuel is primary when a household uses multiple heating fuels. By definition, only one fuel (electricity, natural gas, oil, or wood) is primary. The advantage of listing every possible combination of fuels is that it avoids the need to define a "primary" fuel, which is a difficult and somewhat arbitrary distinction. Also, with all combinations considered, the researcher has the ability to examine the factors that determine households' use of multiple fuels. However, to implement this approach, the researcher needs data that distinguish the alternatives, for example, the cost of heating a house with natural gas and electricity versus the cost with natural gas alone. If the researcher restricts the analysis to choice of primary fuel, then the data requirements are less severe. Only the costs associated with each fuel are needed. Also, a model with four alternatives is inherently easier to estimate and forecast with than a model with the large number of alternatives that arises when every possible combination of fuels is considered. The researcher will need to take these trade-offs into consideration when specifying the choice set.

The same type of issue arises with regard to exhaustiveness. In our case of heating-fuel choice, the researcher can either include "no heating" as an alternative or can redefine the choice situation as being the choice of heating fuel conditional on having heating. The first approach allows the researcher to examine the factors that relate to whether a household has heating. However, this ability is only realized if the researcher has data that meaningfully relate to whether or not a household has heating. Under the second approach, the researcher excludes from the analysis households without heating, and, by doing so, is relieved of the need for data that relate to these households.

As we have just described, the conditions of mutual exclusivity and exhaustiveness can usually be satisfied, and the researcher often has several approaches for doing so. In contrast, the third condition, namely, that the number of alternatives is finite, is actually restrictive. This condition is the defining characteristic of discrete choice models and distinguishes their realm of application from that for regression models. With regression models, the dependent variable is continuous, which means that there is an infinite number of possible outcomes. The outcome might be chosen by a decision maker, such as the decision of how much money to hold in savings accounts. However, the alternatives available to the decision maker, which are every possible monetary value above zero, is not finite (at least not if all fractions are considered, which is an issue we return to later.) When there is an infinite number of alternatives, discrete choice models cannot be applied.

Often regression models and discrete choice models are distinguished by saying that regressions examine choices of "how much" and discrete choice models examine choice of "which." This distinction, while perhaps illustrative, is not actually accurate. Discrete choice models can be and have been used to examine choices of "how much." A prominent example is households' choice of how many cars to own. The alternatives are 0, 1, 2, and so on, up to the largest number that the researcher considers possible (or observes). This choice set contains a finite number of mutually exclusive and exhaustive alternatives, appropriate for analysis via discrete choice models. The researcher can also define the choice set more succinctly as 0, 1, and 2 or more vehicles, if the goals of the research can be met with this specification.

When considered in this way, most choices involving "how many" can be represented in a discrete choice framework. In the case of savings accounts, every one-dollar increment (or even every one-cent increment) can be considered an alternative, and as long as some finite maximum exists, then the choice set fits the criteria for discrete choice. Whether to use regression or discrete choice models in these situations is a specification issue that the researcher must consider. Usually a regression model is more natural and easier. A discrete choice model would be used in these situations only if there were compelling reasons for doing so. As an example, Train *et al.* (1987a) analyzed the number and duration of phone calls that households make, using a discrete choice model instead of a regression model because the discrete choice model allowed greater flexibility in handling the nonlinear price schedules that households face. In general, the researcher needs to consider the goals of the research and the capabilities of alternative methods when deciding whether to apply a discrete choice model.

2.3   Derivation of Choice Probabilities

Discrete choice models are usually derived under an assumption of utility-maximizing behavior by the decision maker. Thurstone (1927) originally developed the concepts in terms of psychological stimuli, leading to a binary probit model of whether respondents can differentiate the level of stimulus. Marschak (1960) interpreted the stimuli as utility and provided a derivation from utility maximization. Following Marschak, models that can be derived in this way are called random utility models (RUMs). It is important to note, however, that models derived from utility maximization can also be used to represent decision making that does not entail utility maximization. The derivation assures that the model is consistent with utility maximization; it does not preclude the model from being consistent with other forms of behavior. The models can also be seen as simply describing the relation of explanatory variables to the outcome of a choice, without reference to exactly how the choice is made.

Random utility models (RUMs) are derived as follows. A decision maker, labeled n, faces a choice among J alternatives. The decision maker would obtain a certain level of utility (or profit) from each alternative. The utility that decision maker n obtains from alternative j is U_{nj}, $j = 1, \ldots, J$. This utility is known to the decision maker but not, as we see in the following, by the researcher. The decision maker chooses the alternative that provides the greatest utility. The behavioral model is therefore: choose alternative i if and only if $U_{ni} > U_{nj} \; \forall j \neq i$.

Consider now the researcher. The researcher does not observe the decision maker's utility. The researcher observes some attributes of the alternatives as faced by the decision maker, labeled x_{nj} $\forall j$, and some attributes of the decision maker, labeled s_n, and can specify a function that relates these observed factors to the decision maker's utility. The function is denoted $V_{nj} = V(x_{nj}, s_n)$ $\forall j$ and is often called *representative utility*. Usually, V depends on parameters that are unknown to the researcher and therefore estimated statistically; however, this dependence is suppressed for the moment.

Since there are aspects of utility that the researcher does not or cannot observe, $V_{nj} \neq U_{nj}$. Utility is decomposed as $U_{nj} = V_{nj} + \varepsilon_{nj}$, where ε_{nj} captures the factors that affect utility but are not included in V_{nj}. This decomposition is fully general, since ε_{nj} is defined as simply the difference between true utility U_{nj} and the part of utility that the researcher captures in V_{nj}. Given its definition, the characteristics of ε_{nj}, such as its distribution, depend critically on the researcher's specification of V_{nj}. In particular, ε_{nj} is not defined for a choice situation *per se*. Rather, it is defined relative to a researcher's representation of that choice situation. This distinction becomes relevant when evaluating the appropriateness of various specific discrete choice models.

The researcher does not know ε_{nj} $\forall j$ and therefore treats these terms as random. The joint density of the random vector $\varepsilon_n = \langle \varepsilon_{n1}, \ldots, \varepsilon_{nJ} \rangle$ is denoted $f(\varepsilon_n)$. With this density, the researcher can make probabilistic statements about the decision maker's choice. The probability that decision maker n chooses alternative i is

$$P_{ni} = \text{Prob}(U_{ni} > U_{nj} \;\forall j \neq i)$$
$$= \text{Prob}(V_{ni} + \varepsilon_{ni} > V_{nj} + \varepsilon_{nj} \;\forall j \neq i)$$
(2.1) $$= \text{Prob}(\varepsilon_{nj} - \varepsilon_{ni} < V_{ni} - V_{nj} \;\forall j \neq i).$$

This probability is a cumulative distribution, namely, the probability that each random term $\varepsilon_{nj} - \varepsilon_{ni}$ is below the observed quantity $V_{ni} - V_{nj}$. Using the density $f(\varepsilon_n)$, this cumulative probability can be rewritten as

$$P_{ni} = \text{Prob}(\varepsilon_{nj} - \varepsilon_{ni} < V_{ni} - V_{nj} \;\forall j \neq i)$$
(2.2) $$= \int_\varepsilon I(\varepsilon_{nj} - \varepsilon_{ni} < V_{ni} - V_{nj} \;\forall j \neq i) f(\varepsilon_n)\, d\varepsilon_n,$$

where $I(\cdot)$ is the indicator function, equaling 1 when the expression in parentheses is true and 0 otherwise. This is a multidimensional integral over the density of the unobserved portion of utility, $f(\varepsilon_n)$. Different discrete choice models are obtained from different specifications of this density, that is, from different assumptions about the distribution of the unobserved portion of utility. The integral takes a closed form only for certain specifications of $f(\cdot)$. Logit and nested logit have closed-form expressions for this integral. They are derived under the assumption that the unobserved portion of utility is distributed iid extreme value and a type of generalized extreme value, respectively. Probit is derived under the assumption that $f(\cdot)$ is a multivariate normal, and mixed logit is based on the assumption that the unobserved portion of utility consists of a part that follows any distribution specified by the researcher plus a part that is iid extreme value. With probit and mixed logit, the resulting integral does not have a closed form and is evaluated numerically through simulation. Each of these models is discussed in detail in subsequent chapters.

The meaning of choice probabilities is more subtle, and more revealing, than it might at first appear. An example serves as illustration. Consider a person who can take either a car or a bus to work. The researcher observes the time and cost that the person would incur under each mode. However, the researcher realizes that there are factors other than time and cost that affect the person's utility and hence his choice. The researcher specifies

$$V_c = \alpha T_c + \beta M_c,$$
$$V_b = \alpha T_b + \beta M_b,$$

where T_c and M_c are the time and cost (in money) that the person incurs traveling to work by car, T_b and M_b are defined analogously for bus, and the subscript n denoting the person is omitted for convenience. The coefficients α and β are either known or estimated by the researcher.

Suppose that, given α and β and the researcher's measures of the time and cost by car and bus, it turns out that $V_c = 4$ and $V_b = 3$. This means that, on observed factors, car is better for this person than bus by 1 unit. (We discuss in following text the normalization of utility that sets the dimension of these units.) It does not mean, however, that the person necessarily chooses car, since there are other factors not observed by the researcher that affect the person. The probability that the person chooses bus instead of car is the probability that the unobserved factors for bus are sufficiently better than those for car to overcome the advantage that car has on observed factors. Specifically, the person will choose bus if the unobserved portion of utility is higher than that for car by at least 1 unit, thus overcoming the 1-unit advantage that car has on observed factors. The probability of this person choosing bus is therefore the probability that $\varepsilon_b - \varepsilon_c > 1$. Likewise, the person will choose car if the unobserved utility for bus is *not* better than that for car by at least 1 unit, that is, if $\varepsilon_b - \varepsilon_c < 1$. Since 1 is the difference between V_c and V_b in our example, the probabilities can be stated more explicitly as

$$P_c = \text{Prob}(\varepsilon_b - \varepsilon_c < V_c - V_b)$$

and

$$P_b = \text{Prob}(\varepsilon_b - \varepsilon_c > V_c - V_b)$$
$$= \text{Prob}(\varepsilon_c - \varepsilon_b < V_b - V_c).$$

These equations are the same as equation (2.1), re-expressed for our car–bus example.

The question arises in the derivation of the choice probabilities: what is meant by the distribution of ε_n? The interpretation that the researcher places on this density affects the researcher's interpretation of the choice probabilities. The most prominent way to think about this distribution is as follows. Consider a population of people who face the same observed utility $V_{nj} \; \forall j$ as person n. Among these people, the values of the unobserved factors differ. The density $f(\varepsilon_n)$ is the distribution of the unobserved portion of utility within the population of people who face the same observed portion of utility. Under this interpretation, the probability P_{ni} is the share of people who choose alternative i within the population of people who face the same observed utility for each alternative as person n. The distribution can also be considered in subjective terms, as representing the researcher's subjective probability that the person's unobserved utility will take given values. In this case, P_{ni} is the probability that the researcher ascribes to the person's choosing alternative i given the researcher's ideas about the unobserved portions of the person's utility. As a third possibility, the distribution can represent the effect of factors that are quixotic to the decision maker himself (representing, e.g., aspects of bounded rationality), so that P_{ni} is the probability that these quixotic factors induce the person to choose alternative i given the observed, nonquixotic factors.

2.4   Specific Models

Logit, GEV, probit, and mixed logit are discussed at length in the subsequent chapters. However, a quick preview of these models is useful at this point, to show how they relate to the general derivation of all choice models and how they differ within this derivation. As stated earlier, different choice models are derived under different specifications of the density of unobserved factors, $f(\varepsilon_n)$. The issues therefore are what distribution is assumed for each model, and what is the motivation for these different assumptions.

Logit (discussed in Chapter 3) is by far the most widely used discrete choice model. It is derived under the assumption that ε_{ni} is iid extreme value for all i. The critical part of the assumption is that the unobserved factors are uncorrelated over alternatives, as well as having the same variance for all alternatives. This assumption, while restrictive, provides a very convenient form for the choice probability. The popularity of the logit model is due to this convenience. However, the assumption of independence can be inappropriate in some situations. Unobserved factors related to one alternative might be similar to those related to another alternative. For example, a person who dislikes travel by bus because of the presence of other riders might have a similar reaction to rail travel; if so, then the unobserved factors affecting bus and rail are corrrelated rather than independent. The assumption of independence also enters when a logit model is applied to sequences of choices over time. The logit model assumes that each choice is independent of the others. In many cases, one would expect that unobserved factors that affect the choice in one period would persist, at least somewhat, into the next period, inducing dependence among the choices over time.

The development of other models has arisen largely to avoid the independence assumption within a logit. Generalized extreme-value models (GEV, discussed in Chapter 4) are based, as the name implies, on a generalization of the extreme-value distribution. The generalization can take many forms, but the common element is that it allows correlation in unobserved factors over alternatives and collapses to the logit model when this correlation is zero. Depending on the type of GEV model, the correlations can be more or less flexible. For example, a comparatively simple GEV model places the alternatives into several groups called nests, with unobserved factors having the same correlation for all alternatives within a nest and no correlation for alternatives in different nests. More complex forms allow essentially any pattern of correlation. GEV models usually have closed forms for the choice probabilities, so that simulation is not required for their estimation.

Probits (Chapter 5) are based on the assumption that the unobserved factors are distributed jointly normal: $\varepsilon'_n = \langle \varepsilon_{n1}, \ldots, \varepsilon_{nJ} \rangle \sim N(0, \Omega)$. With full covariance matrix Ω, any pattern of correlation and heteroskedasticity can be accommodated. When applied to sequences of choices over time, the unobserved factors are assumed to be jointly normal over time as well as over alternatives, with any temporal correlation pattern. The flexibility of the probit model in handling correlations over alternatives and time is its main advantage. Its only functional limitation arises from its reliance on the normal distribution. In some situations, unobserved factors may not be normally distributed. For example, a customer's willingness to pay for a desirable attribute of a product is necessary positive. Assuming that this unobserved factor is normally distributed contradicts the fact that it is positive, since the normal distribution has density on both sides of zero.

Mixed logit (Chapter 6) allows the unobserved factors to follow any distribution. The defining characteristic of a mixed logit is that the unobserved factors can be decomposed into a part that contains all the correlation and heteroskedasticity, and another part that is iid extreme value. The first part can follow any distribution, including non-normal distributions. We will show that mixed logit can approximate any discrete choice model and thus is fully general.

Other discrete choice models (Chapter 7) have been specified by researchers for specific purposes. Often these models are obtained by combining concepts from other models. For example, a mixed probit is obtained by decomposing the unobserved factors into two parts, as in mixed logit, but giving the second part a normal distribution instead of extreme value. This model has the generality of mixed logit and yet for some situations can be easier to estimate. By understanding the derivation and motivation for all the models, each researcher can specify a model that is tailor-made for the situation and goals of her research.

2.5   Identification of Choice Models

Several aspects of the behavioral decision process affect the specification and estimation of any discrete choice model. The issues can be summarized easily in two statements: "Only differences in utility matter" and "The scale of utility is arbitrary." The implications of these statements are far-reaching, subtle, and, in many cases, quite complex. We discuss them below.

2.5.1. Only Differences in Utility Matter

The absolute level of utility is irrelevant to both the decision maker's behavior and the researcher's model. If a constant is added to the utility of all alternatives, the alternative with the highest utility doesn't change. The decision maker chooses the same alternative with $U_{nj} \, \forall j$ as with $U_{nj} + k \, \forall j$ for any constant k. A colloquial way to express this fact is, "A rising tide raises all boats."

The level of utility doesn't matter from the researcher's perspective either. The choice probability is $P_{ni} = \text{Prob}(U_{ni} > U_{nj} \, \forall j \neq i) = \text{Prob}(U_{ni} - U_{nj} > 0 \, \forall j \neq i)$, which depends only on the difference in utility, not its absolute level. When utility is decomposed into the observed and unobserved parts, equation (2.1) expresses the choice probability as $P_{ni} = \text{Prob}(\varepsilon_{nj} - \varepsilon_{ni} < V_{ni} - V_{nj} \, \forall j \neq i)$, which also depends only on differences.

The fact that only differences in utility matter has several implications for the identification and specification of discrete choice models. In general it means that the only parameters that can be estimated (that is, are identified) are those that capture differences across alternatives. This general statement takes several forms.

Alternative-Specific Constants

It is often reasonable to specify the observed part of utility to be linear in parameters with a constant: $V_{nj} = x'_{nj}\beta + k_j \, \forall j$, where x_{nj} is a vector of variables that relate to alternative j as faced by decision maker n, β are coefficients of these variables, and k_j is a constant that is specific to alternative j. The alternative-specific constant for an alternative captures the average effect on utility of all factors that are not included in the model. Thus they serve a similar function to the constant in a regression model, which also captures the average effect of all unincluded factors.

When alternative-specific constants are included, the unobserved portion of utility, ε_{nj}, has zero mean by construction. If ε_{nj} has a nonzero mean when the constants are not included, then adding the constants makes the remaining error have zero mean: that is, if $U_{nj} = x'_{nj}\beta + \varepsilon^*_{nj}$ with $E(\varepsilon_{nj})^* = k_j \neq 0$, then $U_{nj} = x'_{nj}\beta + k_j + \varepsilon_{nj}$ with $E(\varepsilon_{nj}) = 0$. It is reasonable, therefore, to include a constant in V_{nj} for each alternative. However, since only differences in utility matter, only differences in the alternative-specific constants are relevant, not their absolute levels. To reflect this fact, the researcher must set the overall level of these constants.

The concept is readily apparent in the car–bus example. A specification of utility that takes the form

$$U_c = \alpha T_c + \beta M_c + k_c^0 + \varepsilon_c,$$
$$U_b = \alpha T_b + \beta M_b + k_b^0 + \varepsilon_b,$$

with $k_b^0 - k_c^0 = d$, is equivalent to a model with

$$U_c = \alpha T_c + \beta M_c + k_c^1 + \varepsilon_c,$$
$$U_b = \alpha T_b + \beta M_b + k_b^1 + \varepsilon_b,$$

where the difference in the new constants is the same as the difference in the old constants, namely, $k_b^1 - k_c^1 = d = k_b^0 - k_c^0$. Any model with the same difference in constants is equivalent. In terms of estimation, it is impossible to estimate the two constants themselves, since an infinite number of values of the two constants (any values that have the same difference) result in the same choice probabilities.

To account for this fact, the researcher must normalize the absolute levels of the constants. The standard procedure is to normalize one of the constants to zero. For example, the researcher might normalize the constant for the car alternative to zero:

$$U_c = \alpha T_c + \beta M_c + \varepsilon_c,$$
$$U_b = \alpha T_b + \beta M_b + k_b + \varepsilon_b.$$

Under this normalization, the value of k_b is d, which is the difference in the original (unnormalized) constants. The bus constant is interpreted as the average effect of unincluded factors on the utility of bus *relative* to car.

With J alternatives, at most $J - 1$ alternative-specific constants can enter the model, with one of the constants normalized to zero. It is irrelevant which constant is normalized to zero: the other constants are interpreted as being relative to whichever one is set to zero. The researcher could normalize to some value other than zero, of course; however, there would be no point in doing so, since normalizing to zero is easier (the constant is simply left out of the model) and has the same effect.

Sociodemographic Variables

The same issue affects the way that socio-demographic variables enter a model. Attributes of the alternatives, such as the time and cost of travel on different modes, generally vary over alternatives. However, attributes of the decision maker do not vary over alternatives. They can only enter the model if they are specified in ways that create differences in utility over alternatives.

Consider for example the effect of a person's income on the decision whether to take bus or car to work. It is reasonable to suppose that a person's utility is higher with higher income, whether the person takes bus or car. Utility is specified as

$$U_c = \alpha T_c + \beta M_c + \theta_c^0 Y + \varepsilon_c,$$
$$U_b = \alpha T_b + \beta M_b + \theta_b^0 Y + k_b + \varepsilon_b,$$

where Y is income and θ_c^0 and θ_b^0 capture the effects of changes in income on the utility of taking car and bus, respectively. We expect that $\theta_c^0 > 0$ and $\theta_b^0 > 0$, since greater income makes people happier no matter what mode they take. However, $\theta_c^0 \neq \theta_b^0$, since income probably has a different effect on the person depending on his mode of travel. Since only differences in utility matter, the absolute levels of θ_c^0 and θ_b^0 cannot be estimated, only their difference. To set the level, one of these parameters is normalized to zero. The model becomes

$$U_c = \alpha T_c + \beta M_c + \varepsilon_c,$$
$$U_b = \alpha T_b + \beta M_b + \theta_b Y + k_b + \varepsilon_b,$$

where $\theta_b = \theta_b^0 - \theta_c^0$ and is interpreted as the differential effect of income on the utility of bus compared to car. The value of θ_b can be either positive or negative.

Sociodemographic variables can enter utility in other ways. For example, cost is often divided by income:

$$U_c = \alpha T_c + \beta M_c / Y + \varepsilon_c,$$
$$U_b = \alpha T_b + \beta M_b / Y + \theta_b Y + k_b + \varepsilon_b.$$

The coefficient of cost in this specification is β / Y. Since this coefficient decreases in Y, the model reflects the concept that cost becomes less important in a person's decision making, relative to other issues, when income rises.

When sociodemographic variables are interacted with attributes of the alternatives, there is no need to normalize the coefficients. The sociodemographic variables affect the differences in utility through their interaction with the attributes of the alternatives. The difference $U_c - U_b = \ldots \beta(M_c - M_b)/Y \ldots$ varies with income, since costs differ over alternatives.

Number of Independent Error Terms

As given by equation (2.2), the choice probabilities take the form

$$P_{ni} = \int_\varepsilon I(\varepsilon_{nj} - \varepsilon_{ni} < V_{ni} - V_{nj} \ \forall j \neq i) f(\varepsilon_n) d\varepsilon_n.$$

This probability is a J-dimensional integral over the density of the J error terms in $\varepsilon_n = \langle \varepsilon_{n1}, \ldots, \varepsilon_{nJ} \rangle$. The dimension can be reduced, however, through recognizing that only differences in utility matter. With J errors (one for each alternative), there are $J - 1$ error differences. The choice probability can be expressed as a $(J - 1)$-dimensional integral over the density of these error differences:

$$
\begin{aligned}
P_{ni} &= \text{Prob}(U_{ni} > U_{nj} \ \forall j \neq i) \\
&= \text{Prob}(\varepsilon_{nj} - \varepsilon_{ni} < V_{ni} - V_{nj} \ \forall j \neq i) \\
&= \text{Prob}(\tilde{\varepsilon}_{nji} < V_{ni} - V_{nj} \ \forall j \neq i) \\
&= \int I(\tilde{\varepsilon}_{nji} < V_{ni} - V_{nj} \ \forall j \neq i) g(\tilde{\varepsilon}_{ni}) d\tilde{\varepsilon}_{ni}
\end{aligned}
$$

where $\tilde{\varepsilon}_{nji} = \varepsilon_{nj} - \varepsilon_{ni}$ is the difference in errors for alternatives i and j; $\tilde{\varepsilon}_{ni} = \langle \tilde{\varepsilon}_{n1i}, \ldots, \tilde{\varepsilon}_{nJi} \rangle$ is the $(J - 1)$-dimensional vector of error differences, with the $\ldots$ over all alternatives except i; and $g(\cdot)$ is the density of these error differences. Expressed in this way, the choice probability is a $(J - 1)$-dimensional integral.

The density of the error differences $g(\cdot)$, and the density of the original errors, $f(\cdot)$, are related in a particular way. Suppose a model is specified with an error for each alternative: $\varepsilon_n = \langle \varepsilon_{n1}, \ldots, \varepsilon_{nJ} \rangle$ with density $f(\varepsilon_n)$. This model is equivalent to a model with $J - 1$ errors defined as $\tilde{\varepsilon}_{njk} = \varepsilon_{nj} - \varepsilon_{nk}$ for any k and density $g(\tilde{\varepsilon}_{nk})$ derived from $f(\varepsilon_n)$. For any $f(\varepsilon_n)$, the corresponding $g(\tilde{\varepsilon}_{nk})$ can be derived. However, since ε_n has more elements than $\tilde{\varepsilon}_{nk}$, there is an infinite number of densities for the J error terms that give the same density for the $J - 1$ error differences. Stated equivalently, any $g(\tilde{\varepsilon}_{nk})$ is consistent with an infinite number of different $f(\varepsilon_n)$'s. Since choice probabilities can always be expressed as depending only on $g(\tilde{\varepsilon}_{nk})$, one dimension of the density of $f(\varepsilon_n)$ is not identified and must be normalized by the researcher.

The normalization of $f(\varepsilon_n)$ can be handled in various ways. For some models, such as logit, the distribution of the error terms is sufficiently restrictive that the normalization occurs automatically with the assumptions on the distribution. For other models, such as probit, identification is often obtained by specifying the model only in terms of error differences, that is, by parameterizing $g(\cdot)$ without reference to $f(\cdot)$. In all but the simplest models, the researcher needs to consider the fact that only the density of error differences affects the probabilities and therefore is identified. In discussing the various models in subsequent chapters, we will return to this issue and how to handle it.

2.5.2. The Overall Scale of Utility Is Irrelevant

Just as adding a constant to the utility of all alternatives does not change the decision maker's choice, neither does multiplying each alternative's utility by a constant. The alternative with the highest utility is the same no matter how utility is scaled. The model $U_{nj}^0 = V_{nj} + \varepsilon_{nj} \, \forall j$ is equivalent to $U_{nj}^1 = \lambda V_{nj} + \lambda \varepsilon_{nj} \, \forall j$ for any $\lambda > 0$. To take account of this fact, the researcher must normalize the scale of utility.

The standard way to normalize the scale of utility is to normalize the variance of the error terms. The scale of utility and the variance of the error terms are definitionally linked. When utility is multiplied by λ, the variance of each ε_{nj} changes by λ^2: $\mathrm{Var}(\lambda \varepsilon_{nj}) = \lambda^2 \, \mathrm{Var}(\varepsilon_{nj})$. Therefore normalizing the variance of the error terms is equivalent to normalizing the scale of utility.

Normalization with iid Errors

If the error terms are assumed to be independently, identically distributed (iid), then the normalization for scale is straightforward. The researcher normalizes the error variance to some number, which is usually chosen for convenience. Since all the errors have the same variance by assumption, normalizing the variance of any of them sets the variance for them all.

When the observed portion of utility is linear in parameters, the normalization provides a way of interpreting coefficients. Consider the model $U_{nj}^0 = x_{nj}'\beta + \varepsilon_{nj}^0$ where the variance of the error terms is $\text{Var}(\varepsilon_{nj}^0) = \sigma^2$. Suppose the research normalizes the scale by setting the error variance to 1. The original model becomes the following equivalent specification: $U_{nj}^1 = x_{nj}'(\beta/\sigma) + \varepsilon_{nj}^1$ with $\text{Var}(\varepsilon_{nj}^1) = 1$. The original coefficients β are divided by the standard deviation of the unobserved portion of utility. The new coefficients β/σ reflect, therefore, the effect of the observed variables *relative* to the standard deviation of the unobserved factors.

The same concepts apply for whatever number the researcher chooses for normalization. As we will see in the next chapter, the error variances in a standard logit model are traditionally normalized to $\pi^2/6$, which is about 1.6. In this case, the preceding model becomes $U_{nj} = x_{nj}'(\beta/\sigma)$ $\sqrt{1.6} + \varepsilon_{nj}$ with $\text{Var}(\varepsilon_{nj}) = 1.6$. The coefficients still reflect the variance of the unobserved portion of utility. The only difference is that the coefficients are larger by a factor of $\sqrt{1.6}$.

While it is immaterial which number is used by the researcher for normalization, interpretation of model results must take the normalization into consideration. Suppose, for example, that a logit and an independent probit model were both estimated on the same data. As stated earlier, the error variance is normalized to 1.6 for logit. Suppose the researcher normalized the probit to have error variances of 1, which is traditional with independent probits. This difference in normalization must be kept in mind when comparing estimates from the two models. In particular, the coefficients in the logit model will be $\sqrt{1.6}$ times larger than those for the probit model, simply due to the difference in normalization. If the researcher does not take this scale difference into account when comparing the models, she might inadvertently think that the logit model implies that people care more about the attributes (since the coefficients are larger) than implied by the probit model. For example, in a mode choice model, suppose the estimated cost coefficient is -0.55 from a logit model and -0.45 from an independent probit model. It is incorrect to say that the logit model implies more sensitivity to costs than the probit model. The coefficients in one of the models must be adjusted to account for the difference in scale. The logit coefficients can be divided by $\sqrt{1.6}$, so that the error variance is 1, just as in the probit model. With this adjustment, the comparable coefficients are -0.43 for the logit model and -0.45 for the probit model. The logit model implies less price sensitivity than the probit. Instead, the probit coefficients could be converted to the scale of the logit coefficients by multiplying them by $\sqrt{1.6}$, in which case the comparable coefficients would be -0.55 for logit and -0.57 for probit.

A similar issue of interpretation arises when the same model is estimated on different data sets. The relative scale of the estimates from the two data sets reflects the relative variance of unobserved factors in the data sets. Suppose mode choice models were estimated in Chicago and Boston. For Chicago, the estimated cost coefficient is -0.55 and the estimated coefficient of time is -1.78. For Boston, the estimates are -0.81 and -2.69. The ratio of the cost coefficient to the time coefficient is very similar in the two cities: 0.309 in Chicago and 0.301 in Boston. However, the scale of the coefficients is about fifty percent higher for Boston than for Chicago. This scale difference means that the unobserved portion of utility has less variance in Boston than in Chicago: since the coefficients are divided by the standard deviation of the unobserved portion of utility, lower coefficients mean higher standard deviation and hence variance. The models are revealing that factors other than time and cost have less effect on people in Boston than in Chicago. Stated more intuitively, time and cost have more importance, relative to unobserved factors, in Boston than in Chicago, which is consistent with the larger scale of the coefficients for Boston.

Normalization with Heteroskedastic Errors

In some situations, the variance of the error terms can be different for different segments of the population. The researcher cannot set the overall level of utility by normalizing the variance of the errors for all segments, since the variance is different in different segments. Instead, the researcher sets the overall scale of utility by normalizing the variance for one segment, and then estimates the variance (and hence scale) for each segment relative to this one segment.

For example, consider the situation described in the previous section, where the unobserved factors have greater variance in Chicago than in Boston. If separate models are estimated for Chicago and Boston, then the variance of the error term is normalized separately for each model. The scale of the parameters in each model reflects the variance of unincluded factors in that area. Suppose, however, that the researcher wants to estimate a model on data for both Chicago and Boston. She cannot normalize the variance of the unobserved factors for all travelers to the same number, since the variance is different for travelers in Boston than for those in Chicago. Instead, the researcher sets the overall scale of utility by normalizing the variance in one area (say Boston) and then estimates the variance in the other area *relative* to that in the first area (the variance in Chicago relative to that in Boston).

The model in its original form is

$$U_{nj} = \alpha T_{nj} + \beta M_{nj} + \varepsilon_{nj}^{B} \ \forall n \text{ in Boston}$$
$$U_{nj} = \alpha T_{nj} + \beta M_{nj} + \varepsilon_{nj}^{C} \ \forall n \text{ in Chicago,}$$

where the variance of ε_{nj}^{B} is not the same as the variance of ε_{nj}^{C}. Label the ratio of variances as $k = \text{Var}(\varepsilon_{nj}^{C})/\text{Var}(\varepsilon_{nj}^{B})$. We can divide the utility for travelers in Chicago by $\sqrt{k}$; this division doesn't affect their choices, of course, since the scale of utility doesn't matter. However, doing so allows us to rewrite the model as

$$U_{nj} = \alpha T_{nj} + \beta M_{nj} + \varepsilon_{nj} \ \forall n \text{ in Boston}$$
$$U_{nj} = (\alpha/\sqrt{k})T_{nj} + (\beta/\sqrt{k})M_{nj} + \varepsilon_{nj} \ \forall n \text{ in Chicago,}$$

where now the variance of ε_{nj} is the same for all n in both cities (since $\text{Var}(\varepsilon_{nj}^{C}/\sqrt{k}) = (1/k)\text{Var}(\varepsilon_{nj}^{C}) = [\text{Var}(\varepsilon_{nj}^{B})/\text{Var}(\varepsilon_{nj}^{C})]\text{Var}(\varepsilon_{nj}^{C}) = \text{Var}(\varepsilon_{nj}^{B})$. The scale of utility is set by normalizing the variance of ε_{nj}. The parameter k, which is often called the scale parameter, is estimated along with β and α. The estimated value $\hat{k}$ of k tells the researcher the variance of unobserved factors in Chicago relative to that in Boston. For example, $\hat{k} = 1.2$ implies that the variance of unobserved factors is twenty percent greater in Chicago than in Boston.

The variance of the error term can differ over geographic regions, data sets, time, or other factors. In all cases, the researcher sets the overall scale of utility by normalizing one of the variances and then estimating the other variances relative to the normalized one. Swait and Louviere (1993) discuss the role of the scale parameter in discrete choice models, describing the variety of reasons that variances can differ over observations. As well as the traditional concept of variance in unobserved factors, psychological factors can come into play, depending on the choice situation and the interpretation of the researcher. For example, Bradley and Daly (1994) allow the scale parameter to vary over stated preference experiments in order to allow for respondents' fatigue in answering the survey questions. Ben-Akiva and Morikawa (1990) allow the scale parameter to differ for respondents' stated intentions versus their actual market choices.

Normalization with Correlated Errors

In the discussion so far we have assumed that ε_{nj} is independent over alternatives. When the errors are correlated over alternatives, normalizing for scale is more complex. We have talked in terms of setting the scale of utility. However, since only differences in utility matter, it is more appropriate to talk in terms of setting the scale of utility *differences*. When errors are correlated, normalizing the variance of the error for one alternative is not sufficient to set the scale of utility differences.

The issue is most readily described in terms of a four-alternative example. The utility for the four alternatives is $U_{nj} = V_{nj} + \varepsilon_{nj}$, $j = 1, \ldots, 4$. The error vector $\varepsilon_n = \langle \varepsilon_{n1}, \ldots, \varepsilon_{n4} \rangle$ has zero mean and covariance matrix

$$(2.3) \quad \Omega = \begin{pmatrix} \sigma_{11} & \sigma_{12} & \sigma_{13} & \sigma_{14} \\ \cdot & \sigma_{22} & \sigma_{23} & \sigma_{24} \\ \cdot & \cdot & \sigma_{33} & \sigma_{34} \\ \cdot & \cdot & \cdot & \sigma_{44} \end{pmatrix},$$

where the dots refer to the corresponding elements in the upper part of the symmetric matrix.

Since only differences in utility matter, this model is equivalent to one in which all utilities are differenced from, say, the first alternative. The equivalent model is $\tilde{U}_{nj1} = \tilde{V}_{nj1} - \tilde{\varepsilon}_{nj1}$ for $j = 2, 3, 4$, where $\tilde{U}_{nj1} = U_{nj} - U_{n1}$, $\tilde{V}_{nj1} = V_{nj} - V_{n1}$, and the vector of error differences is $\tilde{\varepsilon}_{n1} = \langle (\varepsilon_{n2} - \varepsilon_{n1}), (\varepsilon_{n3} - \varepsilon_{n1}), (\varepsilon_{n4} - \varepsilon_{n1}) \rangle$. The variance of each error difference depends on the variances and covariances of the original errors. For example, the variance of the difference between the first and second errors is $\text{Var}(\tilde{\varepsilon}_{n21}) = \text{Var}(\varepsilon_{n2} - \varepsilon_{n1}) = \text{Var}(\varepsilon_{n1}) + \text{Var}(\varepsilon_{n2}) - 2\,\text{Cov}(\varepsilon_{n1}, \varepsilon_{n2}) = \sigma_{11} + \sigma_{22} - 2\sigma_{12}$. We can similarly calculate the covariance between $\tilde{\varepsilon}_{n21}$, which is the difference between the first and second errors, and $\tilde{\varepsilon}_{n31}$, which is the difference between the first and third errors: $\text{Cov}(\tilde{\varepsilon}_{n21}, \tilde{\varepsilon}_{n31}) = E(\varepsilon_{n2} - \varepsilon_{n1})(\varepsilon_{n3} - \varepsilon_{n1}) = E(\varepsilon_{n2}\varepsilon_{n3} - \varepsilon_{n2}\varepsilon_{n1} - \varepsilon_{n3}\varepsilon_{n1} + \varepsilon_{n1}\varepsilon_{n1}) = \sigma_{23} - \sigma_{21} - \sigma_{31} + \sigma_{11}$. The covariance matrix for the vector of error differences becomes

$$\tilde{\Omega}_1 = \begin{pmatrix} \sigma_{11} + \sigma_{22} - 2\sigma_{12} & \sigma_{11} + \sigma_{23} - \sigma_{12} - \sigma_{13} & \sigma_{11} + \sigma_{24} - \sigma_{12} - \sigma_{14} \\ \cdot & \sigma_{11} + \sigma_{33} - 2\sigma_{13} & \sigma_{11} + \sigma_{34} - \sigma_{13} - \sigma_{14} \\ \cdot & \cdot & \sigma_{11} + \sigma_{44} - 2\sigma_{14} \end{pmatrix}.$$

Setting the variance of one of the original errors is not sufficient to set the variance of the error differences. For example, if the variance for the first alternative is set to some number $\sigma_{11} = k$, the variance of the difference between the errors for the first two alternatives becomes

$k + \sigma_{22} - 2\sigma_{12}$. An infinite number of values for $\sigma_{22} - 2\sigma_{12}$ provide equivalent models.

A common way to set the scale of utility when errors are not iid is to normalize the variance of one of the error differences to some number. Setting the variance of an error difference sets the scale of utility differences and hence of utility. Suppose we normalize the variance of $\tilde{\varepsilon}_{n21}$ to 1. The covariance matrix for the error differences, expressed in terms of the covariances of the original errors, becomes

$$(2.4) \quad \begin{pmatrix} 1 & (\sigma_{11} + \sigma_{23} - \sigma_{12} - \sigma_{13})/m & (\sigma_{11} + \sigma_{24} - \sigma_{12} - \sigma_{14})/m \\ \cdot & (\sigma_{11} + \sigma_{33} - 2\sigma_{13})/m & (\sigma_{11} + \sigma_{34} - \sigma_{13} - \sigma_{14})/m \\ \cdot & \cdot & (\sigma_{11} + \sigma_{44} - 2\sigma_{14})/m \end{pmatrix},$$

where $m = \sigma_{11} + \sigma_{22} - 2\sigma_{12}$. Utility is divided by $\sqrt{\sigma_{11} + \sigma_{22} - 2\sigma_{12}}$ to obtain this scaling.

Note that when the error terms are iid, normalizing the variance of one of these errors automatically normalizes the variance of the error differences. With iid errors, $\sigma_{jj} = \sigma_{ii}$ and $\sigma_{ij} = 0$ for $i \neq j$. Therefore, if σ_{11} is normalized to k, then the variance of the error difference becomes $\sigma_{11} + \sigma_{22} - 2\sigma_{12} = k + k - 0 = 2k$. The variance of the error difference is indeed being normalized, the same as with non-iid errors.

Normalization has implications for the number of parameters that can be estimated in the covariance matrix. The covariance of the original errors, Ω in equation (2.3), has ten elements in our four-alternative example. However, the covariance matrix of the error differences has six elements, one of which is normalized to set the scale of utility differences. The covariance matrix for error differences with the variance of the first error difference normalized to k takes the form

$$(2.5) \quad \tilde{\Omega}_1^* = \begin{pmatrix} k & \omega_{ab} & \omega_{ac} \\ \cdot & \omega_{bb} & \omega_{bc} \\ \cdot & \cdot & \omega_{cc} \end{pmatrix},$$

which has only five parameters. On recognizing that only differences matter and that the scale of utility is arbitrary, the number of covariance parameters drops from ten to five. A model with J alternatives has at most $J(J - 1)/2 - 1$ covariance parameters after normalization.

Interpretation of the model is affected by the normalization. Suppose for example that the elements of matrix (2.5) were estimated. The parameter ω_{bb} is the variance of the difference between the errors for the first and third alternatives *relative* to the variance of the difference between the errors for the first and second alternatives. Complicating interpretation even further is the fact that the variance of the difference between the errors for two alternatives reflects the variances of both as well as their covariance.

As we will see, the normalization of logit and nested logit models is automatic with the distributional assumptions that are placed on the error terms. Interpretation under these assumptions is relatively straightforward. For mixed logit and probit, fewer assumptions are placed on the distribution of error terms, so that normalization is not automatic. The researcher must keep the normalization issues in mind when specifying and interpreting a model. We return to this topic when discussing each discrete choice model in subsequent chapters.

2.6   Aggregation

Discrete choice models operate at the level of individual decision makers. However, the researcher is usually interested in some aggregate measure, such as the average probability within a population or the average response to a change in some factor.

In linear regression models, estimates of aggregate values of the dependent variable are obtained by inserting aggregate values of the explanatory variables into the model. For example, suppose h_n is housing expenditures of person n, y_n is the income of the person, and the model relating them is $h_n = \alpha + \beta y_n$. Since this model is linear, the average expenditure on housing is simply calculated as $\alpha + \beta \bar{y}$, where $\bar{y}$ is average income. Similarly, the average response to a one-unit change in income is simply β, since β is the response for each person.

Discrete choice models are not linear in explanatory variables, and consequently, inserting aggregate values of the explanatory variables into the models will not provide an unbiased estimate of the average probability or average response. The point can be made visually. Consider Figure 2.1, which gives the probabilities of choosing a particular alternative for two individuals with the observed portion of their utility (their *representative utility*) being a and b. The average probability is the average of the probabilities for the two people, namely, $(P_a + P_b)/2$. The average representative utility is $(a + b)/2$, and the probability evaluated at this average is the point on the curve above $(a + b)/2$. As shown for this case, the average probability is greater than the probability evaluated at the average representative utility. In general, the probability evaluated at the average representative utility underestimates the average probability when the individuals' choice probabilities are low and overestimates when they are high.

Estimating the average response by calculating derivatives and elasticities at the average of the explanatory variables is similarly problematic.

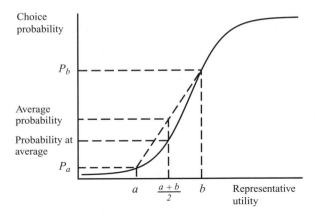

Figure 2.1. Difference between average probability and probability calculated at average representative utility.

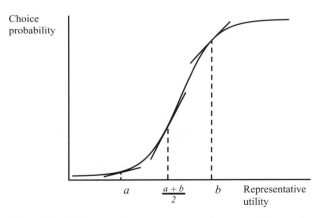

Figure 2.2. Difference between average response and response calculated at average representative utility.

Consider Figure 2.2, depicting two individuals with representative utilities a and b. The derivative of the choice probability for a change in representative utility is small for both of these people (the slope of the curve above a and b). Consequently, the average derivative is also small. However, the derivative at the average representative utility is very large (the slope above $(a + b)/2$). Estimating the average response in this way can be seriously misleading. In fact, Talvitie (1976) found, in a mode choice situation, that elasticities at the average representative utility can be as much as two or three times greater or less than the average of the individual elasticities.

Aggregate outcome variables can be obtained consistently from discrete choice models in two ways, by sample enumeration or segmentation. We discuss each approach in the following sections.

2.6.1. Sample Enumeration

The most straightforward, and by far the most popular, approach is sample enumeration, by which the choice probabilities of each decision maker in a sample are summed, or averaged, over decision makers. Consider a discrete choice model that gives probability P_{ni} that decision maker n will choose alternative i from a set of alternatives. Suppose a sample of N decision makers, labeled $n = 1, \ldots, N$, is drawn from the population for which aggregate statistics are required. (This sample might be the sample on which the model was estimated. However, it might also be a different sample, collected in a different area or at a later date than the estimation sample.) Each sampled decision maker n has some weight associated with him, w_n, representing the number of decision makers similar to him in the population. For samples based on exogenous factors, this weight is the reciprocal of the probability that the decision maker was selected into the sample. If the sample is purely random, then w_n is the same for all n; and if the sample is stratified random, then w_n is the same for all n within a stratum.

A consistent estimate of the total number of decision makers in the population who choose alternative i, labeled $\hat{N}_i$, is simply the weighted sum of the individual probabilities:

$$\hat{N}_i = \sum_n w_n P_{ni}.$$

The average probability, which is the estimated market share, is $\hat{N}_i / N$. Average derivatives and elasticities are similarly obtained by calculating the derivative and elasticity for each sampled person and taking the weighted average.

2.6.2. Segmentation

When the number of explanatory variables is small, and those variables take only a few values, it is possible to estimate aggregate outcomes without utilizing a sample of decision makers. Consider, for example, a model with only two variables entering the representative utility of each alternative: education level and gender. Suppose the education variable consists of four categories: did not complete high school, completed high school but did not attend college, attended college but did not receive a degree, received a college degree. Then the total number of different types of decision makers (called *segments*) is eight: the four education levels for each of the two genders. Choice probabilities vary only over these eight segments, not over individuals within each segment.

If the researcher has data on the number of people in each segment, then the aggregate outcome variables can be estimated by calculating the choice probability for each segment and taking the weighted sum of these probabilities. The number of people estimated to choose alternative i is

$$\hat{N}_i = \sum_{s=1}^{8} w_s P_{si},$$

where P_{si} is the probability that a decision maker in segment s chooses alternative i, and w_s is the number of decision makers in segment s.

2.7   Forecasting

For forecasting into some future year, the procedures described earlier for aggregate variables are applied. However, the exogenous variables and/or the weights are adjusted to reflect changes that are anticipated over time. With sample enumeration, the sample is adjusted so that it *looks like* a sample that would be drawn in the future year. For example, to forecast the number of people who will choose a given alternative five years in the future, a sample drawn from the current year is adjusted to reflect changes in socioeconomic and other factors that are expected to occur over the next five years. The sample is adjusted by (1) changing the value of the variables associated with each sampled decision maker (e.g., increasing each decision maker's income to represent real income growth over time), and/or (2) changing the weight attached to each decision maker to reflect changes over time in the number of decision makers in the population that are similar to the sampled decision maker (e.g., increasing the weights for one-person households and decreasing weights for large households to reflect expected decreases in household size over time).

For the segmentation approach, changes in explanatory variables over time are represented by changes in the number of decision makers in each segment. The explanatory variables themselves cannot logically be adjusted, since the distinct values of the explanatory variables define the segments. Changing the variables associated with a decision maker in one segment simply shifts the decision maker to another segment.

2.8   Recalibration of Constants

As described in Section 2.5.1, alternative-specific constants are often included in a model to capture the average effect of unobserved factors. In forecasting, it is often useful to adjust these constants, to reflect the fact that unobserved factors are different for the forecast area or year compared to the estimation sample. Market-share data from the forecast area can be used to *recalibrate* the constants appropriately. The recalibrated model can then be used to predict changes in market shares due to changes in explanatory factors.

An iterative process is used to recalibrate the constants. Let α_j^0 be the estimated alternative-specific constant for alternative j. The superscript 0 is used to indicate that these are the starting values in the iterative process. Let S_j denote the share of decision makers in the forecast area that choose alternative j in the *base* year (usually, the latest year for which such data are available.) Using the discrete choice model with its original values of $\alpha_j^0 \ \forall j$, predict the share of decision makers in the forecast area who will choose each alternative. Label these predictions $\hat{S}_j^0 \ \forall j$. Compare the predicted shares with the actual shares. If the actual share for an alternative exceeds the predicted share, raise the constant for that alternative. Lower the constant if the actual share is below the predicted. An effective adjustment is

$$\alpha_j^1 = \alpha_j^0 + \ln\left(S_j / \hat{S}_j^0\right).$$

With the new constants, predict the share again, compare with the actual shares, and if needed adjust the constants again. The process is repeated until the forecasted shares are sufficiently close to the actual shares. The model with these recalibrated constants is then used to predict changes from base-year shares due to changes in observed factors that affect decision makers' choices.

3 Logit

3.1 Choice Probabilities

By far the easiest and most widely used discrete choice model is logit. Its popularity is due to the fact that the formula for the choice probabilities takes a closed form and is readily interpretable. Originally, the logit formula was derived by Luce (1959) from assumptions about the characteristics of choice probabilities, namely the *independence from irrelevant alternatives* (IIA) property discussed in Section 3.3.2. Marschak (1960) showed that these axioms implied that the model is consistent with utility maximization. The relation of the logit formula to the distribution of unobserved utility (as opposed to the characteristics of choice probabilities) was developed by Marley, as cited by Luce and Suppes (1965), who showed that the extreme value distribution leads to the logit formula. McFadden (1974) completed the analysis by showing the converse: that the logit formula for the choice probabilities necessarily implies that unobserved utility is distributed extreme value. In his Nobel lecture, McFadden (2001) provides a fascinating history of the development of this path-breaking model.

To derive the logit model, we use the general notation from Chapter 2 and add a specific distribution for unobserved utility. A decision maker, labeled n, faces J alternatives. The utility that the decision maker obtains from alternative j is decomposed into (1) a part labeled V_{nj} that is known by the researcher up to some parameters, and (2) an unknown part ε_{nj} that is treated by the researcher as random: $U_{nj} = V_{nj} + \varepsilon_{nj} \ \forall j$. The logit model is obtained by assuming that each ε_{nj} is independently, identically distributed extreme value. The distribution is also called Gumbel and type I extreme value (and sometimes, mistakenly, Weibull). The density for each unobserved component of utility is

$$(3.1) \quad f(\varepsilon_{nj}) = e^{-\varepsilon_{nj}} e^{-e^{-\varepsilon_{nj}}},$$

and the cumulative distribution is

$$(3.2) \quad F(\varepsilon_{nj}) = e^{-e^{-\varepsilon_{nj}}}.$$

The variance of this distribution is $\pi^2/6$. By assuming the variance is $\pi^2/6$, we are implicitly normalizing the scale of utility, as discussed in Section 2.5. We return to this issue, and its relevance to interpretation, in the next section. The mean of the extreme value distribution is not zero; however, the mean is immaterial, since only differences in utility matter (see Chapter 2), and the difference between two random terms that have the same mean has itself a mean of zero.

The difference between two extreme value variables is distributed logistic. That is, if ε_{nj} and ε_{ni} are iid extreme value, then $\varepsilon^*_{nji} = \varepsilon_{nj} - \varepsilon_{ni}$ follows the logistic distribution

$$(3.3) \quad F\left(\varepsilon^*_{nji}\right) = \frac{e^{\varepsilon^*_{nji}}}{1 + e^{\varepsilon^*_{nji}}}.$$

This formula is sometimes used in describing binary logit models, that is, models with two alternatives. Using the extreme value distribution for the errors (and hence the logistic distribution for the error differences) is nearly the same as assuming that the errors are independently normal. The extreme value distribution gives slightly fatter tails than a normal, which means that it allows for slightly more aberrant behavior than the normal. Usually, however, the difference between extreme value and independent normal errors is indistinguishable empirically.

The key assumption is not so much the shape of the distribution as that the errors are independent of each other. This independence means that the unobserved portion of utility for one alternative is unrelated to the unobserved portion of utility for another alternative. It is a fairly restrictive assumption, and the development of other models such as those described in Chapters 4–6 has arisen largely for the purpose of avoiding this assumption and allowing for correlated errors.

It is important to realize that the independence assumption is not as restrictive as it might at first seem, and in fact can be interpreted as a natural outcome of a well-specified model. Recall from Chapter 2 that ε_{nj} is defined as the difference between the utility that the decision maker actually obtains, U_{nj}, and the representation of utility that the researcher has developed using observed variables, V_{nj}. As such, ε_{nj} and its distribution depend on the researcher's specification of representative utility; it is not defined by the choice situation *per se*. In this light, the assumption of independence attains a different stature. Under independence, the error for one alternative provides no information to the researcher about the error for another alternative. Stated equivalently, the researcher has specified V_{nj} sufficiently that the remaining, unobserved portion of utility is essentially "white noise." In a deep sense, the ultimate goal of the researcher is to represent utility so well that the only remaining aspects constitute simply white noise; that is, the goal is to specify utility well enough that a logit model is appropriate. Seen in this way, the logit model is the ideal rather than a restriction.

If the researcher thinks that the unobserved portion of utility is correlated over alternatives given her specification of representative utility, then she has three options: (1) use a different model that allows for correlated errors, such as those described in Chapters 4–6, (2) respecify representative utility so that the source of the correlation is captured explicitly and thus the remaining errors are independent, or (3) use the logit model under the current specification of representative utility, considering the model to be an approximation. The viability of the last option depends, of course, on the goals of the research. Violations of the logit assumptions seem to have less effect when estimating average preferences than when forecasting substitution patterns. These issues are discussed in subsequent sections.

We now derive the logit choice probabilities, following McFadden (1974). The probability that decision maker n chooses alternative i is

$$P_{ni} = \text{Prob}(V_{ni} + \varepsilon_{ni} > V_{nj} + \varepsilon_{nj} \ \forall j \neq i)$$

(3.4)
$$= \text{Prob}(\varepsilon_{nj} < \varepsilon_{ni} + V_{ni} - V_{nj} \ \forall j \neq i).$$

If ε_{ni} is considered given, this expression is the cumulative distribution for each ε_{nj} evaluated at $\varepsilon_{ni} + V_{ni} - V_{nj}$, which, according to (3.2), is $\exp(-\exp(-(\varepsilon_{ni} + V_{ni} - V_{nj})))$. Since the ε's are independent, this cumulative distribution over all $j \neq i$ is the product of the individual cumulative distributions:

$$P_{ni} \mid \varepsilon_{ni} = \prod_{j \neq i} e^{-e^{-(\varepsilon_{ni} + V_{ni} - V_{nj})}}.$$

Of course, ε_{ni} is not given, and so the choice probability is the integral of $P_{ni} \mid \varepsilon_{ni}$ over all values of ε_{ni} weighted by its density (3.1):

(3.5)
$$P_{ni} = \int \left(\prod_{j \neq i} e^{-e^{-(\varepsilon_{ni} + V_{ni} - V_{nj})}} \right) e^{-\varepsilon_{ni}} e^{-e^{-\varepsilon_{ni}}} \, d\varepsilon_{ni}.$$

Some algebraic manipulation of this integral results in a succinct, closed-form expression:

(3.6)
$$P_{ni} = \frac{e^{V_{ni}}}{\sum_j e^{V_{nj}}},$$

which is the logit choice probability. The algebra that obtains (3.6) from (3.5) is given in the last section of this chapter.

Representative utility is usually specified to be linear in parameters: $V_{nj} = \beta' x_{nj}$, where x_{nj} is a vector of observed variables relating to alternative j. With this specification, the logit probabilities become

$$P_{ni} = \frac{e^{\beta' x_{ni}}}{\sum_j e^{\beta' x_{nj}}}.$$

Under fairly general conditions, any function can be approximated arbitrarily closely by one that is linear in parameters. The assumption is therefore fairly benign. Importantly, McFadden (1974) demonstrated that the log-likelihood function with these choice probabilities is globally concave in parameters β, which helps in the numerical maximization procedures (as discussed in Chapter 8). Numerous computer packages contain routines for estimation of logit models with linear-in-parameters representative utility.

The logit probabilities exhibit several desirable properties. First, P_{ni} is necessarily between zero and one, as required for a probability. When V_{ni} rises, reflecting an improvement in the observed attributes of the alternative, with $V_{nj} \; \forall j \neq i$ held constant, P_{ni} approaches one. And P_{ni} approaches zero when V_{ni} decreases, since the exponential in the numerator of (3.6) approaches zero as V_{ni} approaches $-\infty$. The logit probability for an alternative is never exactly zero. If the researcher believes that an alternative has actually no chance of being chosen by a decision maker, the researcher can exclude that alternative from the choice set. A probability of exactly 1 is obtained only if the choice set consists of a single alternative.

Second, the choice probabilities for all alternatives sum to one: $\sum_{i=1}^{J} P_{ni} = \sum_i \exp(V_{ni})/\sum_j \exp(V_{nj}) = 1$. The decision maker necessarily chooses one of the alternatives. The denominator in (3.6) is simply the sum of the numerator over all alternatives, which gives this summing-up property automatically. With logit, as well as with some more complex models such as the nested logit models of Chapter 4, interpretation of the choice probabilities is facilitated by recognition that the denominator serves to assure that the probabilities sum to one. In other models, such as mixed logit and probit, there is no denominator *per se* to interpret in this way.

The relation of the logit probability to representative utility is sigmoid, or S-shaped, as shown in Figure 3.1. This shape has implications for the impact of changes in explanatory variables. If the representative utility of an alternative is very low compared with other alternatives, a small increase in the utility of the alternative has little effect on the probability of its being chosen: the other alternatives are still sufficiently better such that this small improvement doesn't help much. Similarly, if one alternative

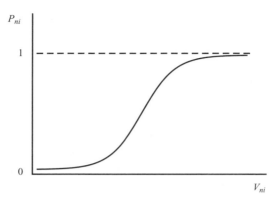

Figure 3.1. Graph of logit curve.

is far superior to the others in observed attributes, a further increase in its representative utility has little effect on the choice probability. The point at which the increase in representative utility has the greatest effect on the probability of its being chosen is when the probability is close to 0.5, meaning a 50–50 chance of the alternative being chosen. In this case, a small improvement tips the balance in people's choices, inducing a large change in probability. The sigmoid shape of logit probabilities is shared by most discrete choice models and has important implications for policy makers. For example, improving bus service in areas where the service is so poor that few travelers take the bus would be less effective, in terms of transit ridership, than making the same improvement in areas where bus service is already sufficiently good to induce a moderate share of travelers to choose it (but not so good that nearly everyone does).

The logit probability formula is easily interpretable in the context of an example. Consider a binary choice situation first: a household's choice between a gas and an electric heating system. Suppose that the utility the household obtains from each type of system depends only on the purchase price, the annual operating cost, and the household's view of the convenience and quality of heating with each type of system and the relative aesthetics of the systems within the house. The first two of these factors can be observed by the researcher, but the researcher cannot observe the others. If the researcher considers the observed part of utility to be a linear function of the observed factors, then the utility of each heating system can be written as: $U_g = \beta_1 PP_g + \beta_2 OC_g + \varepsilon_g$ and $U_e = \beta_1 PP_e + \beta_2 OC_e + \varepsilon_e$, where the subscripts g and e denote gas and electric, PP and OC are the purchase price and operating cost, β_1 and β_2 are scalar parameters, and the subscript n for the household is suppressed. Since higher costs mean less money to spend on other goods, we expect utility to drop as purchase price or operating cost rises (with all else held constant): $\beta_1 < 0$ and $\beta_2 < 0$.

The unobserved component of utility for each alternative, ε_g and ε_e, varies over households depending on how each household views the quality, convenience and aesthetics of each type of system. If these unobserved components are distributed iid extreme value, then the probability that the household will choose gas heating is

$$(3.7) \quad P_g = \frac{e^{\beta_1 PP_g + \beta_2 OC_g}}{e^{\beta_1 PP_g + \beta_2 OC_g} + e^{\beta_1 PP_e + \beta_2 OC_e}}$$

and the probability of electric heating is the same but with $\exp(\beta_1 PP_e + \beta_2 OC_e)$ as the numerator. The probability of choosing a gas system decreases if its purchase price or operating cost rises while that of the electric system remains the same (assuming that β_1 and β_2 are negative, as expected).

As in most discrete choice models, the ratio of coefficients in this example has economic meaning. In particular, the ratio β_2/β_1 represents the household's willingness to pay for operating-cost reductions. If β_1 were estimated as -0.20 and β_2 as -1.14, these estimates would imply that households are willing to pay up to $(-1.14)/(-0.20) = 5.70$ dollars more for a system whose annual operating costs are one dollar less. This relation is derived as follows. By definition, a household's willingness to pay for operating-cost reductions is the increase in purchase price that keeps the household's utility constant given a reduction in operating costs. We take the total derivative of utility with respect to purchase price and operating cost and set this derivative to zero so that utility doesn't change: $dU = \beta_1 \, dPP + \beta_2 \, dOC = 0$. We then solve for the change in purchase price that keeps utility constant (i.e., satisfies this equation) for a change in operating costs: $\partial PP/\partial OC = -\beta_2/\beta_1$. The negative sign indicates that the two changes are in the opposite direction: to keep utility constant, purchase price rises when operating cost decreases.

In this binary choice situation, the choice probabilities can be expressed in another, even more succinct form. Dividing the numerator and denominator of (3.7) by the numerator, and recognizing that $\exp(a)/\exp(b) = \exp(a - b)$, we have

$$P_g = \frac{1}{1 + e^{(\beta_1 PP_e + \beta_2 OC_e) - (\beta_1 PP_g + \beta_2 OC_g)}}.$$

In general, binary logit probabilities with representative utilities V_{n1} and V_{n2} can be written $P_{n1} = 1/(1 + \exp(V_{n2} - V_{n1}))$ and $P_{n2} = 1/(1 + \exp(V_{n1} - V_{n2}))$. If only demographics of the decision maker, s_n, enter the model, and the coefficients of these demographic variables are normalized to zero for the first alternative (as described in Chapter 2), the probability of the first alternative is $P_{n1} = 1/(1 + e^{\alpha' s_n})$, which is the form that is used in most textbooks and computer manuals for binary logit.

Multinomial choice is a simple extension. Suppose there is a third type of heating system, namely oil-fueled. The utility of the oil system is specified as the same form as for the electric and gas systems: $U_o = \beta_1 PP_o + \beta_2 OC_o + \varepsilon_o$. With this extra option available, the probability that the household chooses a gas system is

$$P_g = \frac{e^{\beta_1 PP_g + \beta_2 OC_g}}{e^{\beta_1 PP_g + \beta_2 OC_g} + e^{\beta_1 PP_e + \beta_2 OC_e} + e^{\beta_1 PP_o + \beta_2 OC_o}},$$

which is the same as (3.7) except that an extra term is included in the denominator to represent the oil heater. Since the denominator is larger while the numerator is the same, the probability of choosing a gas system is smaller when an oil system is an option than when not, as one would expect in the real world.

3.2   The Scale Parameter

In the previous section we derived the logit formula under the assumption that the unobserved factors are distributed extreme value with variance $\pi^2/6$. Setting the variance to $\pi^2/6$ is equivalent to normalizing the model for the scale of utility, as discussed in Section 2.5. It is useful to make these concepts more explicit, to show the role that the variance of the unobserved factors plays in logit models.

In general, utility can be expressed as $U_{nj}^* = V_{nj} + \varepsilon_{nj}^*$, where the unobserved portion has variance $\sigma^2 \times (\pi^2/6)$. That is, the variance is any number, re-expressed as a multiple of $\pi^2/6$. Since the scale of utility is irrelevant to behavior, utility can be divided by σ without changing behavior. Utility becomes $U_{nj} = V_{nj}/\sigma + \varepsilon_{nj}$ where $\varepsilon_{nj} = \varepsilon_{nj}^*/\sigma$. Now the unobserved portion has variance $\pi^2/6$: $\text{Var}(\varepsilon_{nj}) = \text{Var}(\varepsilon_{nj}^*/\sigma) = (1/\sigma^2) \text{Var}(\varepsilon_{nj}^*) = (1/\sigma^2) \times \sigma^2 \times (\pi^2/6) = \pi^2/6$. The choice probability is

$$P_{ni} = \frac{e^{V_{ni}/\sigma}}{\sum_j e^{V_{nj}/\sigma}},$$

which is the same formula as in equation (3.6) but with the representative utility divided by σ. If V_{nj} is linear in parameters with coefficient β^*, the choice probabilities become

$$P_{ni} = \frac{e^{(\beta^*/\sigma)'x_{ni}}}{\sum_j e^{(\beta^*/\sigma)'x_{nj}}}.$$

Each of the coefficients is scaled by $1/\sigma$. The parameter σ is called the *scale parameter*, because it scales the coefficients to reflect the variance of the unobserved portion of utility.

Only the ratio β^*/σ can be estimated; β^* and σ are not separately identified. Usually, the model is expressed in its scaled form, with $\beta = \beta^*/\sigma$, which gives the standard logit expression

$$P_{ni} = \frac{e^{\beta' x_{ni}}}{\sum_j e^{\beta' x_{nj}}}.$$

The parameters β are estimated, but for interpretation it is useful to recognize that these estimated parameters are actually estimates of the "original" coefficients β^* divided by the scale parameter σ. The coefficients that are estimated indicate the effect of each observed variable *relative to* the variance of the unobserved factors. A larger variance in unobserved factors leads to smaller coefficients, even if the observed factors have the same effect on utility (i.e., higher σ means lower β even if β^* is the same).

The scale parameter does not affect the ratio of any two coefficients, since it drops out of the ratio; for example, $\beta_1/\beta_2 = (\beta_1^*/\sigma)/(\beta_2^*/\sigma) = \beta_1^*/\beta_2^*$, where the subscripts refer to the first and second coefficients. Willingness to pay, values of time, and other measures of marginal rates of substitution are not affected by the scale parameter. Only the interpretation of the magnitudes of all coefficients is affected.

So far we have assumed that the variance of the unobserved factors is the same for all decision makers, since the same σ is used for all n. Suppose instead that the unobserved factors have greater variance for some decision makers than others. In Section 2.5, we discuss a situation where the variance of unobserved factors is different in Boston than in Chicago. Denote the variance for all decision makers in Boston as $(\sigma^B)^2(\pi^2/6)$ and that for decision makers in Chicago as $(\sigma^C)^2(\pi^2/6)$. The ratio of variance in Chicago to that in Boston is $k = (\sigma^C/\sigma^B)^2$. The choice probabilities for people in Boston become

$$P_{ni} = \frac{e^{\beta' x_{ni}}}{\sum_j e^{\beta' x_{nj}}},$$

and for people in Chicago

$$P_{ni} = \frac{e^{(\beta/\sqrt{k})' x_{ni}}}{\sum_j e^{(\beta/\sqrt{k})' x_{nj}}},$$

where $\beta = \beta^*/\sigma^B$. The ratio of variances k is estimated along with the coefficients β. The estimated β's are interpreted as being relative to the variance of unobserved factors in Boston, and the estimated k provides information on the variance in Chicago relative to that in Boston. More complex relations can be obtained by allowing the variance for an observation to depend on more factors. Also, data from different data sets can often be expected to have different variance for unobserved factors, giving a different scale parameter for each data set. Ben-Akiva and Morikawa (1990) and Swait and Louviere (1993) discuss these issues and provide more examples.

3.3   Power and Limitations of Logit

Three topics elucidate the power of logit models to represent choice behavior, as well as delineating the limits to that power. These topics are: taste variation, substitution patterns, and repeated choices over time. The applicability of logit models can be summarized as follows:

1. Logit can represent systematic taste variation (that is, taste variation that relates to observed characteristics of the decision maker) but not random taste variation (differences in tastes that cannot be linked to observed characteristics).
2. The logit model implies proportional substitution across alternatives, given the researcher's specification of representative utility. To capture more flexible forms of substitution, other models are needed.
3. If unobserved factors are independent over time in repeated choice situations, then logit can capture the dynamics of repeated choice, including state dependence. However, logit cannot handle situations where unobserved factors are correlated over time.

We elaborate each of these statements in the next three subsections.

3.3.1. Taste Variation

The value or importance that decision makers place on each attribute of the alternatives varies, in general, over decision makers. For example, the size of a car is probably more important to households with many members than to smaller households. Low-income households are probably more concerned about the purchase price of a good, relative to its other characteristics, than higher-income households. In choosing which neighborhood to live in, households with young children will be more concerned about the quality of schools than those without children, and so on. Decision makers' tastes also vary for reasons that are not linked to observed demographic characteristics, just because different people are different. Two people who have the same income, education, etc., will make different choices, reflecting their individual preferences and concerns.

Logit models can capture taste variations, but only within limits. In particular, tastes that vary systematically with respect to observed variables can be incorporated in logit models, while tastes that vary with unobserved variables or purely randomly cannot be handled. The following example illustrates the distinction.

Consider households' choice among makes and models of cars to buy. Suppose for simplicity that the only two attributes of cars that the researcher observes are the purchase price, PP_j for make/model j, and inches of shoulder room, SR_j, which is a measure of the interior size of a car. The value that households place on these two attributes varies over households, and so utility is written as

$$(3.8) \quad U_{nj} = \alpha_n SR_j + \beta_n PP_j + \varepsilon_{nj},$$

where α_n and β_n are parameters specific to household n.

The parameters vary over households reflecting differences in taste. Suppose for example that the value of shoulder room varies with the number of members in the households, M_n, but nothing else:

$$\alpha_n = \rho M_n,$$

so that as M_n increases, the value of shoulder room, α_n, also increases. Similarly, suppose the importance of purchase price is inversely related to income, I_n, so that low-income households place more importance on purchase price:

$$\beta_n = \theta / I_n.$$

Substituting these relations into (3.8) produces

$$U_{nj} = \rho(M_n SR_j) + \theta(PP_j / I_n) + \varepsilon_{nj}.$$

Under the assumption that each ε_{nj} is iid extreme value, a standard logit model obtains with two variables entering representative utility, both of which are an interaction of a vehicle attribute with a household characteristic.

Other specifications for the variation in tastes can be substituted. For example, the value of shoulder room might be assumed to increase with household size, but at a decreasing rate, so that $\alpha_n = \rho M_n + \phi M_n^2$ where ρ is expected to be positive and ϕ negative. Then $U_{nj} = \rho(M_n SR_j) + \phi(M_n^2 SR_j) + \theta(PP_j / I_n) + \varepsilon_{nj}$, which results in a logit model with three variables entering the representative utility.

The limitation of the logit model arises when we attempt to allow tastes to vary with respect to unobserved variables or purely randomly. Suppose for example that the value of shoulder room varied with household size plus some other factors (e.g., size of the people themselves, or frequency with which the household travels together) that are unobserved by the researcher and hence considered random:

$$\alpha_n = \rho M_n + \mu_n,$$

where μ_n is a random variable. Similarly, the importance of purchase price consists of its observed and unobserved components:

$$\beta_n = \theta / I_n + \eta_n.$$

Substituting into (3.8) produces

$$U_{nj} = \rho(M_n \text{SR}_j) + \mu_n \text{SR}_j + \theta(\text{PP}_j / I_n) + \eta_n \text{PP}_j + \varepsilon_{nj}.$$

Since μ_n and η_n are not observed, the terms $\mu_n \text{SR}_j$ and $\eta_n \text{PP}_j$ become part of the unobserved component of utility,

$$U_{nj} = \rho(M_n \text{SR}_j) + \theta(\text{PP}_j / I_n) + \tilde{\varepsilon}_{nj},$$

where $\tilde{\varepsilon}_{nj} = \mu_n \text{SR}_j + \eta_n \text{PP}_j + \varepsilon_{nj}$. The new error terms $\tilde{\varepsilon}_{nj}$ cannot possibly be distributed independently and identically as required for the logit formulation. Since μ_n and η_n enter each alternative, $\tilde{\varepsilon}_{nj}$ is necessarily correlated over alternatives: $\text{Cov}(\tilde{\varepsilon}_{nj}, \tilde{\varepsilon}_{nk}) = \text{Var}(\mu_n)\text{SR}_j\text{SR}_k + \text{Var}(\eta_n)\text{PP}_j\text{PP}_k \neq 0$ for any two cars j and k. Furthermore, since SR_j and PP_j vary over alternatives, the variance of $\tilde{\varepsilon}_{nj}$ varies over alternatives, violating the assumption of identically distributed errors: $\text{Var}(\tilde{\varepsilon}_{nj}) = \text{Var}(\mu_n)\text{SR}_j^2 + \text{Var}(\eta_n)\text{PP}_j^2 + \text{Var}(\varepsilon_{nj})$, which is different for different j.

This example illustrates the general point that when tastes vary systematically in the population in relation to observed variables, the variation can be incorporated into logit models. However, if taste variation is at least partly random, logit is a misspecification. As an approximation, logit might be able to capture the average tastes fairly well even when tastes are random, since the logit formula seems to be fairly robust to misspecifications. The researcher might therefore choose to use logit even when she knows that tastes have a random component, for the sake of simplicity. However, there is no guarantee that a logit model will approximate the average tastes. And even if it does, logit does not provide information on the distribution of tastes around the average. This distribution can be important in many situations, such as forecasting the penetration of a new product that appeals to a minority of people rather than to the average tastes. To incorporate random taste variation appropriately and fully, a probit or mixed logit model can be used instead.

3.3.2. Substitution Patterns

When the attributes of one alternative improve (e.g., its price drops), the probability of its being chosen rises. Some of the people who would have chosen other alternatives under the original attributes now choose this alternative instead. Since probabilities sum to one over alternatives, an increase in the probability of one alternative necessarily means a decrease in probability for other alternatives. The pattern of substitution among alternatives has important implications in many situations. For example, when a cell-phone manufacturer launches a new product with extra features, the firm is vitally interested in knowing the extent to which the new product will draw customers away from its other cell phones rather than from competitors' phones, since the firm makes more profit from the latter than from the former. Also, as we will see, the pattern of substitution affects the demand for a product and the change in demand when attributes change. Substitution patterns are therefore important even when the researcher is only interested in market share without being concerned about where the share comes from.

The logit model implies a certain pattern of substitution across alternatives. If substitution actually occurs in this way given the researcher's specification of representative utility, then the logit model is appropriate. However, to allow for more general patterns of substitution and to investigate which pattern is most accurate, more flexible models are needed. The issue can be seen in either of two ways, as a restriction on the ratios of probabilities and/or as a restriction on the cross-elasticities of probabilities. We present each way of characterizing the issue in the following discussion.

The Property of Independence from Irrelevant Alternatives

For any two alternatives i and k, the ratio of the logit probabilities is

$$\frac{P_{ni}}{P_{nk}} = \frac{e^{V_{ni}} / \sum_j e^{V_{nj}}}{e^{V_{nk}} / \sum_j e^{V_{nj}}}$$

$$= \frac{e^{V_{ni}}}{e^{V_{nk}}} = e^{V_{ni} - V_{nk}}.$$

This ratio does not depend on any alternatives other than i and k. That is, the relative odds of choosing i over k are the same no matter what other alternatives are available or what the attributes of the other alternatives are. Since the ratio is independent from alternatives other than i and k, it is said to be independent from *irrelevant* alternatives. The logit model exhibits this *independence from irrelevant alternatives*, or IIA.

In many settings, choice probabilities that exhibit IIA provide an accurate representation of reality. In fact, Luce (1959) considered IIA to be a property of appropriately specified choice probabilities. He derived the logit model directly from an assumption that choice probabilities exhibit IIA, rather than (as we have done) derive the logit formula from an assumption about the distribution of unobserved utility and then observe that IIA is a resulting property.

While the IIA property is realistic in some choice situations, it is clearly inappropriate in others, as first pointed out by Chipman (1960) and Debreu (1960). Consider the famous red-bus–blue-bus problem. A traveler has a choice of going to work by car or taking a blue bus. For simplicity assume that the representative utility of the two modes are the same, such that the choice probabilities are equal: $P_c = P_{bb} = \frac{1}{2}$, where c is car and bb is blue bus. In this case, the ratio of probabilities is one: $P_c / P_{bb} = 1$.

Now suppose that a red bus is introduced and that the traveler considers the red bus to be exactly like the blue bus. The probability that the traveler will take the red bus is therefore the same as for the blue bus, so that the ratio of their probabilities is one: $P_{rb} / P_{bb} = 1$. However, in the logit model the ratio P_c / P_{bb} is the same whether or not another alternative, in this case the red bus, exists. This ratio therefore remains at one. The only probabilities for which $P_c / P_{bb} = 1$ and $P_{rb} / P_{bb} = 1$ are $P_c = P_{bb} = P_{rb} = \frac{1}{3}$, which are the probabilities that the logit model predicts.

In real life, however, we would expect the probability of taking a car to remain the same when a new bus is introduced that is exactly the same as the old bus. We would also expect the original probability of taking bus to be split between the two buses after the second one is introduced. That is, we would expect $P_c = \frac{1}{2}$ and $P_{bb} = P_{rb} = \frac{1}{4}$. In this case, the logit model, because of its IIA property, overestimates the probability of taking either of the buses and underestimates the probability of taking a car. The ratio of probabilities of car and blue bus, P_c / P_{bb}, actually changes with the introduction of the red bus, rather than remaining constant as required by the logit model.

This example is rather stark and unlikely to be encountered in the real world. However, the same kind of misprediction arises with logit models whenever the ratio of probabilities for two alternatives changes with the introduction or change of another alternative. For example, suppose a new transit mode is added that is similar to, but not exactly like, the existing modes, such as an express bus along a line that already has standard bus service. This new mode might be expected to reduce the probability of regular bus by a greater proportion than it reduces the probability of car, so that ratio of probabilities for car and regular bus does not remain constant. The logit model would overpredict demand for the two bus modes in this situation. Other examples are given by, for example, Ortuzar (1983) and Brownstone and Train (1999).

Proportional Substitution

The same issue can be expressed in terms of the cross-elasticities of logit probabilities. Let us consider changing an attribute of alternative j. We want to know the effect of this change on the probabilities for all the *other* alternatives. Section 3.6 derives the formula for the elasticity of P_{ni} with respect to a variable that enters the representative utility of alternative j:

$$E_{iz_{nj}} = -\beta_z z_{nj} P_{nj},$$

where z_{nj} is the attribute of alternative j as faced by person n and β_z is its coefficient (or, if the variable enters representative utility nonlinearly, then β_z is the derivative of V_{nj} with respect to z_{nj}).

This cross-elasticity is the same for all i: i does not enter the formula. An improvement in the attributes of an alternative reduces the probabilities for all the other alternatives by the same percentage. If one alternative's probability drops by ten percent, then all the other alternatives' probabilities also drop by ten percent (except of course the alternative whose attribute changed; its probability rises due to the improvement). A way of stating this phenomenon succinctly is that an improvement in one alternative draws proportionately from the other alternatives. Similarly, for a decrease in the representative utility of an alternative, the probabilities for all other alternatives rise by the same percentage.

This pattern of substitution, which can be called *proportionate shifting*, is a manifestation of the IIA property. The ratio of probabilities for alternatives i and k stays constant when an attribute of alternative j changes only if the two probabilities change by the same proportion. With superscript 0 denoting probabilities before the change and 1 after, the IIA property requires that

$$\frac{P_{ni}^1}{P_{nk}^1} = \frac{P_{ni}^0}{P_{nk}^0}$$

when an attribute of alternative j changes. This equality can only be maintained if each probability changes by the same proportion: $P_{ni}^1 = \lambda P_{ni}^0$ and $P_{nk}^1 = \lambda P_{nk}^0$, where both λ's are the same.

Proportionate substitution can be realistic for some situations, in which case the logit model is appropriate. In many settings, however, other patterns of substitution can be expected, and imposing proportionate substitution through the logit model can lead to unrealistic forecasts. Consider a situation that is important to the California Energy Commission (CEC), which has the responsibility of investigating policies to promote energy efficient vehicles in California and reducing the state's reliance on gasoline for cars. Suppose for the sake of illustration that there are three kinds of vehicles: large gas cars, small gas cars, and small electric cars. Suppose also that under current conditions the probabilities that a household will choose each of these vehicles are .66, .33, and .01, respectively. The CEC is interested in knowing the impact of subsidizing the electric cars. Suppose the subsidy is sufficient to raise the probability for the electric car from .01 to .10. By the logit model, the probability for each of the gas cars would be predicted to drop by the same percentage. The probability for large gas car would drop by ten percent, from .66 to .60, and that for the small gas car would drop by the same ten percent, from .33 to .30. In terms of absolute numbers, the increased probability for the small electric car (.09) is predicted by the logit model to come twice as much from large gas cars (.06) as from small gas cars (0.03).

This pattern of substitution is clearly unrealistic. Since the electric car is small, subsidizing it can be expected to draw more from small gas cars than from large gas cars. In terms of cross-elasticities, we would expect the cross-elasticity for small gas cars with respect to an improvement in small electric cars to be higher than that for large gas cars. This difference is important in the CEC's policy analysis. The logit model will overpredict the gas savings that result from the subsidy, since it overpredicts the substitution away from large gas cars (the "gas guzzlers") and underpredicts the substitution away from small "gas-sipper" cars. From a policy perspective, this misprediction can be critical, causing a subsidy program to seem more beneficial than it actually is. This is the reason that the CEC uses models that are more general than logit to represent substitution across vehicles. The nested logit, probit, and mixed logit models of Chapters 4–6 provide viable options for the researcher.

Advantages of IIA

As just discussed, the IIA property of logit can be unrealistic in many settings. However, when IIA reflects reality (or an adequate approximation to reality), considerable advantages are gained by its employment. First, because of the IIA, it is possible to estimate model parameters consistently on a subset of alternatives for each sampled decision maker. For example, in a situation with 100 alternatives, the researcher might, so as to reduce computer time, estimate on a subset of 10 alternatives for each sampled person, with the person's chosen alternative included as well as 9 alternatives randomly selected from the remaining 99. Since relative probabilities within a subset of alternatives are unaffected by the attributes or existence of alternatives not in the subset, exclusion of alternatives in estimation does not affect the consistency of the estimator. Details of this type of estimation are given in Section 3.7.1. This fact has considerable practical importance. In analyzing choice situations for which the number of alternatives is large, estimation on a subset of alternatives can save substantial amounts of computer time. At an extreme, the number of alternatives might be so large as to preclude estimation altogether if it were not possible to utilize a subset of alternatives.

Another practical use of the IIA property arises when the researcher is only interested in examining choices among a subset of alternatives and not among all alternatives. For example, consider a researcher who is interested in understanding the factors that affect workers' choice between car and bus modes for travel to work. The full set of alternative modes includes walking, bicycling, motorbiking, skateboarding, and so on. If the researcher believed that the IIA property holds adequately well in this case, she could estimate a model with only car and bus as the alternatives and exclude from the analysis sampled workers who used other modes. This strategy would save the researcher considerable time and expense developing data on the other modes, without hampering her ability to examine the factors related to car and bus.

Tests of IIA

Whether IIA holds in a particular setting is an empirical question, amenable to statistical investigation. Tests of IIA were first developed by McFadden et al. (1978). Two types of tests are suggested. First, the model can be reestimated on a subset of the alternatives. Under IIA, the ratio of probabilities for any two alternatives is the same whether or not other alternatives are available. As a result, if IIA holds in reality, then the parameter estimates obtained on the subset of alternatives will not be significantly different from those obtained on the full set of alternatives. A test of the hypothesis that the parameters on the subset are the same as the parameters on the full set constitutes a test of IIA. Hausman and McFadden (1984) provide an appropriate statistic for this type of test. Second, the model can be reestimated with new, cross-alternative variables, that is, with variables from one alternative entering the utility of another alternative. If the ratio of probabilities for alternatives i and k actually depends on the attributes and existence of a third alternative j (in violation of IIA), then the attributes of alternative j will enter significantly the utility of alternatives i or k within a logit specification. A test of whether cross-alternative variables enter the model therefore constitutes a test of IIA. McFadden (1987) developed a procedure for performing this kind of test with regressions: with the dependent variable being the residuals of the original logit model and the explanatory variables being appropriately specified cross-alternative variables. Train et al. (1989) show how this procedure can be performed conveniently within the logit model itself.

The advent of models that do not exhibit IIA, and especially the development of software for estimating these models, makes testing IIA easier than before. For more flexible specifications, such as GEV and mixed logit, the simple logit model with IIA is a special case that arises under certain constraints on the parameters of the more flexible model. In these cases, IIA can be tested by testing these constraints. For example, a mixed logit model becomes a simple logit if the mixing distribution has zero variance. IIA can be tested by estimating a mixed logit and testing whether the variance of the mixing distribution is in fact zero.

A test of IIA as a constraint on a more general model necessarily operates under the maintained assumption that the more general model is itself an appropriate specification. The tests on subsets of alternatives (Hausman and McFadden, 1984) and cross-alternative variables (McFadden, 1987; Train et al., 1989), while more difficult to perform, operate under less restrictive maintained hypotheses. The counterpoint to this advantage, of course, is that, when IIA fails, these tests do not provide as much guidance on the correct specification to use instead of logit.

3.3.3. Panel Data

In many settings, the researcher can observe numerous choices made by each decision maker. For example, in labor studies, sampled people are observed to work or not work in each month over several years. Data on the current and past vehicle purchases of sampled households might be obtained by a researcher who is interested in the dynamics of car choice. In market research surveys, respondents are often asked a series of hypothetical choice questions, called "stated preference" experiments. For each experiment, a set of alternative products with different attributes is described, and the respondent is asked to state which product he would choose. A series of such questions is asked, with the attributes of the products varying so as to determine how the respondent's choice changes when the attributes change. The researcher therefore observes the sequence of choices by each respondent. Data that represent repeated choices like these are called panel data.

If the unobserved factors that affect decision makers are independent over the repeated choices, then logit can be used to examine panel data in the same way as purely cross-sectional data. Any dynamics related to observed factors that enter the decision process, such as state dependence (by which the person's past choices influence their current choices) or lagged response to changes in attributes, can be accommodated. However, dynamics associated with unobserved factors cannot be handled, since the unobserved factors are assumed to be unrelated over choices.

The utility that decision maker n obtains from alternative j in period or choice situation t is

$$U_{njt} = V_{njt} + \varepsilon_{njt} \qquad \forall j, t.$$

If ε_{njt} is distributed extreme value, independent over n, j, and, importantly, t, then, using the same proof as for (3.6), the choice probabilities are

$$(3.9) \qquad P_{nit} = \frac{e^{V_{nit}}}{\sum_j e^{V_{njt}}}.$$

Each choice situation by each decision maker becomes a separate observation. If representative utility for each period is specified to depend only on variables for that period; for example, $V_{njt} = \beta' x_{njt}$, where x_{njt} is a vector of variables describing alternative j as faced by n in period t, then there is essentially no difference between the logit model with panel data and with purely cross-sectional data.

Dynamic aspects of behavior can be captured by specifying representative utility in each period to depend on observed variables from other periods. For example, a lagged price response is represented by entering the price in period $t - 1$ as an explanatory variable in the utility for period t. Prices in future periods can be entered, as by Adamowicz (1994), to capture consumers' anticipation of future price changes. Under the assumptions of the logit model, the dependent variable in previous periods can also be entered as an explanatory variable. Suppose for example that there is inertia, or habit formation, in people's choices such that they tend to stay with the alternative that they have previously chosen unless another alternative provides sufficiently higher utility to warrant a switch. This behavior is captured as $V_{njt} = \alpha y_{nj(t-1)} + \beta x_{njt}$, where $y_{njt} = 1$ if n chose j in period t and 0 otherwise. With $\alpha > 0$, the utility of alternative j in the current period is higher if alternative j was consumed in the previous period. The same specification can also capture a type of variety seeking. If α is negative, the consumer obtains higher utility from *not* choosing the same alternative that he chose in the last period. Numerous variations on these concepts are possible. Adamowicz (1994) enters the *number* of times the alternative has been chosen previously, rather than simply a dummy for the immediately previous choice. Erdem (1996) enters the *attributes* of previously chosen alternatives, with the utility of each alternative in the current period depending on the similarity of its attributes to the previously experienced attributes.

The inclusion of the lagged dependent variable does not induce inconsistency in estimation, since for a logit model the errors are assumed to be independent over time. The lagged dependent variable $y_{nj(t-1)}$ is uncorrelated with the current error ε_{njt} due to this independence. The situation is analogous to linear regression models, where a lagged dependent variable can be added without inducing bias as long as the errors are independent over time.

Of course, the assumption of independent errors over time is severe. Usually, one would expect there to be some factors that are not observed by the researcher that affect each of the decision makers' choices. In particular, if there are dynamics in the observed factors, then the researcher might expect there to be dynamics in the unobserved factors as well. In these situations, the researcher can either use a model such as probit or mixed logit that allows unobserved factors to be correlated over time, or respecify representative utility to bring the sources of the unobserved dynamics into the model explicitly such that the remaining errors are independent over time.

3.4   Nonlinear Representative Utility

In some contexts, the researcher will find it useful to allow parameters to enter representative utility nonlinearly. Estimation is then more difficult, since the log-likelihood function may not be globally concave and computer routines are not as widely available as for logit models with linear-in-parameters utility. However, the aspects of behavior that the researcher is investigating may include parameters that are interpretable only when they enter utility nonlinearly. In these cases, the effort of writing one's own code can be warranted. Two examples illustrate this point.

Example 1: The Goods–Leisure Tradeoff

Consider a workers' choice of mode (car or bus) for trips to work. Suppose that workers also choose the number of hours to work based on the standard trade-off between goods and leisure. Train and McFadden (1978) developed a procedure for examining these interrelated choices. As we see in the following, the parameters of the workers' utility function over goods and leisure enter nonlinearly in the utility for modes of travel.

Assume that workers' preferences regarding goods G and leisure L are represented by a Cobb–Douglas utility function of the form

$$U = (1 - \beta) \ln G + \beta \ln L.$$

The parameter β reflects the worker's relative preference for goods and leisure, with higher β implying greater preference for leisure relative to goods. Each worker has a fixed amount of time (24 hours a day) and faces a fixed wage rate, w. In the standard goods–leisure model, the worker chooses the number of hours to work that maximizes U subject to the constraints that (1) the number of hours worked plus the number of leisure hours equals the number of hours available, and (2) the value of goods consumed equals the wage rate times the number of hours worked.

When mode choice is added to the model, the constraints on time and money change. Each mode takes a certain amount of time and costs a certain amount of money. Conditional on choosing car, the worker maximizes U subject to the constraint that (1) the number of hours worked plus the number of leisure hours equals the number of hours available *after the time spent driving to work in the car is subtracted* and (2) the value of goods consumed equals the wage rate times the number of hours worked *minus the cost of driving to work*. The utility associated with choosing to travel by car is the highest value of U that can be attained under these constraints. Similarly, the utility of taking the bus to work is the maximum value of U that can be obtained given the time and money that are left after the bus time and cost are subtracted. Train and McFadden derived the maximizing values of U conditional on each mode. For the U given above, these values are

$$U_j = -\alpha \left(c_j/w^\beta + w^{1-\beta} t_j \right) \qquad \text{for } j = \text{car and bus}.$$

The cost of travel is divided by w^β, and the travel time is multiplied by $w^{1-\beta}$. The parameter β, which denotes workers' relative preference for goods and leisure, enters the mode choice utility nonlinearly. Since this parameter has meaning, the researcher might want to estimate it within this nonlinear utility rather than use a linear-in-parameters approximation.

Example 2: Geographic Aggregation

Models have been developed and widely used for travelers' choice of destination for various types of trips, such as shopping trips, within a metropolitan area. Usually, the metropolitan area is partitioned into *zones*, and the models give the probability that a person will choose to travel to a particular zone. The representative utility for each zone depends on the time and cost of travel to the zone plus a variety of variables, such as residential population and retail employment, that reflect reasons that people might want to visit the zone. These latter variables are called *attraction* variables; label them by the vector a_j for zone j. Since it is these attraction variables that give rise to parameters entering nonlinearity, assume for simplicity that representative utility depends only on these variables.

The difficulty in specifying representative utility comes in recognizing that the researcher's decision of how large an area to include in each zone is fairly arbitrary. It would be useful to have a model that is not sensitive to the level of aggregation in the zonal definitions. If two zones are combined, it would be useful for the model to give a probability of traveling to the combined zone that is the same as the sum of the probabilities of traveling to the two original zones. This consideration places restrictions on the form of representative utility.

Consider zones j and k, which, when combined, are labeled zone c. The population and employment in the combined zone are necessarily the sums of those in the two original zones: $a_j + a_k = a_c$. In order for the models to give the same probability for choosing these zones before and after their merger, the model must satisfy

$$P_{nj} + P_{nk} = P_{nc},$$

which for logit models takes the form

$$\frac{e^{V_{nj}} + e^{V_{nk}}}{e^{V_{nj}} + e^{V_{nk}} + \sum_{\ell \neq j,k} e^{V_{n\ell}}} = \frac{e^{V_{nc}}}{e^{V_{nc}} + \sum_{\ell \neq j,k} e^{V_{n\ell}}}.$$

This equality holds only when $\exp(V_{nj}) + \exp(V_{nk}) = \exp(V_{nc})$. If representative utility is specified as $V_{n\ell} = \ln(\beta' a_\ell)$ for all zones ℓ, then the equality holds: $\exp(\ln(\beta' a_j)) + \exp(\ln(\beta' a_k)) = \beta' a_j + \beta' a_k = \beta' a_c = \exp(\ln(\beta' a_c))$. Therefore, to specify a destination choice model that is not sensitive to the level of zonal aggregation, representative utility needs to be specified with parameters inside a log operation.

3.5   Consumer Surplus

For policy analysis, the researcher is often interested in measuring the change in consumer surplus that is associated with a particular policy. For example, if a new alternative is being considered, such as building a light rail system in a city, then it is important to measure the benefits of the project to see if they warrant the costs. Similarly, a change in the attributes of an alternative can have an impact on consumer surplus that is important to assess. Degradation of the water quality of rivers harms the anglers who can no longer fish as effectively at the damaged sites. Measuring this harm in monetary terms is a central element of legal action against the polluter. Often the distributional effects of a policy are important to assess, such as how the burden of a tax is borne by different population groups.

Under the logit assumptions, the consumer surplus associated with a set of alternatives takes a closed form that is easy to calculate. By definition, a person's consumer surplus is the utility, in dollar terms, that the person receives in the choice situation. The decision maker chooses the alternative that provides the greatest utility. Consumer surplus is therefore $\mathrm{CS}_n = (1/\alpha_n) \max_j (U_{nj} \, \forall_j)$, where α_n is the marginal utility of income: $dU_n/dY_n = \alpha_n$, with Y_n the income of person n. The division by α_n translates utility into dollars, since $1/\alpha_n = dY_n/dU_n$. The researcher does not observe U_{nj} and therefore cannot use this expression to calculate the decision maker's consumer surplus. Instead, the researcher observes V_{nj} and knows the distribution of the remaining portion of utility. With this information, the researcher is able to calculate the expected consumer surplus:

$$E(\mathrm{CS}_n) = \frac{1}{\alpha_n} E[\max_j (V_{nj} + \varepsilon_{nj} \, \forall_j)],$$

where the expectation is over all possible values of ε_{nj}. Williams (1977) and Small and Rosen (1981) show that, if each ε_{nj} is iid extreme value and utility is linear in income (so that α_n is constant with respect to income), then this expectation becomes

$$(3.10) \quad E(\mathrm{CS}_n) = \frac{1}{\alpha_n} \ln \left(\sum_{j=1}^{J} e^{V_{nj}} \right) + C,$$

where C is an unknown constant that represents the fact that the absolute level of utility cannot be measured. As we see in the following, this constant is irrelevant from a policy perspective and can be ignored.

Note that the argument in parentheses in this expression is the denominator of the logit choice probability (3.6). Aside from the division and addition of constants, expected consumer surplus in a logit model is simply the log of the denominator of the choice probability. It is often called the *log-sum term*. This resemblance between the two formulas has no economic meaning, in the sense that there is nothing about a denominator in a choice probability that makes it necessarily related to consumer surplus. It is simply the outcome of the mathematical form of the extreme value distribution. However, the relation makes calculation of expected consumer surplus very easy, which is another of the many conveniences of logit.

Under the standard interpretation for the distribution of errors, as described in the last paragraph of Section 2.3, $E(\text{CS}_n)$ is the average consumer surplus in the subpopulation of people who have the same representative utilities as person n. The total consumer surplus in the population is calculated as the weighted sum of $E(\text{CS}_n)$ over a sample of decision makers, with the weights reflecting the numbers of people in the population who face the same representative utilities as the sampled person.

The change in consumer surplus that results from a change in the alternatives and/or the choice set is calculated from (3.10). In particular, $E(\text{CS}_n)$ is calculated twice: first under the conditions before the change, and again under the conditions after the change. The difference between the two results is the change in consumer surplus:

$$\Delta E(\text{CS}_n) = \frac{1}{\alpha_n} \left[\ln \left(\sum_{j=1}^{J^1} e^{V_{nj}^1} \right) - \ln \left(\sum_{j=1}^{J^0} e^{V_{nj}^0} \right) \right],$$

where the superscripts 0 and 1 refer to before and after the change. The number of alternatives can change (e.g., a new alternative can be added) as well as the attributes of the alternatives. Since the unknown constant C enters expected consumer surplus both before and after the change, it drops out of the difference and can therefore be ignored when calculating changes in consumer surplus.

To calculate the change in consumer surplus, the researcher must know or have estimated the marginal utility of income, α_n. Usually a price or cost variable enters the representative utility, in which case the negative of its coefficient is α_n by definition. (A price or cost coefficient is negative; the negative of a negative coefficient gives a positive α_n.) For example, in the choice between car and bus, utility is $U_{nj} = \beta_1 t_{nj} + \beta_2 c_{nj}$, where t is time, c is cost, and both β_1 and β_2 are negative, indicating that utility decreases as the time or cost for a trip increases. The negative of the cost coefficient, $-\beta_2$, is the amount that utility rises due to a one-dollar decrease in costs. A one-dollar reduction in costs is equivalent to a one-dollar increase in income, since the person gets to spend the dollar that he saves in travel costs just the same as if he got the extra dollar in income. The amount $-\beta_2$ is therefore the increase in utility from a one-dollar increase in income: the marginal utility of income. It is the same amount in this case for all n. If c_{nj} entered the representative utility interacting with characteristics of the person other than income, as in the product $c_{nj}H_n$, where H_n is household size, then the marginal utility of income would be $-\beta_2 H_n$, which varies over n.

Throughout this discussion, α_n has been assumed to be fixed for a given person independent of his income. The formula (3.10) for expected consumer surplus depends critically on the assumption that the marginal utility of income is independent from income. If the marginal utility of income changes with income, then a more complicated formula is needed, since α_n itself becomes a function of the change in attributes. McFadden (1999) and Karlstrom (2000) provide procedures for calculating changes in consumer surplus under these conditions.

The conditions for using expression (3.10) are actually less severe than stated. Since only changes in consumer surplus are relevant for policy analysis, formula (3.10) can be used if the marginal utility of income is constant over the range of implicit income changes that are considered by the policy. Thus, for policy changes that change consumer surplus by small amounts per person relative to income, the formula can be used even though the marginal utility of income in reality varies with income.

The assumption that α_n does not depend on income has implications for the specification of representative utility. As already discussed, α_n is usually taken as the absolute value of the coefficient of price or cost. Therefore, if the researcher plans to use her model to estimate changes in consumer surplus and wants to apply formula (3.10), this coefficient cannot be specified to depend on income. In the mode choice example, cost can be multiplied by household size, so that the cost coefficient, and hence the marginal utility of income, varies over households of different size. However, if the cost is divided by the household's income, then the coefficient of cost depends on income, violating the assumption needed for expression (3.10). This violation may not be important for small changes in consumer surplus, but certainly becomes important for large changes.

3.6 Derivatives and Elasticities

Since choice probabilities are a function of observed variables, it is often useful to know the extent to which these probabilities change in response to a change in some observed factor. For example, in a household's choice of make and model of car to buy, a natural question is: to what extent will the probability of choosing a given car increase if the vehicle's fuel efficiency is improved? From competing manufacturers' points of view, a related question is: to what extent will the probability of households' choosing, say, a Toyota decrease if the fuel efficiency of a Honda improves?

To address these questions, derivatives of the choice probabilities are calculated. The change in the probability that decision maker n chooses alternative i given a change in an observed factor, z_{ni}, entering the representative utility of that alternative (and holding the representative utility of other alternatives constant) is

$$
\begin{aligned}
\frac{\partial P_{ni}}{\partial z_{ni}} &= \frac{\partial \left(e^{V_{ni}} / \sum_j e^{V_{nj}} \right)}{\partial z_{ni}} \\
&= \frac{e^{V_{ni}}}{\sum e^{V_{nj}}} \frac{\partial V_{ni}}{\partial z_{ni}} - \frac{e^{V_{ni}}}{\left(\sum e^{V_{nj}} \right)^2} e^{V_{ni}} \frac{\partial V_{ni}}{\partial z_{ni}} \\
&= \frac{\partial V_{ni}}{\partial z_{ni}} \left(P_{ni} - P_{ni}^2 \right) \\
&= \frac{\partial V_{ni}}{\partial z_{ni}} P_{ni} (1 - P_{ni}).
\end{aligned}
$$

If representative utility is linear in z_{ni} with coefficient β_z, the derivative becomes $\beta_z P_{ni}(1 - P_{ni})$. This derivative is largest when $P_{ni} = 1 - P_{ni}$, which occurs when $P_{ni} = .5$. It becomes smaller as P_{ni} approaches zero or one. The sigmoid probability curve in Figure 3.1 is consistent with these facts. Stated intuitively, the effect of a change in an observed variable is largest when the choice probabilities indicate a high degree of uncertainty regarding the choice. As the choice becomes more certain (i.e., the probabilities approach zero or one), the effect of a change in an observed variable lessens.

One can also determine the extent to which the probability of choosing a particular alternative changes when an observed variable relating to *another* alternative changes. Let z_{nj} denote an attribute of alternative j. How does the probability of choosing alternative i change as z_{nj} increases? We have

$$
\begin{aligned}
\frac{\partial P_{ni}}{\partial z_{nj}} &= \frac{\partial \left(e^{V_{ni}} / \sum_k e^{V_{nk}} \right)}{\partial z_{nj}} \\
&= -\frac{e^{V_{ni}}}{\left(\sum e^{V_{nk}} \right)^2} e^{V_{nj}} \frac{\partial V_{nj}}{\partial z_{nj}} \\
&= -\frac{\partial V_{nj}}{\partial z_{nj}} P_{ni} P_{nj}.
\end{aligned}
$$

When V_{nj} is linear in z_{nj} with coefficient β_z, then this cross-derivative becomes $-\beta_z P_{ni} P_{nj}$. If z_{nj} is a desirable attribute, so that β_z is positive, then raising z_{nj} decreases the probability of choosing each alternative other than j. Furthermore, the decrease in probability is proportional to the value of the probability before z_{nj} was changed.

A logically necessary aspect of derivatives of choice probabilities is that, when an observed variable changes, the changes in the choice probabilities sum to zero. This is a consequence of the fact that the probabilities must sum to one before and after the change; it is demonstrated for logit models as follows:

$$
\begin{aligned}
\sum_{i=1}^{J} \frac{\partial P_{ni}}{\partial z_{nj}} &= \frac{\partial V_{nj}}{\partial z_{nj}} P_{nj}(1 - P_{nj}) + \sum_{i \neq j} \left(-\frac{\partial V_{nj}}{\partial z_{nj}} \right) P_{nj} P_{ni} \\
&= \frac{\partial V_{nj}}{\partial z_{nj}} P_{nj} \left[(1 - P_{nj}) - \sum_{i \neq j} P_{ni} \right] \\
&= \frac{\partial V_{nj}}{\partial z_{nj}} P_{nj} [(1 - P_{nj}) - (1 - P_{nj})] \\
&= 0.
\end{aligned}
$$

In practical terms, if one alternative is improved so that the probability of its being chosen increases, the additional probability is necessarily drawn from other alternatives. To increase the probability of one alternative necessitates decreasing the probability of another alternative. While obvious, this fact is often forgotten by planners who want to improve demand for one alternative without reducing demand for other alternatives.

Economists often measure response by elasticities rather than derivatives, since elasticities are normalized for the variables' units. An elasticity is the percentage change in one variable that is associated with a one-percent change in another variable. The elasticity of P_{ni} with respect to z_{ni}, a variable entering the utility of alternative i, is

$$
\begin{aligned}
E_{iz_{ni}} &= \frac{\partial P_{ni}}{\partial z_{ni}} \frac{z_{ni}}{P_{ni}} \\
&= \frac{\partial V_{ni}}{\partial z_{ni}} P_{ni}(1 - P_{ni}) \frac{z_{ni}}{P_{ni}} \\
&= \frac{\partial V_{ni}}{\partial z_{ni}} z_{ni}(1 - P_{ni}).
\end{aligned}
$$

If representative utility is linear in z_{ni} with coefficient β_z, then $E_{iz_{ni}} = \beta_z z_{ni}(1 - P_{ni})$.

The cross-elasticity of P_{ni} with respect to a variable entering alternative j is

$$E_{iz_{nj}} = \frac{\partial P_{ni}}{\partial z_{nj}} \frac{z_{nj}}{P_{ni}}$$

$$= -\frac{\partial V_{nj}}{\partial z_{nj}} z_{nj} P_{nj},$$

which in the case of linear utility reduces to $E_{iz_{nj}} = -\beta_z z_{nj} P_{nj}$. As discussed in Section 3.3.2, this cross-elasticity is the same for all i: a change in an attribute of alternative j changes the probabilities for all other alternatives by the same percent. This property of the logit cross-elasticities is a manifestation, or restatement, of the IIA property of the logit choice probabilities.

3.7   Estimation

Manski and McFadden (1981) and Cosslett (1981) describe estimation methods under a variety of sampling procedures. We discuss in this section estimation under the most prominent of these sampling schemes. We first describe estimation when the sample is exogenous and all alternatives are used in estimation. We then discuss estimation on a subset of alternatives and with certain types of choice-based (i.e., nonexogenous) samples.

3.7.1. Exogenous Sample

Consider first the situation in which the sample is exogenously drawn, that is, is either random or stratified random with the strata defined on factors that are exogenous to the choice being analyzed. If the sampling procedure is related to the choice being analyzed (for example, if mode choice is being examined and the sample is drawn by selecting people on buses and pooling them with people selected at toll booths), then more complex estimation procedures are generally required, as discussed in the next section. We also assume that the explanatory variables are exogenous to the choice situation. That is, the variables entering representative utility are independent of the unobserved component of utility.

A sample of N decision makers is obtained for the purpose of estimation. Since the logit probabilities take a closed form, the traditional maximum-likelihood procedures can be applied. The probability of person n choosing the alternative that he was actually observed to choose can be expressed as

$$\prod_i (P_{ni})^{y_{ni}},$$

where $y_{ni} = 1$ if person n chose i and zero otherwise. Note that since $y_{ni} = 0$ for all nonchosen alternatives and P_{ni} raised to the power of zero is 1, this term is simply the probability of the chosen alternative.

Assuming that each decision maker's choice is independent of that of other decision makers, the probability of each person in the sample choosing the alternative that he was observed actually to choose is

$$L(\beta) = \prod_{n=1}^{N} \prod_i (P_{ni})^{y_{ni}},$$

where β is a vector containing the parameters of the model. The log-likelihood function is then

$$(3.11) \quad LL(\beta) = \sum_{n=1}^{N} \sum_i y_{ni} \ln P_{ni}$$

and the estimator is the value of β that maximizes this function. McFadden (1974) shows that $LL(\beta)$ is globally concave for linear-in-parameters utility, and many statistical packages are available for estimation of these models. When parameters enter the representative utility nonlinearly, the researcher may need to write her own estimation code using the procedures described in Chapter 8.

Maximum likelihood estimation in this situation can be reexpressed and reinterpreted in a way that assists in understanding the nature of the estimates. At the maximum of the likelihood function, its derivative with respect to each of the parameters is zero:

$$(3.12) \quad \frac{dLL(\beta)}{d\beta} = 0.$$

The maximum likelihood estimates are therefore the values of β that satisfy this first-order condition. For convenience, let the representative utility be linear in parameters: $V_{nj} = \beta' x_{nj}$. This specification is not required, but makes the notation and discussion more succinct. Using (3.11) and the formula for the logit probabilities, we show at the end of this subsection that the first-order condition (3.12) becomes

$$(3.13) \quad \sum_n \sum_i (y_{ni} - P_{ni}) x_{ni} = 0.$$

Rearranging and dividing both sides by N, we have

$$(3.14) \quad \frac{1}{N} \sum_n \sum_i y_{ni} x_{ni} = \frac{1}{N} \sum_n \sum_i P_{ni} x_{ni}.$$

This expression is readily interpretable. Let $\bar{x}$ denote the average of x over the alternatives chosen by the sampled individuals: $\bar{x} = (1/N) \sum_n \sum_i y_{ni} x_{ni}$. Let $\hat{x}$ be the average of x over the predicted choices of the sampled decision makers: $\hat{x} = (1/N) \sum_n \sum_i P_{ni} x_{ni}$. The observed average of x in the sample is $\bar{x}$, while $\hat{x}$ is the predicted average. By (3.14), these two averages are equal at the maximum likelihood estimates. That is, the maximum likelihood estimates of β are those that make the predicted average of each explanatory variable equal to the observed average in the sample. In this sense, the estimates induce the model to reproduce the observed averages in the sample.

This property of the maximum likelihood estimator for logit models takes on a special meaning for the alternative-specific constants. An alternative-specific constant is the coefficient of a dummy variable that identifies an alternative. A dummy for alternative j is a variable whose value in the representative utility of alternative i is $d_i^j = 1$ for $i = j$ and zero otherwise. By (3.14), the estimated constant is the one that gives

$$\frac{1}{N} \sum_n \sum_i y_{ni} d_i^j = \frac{1}{N} \sum_n \sum_i P_{ni} d_i^j,$$

$$S_j = \hat{S}_j,$$

where S_j is the share of people in the sample who chose alternative j, and $\hat{S}_j$ is the predicted share for alternative j. With alternative-specific constants, the predicted shares for the sample equal the observed shares. The estimated model is therefore correct on average within the sample. This feature is similar to the function of a constant in a linear regression model, where the constant assures that the average of the predicted value of the dependent variable equals its observed average in the sample.

The first-order condition (3.13) provides yet another important interpretation. The difference between a person's actual choice, y_{ni}, and the probability of that choice, P_{ni}, is a modeling error, or residual. The left-hand side of (3.13) is the sample covariance of the residuals with the explanatory variables. The maximum likelihood estimates are therefore the values of the β's that make this covariance zero, that is, make the residuals uncorrelated with the explanatory variables. This condition for logit estimates is the same as applies in linear regression models. For a regression model $y_n = \beta' x_n + \varepsilon_n$, the ordinary least squares estimates are the values of β that set $\sum_n (y_n - \beta' x_n) x_n = 0$. This fact is verified by solving for β: $\beta = (\sum_n x_n x_n')^{-1} (\sum_n x_n y_n)$, which is the formula for the ordinary least squares estimator. Since $y_n - \beta'x_n$ is the residual in the regression model, the estimates make the residuals uncorrelated with the explanatory variables.

Under this interpretation, the estimates can be motivated as providing a sample analog to population characteristics. We have assumed that the explanatory variables are exogenous, meaning that they are uncorrelated in the population with the model errors. Since the variables and errors are uncorrelated in the population, it makes sense to choose estimates that make the variables and residuals uncorrelated in the sample. The estimates do exactly that: they provide a model that reproduces in the sample the zero covariances that occur in the population.

Estimators that solve equations of the form (3.13) are called method-of-moments estimators, since they use moment conditions (correlations in this case) between residuals and variables to define the estimator. We will return to these estimators when discussing simulation-assisted estimation in Chapter 10.

We asserted without proof that (3.13) is the first-order condition for the maximum likelihood estimator of the logit model. We give that proof now. The log-likelihood function (3.11) can be reexpressed as

$$
\begin{aligned}
LL(\beta) &= \sum_n \sum_i y_{ni} \ln P_{ni} \\
&= \sum_n \sum_i y_{ni} \ln\left(\frac{e^{\beta'x_{ni}}}{\sum_j e^{\beta'x_{nj}}}\right) \\
&= \sum_n \sum_i y_{ni}(\beta'x_{ni}) - \sum_n \sum_i y_{ni} \ln\left(\sum_j e^{\beta'x_{nj}}\right).
\end{aligned}
$$

The derivative of the log-likelihood function then becomes

$$
\begin{aligned}
\frac{dLL(\beta)}{d\beta} &= \frac{\sum_n \sum_i y_{ni}(\beta'x_{ni})}{d\beta} - \frac{\sum_n \sum_i y_{ni} \ln\left(\sum_j e^{\beta'x_{nj}}\right)}{d\beta} \\
&= \sum_n \sum_i y_{ni}x_{ni} - \sum_n \sum_i y_{ni} \sum_j P_{nj}x_{nj} \\
&= \sum_n \sum_i y_{ni}x_{ni} - \sum_n \left(\sum_j P_{nj}x_{nj}\right) \sum_i y_{ni} \\
&= \sum_n \sum_i y_{ni}x_{ni} - \sum_n \left(\sum_j P_{nj}x_{nj}\right) \\
&= \sum_n \sum_i (y_{ni} - P_{ni})x_{ni}.
\end{aligned}
$$

Setting this derivative to zero gives the first-order condition (3.13).

Estimation on a Subset of Alternatives

In some situations, the number of alternatives facing the decision maker is so large that estimating model parameters is very expensive or even impossible. With a logit model, estimation can be performed on a subset of alternatives without inducing inconsistency. For example, a researcher examining a choice situation that involves 100 alternatives can estimate on a subset of 10 alternatives for each sampled decision maker, with the person's chosen alternative included as well as 9 alternatives randomly selected from the remaining 99. If all alternatives have the same chance of being selected into the subset, then estimation proceeds on the subset of alternatives as if it were the full set. If alternatives have unequal probability of being selected, more complicated estimation procedures may be required. The procedure is described as follows.

Suppose that the researcher has used some specific method for randomly selecting alternatives into the subset that is used in estimation for each sampled decision maker. Denote the full set of alternatives as F and a subset of alternatives as K. Let $q(K \mid i)$ be the probability under the researcher's selection method that subset K is selected given that the decision maker chose alternative i. Assuming that the subset necessarily includes the chosen alternative, we have $q(K \mid i) = 0$ for any K that does not include i. The probability that person n chooses alternative i from the full set is P_{ni}. Our goal is to derive a formula for the probability that the person chooses alternative i *conditional* on the researcher selecting subset K for him. This conditional probability is denoted $P_n(i \mid K)$.

This conditional probability is derived as follows. The joint probability that the researcher selects subset K and the decision maker chooses alternative i is $\text{Prob}(K, i) = q(K \mid i)P_{ni}$. The joint probability can also be expressed with the opposite conditioning as $\text{Prob}(K, i) = P_n(i \mid K)Q(K)$ where $Q(K) = \sum_{j \in F} P_{nj}q(K \mid j)$ is the probability of the researcher selecting subset K marginal over all the alternatives that the person could choose. Equating these two expressions and solving for $P_n(i \mid K)$, we have

$$P_n(i \mid K) = \frac{P_{ni}q(K \mid i)}{\sum_{j \in F} P_{nj}q(K \mid j)}$$

$$= \frac{e^{V_{ni}}q(K \mid i)}{\sum_{j \in F} e^{V_{nj}}q(K \mid j)}$$

(3.15)
$$= \frac{e^{V_{ni}}q(K \mid i)}{\sum_{k \in K} e^{V_{nk}}q(K \mid j)},$$

where the second line has canceled out the denominators of P_{ni} and

P_{nj} $\forall j$, and the third equality uses the fact that $q(K \mid j) = 0$ for any j not in K.

Suppose that the researcher has designed the selection procedure so that $q(K \mid j)$ is the same for all $j \in K$. This property occurs if, for example, the researcher assigns an equal probability of selection to all nonchosen alternatives, so that the probability of selecting j into the subset when i is chosen by the decision maker is the same as for selecting i into the subset when j is chosen. McFadden (1978) calls this the "uniform conditioning property," since the subset of alternatives has a uniform (equal) probability of being selected conditional on any of its members being chosen by the decision maker. When this property is satisfied, $q(K \mid j)$ cancels out of the preceding expression, and the probability becomes

$$P_n(i \mid K) = \frac{e^{V_{ni}}}{\sum_{j \in K} e^{V_{nj}}},$$

which is simply the logit formula for a person who faces the alternatives in subset K.

The conditional likelihood function under the uniform conditioning property is

$$\text{CLL}(\beta) = \sum_n \sum_{i \in K_n} y_{ni} \ln \frac{e^{V_{ni}}}{\sum_{j \in K_n} e^{V_{nj}}},$$

where K_n is the subset selected for person n. This function is the same as the log-likelihood function given in (3.11) except that the subset of alternatives K_n replaces, for each sampled person, the complete set. Maximization of CLL provides a consistent estimator of β. However, since information is excluded from CLL that LL incorporates (i.e., information on alternatives not in each subset), the estimator based on CLL is not efficient.

Suppose that the researcher designs a selection process that does not exhibit the uniform conditioning property. In this case, the probability $q(K \mid i)$ can be incorporated into the model as a separate variable. The expression in (3.15) can be rewritten as

$$P_n(i \mid K) = \frac{e^{V_{ni} + \ln q(K \mid i)}}{\sum_{j \in K} e^{V_{nj} + \ln q(K \mid j)}}.$$

A variable z_{nj} calculated as $\ln q(K_n \mid j)$ is added to the representative utility of each alternative. The coefficient of this variable is constrained to 1 in estimation.

The question arises: why would a researcher ever want to design a selection procedure that does not satisfy the uniform conditioning property, since satisfying the property makes estimation so straightforward? An illustration of the potential benefit of nonuniform conditioning is provided by Train *et al.* (1987a) in their study of telecommunications demand. The choice situation in their application included an enormous number of alternatives representing portfolios of calls by time of day, distance, and duration. The vast majority of alternatives were hardly ever chosen by anyone in the population. If alternatives had been selected with equal probability for each alternative, it was quite likely than the resulting subsets would consist nearly entirely of alternatives that were hardly ever chosen, coupled with the person's chosen alternative. Comparing a person's chosen alternative with a group of highly undesirable alternatives provides little information about the reasons for a person's choice. To avoid this problem, alternatives were selected in proportion to the shares for the alternatives in the population (or, to be precise, estimates of the population shares). This procedure increased the chance that relatively desirable alternatives would be in each subset of alternatives that was used in estimation.

3.7.2. Choice-Based Samples

In some situations, a sample drawn on the basis of exogenous factors would include few people who have chosen particular alternatives. For example, in the choice of water heaters, a random sample of households in most areas would include only a small number who had chosen solar water-heating systems. If the researcher is particularly interested in factors that affect the penetration of solar devices, a random sample would need to be very large to assure a reasonable number of households with solar heat.

In situations such as these, the researcher might instead select the sample, or part of the sample, on the basis of the choice being analyzed. For example, the researcher examining water heaters might supplement a random sample of households with households that are known (perhaps through sales records at stores if the researcher has access to these records) to have recently installed solar water heaters.

Samples selected on the basis of decision makers' choices can be purely choice-based or a hybrid of choice-based and exogenous. In a purely choice-based sample, the population is divided into those that choose each alternative, and decision makers are drawn randomly within each group, though at different rates. For example, a researcher who is examining the choice of home location and is interested in identifying the factors that contribute to people choosing one particular community might draw randomly from within that community at the rate of one out of L households, and draw randomly from all other communities at a rate of one out of M, where M is larger than L. This procedure assures that the researcher has an adequate number of people in the sample from the area of interest. A hybrid sample is like the one drawn by the researcher interested in solar water heating, in which an exogenous sample is supplemented with a sample drawn on the basis of the households' choices.

Estimation of model parameters with samples drawn at least partially on the basis of the decision maker's choice is fairly complex in general, and varies with the exact form of the sampling procedure. For interested readers, Ben-Akiva and Lerman (1985, pp. 234–244) provide a useful discussion. One result is particularly significant, since it allows researchers to estimate logit models on choice-based samples without becoming involved in complex estimation procedures. This result, due to Manski and Lerman (1977), can be stated as follows. If the researcher is using a *purely* choice-based sample and includes an alternative-specific constant in the representative utility for each alternative, then estimating a logit model as if the sample were exogenous produces consistent estimates for all the model parameters except the alternative-specific constants. Furthermore, these constants are biased by a known factor and can therefore be adjusted so that the adjusted constants are consistent. In particular, the expectation of the estimated constant for alternative j, labeled $\hat{\alpha}_j$, is related to the true constant α_j^* by

$$E(\hat{\alpha}_j) = \alpha_j^* - \ln(A_j/S_j),$$

where A_j is the share of decision makers in the population who chose alternative j, and S_j is the share in the choice-based sample who chose alternative j. Consequently, if A_j is known (that is, if population shares are known for each alternative), then a consistent estimate of the alternative-specific constant is the constant $\hat{\alpha}_j$ that is estimated on the choice-based sample *plus* the log of the ratio of the population share to the sample share.

3.8   Goodness of Fit and Hypothesis Testing

We discuss goodness of fit and hypothesis testing in the context of logit models, where the log-likelihood function is calculated exactly. The concepts apply to other models, with appropriate adjustment for simulation variance, when the log-likelihood function is simulated rather than calculated exactly.

3.8.1. Goodness of Fit

A statistic called the *likelihood ratio index* is often used with discrete choice models to measure how well the models fit the data. Stated more precisely, the statistic measures how well the model, with its estimated parameters, performs compared with a model in which all the parameters are zero (which is usually equivalent to having no model at all). This comparison is made on the basis of the log-likelihood function, evaluated at both the estimated parameters and at zero for all parameters.

The likelihood ratio index is defined as

$$\rho = 1 - \frac{\text{LL}(\hat{\beta})}{\text{LL}(0)},$$

where $\text{LL}(\hat{\beta})$ is the value of the log-likelihood function at the estimated parameters and $\text{LL}(0)$ is its value when all the parameters are set equal to zero. If the estimated parameters do no better, in terms of the likelihood function, than zero parameters (that is, if the estimated model is no better than no model), then $\text{LL}(\hat{\beta}) = \text{LL}(0)$ and so $\rho = 0$. This is the lowest value that ρ can take (since if $\text{LL}(\hat{\beta})$ were less than $\text{LL}(0)$, then $\hat{\beta}$ would not be the maximum likelihood estimate).

At the other extreme, suppose the estimated model was so good that each sampled decision maker's choice could be predicted perfectly. In this case, the likelihood function at the estimated parameters would be one, since the probability of observing the choices that were actually made is one. And, since the log of one is zero, the log-likelihood function would be zero at the estimated parameters. With $\text{LL}(\hat{\beta}) = 0$, $\rho = 1$. This is the highest value that ρ can take. In summary, the likelihood ratio index ranges from zero, when the estimated parameters are no better than zero parameters, to one, when the estimated parameters perfectly predict the choices of the sampled decision makers.

It is important to note that the likelihood ratio index is not at all similar in its interpretation to the R^2 used in regression, despite both statistics having the same range. R^2 indicates the percentage of the variation in the dependent variable that is "explained" by the estimated model. The likelihood ratio has no intuitively interpretable meaning for values between the extremes of zero and one. It is the percentage increase in the log-likelihood function above the value taken at zero parameters (since $\rho = 1 - \text{LL}(\hat{\beta})/\text{LL}(0) = (\text{LL}(0) - \text{LL}(\hat{\beta}))/\text{LL}(0))$. However, the meaning of such a percentage increase is not clear. In comparing two models estimated on the same data and with the same set of alternatives (such that LL(0) is the same for both models), it is usually valid to say that the model with the higher ρ fits the data better. But this is saying no more than that increasing the value of the log-likelihood function is preferable. Two models estimated on samples that are not identical or with a different set of alternatives for any sampled decision maker cannot be compared via their likelihood ratio index values.

Another goodness-of-fit statistic that is sometimes used, but should actually be avoided, is the "percent correctly predicted." This statistic is calculated by identifying for each sampled decision maker the alternative with the highest probability, based on the estimated model, and determining whether or not this was the alternative that the decision maker actually chose. The percentage of sampled decision makers for which the highest-probability alternative and the chosen alternative are the same is called the percent correctly predicted.

This statistic incorporates a notion that is opposed to the meaning of probabilities and the purpose of specifying choice probabilities. The statistic is based on the idea that the decision maker is predicted by the researcher to choose the alternative for which the model gives the highest probability. However, as discussed in the derivation of choice probabilities in Chapter 2, the researcher does not have enough information to predict the decision maker's choice. The researcher has only enough information to state the probability that the decision maker will choose each alternative. In stating choice probabilities, the researcher is saying that if the choice situation were repeated numerous times (or faced by numerous people with the same attributes), each alternative would be chosen a certain proportion of the time. This is quite different from saying that the alternative with the highest probability will be chosen each time.

An example may be useful. Suppose an estimated model predicts choice probabilities of .75 and .25 in a two-alternative situation. Those probabilities mean that if 100 people faced the representative utilities that gave these probabilities (or one person faced these representative utilities 100 times), the researcher's best prediction of how many people would choose each alternative are 75 and 25. However, the "percent correctly predicted" statistic is based on the notion that the best prediction for each person is the alternative with the highest probability. This notion would predict that one alternative would be chosen by all 100 people while the other alternative would never be chosen. The procedure misses the point of probabilities, gives obviously inaccurate market shares, and seems to imply that the researcher has perfect information.

3.8.2. Hypothesis Testing

As with regressions, standard t-statistics are used to test hypotheses about individual parameters in discrete choice models, such as whether the parameter is zero. For more complex hypotheses, a likelihood ratio test can nearly always be used, as follows. Consider a null hypothesis H that can be expressed as constraints on the values of the parameters. Two of the most common hypotheses are (1) several parameters are zero, and (2) two or more parameters are equal. The constrained maximum likelihood estimate of the parameters (labeled $\hat{\beta}^H$) is that value of β that gives the highest value of LL without violating the constraints of the null hypothesis H. Define the ratio of likelihoods, $R = L(\hat{\beta}^H)/L(\hat{\beta})$, where $\hat{\beta}^H$ is the (constrained) maximum value of the likelihood function (not logged) under the null hypothesis H, and $\hat{\beta}$ is the unconstrained maximum of the likelihood function. As in likelihood ratio tests for models other than those of discrete choice, the test statistic defined as $-2 \log R$ is distributed chi-squared with degrees of freedom equal to the number of restrictions implied by the null hypothesis. Therefore, the test statistic is $-2(LL(\hat{\beta}^H) - LL(\hat{\beta}))$. Since the log likelihood is always negative, this is simply two times the (magnitude of the) difference between the constrained and unconstrained maximums of the log-likelihood function. If this value exceeds the critical value of chi-squared with the appropriate degrees of freedom, then the null hypothesis is rejected.

Null Hypothesis I: The Coefficients of Several
Explanatory Variables Are Zero

To test this hypothesis, estimate the model twice: once with these explanatory variables included, and a second time without them (since excluding the variables forces their coefficients to be zero). Observe the maximum value of the log-likelihood function for each estimation; two times the difference in these maximum values is the value of the test statistic. Compare the test statistic with the critical value of chi-squared with degrees of freedom equal to the number of explanatory variables excluded from the second estimation.

Null Hypothesis II: The Coefficients of the First
Two Variables Are the Same

To test this hypothesis, estimate the model twice: once with each of the explanatory variables entered separately, including the first two;

then with the first two variables replaced by one variable that is the sum of the two variables (since adding the variables forces their coefficients to be equal). Observe the maximum value of the log-likelihood function for each of the estimations. Multiply the difference in these maximum values by two, and compare this figure with the critical value of chi-squared with one degree of freedom.

3.9   Case Study: Forecasting for a New Transit System

One of the earliest applications of logit models, and a prominent test of their capabilities, arose in the mid-1970s in the San Francisco Bay area. A new rail system, called the Bay Area Rapid Transit (BART), had been built. Daniel McFadden obtained a grant from the National Science Foundation to apply logit models to commuters' mode choices in the Bay area and to use the models to predict BART ridership. I was lucky enough to serve as his research assistant on this project. A sample of commuters was taken before BART was open for service. Mode choice models were estimated on this sample. These estimates provided important information on the factors that enter commuters' decisions, including their value of time savings. The models were then used to forecast the choices that the sampled commuters would make once BART became available. After BART had opened, the commuters were recontacted and their mode choices were observed. The predicted share taking BART was compared with the observed share. The models predicted quite well, far more accurately than the procedures used by the BART consultants, who had not used discrete choice models.

The project team collected data on 771 commuters before BART was opened. Four modes were considered to be available for the trip to work: (1) driving a car by oneself, (2) taking the bus and walking to the bus stop, (3) taking the bus and driving to the bus stop, and (4) carpooling. The time and cost of travel on each mode were determined for each commuter, based on the location of the person's home and work. Travel time was differentiated as walk time (for the bus–walk mode), wait time (for both bus modes), and on-vehicle time (for all the modes). Characteristics of the commuter were also collected, including income, household size, number of cars and drivers in the household, and whether the commuter was the head of the household. A logit model with linear-in-parameters utility was estimated on these data.

The estimated model is shown in Table 3.1, which is reproduced from Train (1978). The cost of travel was divided by the commuter's wage to reflect the expectation that workers with lower wages are more

Table 3.1. *Logit model of work trip mode choice*

Explanatory Variable[a]	Coefficient	t-Statistic
Cost divided by post-tax wage, cents per minute (1–4)	−0.0284	4.31
Auto on-vehicle time, minutes (1, 3, 4)	−0.0644	5.65
Transit on-vehicle time, minutes (2, 3)	−0.0259	2.94
Walk time, minutes (2, 3)	−0.0689	5.28
Transfer wait time, minutes (2, 3)	−0.0538	2.30
Number of transfers (2, 3)	−0.1050	0.78
Headway of first bus, minutes (2, 3)	−0.0318	3.18
Family income with ceiling $7500 (1)	0.00000454	0.05
Family income – $7500 with floor 0, ceiling $3000 (1)	−0.0000572	0.43
Family income – $10,500 with floor 0, ceiling $5000 (1)	−0.0000543	0.91
Number of drivers in household (1)	1.02	4.81
Number of drivers in household (3)	0.990	3.29
Number of drivers in household (4)	0.872	4.25
Dummy if worker is head of household (1)	0.627	3.37
Employment density at work location (1)	−0.0016	2.27
Home location in or near central business district (1)	−0.502	4.18
Autos per driver with ceiling one (1)	5.00	9.65
Autos per driver with ceiling one (3)	2.33	2.74
Autos per driver with ceiling one (4)	2.38	5.28
Auto alone dummy (1)	−5.26	5.93
Bus with auto access dummy (3)	−5.49	5.33
Carpool dummy (4)	−3.84	6.36
Likelihood ratio index	0.4426	
Log likelihood at convergence	−595.8	
Number of observations	771	
Value of time saved as a percentage of wage:		
Auto on-vehicle time	227	3.20
Transit on-vehicle time	91	2.43
Walk time	243	3.10
Transfer wait time	190	2.01

[a] Variable enters modes in parentheses and is zero in other modes. Modes: 1. Auto alone. 2. Bus with walk access. 3. Bus with auto access. 4. Carpool.

concerned about cost than higher-paid workers. On-vehicle time enters separately for car and bus travel to indicate that commuters might find time spent on the bus to be more, or less, bothersome than time spent driving in a car. Bus travel often involves transfers, and these transfers can be onerous for travelers. The model therefore includes the number of transfers and the expected wait time at the transfers. The headway (i.e., the time between scheduled buses) for the first bus line that the commuter would take is included as a measure of the maximum amount of time that the person would need to wait for this bus.

The estimated coefficients of cost and the various time components provide information on the value of time. By definition, the value of time is the extra cost that a person would be willing to incur to save time. The utility takes the form $U_{nj} = \alpha c_{nj}/w_n + \beta t_{nj} + \ldots$, where c is cost and t is time. The total derivative with respect to changes in time and cost is $dU_{nj} = (\alpha/w_n)\,dc_{nj} + \beta\,dt_{nj}$, which we set equal to zero and solve for dc/dt to find the change in cost that keeps utility unchanged for a change in time: $dc/dt = -(\beta/\alpha)w_n$. The value of time is therefore a proportion β/α of the person's wage. The estimated values of time are reported at the bottom of Table 3.1. The time saved from riding on the bus is valued at 91 percent of wage $((-.0259/-.0284) \times 100)$, while the time saved from driving in a car is worth more than twice as much: 227 percent of wage. This difference suggests that commuters consider driving to be considerably more onerous than riding the bus, when evaluated on a per-minute basis. Commuters apparently choose cars not because they like driving *per se* but because driving is usually quicker. Walking is considered more bothersome than waiting for a bus (243 percent of wage versus 190 percent), and waiting for a bus is more bothersome than riding the bus.

Income enters the representative utility of the auto-alone alternative. It enters in a piecewise linear fashion to allow for the possibility that additional income has a different impact depending on the overall level of income. None of the income variables enters significantly. Apparently dividing travel cost by wage picks up whatever effect income might have on the mode choice of a commuter. That is, higher wages induce the commuter to be less concerned about travel costs but do not induce a predilection for driving beyond the impact through cost. The number of people and the number of vehicles per driver in the household have a significant effect on mode choice, as expected. Alternative-specific constants are included, with the constant for the bus–walk alternative normalized to zero.

The model in Table 3.1 was used to predict the mode choices of the commuters after BART was open for service. The choice set was considered to be the four modes listed previously plus two BART modes, differentiated by whether the person takes the bus or drives to the BART station. Table 3.2 presents the forecasted and actual shares for each mode. BART demand was forecast to be 6.3 percent, compared with an actual share of 6.2 percent. This close correspondence is remarkable.

The figures in Table 3.2 tend to mask several complications that arose in the forecasting. For example, walking to the BART station was

Table 3.2. *Predictions for after BART opened*

	Actual Share	Predicted Share
Auto alone	59.90	55.84
Bus with walk access	10.78	12.51
Bus with auto access	1.426	2.411
BART with bus access	0.951	1.053
BART with auto access	5.230	5.286
Carpool	21.71	22.89

originally included as a separate mode. The model forecasted this option very poorly, overpredicting the number of people who would walk to BART by a factor of twelve. The problem was investigated and found to be primarily due to differences between the experience of walking to BART stations and that of walking to the bus, given the neighborhoods in which the BART stations are located. These issues are discussed at greater length by McFadden *et al.* (1977).

3.10   Derivation of Logit Probabilities

It was stated without proof in Section 3.1 that if the unobserved component of utility is distributed iid extreme value for each alternative, then the choice probabilities take the form of equation (3.6). We now derive this result. From (3.5) we have

$$P_{ni} = \int_{s=-\infty}^{\infty} \left(\prod_{j \neq i} e^{-e^{-(s+V_{ni}-V_{nj})}} \right) e^{-s} e^{-e^{-s}} ds,$$

where s is ε_{ni}. Our task is to evaluate this integral. Noting that $V_{ni} - V_{ni} = 0$ and then collecting terms in the exponent of e, we have

$$P_{ni} = \int_{s=-\infty}^{\infty} \left(\prod_{j} e^{-e^{-(s+V_{ni}-V_{nj})}} \right) e^{-s} ds$$

$$= \int_{s=-\infty}^{\infty} \exp\left(-\sum_{j} e^{-(s+V_{ni}-V_{nj})} \right) e^{-s} ds$$

$$= \int_{s=-\infty}^{\infty} \exp\left(-e^{-s} \sum_{j} e^{-(V_{ni}-V_{nj})} \right) e^{-s} ds.$$

Define $t = \exp(-s)$ such that $-\exp(-s)\, ds = dt$. Note that as s approaches infinity, t approaches zero, and as s approaches negative infinity, t becomes infinitely large. Using this new term,

$$
\begin{aligned}
P_{ni} &= \int_{\infty}^{0} \exp\left(-t \sum_j e^{-(V_{ni}-V_{nj})}\right)(-dt) \\
&= \int_{0}^{\infty} \exp\left(-t \sum_j e^{-(V_{ni}-V_{nj})}\right) dt \\
&= \frac{\exp\left(-t \sum_j e^{-(V_{ni}-V_{nj})}\right)}{-\sum_j e^{-(V_{ni}-V_{nj})}} \Bigg|_{0}^{\infty} \\
&= \frac{1}{\sum_j e^{-(V_{ni}-V_{nj})}} = \frac{e^{V_{ni}}}{\sum_j e^{V_{nj}}},
\end{aligned}
$$

as required.

4   GEV

4.1   Introduction

The standard logit model exhibits independence from irrelevant alternatives (IIA), which implies proportional substitution across alternatives. As we discussed in Chapter 3, this property can be seen either as a restriction imposed by the model or as the natural outcome of a well-specified model that captures all sources of correlation over alternatives into representative utility, so that only white noise remains. Often the researcher is unable to capture all sources of correlation explicitly, so that the unobserved portions of utility are correlated and IIA does not hold. In these cases, a more general model than standard logit is needed.

Generalized extreme value (GEV) models constitute a large class of models that exhibit a variety of substitution patterns. The unifying attribute of these models is that the unobserved portions of utility for all alternatives are jointly distributed as a generalized extreme value. This distribution allows for correlations over alternatives and, as its name implies, is a generalization of the univariate extreme value distribution that is used for standard logit models. When all correlations are zero, the GEV distribution becomes the product of independent extreme value distributions and the GEV model becomes standard logit. The class therefore includes logit but also includes a variety of other models. Hypothesis tests on the correlations within a GEV model can be used to examine whether the correlations are zero, which is equivalent to testing whether standard logit provides an accurate representation of the substitution patterns.

The most widely used member of the GEV family is called *nested logit*. This model has been applied by many researchers in a variety of situations, including energy, transportation, housing, telecommunications, and a host of other fields; see, for example, Ben-Akiva (1973), Train (1986, Chapter 8), Train *et al.* (1987a), Forinash and Koppelman (1993), and Lee (1999). Its functional form is simple compared to other types of GEV models, and it provides a rich set of possible substitution patterns. Sections 4.2 and 4.3 describe the specification and estimation of nested logit models. This description is useful in itself, since nested logit models are so prominent, and also as background for understanding more complex GEV models. In Section 4.4, we turn to other GEV models that researchers have implemented, with special emphasis on two of the most promising of these, namely, the paired combinatorial logit (PCL) and generalized nested logit (GNL). The chapter's final section describes the entire class of GEV models and how new specifications within the class are generated.

Only a small portion of the possible models within the GEV class have ever been implemented. This means that the full capabilities of this class have not yet been fully exploited and that new research in this area has the potential to find even more powerful models than those already used. An example of this potential is evidenced by Karlstrom (2001), who specified a GEV model of a different form than had ever been used before and found that it fitted his data better than previously implemented types of GEV models. GEV models have the advantage that the choice probabilities usually take a closed form, so that they can be estimated without resorting to simulation. For this reason alone, GEV models will continue to be the source of new and powerful specifications to meet researchers' needs.

4.2   Nested Logit

4.2.1. Substitution Patterns

A nested logit model is appropriate when the set of alternatives faced by a decision maker can be partitioned into subsets, called *nests*, in such a way that the following properties hold:

1. For any two alternatives that are in the *same* nest, the ratio of probabilities is independent of the attributes or existence of all other alternatives. That is, IIA holds within each nest.
2. For any two alternatives in *different* nests, the ratio of probabilities can depend on the attributes of other alternatives in the two nests. IIA does not hold in general for alternatives in different nests.

An example can best explain whether a set of alternatives can be so partitioned. Suppose the set of alternatives available to a worker for his commute to work consists of driving an auto alone, carpooling, taking the bus, and taking rail. If any alternative were removed, the probabilities of

Table 4.1. *Example of IIA holding within nests of alternatives: Change in probabilities when one alternative is removed*

		Probability			
		With Alternative Removed			
Alternative	Original	Auto Alone	Carpool	Bus	Rail
Auto alone	.40	—	.45 (+12.5%)	.52 (+30%)	.48 (+20%)
Carpool	.10	.20 (+100%)	—	.13 (+30%)	.12 (+20%)
Bus	.30	.48 (+60%)	.33 (+10%)	—	.40 (+33%)
Rail	.20	.32 (+60%)	.22 (+10%)	.35 (+70%)	—

the other alternatives would increase (e.g., if the worker's car were being repaired, so that he could not drive to work by himself, then the probabilities of carpool, bus, and rail would increase). The relevant question in partitioning these alternatives is: by what proportion would each probability increase when an alternative is removed? Suppose the changes in probabilities occur as set forth in Table 4.1. Note that the probabilities for bus and rail always rise by the same proportion whenever one of the other alternatives is removed. IIA therefore holds between these two alternatives. Let us put these alternatives in a nest and call the nest "transit." Similarly, the probability of auto alone and carpool rise by the same proportion whenever one of the other alternatives is removed. IIA holds between these two alternatives, and so we put them into a nest called "auto." IIA does not hold between either of the auto alternatives and either of the transit alternatives. For example, when the auto-alone alternative is removed, the probability of carpool rises proportionately more than the probability of bus or rail. With our two nests, we can state the patterns of substitution succinctly as: IIA holds within each nest but not across nests. A nested logit model with the two auto alternatives in one nest and the two transit alternatives in another nest is appropriate to represent this situation.

A convenient way to picture the substitution patterns is with a tree diagram. In such a tree, each branch denotes a subset of alternatives within which IIA holds, and every leaf on each branch denotes an alternative. For example, the tree diagram for the worker's choice of mode just described is given in Figure 4.1. The (upside down) tree consists of two branches, labeled "auto" and "transit," for the two subsets of alternatives, and each of the branches contains two twigs for the two alternatives within the subset. There is proportional substitution across twigs within a branch but not across branches.

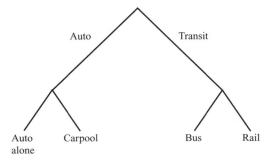

Figure 4.1. Tree diagram for mode choice.

4.2.2. Choice Probabilities

Daly and Zachary (1978), McFadden (1978), and Williams (1977) showed, independently and using different proofs, that the nested logit model is consistent with utility maximization. Let the set of alternatives j be partitioned into K nonoverlapping subsets denoted B_1, $B_2, \ldots, B_K$ and called nests. The utility that person n obtains from alternative j in nest B_k is denoted, as usual, as $U_{nj} = V_{nj} + \varepsilon_{nj}$, where V_{nj} is observed by the researcher and ε_{nj} is a random variable whose value is not observed by the researcher. The nested logit model is obtained by assuming that the vector of unobserved utility, $\varepsilon_n = \langle \varepsilon_{n1}, \ldots, \varepsilon_{nJ} \rangle$, has cumulative distribution

$$(4.1) \quad \exp\left(-\sum_{k=1}^{K} \left(\sum_{j \in B_k} e^{-\varepsilon_{nj}/\lambda_k} \right)^{\lambda_k} \right).$$

This distribution is a type of GEV distribution. It is a generalization of the distribution that gives rise to the logit model. For logit, each ε_{nj} is independent with a univariate extreme value distribution. For this GEV, the marginal distribution of each ε_{nj} is univariate extreme value. However, the ε_{nj}'s are correlated within nests. For any two alternatives j and m in nest B_k, ε_{nj} is correlated with ε_{nm}. For any two alternatives in different nests, the unobserved portion of utility is still uncorrelated: $\text{Cov}(\varepsilon_{nj}, \varepsilon_{nm}) = 0$ for any $j \in B_k$ and $m \in B_\ell$ with $\ell \neq k$.

The parameter λ_k is a measure of the degree of independence in unobserved utility among the alternatives in nest k. A higher value of λ_k means greater independence and less correlation. The statistic $1 - \lambda_k$ is a measure of correlation, in the sense that as λ_k rises, indicating less correlation, this statistic drops. As McFadden (1978) points out, the correlation is actually more complex than $1 - \lambda_k$, but $1 - \lambda_k$ can be used as an indication of correlation. A value of $\lambda_k = 1$ indicates complete independence within nest k, that is, no correlation. When $\lambda_k = 1$ for all k, representing independence among all the alternatives in all nests, the GEV distribution becomes the product of independent extreme value terms, whose distribution is given in (3.2). In this case, the nested logit model reduces to the standard logit model.

As shown by the authors cited earlier, this distribution for the unobserved components of utility gives rise to the following choice probability for alternative $i \in B_k$:

$$
(4.2) \quad P_{ni} = \frac{e^{V_{ni}/\lambda_k} \left(\sum_{j \in B_k} e^{V_{nj}/\lambda_k} \right)^{\lambda_k - 1}}{\sum_{\ell=1}^{K} \left(\sum_{j \in B_\ell} e^{V_{nj}/\lambda_\ell} \right)^{\lambda_\ell}}.
$$

We can use this formula to show that IIA holds within each subset of alternatives but not across subsets. Consider alternatives $i \in B_k$ and $m \in B_\ell$. Since the denominator of (4.2) is the same for all alternatives, the ratio of probabilities is the ratio of numerators:

$$
\frac{P_{ni}}{P_{nm}} = \frac{e^{V_{ni}/\lambda_k} \left(\sum_{j \in B_k} e^{V_{nj}/\lambda_k} \right)^{\lambda_k - 1}}{e^{V_{nm}/\lambda_\ell} \left(\sum_{j \in B_\ell} e^{V_{nj}/\lambda_\ell} \right)^{\lambda_\ell - 1}}.
$$

If $k = \ell$ (i.e., i and m are in the same nest) then the factors in parentheses cancel out and we have

$$
\frac{P_{ni}}{P_{nm}} = \frac{e^{V_{ni}/\lambda_k}}{e^{V_{nm}/\lambda_\ell}}
$$

This ratio is independent of all other alternatives. For $k \neq \ell$ (i.e., i and m are in different nests), the factors in parentheses do not cancel out. The ratio of probabilities depends on the attributes of all alternatives in the nests that contain i and m. Note, however, that the ratio does not depend on the attributes of alternatives in nests other than those containing i and m. A form of IIA holds, therefore, even for alternatives in different nests. This form of IIA can be loosely described as "independence from irrelevant nests" or IIN. With a nested logit model, IIA holds over alternatives in each nest and IIN holds over alternatives in different nests. This property of nested logit models is reinforced in the next section when we decompose the nested logit probability into two standard logit probabilities.

When $\lambda_k = 1$ for all k (and hence $1 - \lambda_k = 0$), indicating no correlation among the unobserved components of utility for alternatives within a nest, the choice probabilities become simply logit. The nested logit model is a generalization of logit that allows for a particular pattern of correlation in unobserved utility.

The parameter λ_k can differ over nests, reflecting different correlation among unobserved factors within each nest. The researcher can constrain the λ_k's to be the same for all (or some) nests, indicating that the correlation is the same in each of these nests. Hypothesis testing can be used to determine whether constraints on the λ_k's are reasonable. Testing the constraint $\lambda_k = 1 \; \forall k$ is equivalent to testing whether the standard logit model is a reasonable specification against the more general nested logit. These tests are performed most readily with the likelihood ratio statistic described in Section 3.8.2.

The value of λ_k must be within a particular range for the model to be consistent with utility-maximizing behavior. If $\lambda_k \; \forall k$ is between zero and one, the model is consistent with utility maximization for all possible values of the explanatory variables. For λ_k greater than one, the model is consistent with utility-maximizing behavior for some range of the explanatory variables but not for all values. Kling and Herriges (1995) and Herriges and Kling (1996) provide tests of consistency of nested logit with utility maximization when $\lambda_k > 1$; and Train et al. (1987a) and Lee (1999) provide examples of models for which $\lambda_k > 1$. A negative value of λ_k is inconsistent with utility maximization and implies that improving the attributes of an alternative (such as lowering its price) can decrease the probability of the alternative being chosen. With positive λ_k, the nested logit approaches the "elimination by aspects" model of Tversky (1972) as $\lambda_k \to 0$.

In the notation that we have been using, each λ_k is a fixed parameter, which implies that all decision makers have the same correlations among unobserved factors. In reality, correlations might differ over decision makers based on their observed characteristics. To accommodate this possibility, each λ_k can be specified to be a parametric function of observed demographics or other variables, as long as the function maintains a positive value. For example, Bhat (1997) specifies $\lambda = \exp(\alpha z_n)$, where z_n is a vector of characteristics of decision maker n, and α is a vector of parameters to be estimated along with the parameters that enter representative utility. The exponential transformation assures that λ is positive.

4.2.3. Decomposition into Two Logits

Expression (4.2) is not very illuminating as a formula. However, the choice probabilities can be expressed in an alternative fashion that is quite simple and readily interpretable. Without loss of generality, the observed component of utility can be decomposed into two parts: (1) a part labeled W that is constant for all alternatives within a nest, and

(2) a part labeled Y that varies over alternatives within a nest. Utility is written as

(4.3) $U_{nj} = W_{nk} + Y_{nj} + \varepsilon_{nj}$

for $j \in B_k$, where:

W_{nk} depends only on variables that describe nest k. These variables differ over nests but not over alternatives within each nest.

Y_{nj} depends on variables that describe alternative j. These variables vary over alternatives within nest k.

Note that this decomposition is fully general, since for any W_{nk}, Y_{nj} is defined as $V_{nj} - W_{nk}$.

With this decomposition of utility, the nested logit probability can be written as the product of two standard logit probabilities. Let the probability of choosing alternative $i \in B_k$ be expressed as the product of two probabilities, namely, the probability that an alternative within nest B_k is chosen and the probability that the alternative i is chosen given that an alternative in B_k is chosen:

$$P_{ni} = P_{ni \mid B_k} P_{nB_k},$$

where $P_{ni \mid B_k}$ is the conditional probability of choosing alternative i given that an alternative in nest B_k is chosen, and P_{nB_k} is the marginal probability of choosing an alternative in nest B_k (with the marginality being over all alternatives in B_k). This equality is exact, since any probability can be written as the product of a marginal and a conditional probability.

The reason for decomposing P_{ni} into a marginal and a conditional probability is that, with the nested logit formula for P_{ni}, the marginal and conditional probabilities take the form of logits. In particular, the marginal and conditional probabilities can be expressed as

(4.4) $P_{nB_k} = \dfrac{e^{W_{nk} + \lambda_k I_{nk}}}{\sum_{\ell=1}^{K} e^{W_{n\ell} + \lambda_\ell I_{n\ell}}},$

(4.5) $P_{ni \mid B_k} = \dfrac{e^{Y_{ni} / \lambda_k}}{\sum_{j \in B_k} e^{Y_{nj} / \lambda_k}},$

where

$$I_{nk} = \ln \sum_{j \in B_k} e^{Y_{nj} / \lambda_k}.$$

The derivation of these expressions from the choice probability (4.2) simply involves algebraic rearrangement. For interested readers, it is given in Section 4.2.5.

Stated in words, the probability of choosing an alternative in B_k takes the form of the logit formula, as if it resulted from a model for a choice among nests. This probability includes variables W_{nk} that vary over nests but not over alternatives within each nest. It also includes a quantity called I_{nk}, whose meaning we elucidate in subsequent text. The conditional probability of choosing i given that an alternative in B_k is chosen is also given by a logit formula, as if it resulted from a model for the choice among the alternatives within the nest. This conditional probability includes variables Y_{nj} that vary over alternatives within the nest. Note that these variables are divided by λ_k, so that, when Y_{nj} is linear in parameters, the coefficients that enter this conditional probability are the original coefficients divided by λ_k. It is customary to refer to the marginal probability (choice of nest) as the *upper model* and to the conditional probability (choice of alternative within the nest) as the *lower model*, reflecting their relative positions in Figure 4.1.

The quantity I_{nk} links the upper and lower models by bringing information from the lower model into the upper model. Ben-Akiva (1973) first identified the correct formula for this link. In particular, I_{nk} is the log of the denominator of the lower model. This formula has an important meaning. Recall from the discussion of consumer surplus for a logit model (Section 3.5) that the log of the denominator of the logit model is the expected utility that the decision maker obtains from the choice situation, as shown by Williams (1977) and Small and Rosen (1981). The same interpretation applies here: $\lambda_k I_{nk}$ is the expected utility that decision maker n receives from the choice among the alternatives in nest B_k. The formula for expected utility is the same here as for a logit model because, conditional on the nest, the choice of alternatives within the nest is indeed a logit, as given by equation (4.5). I_{nk} is often called the *inclusive value* or *inclusive utility* of nest B_k. It is also called the "log-sum term" because it is the log of a sum (of exponentiated representative utilities). The term "inclusive price" is sometimes used; however, the *negative* of I_{nk} more closely resembles a price.

The coefficient λ_k of I_{nk} in the upper model is often called the log-sum coefficient. As discussed, λ_k reflects the degree of independence among the unobserved portions of utility for alternatives in nest B_k, with a lower λ_k indicating less independence (more correlation).

It is appropriate that the inclusive value enters as an explanatory variable in the upper model. Stated loosely, the probability of choosing nest

B_k depends on the expected utility that the person receives from that nest. This expected utility includes the utility that he receives no matter which alternative he chooses in the nest, which is W_{nk}, plus the expected extra utility that he receives by being able to choose the best alternative in the nest, which is $\lambda_k I_{nk}$.

Recall that the coefficients that enter the lower model are divided by λ_k, as given in equation (4.5). Models have been specified and estimated without dividing by λ_k in the lower model. Daly (1987) and Greene (2000) describe such a model, and the software package STATA includes it as its nested logit model in the nlogit command. The package NLOGIT allows either specification. If the coefficients in the lower model are not divided by λ_k, the choice probabilities are not the same as those given in equation (4.2). As shown in the derivation in Section 4.2.5, the division by λ_k is needed for the product of the conditional and marginal probabilities to equal the nested logit probabilities given by equation (4.2). However, the fact that the model does not give the probabilities in equation (4.2) does not necessarily mean that the model is inappropriate. Koppelman and Wen (1998) and Hensher and Greene (2002) compare the two approaches (dividing by λ_k versus not) and show that the latter model is not consistent with utility maximization when any coefficients are common across nests (such as a cost coefficient that is the same for bus and car modes). Heiss (2002) points out the converse: if no coefficients are common over nests, then the latter model is consistent with utility maximization, since the necessary division by λ_k in each nest is accomplished implicitly (rather than explicitly) by allowing separate coefficients in each nests such that the scale of coefficients differs over nests. When coefficients are common over nests, she found that not dividing by λ_k leads to counterintuitive implications.

4.2.4. Estimation

The parameters of a nested model can be estimated by standard maximum likelihood techniques. Substituting the choice probabilities of expression (4.2) into the log-likelihood function gives an explicit function of the parameters of this model. The values of the parameters that maximize this function are, under fairly general conditions, consistent and efficient (Brownstone and Small, 1989).

Computer routines are available in commercial software packages for estimating nested models by maximum likelihood. Hensher and Greene (2002) provide a guide for nested logits using available software. Numerical maximization is sometimes difficult, since the log-likelihood function is not globally concave and even in concave areas is not close to a quadratic. The researcher may need to help the routines by trying different algorithms and/or starting values, as discussed in Chapter 8.

Instead of performing maximum likelihood, nested logit models can be estimated consistently (but not efficiently) in a sequential fashion, exploiting the fact that the choice probabilities can be decomposed into marginal and conditional probabilities that are logit. This sequential estimation is performed "bottom up." The lower models (for the choice of alternative within a nest) are estimated first. Using the estimated coefficients, the inclusive value is calculated for each lower model. Then the upper model (for choice of nest) is estimated, with the inclusive value entering as explanatory variables.

Sequential estimation creates two difficulties that argue against its use. First, the standard errors of the upper-model parameters are biased downward, as Amemiya (1978) first pointed out. This bias arises because the variance of the inclusive value estimate that enters the upper model is not incorporated into the calculation of standard errors. With downwardly biased standard errors, smaller confidence bounds and larger t-statistics are estimated for the parameters than are true, and the upper model will appear to be better than it actually is. Ben-Akiva and Lerman (1985, p. 298) give a procedure for adjusting the standard errors to eliminate the bias.

Second, it is usually the case that some parameters appear in several submodels. Estimating the various upper and lower models separately provides separate estimates of whatever common parameters appear in the model. Simultaneous estimation by maximum likelihood assures that the common parameters are constrained to be the same wherever they appear in the model.

These two complications are symptoms of a more general circumstance, namely, that sequential estimation of nested logit models, while consistent, is not as efficient as simultaneous estimation by maximum likelihood. With simultaneous estimation, all information is utilized in the estimation of each parameter, and parameters that are common across components are necessarily constrained to be equal. Since commercial software is available for simultaneous estimation, there is little reason to estimate a nested logit sequentially. If problems arise in simultaneous estimation, then the researcher might find it useful to estimate the model sequentially and then use the sequential estimates as starting values in the simultaneous estimation. The main value of the decomposition of the nested logit into its upper and lower components comes not in its use as an estimation tool but rather as an heuristic device: the decomposition helps greatly in understanding the meaning and structure of the nested logit model.

4.2.5. Equivalence of Nested Logit Formulas

We asserted in Section 4.2.3 that the product of the marginal and conditional probabilities in (4.4) and (4.5) equals the joint probability in (4.2). We now verify this assertion:

$$
\begin{aligned}
P_{ni} &= \frac{e^{V_{ni}/\lambda_k}\left(\sum_{j\in B_k} e^{V_{nj}/\lambda_k}\right)^{\lambda_k-1}}{\sum_{\ell=1}^{K}\left(\sum_{j\in B_\ell} e^{V_{nj}/\lambda_\ell}\right)^{\lambda_\ell}} \qquad \text{by (4.2)}\\[2ex]
&= \frac{e^{V_{ni}/\lambda_k}}{\sum_{j\in B_k} e^{V_{nj}/\lambda_k}} \frac{\left(\sum_{j\in B_k} e^{V_{nj}/\lambda_k}\right)^{\lambda_k}}{\sum_{\ell=1}^{K}\left(\sum_{j\in B_\ell} e^{V_{nj}/\lambda_\ell}\right)^{\lambda_\ell}}\\[2ex]
&= \frac{e^{(W_{nk}+Y_{ni})/\lambda_k}}{\sum_{j\in B_k} e^{(W_{nk}+Y_{nj})/\lambda_k}} \frac{\left(\sum_{j\in B_k} e^{(W_{nk}+Y_{nj})/\lambda_k}\right)^{\lambda_k}}{\sum_{\ell=1}^{K}\left(\sum_{j\in B_\ell} e^{(W_{n\ell}+Y_{nj})/\lambda_\ell}\right)^{\lambda_\ell}} \qquad \text{by (4.3)}\\[2ex]
&= \frac{e^{W_{nk}/\lambda_k} e^{Y_{ni}/\lambda_k}}{e^{W_{nk}/\lambda_k}\sum_{j\in B_k} e^{Y_{nj}/\lambda_k}} \frac{e^{W_{nk}}\left(\sum_{j\in B_k} e^{Y_{nj}/\lambda_k}\right)^{\lambda_k}}{\sum_{\ell=1}^{K} e^{W_{n\ell}}\left(\sum_{j\in B_\ell} e^{Y_{nj}/\lambda_\ell}\right)^{\lambda_\ell}}\\[2ex]
&= \frac{e^{Y_{ni}/\lambda_k}}{\sum_{j\in B_k} e^{Y_{nj}/\lambda_k}} \frac{e^{W_{nk}+\lambda_k I_{nk}}}{\sum_{\ell=1}^{K} e^{W_{n\ell}+\lambda_\ell I_{n\ell}}}\\[2ex]
&= P_{ni\mid B_k} P_{nB_k},
\end{aligned}
$$

where the next-to-last equality is because $I_{nk} = \ln \sum_{j\in B_k} e^{Y_{nj}/\lambda_k}$, recognizing that $e^x b^c = e^{x+c\ln b}$.

4.3   Three-Level Nested Logit

The nested logit model that we have discussed up to this point is called a two-level nested logit model, because there are two levels of modeling: the marginal probabilities (upper model) and the conditional probabilities (lower models). In the case of the mode choice, the two levels are the marginal model of auto versus transit and the conditional models of type of auto or transit (auto alone or carpool given auto, and bus or rail given transit).

In some situations, three- or higher-level nested logit models are appropriate. Three-level models are obtained by partitioning the set of alternatives into nests and then partitioning each nest into subsets. The probability formula is a generalization of (4.2) with extra sums for the subsets within the sums for nests. See McFadden (1978) or Ben-Akiva and Lerman (1985) for the formula.

As with a two-level nested logit, the choice probabilities for a three-level model can be expressed as a series of logits. The top model

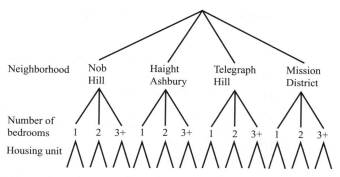

Figure 4.2. Three-level nested logit.

describes the choice of nest; the middle models describe the choice of subnest within each nest; and the bottom models describe the choice of alternative within each subnest. The top model includes an inclusive value for each nest. This value represents the expected utility that the decision maker can obtain from the subnests within the nest. It is calculated as the log of the denominator of the middle model for that nest. Similarly, the middle models include an inclusive value for each subnest, which represents the expected utility that the decision maker can obtain from the alternatives within the subnest. It is calculated as the log of the denominator of the bottom model for the subnest.

As an example, consider a household's choice of housing unit within a metropolitan area. The household has a choice among all the available housing units in the city. The housing units are available in different neighborhoods in the city and with different numbers of bedrooms. It is reasonable to assume that there are unobserved factors that are common to all units in the same neighborhood, such as the proximity to shopping and entertainment. The unobserved portion of utility is therefore expected to be correlated over all units in a given neighborhood. There are also unobserved factors that are common to all units with the same number of bedrooms, such as the convenience of working at home. We therefore expect the unobserved utility to be even more highly correlated among units of the same size in the same neighborhood than between units of different size in the same neighborhood. This pattern of correlation can be represented by nesting the units by neighborhood and then subnesting them by number of bedrooms. A tree diagram depicting this situation is given in Figure 4.2 for San Francisco. There are three levels of submodels: the probability for choice of neighborhood, the probability for choice of number of bedrooms given the neighborhood, and the choice of unit given the neighborhood and number of bedrooms.

A nested logit model with this nesting structure embodies IIA in the following ways.

1. The ratio of probabilities of two housing units in the same neighborhood and with the same number of bedrooms is independent of the characteristics of all other units. For example, lowering the price of a two-bedroom apartment in Pacific Heights draws proportionately from all one-bedroom units on Russian Hill.

2. The ratio of probabilities of two housing units in the same neighborhood but with different numbers of bedrooms is independent of the characteristics of units in other neighborhoods but depends on the characteristics of units in the same neighborhood that have the same number of bedrooms as either of these units. Lowering the price of a two-bedroom apartment in Pacific Heights draws proportionately from one- and two-bedroom units on Russian Hill, but draws disproportionately from two-bedroom units in Pacific Heights relative to one-bedroom units in Pacific Heights.

3. The ratio of probabilities of two housing units in different neighborhoods depends on the characteristics of all the other housing units in those neighborhoods but not on the characteristics of units in other neighborhoods. Lowering the price of a two-bedroom apartment in Pacific Heights draws proportionately from all units outside Pacific Heights but draws disproportionately from units in Pacific Heights relative to units outside Pacific Heights.

Each layer of a nesting in a nested logit introduces parameters that represent the degree of correlation among alternatives within the nests. With the full set of alternatives partitioned into nests, the parameter λ_k is introduced for nest k, as described for two-level models. If the nests are further partitioned into subnests, then a parameter σ_{mk} is introduced for subnest m of nest k. Using the decomposition of the probability into a series of logit models, σ_{mk} is the coefficient of the inclusive value in the middle model, and $\lambda_k \sigma_{mk}$ is the coefficient of the inclusive value in the top model. Just as for a two-level nested logit, the values of these parameters must be in certain ranges to be consistent with utility maximization. If $0 < \lambda_k < 1$ and $0 < \sigma_{mk} < 1$, then the model is consistent with utility maximization for all levels of the explanatory variables. A negative value for either parameter is inconsistent with utility maximization. And values greater than one are consistent for a range of explanatory variables.

4.4   Overlapping Nests

For the nested logit models that we have considered, each alternative is a member of only one nest (and, for three-level models, only one subnest). This aspect of nested logit models is a restriction that is sometimes inappropriate. For example, in our example of mode choice, we put carpool and auto alone into a nest because they have some similar unobserved attributes. However, carpooling also has some unobserved attributes that are similar to bus and rail, such as a lack of flexibility in scheduling (the worker cannot go to work whenever he wants each day but rather has to go at the time that the carpool has decided, similarly to taking a bus or rail line with fixed departure times). It would be useful to have a model in which the unobserved utility for the carpool alternative could be correlated with that of auto alone and also correlated, though to a different degree, with that of bus and rail. Stated equivalently, it would be useful for the carpool alternative to be in two nests: one with auto alone and another with bus and rail.

Several kinds of GEV models have been specified with overlapping nests, so that an alternative can be a member of more than one nest. Vovsha (1997), Bierlaire (1998), and Ben-Akiva and Bierlaire (1999) have proposed various models called cross-nested logits (CNLs) that contain multiple overlapping nests. Small (1987) considered a situation where the alternatives have a natural order, such as the number of cars that a household owns (0, 1, 2, 3, . . .) or the destination for shopping trips, with the shopping areas ordered by distance from the household's home. He specified a model, called ordered generalized extreme value (OGEV), in which the correlation in unobserved utility between any two alternatives depends on their proximity in the ordering. This model has overlapping nests like the CNLs, but each nest consists of two alternatives, and a pattern is imposed on the correlations (higher correlation for closer pairs). Small (1994) and Bhat (1998b) described a nested version of the OGEV, which is similar to a nested logit except that the lower models (for the alternatives given the nests) are OGEV rather than standard logit. Chu (1981, 1989) proposed a model called the paired combinatorial logit (PCL) in which each pair of alternatives constitutes a nest with its own correlation. With J alternatives, each alternative is a member of $J - 1$ nests, and the correlation of its unobserved utility with each other alternative is estimated. Wen and Koppelman (2001) have developed a generalized nested logit (GNL) model that includes the PCL and other cross-nested models as special cases. I describe in the following subsections the PCL and GNL, the former because of its simplicity and the latter because of its generality.

94   Behavioral Models

4.4.1. Paired Combinatorial Logit

Each pair of alternatives is considered to be a nest. Since each alternative is paired with each of the other alternatives, each alternative is member of $J - 1$ nests. A parameter labeled λ_{ij} indicates the degree of independence between alternatives i and j. Stated equivalently: $1 - \lambda_{ij}$ is a measure of the correlation between the unobserved utility of alternative i and that of alternative j. This parameter is analogous to the λ_k in a nested logit model, where λ_k indicates the degree of independence of alternatives within the nest and $1 - \lambda_k$ is a measure of correlation within the nest. And as with nested logit, the PCL model becomes a standard logit when $\lambda_{ij} = 1$ for all pairs of alternatives.

The choice probabilities for the PCL model are

$$(4.6) \quad P_{ni} = \frac{\sum_{j \neq i} e^{V_{ni}/\lambda_{ij}} (e^{V_{ni}/\lambda_{ij}} + e^{V_{nj}/\lambda_{ij}})^{\lambda_{ij}-1}}{\sum_{k=1}^{J-1} \sum_{\ell=k+1}^{J} (e^{V_{nk}/\lambda_{k\ell}} + e^{V_{n\ell}/\lambda_{k\ell}})^{\lambda_{k\ell}}}.$$

The sum in the numerator is over all $J - 1$ nests that alternative i is in. For each of these nests, the term being added is the same as the numerator of the nested logit probability (4.2). Thus, the PCL is like the nested logit except that it allows i to be in more than one nest. The denominator in the PCL also takes the same form as in a nested logit: it is the sum over all nests of the sum of the $\exp(V/\lambda)$'s within the nest, raised to the appropriate power λ. If λ_{ij} is between zero and one for all ij pairs, then the model is consistent with utility maximization for all levels of the data. It is easy to verify that P_{ni} becomes the standard logit formula when $\lambda_{ij} = 1 \ \forall i, j$. In their application, Koppelman and Wen (2000) found PCL to perform better than nested logit or standard logit.

The researcher can test the hypothesis that $\lambda_{ij} = 1$ for some or all of the pairs, using the likelihood ratio test of Section 3.8.2. Acceptance of the hypothesis for a pair of alternatives implies that there is no significant correlation in the unobserved utility for that pair. The researcher can also place structure on the pattern of correlation. For example, correlations can be assumed to be the same among a group of alternatives; this assumption is imposed by setting $\lambda_{ij} = \lambda_{k\ell}$ for all i, j, k, and ℓ in the group. Small's OGEV model is a PCL model in which λ_{ij} is specified to be a function of the proximity between i and j. With a large number of alternatives, the researcher will probably need to impose some form of structure on the λ_{ij}'s, simply to avoid the proliferation of parameters that arises with large J. This proliferation of parameters, one for each pair of alternatives, is what makes the PCL so flexible. The researcher's goal is to apply this flexibility meaningfully for his particular situation.

As discussed near the end of Section 2.5, since the scale and level of utility are immaterial, at most $J(J-1)/2 - 1$ covariance parameters can be estimated in a discrete choice model. A PCL model contains $J(J-1)/2$ λ's: one for each alternative paired with each other alternative, recognizing that i paired with j is the same as j paired with i. The number of λ's exceeds the number of identifiable covariance parameters by exactly one. The researcher must therefore place at least one constraint on the λ's. This can be accomplished by normalizing one of the λ's to 1. If structure is imposed on the pattern of correlation, as described in the previous paragraph, then this structure will usually impose the normalization automatically.

4.4.2. Generalized Nested Logit

Nests of alternatives are labeled $B_1, B_2, \ldots, B_K$. Each alternative can be a member of more than one nest. Importantly, an alternative can be in a nest to varying degrees. Stated differently, an alternative is allocated among the nests, with the alternative being in some nests more than other nests. An *allocation* parameter α_{jk} reflects the extent to which alternative j is a member of nest k. This parameter must be nonnegative: $\alpha_{jk} \geq 0 \,\forall j, k$. A value of zero means that the alternative is not in the nest at all. Interpretation is facilitated by having the allocation parameters sum to one over nests for any alternative: $\sum_k \alpha_{jk} = 1 \,\forall j$. Under this condition, α_{jk} reflects the portion of the alternative that is allocated to each nest.

A parameter λ_k is defined for each nest and serves the same function as in nested logit models, namely to indicate the degree of independence among alternatives within the nest: higher λ_k translates into greater independence and less correlation.

The probability that person n chooses alternative i is

$$(4.7) \quad P_{ni} = \frac{\sum_k \left(\alpha_{ik} e^{V_{ni}}\right)^{1/\lambda_k} \left(\sum_{j \in B_k} \left(\alpha_{jk} e^{V_{nj}}\right)^{1/\lambda_k}\right)^{\lambda_k - 1}}{\sum_{\ell=1}^{K} \left(\sum_{j \in B_\ell} \left(\alpha_{j\ell} e^{V_{nj}}\right)^{1/\lambda_\ell}\right)^{\lambda_\ell}}.$$

This formula is similar to the nested logit probability given in equation (4.2), except that the numerator is a sum over all the nests that contains alternative i, with weights applied to these nests. If each alternative enters only one nest, with $\alpha_{jk} = 1$ for $j \in B_k$ and zero otherwise, the model becomes a nested logit model. And if, in addition, $\lambda_k = 1$ for all nests, then the model becomes standard logit. Wen and Koppelman (2001) derive various cross-nested models as special cases of the GNL.

To facilitate interpretation, the GNL probability can be decomposed as

$$P_{ni} = \sum_k P_{ni \mid B_k} P_{nk},$$

where the probability of nest k is

$$P_{nk} = \frac{\left(\sum_{j \in B_k}\left(\alpha_{jk}e^{V_{nj}}\right)^{1/\lambda_k}\right)^{\lambda_k}}{\sum_{\ell=1}^{K}\left(\sum_{j \in B_\ell}\left(\alpha_{j\ell}e^{V_{nj}}\right)^{1/\lambda_\ell}\right)^{\lambda_\ell}}$$

and the probability of alternative i given nest k is

$$P_{ni \mid B_k} = \frac{\left(\alpha_{ik}e^{V_{ni}}\right)^{1/\lambda_k}}{\sum_{j \in B_k}\left(\alpha_{jk}e^{V_{nj}}\right)^{1/\lambda_k}}.$$

4.5   Heteroskedastic Logit

Instead of capturing correlations among alternatives, the researcher may simply want to allow the variance of unobserved factors to differ over alternatives. Steckel and Vanhonacker (1988), Bhat (1995), and Recker (1995) describe a type of GEV model, called *heteroskedastic extreme value* (HEV), that is the same as logit except for having a different variance for each alternative. Utility is specified as $U_{nj} = V_{nj} + \varepsilon_{nj}$, where ε_{nj} is distributed independently extreme value with variance $(\theta_j \pi)^2/6$. There is no correlation in unobserved factors over alternatives; however, the variance of the unobserved factors is different for different alternatives. To set the overall scale of utility, the variance for one alternative is normalized to $\pi^2/6$, which is the variance of the standardized extreme value distribution. The variances for the other alternatives are then estimated relative to the normalized variance.

The choice probabilities for this heteroskedastic logit are (Bhat, 1995)

$$P_{ni} = \int \left[\prod_{j \neq i} e^{-e^{-(V_{ni}-V_{nj}+\theta_i w)/\theta_j}}\right] e^{-e^{-w}}e^{-w}dw,$$

where $w = \varepsilon_{ni}/\theta_i$. The integral does not take a closed form; however, it can be approximated by simulation. Note that $\exp(-\exp(-w))\exp(-w)$ is the extreme value density, given in Section 3.1. P_{ni} is therefore the integral of the factor in square brackets over the extreme value density. It can be simulated as follows: (1) Take a draw from the extreme value distribution, using the procedure described in Section 9.2.3. (2) For this draw of w, calculate the factor in brackets, namely, $\prod_{j \neq i} \exp(-\exp(-(v_{ni} - V_{nj} + \theta_i w)/\theta_j))$. (3) Repeat steps 1 and 2 many times, and average the results. This average is an approximation to P_{ni}. Bhat (1995) shows that, since the integral is only one-dimensional, the heteroskedastic logit probabilities can be calculated effectively with quadrature rather than simulation.

4.6   The GEV Family

We now describe the processs that McFadden (1978) developed to generate GEV models. Using this process, the researcher is able to develop new GEV models that best fit the specific circumstances of his choice situation. As illustration, we show how the procedure is used to generate models that we have already discussed, namely logit, nested logit, and paired combinatorial logit. The same procedure can be applied by a researcher to generate new models with properties that meet his research needs.

For notational simplicity, we will omit the subscript n denoting the decision maker. Also, since we will be using $\exp(V_j)$ repeatedly, let's denote it more compactly by Y_j. That is, let $Y_j \equiv \exp(V_j)$. Note that Y_j is necessarily positive.

Consider a function G that depends on Y_j for all j. We denote this function $G = G(Y_1, \ldots, Y_J)$. Let G_i be the derivative of G with respect to Y_i: $G_i = \partial G / \partial Y_i$. If this function meets certain conditions, then a discrete choice model can be based upon it. In particular, if G satisfies the conditions that are listed in the next paragraph, then

$$(4.8) \qquad P_i = \frac{Y_i G_i}{G}$$

is the choice probability for a discrete choice model that is consistent with utility maximization. Any model that can be derived in this way is a GEV model. This formula therefore defines the family of GEV models.

The properties that the function must exhibit are the following:

1. $G \geq 0$ for all positive values of $Y_j \; \forall j$.
2. G is homogeneous of degree one. That is, if each Y_j is raised by some proportion ρ, G rises by proportion ρ also: $G(\rho Y_1, \ldots, \rho Y_J) = \rho G(Y_1, \ldots, Y_J)$. Actually, Ben-Akiva and Francois (1983) showed that this condition can be relaxed to allow any degree of homogeneity. We retain the usage of degree one, since doing so makes the condition easier to interpret and is consistent with McFadden's original description.
3. $G \to \infty$ as $Y_j \to \infty$ for any j.
4. The cross partial derivatives of G change signs in a particular way. That is, $G_i \geq 0$ for all i, $G_{ij} = \partial G_i / \partial Y_j \leq 0$ for all $j \neq i$, $G_{ijk} = \partial G_{ij} / \partial Y_k \geq 0$ for any distinct i, j, and k, and so on for higher-order cross-partials.

There is little economic intuition to motivate these properties, particularly the last one. However, it is easy to verify whether a function exhibits these properties. The lack of intuition behind the properties is a blessing and a curse. The disadvantage is that the researcher has little guidance on how to specify a G that provides a model that meets the needs of his research. The advantage is that the purely mathematical approach allows the researcher to generate models that he might not have developed while relying only on his economic intuition. Karlstrom (2001) provides an example: he arbitrarily specified a G (in the sense that it was not based on behavioral concepts) and found that the resulting probability formula fitted his data better than logit, nested logit, and PCL.

We can now show how logit, nested logit, and PCL models are obtained under appropriate specifications of G.

Logit

Let $G = \sum_{j=1}^{J} Y_j$. This G exhibits the four required properties: (1) The sum of positive Y_j's is positive. (2) If all Y_j's are raised by a factor ρ, G rises by that same factor. (3) If any Y_j rises without bound, then G does also. (4) The first partial derivative is $G_i = \partial G / \partial Y_i = 1$, which meets the criterion that $G_i \geq 0$. And the higher-order derivatives are all zero, which clearly meets the criterion, since they are ≥ 0 or ≤ 0 as required.

Inserting this G and its first derivative G_i into (4.8), the resulting choice probability is

$$
\begin{aligned}
P_i &= \frac{Y_i G_i}{G} \\
&= \frac{Y_i}{\sum_{j=1}^{J} Y_j} \\
&= \frac{e^{V_i}}{\sum_{j=1}^{J} e^{V_j}},
\end{aligned}
$$

which is the logit formula.

Nested Logit

The J alternatives are partitioned into K nests labeled $B_1, \ldots, B_K$. Let

$$
G = \sum_{\ell=1}^{K} \left(\sum_{j \in B_\ell} Y_j^{1/\lambda_\ell} \right)^{\lambda_\ell},
$$

with each λ_k between zero and one. The first three properties are easy to verify. For the fourth property, we calculate the first partial derivative

$$G_i = \lambda_k \left(\sum_{j \in B_k} Y_j^{1/\lambda_k} \right)^{\lambda_k - 1} \frac{1}{\lambda_k} Y_i^{(1/\lambda_k) - 1}$$

$$= Y_i^{(1/\lambda_k) - 1} \left(\sum_{j \in B_k} Y_j^{1/\lambda_k} \right)^{\lambda_k - 1}$$

for $i \in B_k$. Since $Y_j \geq 0 \ \forall j$, we have $G_i \geq 0$, as required. The second cross partial derivative is

$$G_{im} = \frac{\partial G_i}{\partial Y_m}$$

$$= (\lambda_k - 1) Y_i^{(1/\lambda_k) - 1} \left(\sum_{j \in B_k} Y_j^{1/\lambda_k} \right)^{\lambda_k - 2} \frac{1}{\lambda_k} Y_m^{(1/\lambda_k) - 1}$$

$$= \frac{\lambda_k - 1}{\lambda_k} (Y_i Y_m)^{(1/\lambda_k) - 1} \left(\sum_{j \in B_k} Y_j^{1/\lambda_k} \right)^{\lambda_k - 2}$$

for $m \in B_k$ and $m \neq i$. With $\lambda_k \leq 1$, $G_{ij} \leq 0$, as required. For j in a different nest than i, $G_{ij} = 0$, which also meets the criterion. Higher cross-partials are calculated similarly; they exhibit the required property if $0 < \lambda_k \leq 1$.

The choice probability becomes

$$P_i = \frac{Y_i G_i}{G}$$

$$= \frac{Y_i Y_i^{(1/\lambda_k) - 1} \left(\sum_{j \in B_k} Y_j^{1/\lambda_\ell} \right)^{\lambda_k - 1}}{\sum_{\ell=1}^{K} \left(\sum_{j \in B_\ell} Y_j^{1/\lambda_\ell} \right)^{\lambda_\ell}}$$

$$= \frac{Y_i^{1/\lambda_k} \left(\sum_{j \in B_k} Y_j^{1/\lambda_\ell} \right)^{\lambda_k - 1}}{\sum_{\ell=1}^{K} \left(\sum_{j \in B_\ell} Y_j^{1/\lambda_\ell} \right)^{\lambda_\ell}}$$

$$= \frac{(e^{V_i})^{1/\lambda_k} \left(\sum_{j \in B_k} (e^{V_j})^{1/\lambda_\ell} \right)^{\lambda_k - 1}}{\sum_{\ell=1}^{K} \left(\sum_{j \in B_\ell} (e^{V_j})^{1/\lambda_\ell} \right)^{\lambda_\ell}}$$

$$= \frac{e^{V_i/\lambda_k} \left(\sum_{j \in B_k} e^{V_j/\lambda_\ell} \right)^{\lambda_k - 1}}{\sum_{\ell=1}^{K} \left(\sum_{j \in B_\ell} e^{V_j/\lambda_\ell} \right)^{\lambda_\ell}},$$

which is the nested logit formula (4.2).

Paired Combinatorial Logit

Let

$$G = \sum_{k=1}^{J-1} \sum_{\ell=k+1}^{J} \left(Y_k^{1/\lambda_{k\ell}} + Y_\ell^{1/\lambda_{k\ell}} \right)^{\lambda_{k\ell}}.$$

The required properties are verified in the same way as for the nested logit. We have

$$G_i = \sum_{j \neq i} \lambda_{ji} \left(Y_i^{1/\lambda_{ij}} + Y_j^{1/\lambda_{ij}} \right)^{\lambda_{ij}-1} \frac{1}{\lambda_{ij}} Y_i^{(1/\lambda_{ij})-1}$$

$$= \sum_{j \neq i} Y_i^{(1/\lambda_{ij})-1} \left(Y_i^{1/\lambda_{ij}} + Y_j^{1/\lambda_{ij}} \right)^{\lambda_{ij}-1}.$$

And so the choice probability is

$$P_i = \frac{Y_i G_i}{G}$$

$$= \frac{Y_i \sum_{j \neq i} Y_i^{(1/\lambda_{ij})-1} \left(Y_i^{1/\lambda_{ij}} + Y_j^{1/\lambda_{ij}} \right)^{\lambda_{ij}-1}}{\sum_{k=1}^{J-1} \sum_{\ell=k+1}^{J} \left(Y_k^{1/\lambda_{k\ell}} + Y_\ell^{1/\lambda_{k\ell}} \right)^{\lambda_{k\ell}}}$$

$$= \frac{\sum_{j \neq i} Y_i^{(1/\lambda_{ij})} \left(Y_i^{1/\lambda_{ij}} + Y_j^{1/\lambda_{ij}} \right)^{\lambda_{ij}-1}}{\sum_{k=1}^{J-1} \sum_{\ell=k+1}^{J} \left(Y_k^{1/\lambda_{k\ell}} + Y_\ell^{1/\lambda_{k\ell}} \right)^{\lambda_{k\ell}}}$$

$$= \frac{\sum_{j \neq i} e^{V_i/\lambda_{ij}} (e^{V_i/\lambda_{ij}} + e^{V_j/\lambda_{ij}})^{\lambda_{ij}-1}}{\sum_{k=1}^{J-1} \sum_{\ell=k+1}^{J} (e^{V_k/\lambda_{k\ell}} + e^{V_\ell/\lambda_{k\ell}})^{\lambda_{k\ell}}},$$

which is the PCL formula (4.6).

Generalized Nest Logit

The reader can verify that the GNL probabilities in equation (4.7) are derived from

$$G = \sum_{k=1}^{K} \left(\sum_{j \in B_k} (\alpha_{jk} Y_j)^{1/\lambda_k} \right)^{\lambda_k}.$$

Using the same process, researchers can generate other GEV models.

5 Probit

5.1 Choice Probabilities

The logit model is limited in three important ways. It cannot represent random taste variation. It exhibits restrictive substitution patterns due to the IIA property. And it cannot be used with panel data when unobserved factors are correlated over time for each decision maker. GEV models relax the second of these restrictions, but not the other two. Probit models deal with all three. They can handle random taste variation, they allow any pattern of substitution, and they are applicable to panel data with temporally correlated errors.

The only limitation of probit models is that they require normal distributions for all unobserved components of utility. In many, perhaps most situations, normal distributions provide an adequate representation of the random components. However, in some situations, normal distributions are inappropriate and can lead to perverse forecasts. A prominent example relates to price coefficients. For a probit model with random taste variation, the coefficient of price is assumed to be normally distributed in the population. Since the normal distribution has density on both sides of zero, the model necessarily implies that some people have a positive price coefficient. The use of a distribution that has density only on one side of zero, such as the lognormal, is more appropriate and yet cannot be accommodated within probit. Other than this restriction, the probit model is quite general.

The probit model is derived under the assumption of jointly normal unobserved utility components. The first derivation, by Thurstone (1927) for a binary probit, used the terminology of psychological stimuli, which Marschak (1960) translated into economic terms as utility. Hausman and Wise (1978) and Daganzo (1979) elucidated the generality of the specification for representing various aspects of choice behavior. Utility is decomposed into observed and unobserved parts: $U_{nj} = V_{nj} + \varepsilon_{nj} \; \forall j$. Consider the vector composed of each ε_{nj}, labeled $\varepsilon'_n = \langle \varepsilon_{n1}, \ldots, \varepsilon_{nJ} \rangle$.

We assume that ε_n is distributed normal with a mean vector of zero and covariance matrix Ω. The density of ε_n is

$$\phi(\varepsilon_n) = \frac{1}{(2\pi)^{J/2}|\Omega|^{1/2}} e^{-\frac{1}{2}\varepsilon_n' \Omega^{-1} \varepsilon_n}.$$

The covariance Ω can depend on variables faced by decision maker n, so that Ω_n is the more appropriate notation; however, we omit the subscript for the sake of simplicity.

The choice probability is

$$P_{ni} = \text{Prob}(V_{ni} + \varepsilon_{ni} > V_{nj} + \varepsilon_{nj} \ \forall j \neq i)$$

$$(5.1) \qquad = \int I(V_{ni} + \varepsilon_{ni} > V_{nj} + \varepsilon_{nj} \ \forall j \neq i)\phi(\varepsilon_n)\,d\varepsilon_n,$$

where $I(\cdot)$ is an indicator of whether the statement in parentheses holds, and the integral is over all values of ε_n. This integral does not have a closed form. It must be evaluated numerically through simulation.

The choice probabilities can be expressed in a couple of other ways that are useful for simulating the integral. Let B_{ni} be the set of error terms ε_n that result in the decision maker choosing alternative i: $B_{ni} = \{\varepsilon_n \text{ s.t. } V_{ni} + \varepsilon_{ni} > V_{nj} + \varepsilon_{nj} \ \forall j \neq i\}$. Then

$$(5.2) \qquad P_{ni} = \int_{\varepsilon_n \in B_{ni}} \phi(\varepsilon_n)\,d\varepsilon_n,$$

which is an integral over only some of the values of ε_n rather than all possible values, namely, the ε_n's in B_{ni}.

Expressions (5.1) and (5.2) are J-dimensional integrals over the J errors ε_{nj}, $j = 1, \ldots, J$. Since only differences in utility matter, the choice probabilities can be equivalently expressed as $(J - 1)$-dimensional integrals over the differences between the errors. Let us difference against alternative i, the alternative for which we are calculating the probability. Define $\tilde{U}_{nji} = U_{nj} - U_{ni}$, $\tilde{V}_{nji} = V_{nj} - V_{ni}$, and $\tilde{\varepsilon}_{nji} = \varepsilon_{nj} - \varepsilon_{ni}$. Then $P_{ni} = \text{Prob}(\tilde{U}_{nji} < 0 \ \forall j \neq i)$. That is, the probability of choosing alternative i is the probability that all the utility differences, when differenced against i, are negative. Define the vector $\tilde{\varepsilon}_{ni} = \langle \tilde{\varepsilon}_{n1i}, \ldots, \tilde{\varepsilon}_{nJi} \rangle$ where the "$\ldots$" is over all alternatives except i, so that $\tilde{\varepsilon}_{ni}$ has dimension $J - 1$. Since the difference between two normals is normal, the density of the error differences is

$$\phi(\tilde{\varepsilon}_{ni}) = \frac{1}{(2\pi)^{\frac{1}{2}(J-1)}|\tilde{\Omega}_i|^{1/2}} e^{-\frac{1}{2}\tilde{\varepsilon}_{ni}' \tilde{\Omega}_i \tilde{\varepsilon}_{ni}},$$

where $\tilde{\Omega}_i$ is the covariance of $\tilde{\varepsilon}_{ni}$, derived from Ω. Then the choice probability expressed in utility differences is

$$(5.3) \quad P_{ni} = \int I(\tilde{V}_{nji} + \tilde{\varepsilon}_{nji} < 0 \; \forall j \neq i) \phi(\tilde{\varepsilon}_{ni}) \, d\tilde{\varepsilon}_{ni},$$

which is a $(J-1)$-dimensional integral over all possible values of the error differences. An equivalent expression is

$$(5.4) \quad P_{ni} = \int_{\tilde{\varepsilon}_{ni} \in \tilde{B}_{ni}} \phi(\tilde{\varepsilon}_{ni}) \, d\tilde{\varepsilon}_{ni},$$

where $\tilde{B}_{ni} = \{\tilde{\varepsilon}_{ni} \text{ s.t. } \tilde{V}_{nji} + \tilde{\varepsilon}_{nji} < 0 \; \forall j \neq i\}$, which is a $(J-1)$-dimensional integral over the error differences in $\tilde{B}_{ni}$.

Expressions (5.3) and (5.4) utilize the covariance matrix $\tilde{\Omega}_i$ of the error differences. There is a straightforward way to derive $\tilde{\Omega}_i$ from the covariance of the errors themselves, Ω. Let M_i be the $(J-1)$ identity matrix with an extra column of -1's added as the ith column. The extra column makes the matrix have size $J-1$ by J. For example, with $J = 4$ alternatives and $i = 3$,

$$M_i = \begin{pmatrix} 1 & 0 & -1 & 0 \\ 0 & 1 & -1 & 0 \\ 0 & 0 & -1 & 1 \end{pmatrix}.$$

This matrix can be used to transform the covariance matrix of errors into the covariance matrix of error differences: $\tilde{\Omega}_i = M_i \Omega M_i'$. Note that $\tilde{\Omega}_i$ is $(J-1) \times (J-1)$ while Ω is $J \times J$, since M_i is $(J-1) \times J$. As an illustration, consider a three-alternative situation with errors $\langle \varepsilon_{n1}, \varepsilon_{n2}, \varepsilon_{n3} \rangle$ that have covariance

$$\Omega = \begin{pmatrix} \sigma_{11} & \sigma_{12} & \sigma_{13} \\ \sigma_{12} & \sigma_{22} & \sigma_{23} \\ \sigma_{13} & \sigma_{23} & \sigma_{33} \end{pmatrix}.$$

Suppose we takes differences against alternative 2. We know from first principles that the error differences $\langle \tilde{\varepsilon}_{n12}, \tilde{\varepsilon}_{n32} \rangle$ have covariance

$$\tilde{\Omega}_2 = \text{Cov}\begin{pmatrix} \varepsilon_{n1} - \varepsilon_{n2} \\ \varepsilon_{n3} - \varepsilon_{n2} \end{pmatrix}$$

$$= \begin{pmatrix} \sigma_{11} + \sigma_{22} - 2\sigma_{12} & \sigma_{13} + \sigma_{22} - \sigma_{12} - \sigma_{23} \\ \sigma_{13} + \sigma_{22} - \sigma_{12} - \sigma_{23} & \sigma_{33} + \sigma_{22} - 2\sigma_{23} \end{pmatrix}.$$

This covariance matrix can also be derived by the transformation $\tilde{\Omega}_2 = M_2\Omega M_2'$:

$$\tilde{\Omega}_n = \begin{pmatrix} 1 & -1 & 0 \\ 0 & -1 & 1 \end{pmatrix} \begin{pmatrix} \sigma_{11} & \sigma_{12} & \sigma_{13} \\ \sigma_{12} & \sigma_{22} & \sigma_{23} \\ \sigma_{13} & \sigma_{23} & \sigma_{33} \end{pmatrix} \begin{pmatrix} 1 & 0 \\ -1 & -1 \\ 0 & 1 \end{pmatrix}$$

$$= \begin{pmatrix} \sigma_{11} - \sigma_{12} & \sigma_{12} - \sigma_{22} & \sigma_{13} - \sigma_{23} \\ -\sigma_{12} + \sigma_{13} & -\sigma_{22} + \sigma_{23} & -\sigma_{23} + \sigma_{33} \end{pmatrix} \begin{pmatrix} 1 & 0 \\ -1 & -1 \\ 0 & 1 \end{pmatrix}$$

$$= \begin{pmatrix} \sigma_{11} - \sigma_{12} - \sigma_{12} + \sigma_{22} & -\sigma_{12} + \sigma_{22} + \sigma_{13} - \sigma_{23} \\ -\sigma_{12} + \sigma_{13} + \sigma_{22} - \sigma_{23} & \sigma_{22} - \sigma_{23} - \sigma_{23} + \sigma_{33} \end{pmatrix}$$

$$= \begin{pmatrix} \sigma_{11} + \sigma_{22} - 2\sigma_{12} & \sigma_{13} + \sigma_{22} - \sigma_{12} - \sigma_{23} \\ \sigma_{13} + \sigma_{22} - \sigma_{12} - \sigma_{23} & \sigma_{33} + \sigma_{22} - 2\sigma_{23} \end{pmatrix}.$$

As we will see, this transformation by M_i comes in handy when simulating probit probabilities.

5.2   Identification

As described in Section 2.5, any discrete choice model must be normalized to take account of the fact that the level and scale of utility are irrelevant. The level of utility is immaterial because a constant can be added to the utility of all alternatives without changing which alternative has the highest utility: the alternative with the highest utility before the constant is added still has the highest utility afterward. Similarly, the scale of utility doesn't matter because the utility of each alternative can be multiplied by a (positive) constant without changing which alternative has the highest utility. In logit and nested logit models, the normalization for scale and level occurs automatically with the distributional assumptions that are placed on the error terms. As a result, normalization does not need to be considered explicitly for these models. With probit models, however, normalization for scale and level does not occur automatically. The researcher must normalize the model directly.

Normalization of the model is related to parameter identification. A parameter is *identified* if it can be estimated, and is *unidentified* if it cannot be estimated. An example of an unidentified parameter is k in the utility specification $U_{nj} = V_{nj} + k + \varepsilon_{nj}$. While the researcher might write utility in this way, and might want to estimate k to obtain a measure of the overall level of utility, doing so is impossible. The behavior of the decision maker is unaffected by k, and so the researcher cannot infer its value from the choices that decision makers have made. Stated directly, parameters that do not affect the behavior of decision makers cannot be estimated. In an unnormalized model, parameters can appear that are not identified; these parameters relate to the scale and level of utility, which do not affect behavior. Once the model is normalized, these parameters disappear. The difficulty arises because it is not always obvious which parameters relate to scale and level. In the preceding example, the fact that k is unidentified is fairly obvious. In many cases, it is not at all obvious which parameters are identified. Bunch and Kitamura (1989) have shown that the probit models in several published articles are not normalized and contain unidentified parameters. The fact that neither the authors nor the reviewers of these articles could tell that the models were unnormalized is testimony to the complexity of the issue.

I provide in the following a procedure that can always be used to normalize a probit model and assure that all parameters are identified. It is not the only procedure that can be used; see, for example, Bunch (1991). In some cases a researcher might find other normalization procedures more convenient. However, the procedure I give can always be used, either by itself or as a check on another procedure.

I describe the procedure in terms of a four-alternative model. Generalization to more alternatives is obvious. As usual, utility is expressed as $U_{nj} = V_{nj} + \varepsilon_{nj}$, $j = 1, \ldots, 4$. The vector of errors is $\varepsilon'_n = \langle \varepsilon_{n1}, \ldots, \varepsilon_{n4} \rangle$. It is normally distributed with zero mean and a covariance matrix that can be expressed explicitly as

$$(5.5) \quad \Omega = \begin{pmatrix} \sigma_{11} & \sigma_{12} & \sigma_{13} & \sigma_{14} \\ \cdot & \sigma_{22} & \sigma_{23} & \sigma_{24} \\ \cdot & \cdot & \sigma_{33} & \sigma_{34} \\ \cdot & \cdot & \cdot & \sigma_{44} \end{pmatrix},$$

where the dots refer to the corresponding elements on the upper part of the matrix. Note that there are ten elements in this matrix, that is, ten distinct σ's representing the variances and covariances among the four errors. In general, a model with J alternatives has $J(J+1)/2$ distinct elements in the covariance matrix of the errors.

To take account of the fact that the level of utility is irrelevant, we take utility differences. In my procedure, I always take differences with respect to the first alternative, since that simplifies the analysis in a way that we will see. Define error differences as $\tilde{\varepsilon}_{nj1} = \varepsilon_{nj} - \varepsilon_{n1}$ for $j = 2, 3, 4$, and define the vector of error differences as $\tilde{\varepsilon}_{n1} = \langle \tilde{\varepsilon}_{n21}, \tilde{\varepsilon}_{n31}, \tilde{\varepsilon}_{n41} \rangle$. Note that the subscript 1 in $\tilde{\varepsilon}_{n1}$ means that the error differences are against the first alternative, rather than that the errors are for the first alternative.

The covariance matrix for the vector of error differences takes the form

$$\tilde{\Omega}_1 = \begin{pmatrix} \theta_{22} & \theta_{23} & \theta_{24} \\ \cdot & \theta_{33} & \theta_{34} \\ \cdot & \cdot & \theta_{44} \end{pmatrix},$$

where the θ's relate to the original σ's as follows:

$$\theta_{22} = \sigma_{22} + \sigma_{11} - 2\sigma_{12},$$
$$\theta_{33} = \sigma_{33} + \sigma_{11} - 2\sigma_{13},$$
$$\theta_{44} = \sigma_{44} + \sigma_{11} - 2\sigma_{14},$$
$$\theta_{23} = \sigma_{23} + \sigma_{11} - \sigma_{12} - \sigma_{13},$$
$$\theta_{24} = \sigma_{24} + \sigma_{11} - \sigma_{12} - \sigma_{14},$$
$$\theta_{34} = \sigma_{34} + \sigma_{11} - \sigma_{13} - \sigma_{14}.$$

Computationally, this matrix can be obtained using the transformation matrix M_i defined in Section 5.1 as $\tilde{\Omega}_1 = M_1 \Omega M_1'$.

To set the scale of utility, one of the diagonal elements is normalized. I set the top-left element of $\tilde{\Omega}_1$, which is the variance of $\tilde{\varepsilon}_{n21}$, to 1. This normalization for scale gives us the following covariance matrix:

$$(5.6) \quad \tilde{\Omega}_1^* = \begin{pmatrix} 1 & \theta_{23}^* & \theta_{24}^* \\ \cdot & \theta_{33}^* & \theta_{34}^* \\ \cdot & \cdot & \theta_{44}^* \end{pmatrix}.$$

The θ^*'s relate to the original σ's as follows:

$$\theta_{33}^* = \frac{\sigma_{33} + \sigma_{11} - 2\sigma_{13}}{\sigma_{22} + \sigma_{11} - 2\sigma_{12}},$$

$$\theta_{44}^* = \frac{\sigma_{44} + \sigma_{11} - 2\sigma_{14}}{\sigma_{22} + \sigma_{11} - 2\sigma_{12}},$$

$$\theta_{23}^* = \frac{\sigma_{23} + \sigma_{11} - \sigma_{12} - \sigma_{13}}{\sigma_{22} + \sigma_{11} - 2\sigma_{12}},$$

$$\theta_{24}^* = \frac{\sigma_{24} + \sigma_{11} - \sigma_{12} - \sigma_{14}}{\sigma_{22} + \sigma_{11} - 2\sigma_{12}},$$

$$\theta_{34}^* = \frac{\sigma_{34} + \sigma_{11} - \sigma_{13} - \sigma_{14}}{\sigma_{22} + \sigma_{11} - 2\sigma_{12}}.$$

There are five elements in $\tilde{\Omega}_1^*$. These are the only identified parameters in the model. This number is less than the ten elements that enter Ω. Each θ^* is a function of the σ's. Since there are five θ^*'s and ten σ's, it is not possible to solve for all the σ's from estimated values of the θ^*'s. It is therefore not possible to obtain estimates of all the σ's.

In general, a model with J alternatives and an unrestricted covariance matrix will have $[(J-1)J/2]-1$ covariance parameters when normalized, compared to the $J(J+1)/2$ parameters when unnormalized. Only $[(J-1)J/2]-1$ parameters are identified. This reduction in the number of parameters is *not* a restriction. The reduction in the number of parameters is a normalization that simply eliminates irrelevant aspects of the original covariance matrix, namely the scale and level of utility. The ten elements in Ω allow for variance and covariance that is due simply to scale and level, which has no relevance for behavior. Only the five elements in $\tilde{\Omega}_1^*$ contain information about the variance and covariance of errors independent of scale and level. In this sense, only the five parameters have economic content, and only the five parameters can be estimated.

Suppose now that the researcher imposes structure on the covariance matrix. That is, instead of allowing a full covariance matrix for the errors, the researcher believes that the errors follow a pattern that implies particular values for, or relations among, the elements in the covariance matrix. The researcher restricts the covariance matrix to incorporate this pattern.

The structure can take various forms, depending on the application. Yai *et al.* (1997) estimate a probit model of route choice where the covariance between any two routes depends only on the length of shared route segments; this structure reduces the number of covariance parameters to only one, which captures the relation of the covariance to shared length. Bolduc *et al.* (1996) estimate a model of physicians' choice of location where the covariance among locations is a function of their proximity to one another, using what Bolduc (1992) has called a "generalized autoregressive" structure. Haaijer *et al.* (1998) impose a factor-analytic structure that arises from random coefficients of explanatory variables; this type of structure is described in detail in Section 5.3. Elrod and Keane (1995) impose a factor-analytic structure, but one that arises from error components rather than random coefficients *per se*.

Often the structure that is imposed will be sufficient to normalize the model. That is, the restrictions that the researcher imposes on the covariance matrix to fit her beliefs about the way the errors relate to each other will also serve to normalize the model. However, this is not always the case. The examples cited by Bunch and Kitamura (1989) are cases where the restrictions that the researcher placed on the covariance matrix seemed sufficient to normalize the model but actually were not.

The procedure that I give in the preceding text can be used to determine whether the restrictions on the covariance matrix are sufficient to normalize the model. The researcher specifies Ω with her restrictions on its elements. Then the stated procedure is used to derive $\tilde{\Omega}_1^*$, which is normalized for scale and level. We know that each element of $\tilde{\Omega}_1^*$ is identified. If each of the restricted elements of Ω can be calculated from the elements of $\tilde{\Omega}_1^*$, then the restrictions are sufficient to normalize the model. In this case, each parameter in the restricted Ω is identified. On the other hand, if the elements of Ω cannot be calculated from the elements of $\tilde{\Omega}_1^*$, then the restrictions are not sufficient to normalize the model and the parameters in Ω are not identified.

To illustrate this approach, suppose the researcher is estimating a four-alternative model and assumes that the covariance matrix for the errors has the following form:

$$\Omega = \begin{pmatrix} 1+\rho & \rho & 0 & 0 \\ \cdot & 1+\rho & 0 & 0 \\ \cdot & \cdot & 1+\rho & \rho \\ \cdot & \cdot & \cdot & 1+\rho \end{pmatrix}.$$

This covariance matrix allows the first and second errors to be correlated, the same as the third and fourth alternatives, but allows no other correlation. The correlation between the appropriate pairs is $\rho/(1+\rho)$. Note that by specifying the diagonal elements as $1 + \rho$, the researcher assures that the correlation is between -1 and 1 for any value of ρ, as required for a correlation. Is this model, as specified, normalized for scale and level? To answer the question, we apply the described procedure. First, we take differences with respect to the first alternative. The covariance matrix of error differences is

$$\tilde{\Omega}_1 = \begin{pmatrix} \theta_{22} & \theta_{23} & \theta_{24} \\ \cdot & \theta_{33} & \theta_{34} \\ \cdot & \cdot & \theta_{44} \end{pmatrix},$$

where the θ's relate to the original σ's as follows:

$\theta_{22} = 2,$

$\theta_{33} = 2 + 2\rho,$

$\theta_{44} = 2 + 2\rho,$

$\theta_{23} = 1,$

$\theta_{24} = 1,$

$\theta_{34} = 1 + 2\rho.$

We then normalize for scale by setting the top-left element to 1. The normalized covariance matrix is

$$\tilde{\Omega}_1^* = \begin{pmatrix} 1 & \theta_{23}^* & \theta_{24}^* \\ \cdot & \theta_{33}^* & \theta_{34}^* \\ \cdot & \cdot & \theta_{44}^* \end{pmatrix},$$

where the θ^*'s relate to the original σ's as follows:

$$\theta_{33}^* = 1 + \rho,$$
$$\theta_{44}^* = 1 + \rho,$$
$$\theta_{23}^* = \tfrac{1}{2},$$
$$\theta_{24}^* = \tfrac{1}{2},$$
$$\theta_{34}^* = \tfrac{1}{2} + \rho.$$

Note that $\theta_{33}^* = \theta_{44}^* = \theta_{34}^* + \frac{1}{2}$ and that the other θ^*'s have fixed values. There is one parameter in $\tilde{\Omega}_1^*$, as there is in Ω. Define $\theta = 1 + \rho$. Then $\tilde{\Omega}_1^*$ is

$$\tilde{\Omega}_1^* = \begin{pmatrix} 1 & \tfrac{1}{2} & \tfrac{1}{2} \\ \cdot & \theta & \theta - \tfrac{1}{2} \\ \cdot & \cdot & \theta \end{pmatrix}.$$

The original ρ can be calculated directly from θ. For example, if θ is estimated to be 2.4, then the estimate of ρ is $\theta - 1 = 1.4$ and the correlation is $1.4/2.4 = .58$. The fact that the parameters that enter Ω can be calculated from the parameters that enter the normalized covariance matrix $\tilde{\Omega}_1^*$ means that the original model is normalized for scale and level. That is, the restrictions that the researcher placed on Ω also provided the needed normalization.

Sometimes restrictions on the original covariance matrix can appear to be sufficient to normalize the model when in fact they do not. Applying our procedure will determine whether this is the case. Consider the same model, but now suppose that the researcher allows a different correlation between the first and second errors than between the third and fourth errors. The covariance matrix of errors is specified to be

$$\Omega = \begin{pmatrix} 1 + \rho_1 & \rho_1 & 0 & 0 \\ \cdot & 1 + \rho_1 & 0 & 0 \\ \cdot & \cdot & 1 + \rho_2 & \rho_2 \\ \cdot & \cdot & \cdot & 1 + \rho_2 \end{pmatrix}.$$

The correlation between the first and second errors is $\rho_1/(1 + \rho_1)$, and the correlation between the third and fourth errors is $\rho_2/(1 + \rho_2)$. We can derive $\tilde{\Omega}_1$ for error differences and then derive $\tilde{\Omega}_1^*$ by setting the top-left element of $\tilde{\Omega}_1$ to 1. The resulting matrix is

$$\tilde{\Omega}_1^* = \begin{pmatrix} 1 & \frac{1}{2} & \frac{1}{2} \\ \cdot & \theta & \theta - \frac{1}{2} \\ \cdot & \cdot & \theta \end{pmatrix},$$

where now $\theta = 1 + (\rho_1 + \rho_2)/2$. The values of ρ_1 and ρ_2 cannot be calculated from a value of θ. The original model is therefore not normalized for scale and level, and the parameters ρ_1 and ρ_2 are not identified. This fact is somewhat surprising, since only two parameters enter the original covariance matrix Ω. It would seem, unless the researcher explicitly tested in the manner we have just done, that restricting the covariance matrix to consist of only two elements would be sufficient to normalize the model. In this case, however, it is not.

In the normalized model, only the average of the ρ's appears: $(\rho_1 + \rho_2)/2$. It is possible to calculate the average ρ from θ, simply as $\theta - 1$. This means that the average ρ is identified, but not the individual values. When $\rho_1 = \rho_2$, as in the previous example, the model is normalized because each ρ is equal to the average ρ. However, as we now see, any model with the same average ρ's is equivalent, after normalizing for scale and level. Hence, assuming that $\rho_1 = \rho_2$ is no different than assuming that $\rho_1 = 3\rho_2$, or any other relation. All that matters for behavior is the average of these parameters, not their values relative to each other. This fact is fairly surprising and would be hard to realize without using our procedure for normalization.

Now that we know how to assure that a probit model is normalized for level and scale, and hence contains only economically meaningful information, we can examine how the probit model is used to represent various types of choice situations. We look at three situations in which logit models are limited and show how the limitation is overcome with probit. These situations are taste variation, substitution patterns, and repeated choices over time.

5.3   Taste Variation

Probit is particularly well suited for incorporating random coefficients, provided that the coefficients are normally distributed. Hausman and Wise (1978) were the first, to my knowledge, to give this derivation. Haaijer et al. (1998) provide a compelling application. Assume that representative utility is linear in parameters and that the coefficients vary randomly over decision makers instead of being fixed as we have assumed so far in this book. The utility is $U_{nj} = \beta'_n x_{nj} + \varepsilon_{nj}$, where β_n is the vector of coefficients for decision maker n representing that person's tastes. Suppose the β_n is normally distributed in the population with mean b and covariance W: $\beta_n \sim N(b, W)$. The goal of the research is to estimate the parameters b and W.

The utility can be rewritten with β_n decomposed into its mean and deviations from its mean: $U_{nj} = b' x_{nj} + \tilde{\beta}'_n x_{nj} + \varepsilon_{nj}$, where $\tilde{\beta}_n = \beta_n - b$. The last two terms in the utility are random; denote their sum as η_{nj} to obtain $U_{nj} = b' x_{nj} + \eta_{nj}$. The covariance of the η_{nj}'s depends on W as well as the x_{nj}'s, so that the covariance differs over decision makers.

The covariance of the η_{nj}'s can be described easily for a two-alternative model with one explanatory variable. In this case, the utility is

$$U_{n1} = \beta_n x_{n1} + \varepsilon_{n1},$$
$$U_{n2} = \beta_n x_{n2} + \varepsilon_{n2}.$$

Assume that β_n is normally distributed with mean b and variance σ_β. Assume that ε_{n1} and ε_{n2} are independently identically distributed with variance σ_ε. The assumption of independence is for this example and is not needed in general. The utility is then rewritten as

$$U_{n1} = b x_{n1} + \eta_{n1},$$
$$U_{n2} = b x_{n2} + \eta_{n2},$$

where η_{n1} and η_{n2} are jointly normally distributed. Each has zero mean: $E(\eta_{nj}) = E(\tilde{\beta}_n x_{nj} + \varepsilon_{nj}) = 0$. The covariance is determined as follows. The variance of each is $V(\eta_{nj}) = V(\tilde{\beta}_n x_{nj} + \varepsilon_{nj}) = x_{nj}^2 \sigma_\beta + \sigma_\varepsilon$. Their covariance is

$$\text{Cov}(\eta_{n1}, \eta_{n2}) = E[(\tilde{\beta}_n x_{n1} + \varepsilon_{n1})(\tilde{\beta}_n x_{n2} + \varepsilon_{n2})]$$
$$= E(\tilde{\beta}_n^2 x_{n1} x_{n2} + \varepsilon_{n1}\varepsilon_{n2} + \varepsilon_{n1}\tilde{\beta}_b x_{n2} + \varepsilon_{n2}\tilde{\beta}_n x_{n1})$$
$$= x_{n1} x_{n2} \sigma_\beta.$$

The covariance matrix is

$$\Omega = \begin{pmatrix} x_{n1}^2 \sigma_\beta + \sigma_\varepsilon & x_{n1} x_{n2} \sigma_\beta \\ x_{n1} x_{n2} \sigma_\beta & x_{n2}^2 \sigma_\beta + \sigma_\varepsilon \end{pmatrix}$$
$$= \sigma_\beta \begin{pmatrix} x_{n1}^2 & x_{n1} x_{n2} \\ x_{n1} x_{n2} & x_{n2}^2 \end{pmatrix} + \sigma_\varepsilon \begin{pmatrix} 1 & 0 \\ 0 & 1 \end{pmatrix}.$$

One last step is required for estimation. Recall that behavior is not affected by a multiplicative transformation of utility. We therefore need to set the scale of utility. A convenient normalization for this case is

$\sigma_\varepsilon = 1$. Under this normalization,

$$\Omega = \sigma_\beta \begin{pmatrix} x_{n1}^2 & x_{n1}x_{n2} \\ x_{n1}x_{n2} & x_{n2}^2 \end{pmatrix} + \begin{pmatrix} 1 & 0 \\ 0 & 1 \end{pmatrix}.$$

The values of x_{n1} and x_{n2} are observed by the researcher, and the parameters b and σ_β are estimated. Thus, the researcher learns both the mean and the variance of the random coefficient in the population. Generalization to more than one explanatory variable and more than two alternatives is straightforward.

5.4   Substitution Patterns and Failure of IIA

Probit can represent any substitution pattern. The probit probabilities do not exhibit the IIA property that gives rise to the proportional substitution of logit. Different covariance matrices Ω provide different substitution patterns, and by estimating the covariance matrix, the researcher determines the substitution pattern that is most appropriate for the data.

A full covariance matrix can be estimated, or the researcher can impose structure on the covariance matrix to represent particular sources of nonindependence. This structure usually reduces the number of the parameters and facilitates their interpretation. We consider first the situation where the researcher estimates a full covariance matrix, and then turn to a situation where the researcher imposes structure on the covariance matrix.

Full Covariance: Unrestricted Substitution Patterns

For notational simplicity, consider a probit model with four alternatives. A full covariance matrix for the unobserved components of utility takes the form of Ω in (5.5). When normalized for scale and level, the covariance matrix becomes $\tilde{\Omega}_1^*$ in (5.6). The elements of $\tilde{\Omega}_1^*$ are estimated. The estimated values can represent any substitution pattern; importantly, the normalization for scale and level does not restrict the substitution patterns. The normalization only eliminates aspects of Ω that are irrelevant to behavior.

Note, however, that the estimated values of the θ^*'s provide essentially no interpretable information in themselves (Horowitz, 1991). For example, suppose θ_{33}^* is estimated to be larger than θ_{44}^*. It might be tempting to interpret this result as indicating that the variance in unobserved utility of the third alternative is greater than that for the fourth alternative; that is, that $\sigma_{33} > \sigma_{44}$. However, this interpretation is incorrect. It is quite possible that $\theta_{33}^* > \theta_{44}^*$ and yet $\sigma_{44} > \sigma_{33}$, if the covariance σ_{14} is sufficiently greater than σ_{13}. Similarly, suppose that θ_{23} is estimated to be negative. This does not mean that unobserved utility for the second alternative is negatively correlated with unobserved utility for the third alternative (that is, $\sigma_{23} < 0$). It is possible that σ_{23} is positive and yet σ_{12} and σ_{13} are sufficiently large to make θ^*_{23} negative. The point here is that estimating a full covariance matrix allows the model to represent any substitution pattern, but renders the estimated parameters essentially uninterpretable.

Structured Covariance: Restricted Substitution Patterns

By imposing structure on the covariance matrix, the estimated parameters usually become more interpretable. The structure is a restriction on the covariance matrix and, as such, reduces the ability of the model to represent various substitution patterns. However, if the structure is correct (that is, actually represents the behavior of the decision makers), then the true substitution pattern will be able to be represented by the restricted covariance matrix.

Structure is necessarily situation-dependent: an appropriate structure for a covariance matrix depends on the specifics of the situation being modeled. Several studies using different kinds of structure were described in Section 5.2. As an example of how structure can be imposed on the covariance matrix and hence substitution patterns, consider a homebuyer's choice among purchase-money mortgages. Suppose four mortgages are available to the homebuyer from four different institutions: one with a fixed rate, and three with variable rates. Suppose the unobserved portion of utility consists of two parts: the homebuyer's concern about the risk of rising interest rates, labeled r_n, which is common to all the variable-rate loans; and all other unobserved factors, labeled collectively η_{nj}. The unobserved component of utility is then

$$\varepsilon_{nj} = -r_n d_j + \eta_{nj},$$

where $d_j = 1$ for the variable-rate loans and 0 for the fixed-rate loan, and the negative sign indicates that utility decreases as concern about risk rises. Assume that r_n is normally distributed over homebuyers with variance σ, and that $\eta_{nj} \, \forall j$ is iid normal with zero mean and variance ω. Then the covariance matrix for $\varepsilon_n = \langle \varepsilon_{n1}, \ldots, \varepsilon_{n4} \rangle$ is

$$\Omega = \begin{pmatrix} 0 & 0 & 0 & 0 \\ \cdot & \sigma & \sigma & \sigma \\ \cdot & \cdot & \sigma & \sigma \\ \cdot & \cdot & \cdot & \sigma \end{pmatrix} + \omega \begin{pmatrix} 1 & 0 & 0 & 0 \\ \cdot & 1 & 0 & 0 \\ \cdot & \cdot & 1 & 0 \\ \cdot & \cdot & \cdot & 1 \end{pmatrix}.$$

The model needs to normalized for scale but, as we will see, is already normalized for level. The covariance of error differences is

$$\tilde{\Omega}_1 = \begin{pmatrix} \sigma & \sigma & \sigma \\ \cdot & \sigma & \sigma \\ \cdot & \cdot & \sigma \end{pmatrix} + \omega \begin{pmatrix} 2 & 1 & 1 \\ \cdot & 2 & 1 \\ \cdot & \cdot & 2 \end{pmatrix}.$$

This matrix has no fewer parameters than Ω. That is to say, the model was already normalized for level. To normalize for scale, set $\sigma + 2\omega = 1$. Then the covariance matrix becomes

$$\tilde{\Omega}_1^* = \begin{pmatrix} 1 & \theta & \theta \\ \cdot & 1 & \theta \\ \cdot & \cdot & 1 \end{pmatrix},$$

where $\theta = (\sigma + \omega)/(\sigma + 2\omega)$. The values of σ and ω cannot be calculated from θ. However, the parameter θ provides information about the variance in utility due to concern about risk relative to that due to all other unobserved factors. For example, suppose θ is estimated to be 0.75. This estimate can be intrepreted as indicating that the variance in utility attributable to concern about risk is twice as large as the variance in utility attributable to all other factors:

$$\theta = 0.75,$$
$$\frac{\sigma + \omega}{\sigma + 2\omega} = 0.75,$$
$$\sigma + \omega = 0.75\sigma + 1.5\omega,$$
$$0.25\sigma = 0.5\omega,$$
$$\sigma = 2\omega.$$

Stated equivalently, $\hat{\theta} = 0.75$ means that concern about risk accounts for two-thirds of the variance in the unobserved component of utility.

Since the original model was already normalized for level, the model could be estimated without reexpressing the covariance matrix in terms of error differences. The normalization for scale could be accomplished simply by setting $\omega = 1$ in the original Ω. Under this procedure, the parameter σ is estimated directly. Its value relative to 1 indicates the variance due to concern about risk relative to the variance due to perceptions about ease of dealing with each institution. An estimate $\hat{\theta} = 0.75$ corresponds to an estimate $\hat{\sigma} = 2$.

5.5   Panel Data

Probit with repeated choices is similar to probit on one choice per decision maker. The only difference is that the dimension of the covariance matrix of the errors is expanded. Consider a decision maker who faces a choice among J alternatives in each of T time periods or choices situations. The alternatives can change over time, and J and T can differ for different decision makers; however, we suppress the notation for these possibilities. The utility that decision maker n obtains from alternative j in period t is $U_{njt} = V_{njt} + \varepsilon_{njt}$. In general, one would expect ε_{njt} to be correlated over time as well as over alternatives, since factors that are not observed by the researcher can persist over time. Denote the vector of errors for all alternatives in all time periods as $\varepsilon_n = \langle \varepsilon_{n11}, \ldots, \varepsilon_{nJ1}, \varepsilon_{n12}, \ldots, \varepsilon_{nJ2}, \ldots, \varepsilon_{n1T}, \ldots, \varepsilon_{nJT} \rangle$. The covariance matrix of this vector is denoted Ω, which has dimension $JT \times JT$.

Consider a sequence of alternatives, one for each time period, $\mathbf{i} = \{i_1, \ldots, i_T\}$. The probability that the decision maker makes this sequence of choices is

$$P_{ni} = \text{Prob}(U_{ni_t t} > U_{njt} \; \forall j \neq i_t, \forall t)$$
$$= \text{Prob}(V_{ni_t t} + \varepsilon_{ni_t t} > V_{njt} + \varepsilon_{njt} \; \forall j \neq i_t, \forall t)$$
$$= \int_{\varepsilon_n \in B_n} \phi(\varepsilon_n) \, d\varepsilon_n.$$

where $B_n = \{\varepsilon_n \text{ s.t. } V_{ni_t t} + \varepsilon_{ni_t t} > V_{njt} + \varepsilon_{njt} \; \forall j \neq i_t, \forall t\}$ and $\phi(\varepsilon_n)$ is the joint normal density with zero mean and covariance Ω. Compared to the probit probability for one choice situation, the integral is simply expanded to be over JT dimensions rather than J.

It is often more convenient to work in utility differences. The probability of sequence $\mathbf{i}$ is the probability that the utility differences are negative for each alternative in each time period, when the differences in each time period are taken against the alternative identified by $\mathbf{i}$ for that time period:

$$P_{ni} = \text{Prob}(\tilde{U}_{nji_t t} < 0 \; \forall j \neq i_t, \forall t)$$
$$= \int_{\tilde{\varepsilon}_n \in \tilde{B}_n} \phi(\tilde{\varepsilon}_n) \, d\tilde{\varepsilon}_n,$$

where $\tilde{U}_{nji_t t} = U_{njt} - U_{ni_t t}$; $\tilde{\varepsilon}_n' = \langle(\varepsilon_{n11} - \varepsilon_{ni_1 1}), \ldots, (\varepsilon_{nJ1} - \varepsilon_{ni_1 1}), \ldots,$ $(\varepsilon_{n1T} - \varepsilon_{ni_T T}), \ldots, (\varepsilon_{nJT} - \varepsilon_{ni_T T})\rangle$ with each . . . being over all alternatives except i_t, and the matrix $\tilde{B}_n$ is the set of $\tilde{\varepsilon}_n$'s for which $\tilde{U}_{nji_t t} < 0 \; \forall j \neq i_t, \forall t$. This is a $(J-1)T$-dimensional integral. The density $\phi(\tilde{\varepsilon}_n)$ is joint normal with covariance matrix derived from Ω. The simulation of the choice probability is the same as for situations with one choice per decision maker, which we describe in Section 5.6, but with a larger dimension for the covariance matrix and integral. Borsch-Supan et al. (1991) provide an example of a multinomial probit on panel data that allows covariance over time and over alternatives.

For binary choices, such as whether a person buys a particular product in each time period or works at a paid job each month, the probit model simplifies considerably (Gourieroux and Monfort, 1993). The net utility of taking the action (e.g., working) in period t is $U_{nt} = V_{nt} + \varepsilon_{nt}$, and the person takes the action if $U_{nt} > 0$. This utility is called *net* utility because it is the difference between the utility of taking the action and that of not taking the action. As such, it is already expressed in difference terms. The errors are correlated over time, and the covariance matrix for $\varepsilon_{n1}, \ldots, \varepsilon_{nT}$ is Ω, which is $T \times T$.

A sequence of binary choices is most easily represented by a set of T dummy variables: $d_{nt} = 1$ if person n took the action in period t, and $d_{nt} = -1$ otherwise. The probability of the sequence of choices $d_n = d_{n1}, \ldots, d_{nT}$ is

$$
\begin{aligned}
P_{nd_n} &= \text{Prob}(U_{nt}d_{nt} > 0 \; \forall t) \\
&= \text{Prob}(V_{nt}d_{nt} + \varepsilon_{nt}d_{nt} > 0 \; \forall t) \\
&= \int_{\varepsilon_n \in B_n} \phi(\varepsilon_n)\, d\varepsilon_n,
\end{aligned}
$$

where B_n is the set of ε_n's for which $V_{nt}d_{nt} + \varepsilon_{nt}d_{nt} > 0 \; \forall t$, and $\phi(\varepsilon_n)$ is the joint normal density with covariance Ω.

Structure can be placed on the covariance of the errors over time. Suppose in the binary case, for example, that the error consists of a portion that is specific to the decision maker, reflecting his proclivity to take the action, and a part that varies over time for each decision maker: $\varepsilon_{nt} = \eta_n + \mu_{nt}$, where μ_{nt} is iid over time and people with a standard normal density, and η_n is iid over people with a normal density with zero mean and variance σ. The variance of the error in each period is $V(\varepsilon_{nt}) = V(\eta_n + \mu_{nt}) = \sigma + 1$. The covariance between the errors in two different periods t and s is $\text{Cov}(\varepsilon_{nt}, \varepsilon_{ns}) = E(\eta_n + \mu_{nt})(\eta_n + \mu_{ns}) = \sigma$. The covariance matrix therefore takes the form

$$
\Omega = \begin{pmatrix}
\sigma + 1 & \sigma & \cdots & \cdots & \sigma \\
\sigma & \sigma + 1 & \sigma & \cdots & \sigma \\
\cdots & \cdots & \cdots & \cdots & \cdots \\
\sigma & \cdots & \cdots & \sigma & \sigma + 1
\end{pmatrix}.
$$

Only one parameter, σ, enters the covariance matrix. Its value indicates the variance in unobserved utility across individuals (the variance of η_n) relative to the variance across time for each individual (the variance of μ_{nt}). It is often called the *cross-subject variance relative to the within-subject variance*.

The choice probabilities under this structure on the errors can be easily simulated using the concepts of convenient error partitioning from Section 1.2. Conditional on η_n, the probability of *not* taking the action in period t is $\text{Prob}(V_{nt} + \eta_n + \mu_{nt} < 0) = \text{Prob}(\mu_{nt} < -(V_{nt} + \eta_n)) = \Phi(-(V_{nt} + \eta_n))$, where $\Phi(\cdot)$ is the cumulative standard normal function. Most software packages include routines to calculate this function. The probability of taking the action, conditional on η_n, is then $1 - \Phi(-(V_{nt} + \eta_n)) = \Phi(V_{nt} + \eta_n)$. The probability of the sequence of choices d_n, conditional on η_n, is therefore $\prod_t \Phi((V_{nt} + \eta_n)d_{nt})$, which we can label $H_{nd_n}(\eta_n)$.

So far we have conditioned on η_n, when in fact η_n is random. The *unconditional* probability is the integral of the conditional probability $H_{nd_n}(\eta_n)$ over all possible values of η_n:

$$P_{nd_n} = \int H_{nd_n}(\eta_n)\phi(\eta_n)\,d\eta_n$$

where $\phi(\eta_n)$ is the normal density with zero mean and variance σ. This probability can be simulated very simply as follows:

1. Take a draw from a standard normal density using a random number generator. Multiply the draw by $\sqrt{\sigma}$, so that it becomes a draw of η_n from a normal density with variance σ.
2. For this draw of η_n, calculate $H_{nd_n}(\eta_n)$.
3. Repeat steps 1–2 many times, and average the results. This average is a simulated approximation to P_{nd_n}.

This simulator is much easier to calculate than the general probit simulators described in the next section. The ability to use it arises from the structure that we imposed on the model, namely, that the time dependence of the unobserved factors is captured entirely by a random component η_n that remains constant over time for each person. Gourieroux and Monfort (1993) provide an example of the use of this simulator with a probit model of this form.

The representative utility in one time period can include exogenous variables for other time periods, the same as we discussed with respect to logit models on panel data (Section 3.3.3). That is, V_{nt} can include exogenous variables that relate to periods other than t. For example, a lagged response to price changes can be represented by including prices from previous periods in the current period's V. Anticipatory behavior (by which, for example, a person buys a product now because he correctly anticipates that the price will rise in the future) can be represented by including prices in future periods in the current period's V.

Entering a lagged dependent variable is possible, but introduces two difficulties that the researcher must address. First, since the errors are correlated over time, the choice in one period is correlated with the errors in subsequent periods. As a result, inclusion of a lagged dependent variable without adjusting the estimation procedure appropriately results in inconsistent estimates. This issue is analogous to regression analysis, where the ordinary least squares estimator is inconsistent when a lagged dependent variable is included and the errors are serially correlated. To estimate a probit consistently in this situation, the researcher must determine the distribution of each ε_{nt} conditional on the value of the lagged dependent variables. The choice probability is then based on this conditional distribution instead of the unconditional distribution $\phi(\cdot)$ that we used earlier. Second, often the researcher does not observe the decision makers' choices from the very first choice that was available to them. For example, a researcher studying employment patterns will perhaps observe a person's employment status over a period of time (e.g., 1998–2001), but usually will not observe the person's employment status starting with the very first time the person could have taken a job (which might precede 1998 by many years). In this case, the probability for the first period that the researcher observes depends on the choices of the person in the earlier periods that the researcher does not observe. The researcher must determine a way to represent the first choice probability that allows for consistent estimation in the face of missing data on earlier choices. This is called the *initial conditions problem* of dynamic choice models. Both of these issues, as well as potential approaches to dealing with them, are addressed by Heckman (1981b, 1981a) and Heckman and Singer (1986). Due to their complexity, I do not describe the procedures here and refer interested and brave readers to these articles.

Papatla and Krishnamurthi (1992) avoid these issues in their probit model with lagged dependent variables by assuming that the unobserved factors are independent over time. As we discussed in relation to logit on panel data (Section 3.3.3), lagged dependent variables are not correlated with the current errors when the errors are independent over time, and they can therefore be entered without inducing inconsistency. Of course, this procedure is only appropriate if the assumption of errors being independent over time is true in reality, rather than just by assumption.

5.6   Simulation of the Choice Probabilities

The probit probabilities do not have a closed-form expression and must be approximated numerically. Several nonsimulation procedures have been used and can be effective in certain circumstances.

Quadrature methods approximate the integral by a weighted function of specially chosen evaluation points. A good explanation for these procedures is provided by Geweke (1996). Examples of their use for probit include Butler and Moffitt (1982) and Guilkey and Murphy (1993). Quadrature operates effectively when the dimension of the integral is small, but not with higher dimensions. It can be used for probit if the number of alternatives (or, with panel data, the number of alternatives times the number of time periods) is no more than four or five. It can also be used if the researcher has specified an error-component structure with no more than four or five terms. However, it is not effective for general probit models. And even with low-dimensional integration, simulation is often easier.

Another nonsimulation procedure that has been suggested is the Clark algorithm, introduced by Daganzo et al. (1977). This algorithm utilizes the fact, shown by Clark (1961), that the maximum of several normally distributed variables is itself approximately normally distributed. Unfortunately, the approximation can be highly inaccurate in some situations (as shown by Horowitz et al., 1982), and the degree of accuracy is difficult to assess in any given setting.

Simulation has proven to be very general and useful for approximating probit probabilities. Numerous simulators have been proposed for probit models; a summary is given by Hajivassiliou et al. (1996). In the preceding section, I described a simulator that is appropriate for a probit model that has a particularly convenient structure, namely a binary probit on panel data where the time dependence is captured by one random factor. In the current section, I describe three simulators that are applicable for probits of any form: accept–reject, smoothed accept–reject, and GHK. The GHK simulator is by far the most widely used probit simulator, for reasons that we discuss. The other two methods are valuable pedagogically. They also have relevance beyond probit and can be applied in practically any situation. They can be very useful when the researcher is developing her own models rather than using probit or any other model in this book.

5.6.1. Accept–Reject Simulator

The accept–reject (AR) is the most straightforward simulator. Consider simulating P_{ni}. Draws of the random terms are taken from their distributions. For each draw, the researcher determines whether those values of the errors, when combined with the observed variables as faced by person n, would result in alternative i being chosen. If so, the draw is called an *accept*. If the draw would result in some other alternative being chosen, the draw is a *reject*. The simulated probability is the proportion of draws that are accepts. This procedure can be applied to any choice model with any distribution for the random terms. It was originally proposed for probits (Manski and Lerman, 1981), and we give the details of the approach in terms of the probit model. Its use for other models is obvious.

We use expression (5.1) for the probit probabilities:

$$P_{ni} = \int I(V_{ni} + \varepsilon_{ni} > V_{nj} + \varepsilon_{nj} \ \forall j \neq i) \phi(\varepsilon_n) \, d\varepsilon_n,$$

where $I(\cdot)$ is an indicator of whether the statement in parentheses holds, and $\phi(\varepsilon_n)$ is the joint normal density with zero mean and covariance Ω. The AR simulator of this integral is calculated as follows:

1. Draw a value of the J-dimensional vector of errors, ε_n, from a normal density with zero mean and covariance Ω. Label the draw ε_n^r with $r = 1$, and the elements of the draw as $\varepsilon_{n1}^r, \ldots, \varepsilon_{nJ}^r$.
2. Using these values of the errors, calculate the utility that each alternative obtains with these errors. That is, calculate $U_{nj}^r = V_{nj} + \varepsilon_{nj}^r \ \forall j$.
3. Determine whether the utility of alternative i is greater than that for all other alternatives. That is, calculate $I^r = 1$ if $U_{ni}^r > U_{nj}^r$, indicating an accept, and $I^r = 0$ otherwise, indicating a reject.
4. Repeat steps 1–3 many times. Label the number of repetitions (including the first) as R, so that r takes values of 1 through R.
5. The simulated probability is the proportion of draws that are accepts: $\check{P}_{ni} = \frac{1}{R} \sum_{r=1}^{R} I^r$.

The integral $\int I(\cdot) \phi(\varepsilon_n) \, d\varepsilon$ is approximated by the average $\frac{1}{R} \sum I^r(\cdot)$ for draws from $\phi(\cdot)$. Obviously, $\check{P}_{ni}$ is unbiased for P_{ni}: $E(\check{P}_{ni}) = \frac{1}{R} \sum E[I^r(\cdot)] = \frac{1}{R} \sum P_{ni} = P_{ni}$, where the expectation is over different sets of R draws. The variance of $\check{P}_{ni}$ over different sets of draws diminishes as the number of draws rises. The simulator is often called the "crude frequency simulator," since it is the frequency of times that draws of the errors result in the specified alternative being chosen. The word "crude" distinguishes it from the *smoothed* frequency simulator that we describe in the next section.

The first step of the AR simulator for a probit model is to take a draw from a joint normal density. The question arises: how are such draws obtained? The most straightforward procedure is that described in Section 9.2.5, which uses the Choleski factor. The covariance matrix for the errors is Ω. A Choleski factor of Ω is a lower-triangular matrix L such that $LL' = \Omega$. It is sometimes called the generalized square root of

Ω. Most statistical software packages contain routines to calculate the Choleski factor of any symmetric matrix. Now suppose that η is a vector of J iid standard normal deviates such that $\eta \sim N(0, I)$, where I is the identity matrix. This vector can be obtained by taking J draws from a random number generator for the standard normal and stacking them into a vector. We can construct a vector ε that is distributed $N(O, \Omega)$ by using the Choleski factor to tranform η. In particular, calculate $\varepsilon = L\eta$. Since the sum of normals is normal, ε is normally distributed. Since η has zero mean, so does ε. The covariance of ε is $\text{Cov}(\varepsilon) = E(\varepsilon\varepsilon') = E(L\eta(L\eta)') = E(L\eta\eta'L') = LE(\eta\eta')L' = LIL' = LL' = \Omega$.

Using the Choleski factor L of Ω, the first step of the AR simulator becomes two substeps:

1A. Draw J values from a standard normal density, using a random number generator. Stack these values into a vector, and label the vector η^r.

1B. Calculate $\varepsilon_n^r = L\eta^r$.

Then, using ε_n^r, calculate the utility of each alternative and see whether alternative i has the highest utility.

The procedure that we have described operates on utilities and expression (5.1), which is a J-dimensional integral. The procedure can be applied analogously to utility differences, which reduces the dimension of the integral to $J - 1$. As given in (5.3), the choice probabilities can be expressed in terms of utility differences:

$$P_{ni} = \int I(\tilde{V}_{nji} + \tilde{\varepsilon}_{nji} < 0 \; \forall j \neq i) \phi(\tilde{\varepsilon}_{ni}) \, d\tilde{\varepsilon}_{ni},$$

where $\phi(\tilde{\varepsilon}_{ni})$ is the joint normal density with zero mean and covariance $\tilde{\Omega}_i = M_i \Omega M_i'$. This integral can be simulated with AR methods through the following steps:

1. Draw $\tilde{\varepsilon}_{ni}^r = L_i \eta^r$ as follows:
   (a) Draw $J - 1$ values from a standard normal density using a random number generator. Stack these values into a vector, and label the vector η^r.
   (b) Calculate $\tilde{\varepsilon}_{ni}^r = L_i \eta^r$, where L_i is the Choleski factor of $\tilde{\Omega}_i$.
2. Using these values of the errors, calculate the utility difference for each alternative, differenced against the utility of alternative i. That is, calculate $\tilde{U}_{nji}^r = V_{nj} - V_{ni} + \tilde{\varepsilon}_{nji}^r \; \forall j \neq i$.
3. Determine whether each utility difference is negative. That is, calculate $I^r = 1$ if $U_{nji}^r < 0 \; \forall j \neq i$, indicating an accept, and $I^r = 0$ otherwise, indicating a reject.

4. Repeat steps 1–3 R times.
5. The simulated probability is the number of accepts divided by the number of repetitions: $\check{P}_{ni} = \frac{1}{R} \sum_{r=1}^{R} I^r$.

Using utility differences is slightly faster computationally than using the utilities themselves, since one dimension is eliminated. However, it is often easier conceptually to remain with utilities.

As just stated, the AR simulator is very general. It can be applied to any model for which draws can be obtained for the random terms and the behavior that the decision maker would exhibit with these draws can be determined. It is also very intuitive, which is an advantage from a programming perspective, since debugging becomes comparatively easy. However, the AR simulator has several disadvantages, particularly when used in the context of maximum likelihood estimation.

Recall that the log-likelihood function is LL $= \sum_n \sum_j d_{nj} \log P_{nj}$, where $d_{nj} = 1$ if n chose j and 0 otherwise. When the probabilities cannot be calculated exactly, as in the case of probit, the simulated log-likelihood function is used instead, with the true probabilities replaced with the simulated probabilities: SLL $= \sum_n \sum_j d_{nj} \log \check{P}_{nj}$. The value of the parameters that maximizes SLL is called the maximum simulated likelihood estimator (MSLE). It is by far the most widely used simulation-based estimation procedure. Its properties are described in Chapter 8. Unfortunately, using the AR simulator in SLL can be problematic.

There are two issues. First, $\check{P}_{ni}$ can be zero for any finite number of draws R. That is, it is possible that each of the R draws of the error terms result in a reject, so that the simulated probability is zero. Zero values for $\check{P}_{ni}$ are problematic because the log of $\check{P}_{ni}$ is taken when it enters the log-likelihood function and the log of zero is undefined. SLL cannot be calculated if the simulated probability is zero for any decision maker in the sample.

The occurrence of a zero simulated probability is particularly likely when the true probability is low. Often at least one decision maker in a sample will have made a choice that has a low probability. With numerous alternatives (such as thousands of makes and models for the choice of car), each alternative has a low probability. With repeated choices, the probability for any sequence of choices can be extremely small; for example, if the probability of choosing an alternative is 0.25 in each of 10 time periods, the probability of the sequence is $(0.25)^{10}$, which is less than 0.000001.

Furthermore, SLL needs to be calculated at each step in the search for its maximum. Some of the parameter values at which SLL is

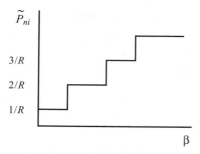

Figure 5.1. The AR simulator is a step function in parameters.

calculated can be far from the true values. Low probabilities can occur at these parameter values even when they do not occur at the maximizing values.

Nonzero simulated probabilities can always be obtained by taking enough draws. However, if the researcher continues taking draws until at least one accept is obtained for each decision maker, then the number of draws becomes a function of the probabilities. The simulation process is then not independent of the choice process that is being modeled, and the properties of the estimator become more complex.

There is a second difficulty with the AR simulator for MSLE. The simulated probabilities are not smooth in the parameters; that is, they are not twice differentiable. As explained in Chapter 8, the numerical procedures that are used to locate the maximum of the log-likelihood function rely on the first derivatives, and sometimes the second derivatives, of the choice probabilities. If these derivatives do not exist, or do not point toward the maximum, then the numerical procedure will not perform effectively.

The AR simulated probability is a step function, as depicted in Figure 5.1. $\check{P}_{ni}$ is the proportion of draws for which alternative i has the highest utility. An infinitesimally small change in a parameter will usually not change any draw from a reject to an accept or vice versa. If U_{ni}^r is below U_{nj}^r for some j at a given level of the parameters, then it will also be so for an infinitesimally small change in any parameter. So, usually, $\check{P}_{nj}$ is constant with respect to small changes in the parameters. Its derivatives with respect to the parameters are zero in this range. If the parameters change in such a way that a reject becomes an accept, then $\check{P}_{nj}$ rises by a discrete amount, from M/R to $(M + 1)/R$, where M is the number of accepts at the original parameter values. $\check{P}_{nj}$ is constant (zero slope) until an accept becomes a reject or vice versa, at which point $\check{P}_{nj}$ jumps by $1/R$. Its slope at this point is undefined. The first derivative of $\check{P}_{nj}$ with respect to the parameters is either zero or undefined.

This fact hinders the numerical procedures that are used to locate the maximum of SLL. As discussed in Chapter 8, the maximization procedures use the gradient at trial parameter values to determine the direction to move to find parameters with higher SLL. With the slope $\check{P}_{nj}$ for each n either zero or undefined, the gradient of SLL is either zero or undefined. This gradient provides no help in finding the maximum.

This problem is not actually as drastic as it seems. The gradient of SLL can be approximated as the change in SLL for a non-infinitesimally small change in the parameters. The parameters are changed by an amount that is large enough to switch accepts to rejects and vice versa for at least some of the observations. The approximate gradient, which can be called an arc gradient, is calculated as the amount that SLL changes divided by the change in the parameters. To be precise: for parameter vector β of length K, the derivate of SLL with respect to the kth parameter is calculated as $(SLL^1 - SLL^0)/(\beta_k^1 - \beta_k^0)$, where SLL^0 is calculated at the original β with kth element β_k^0 and SLL^1 is calculated at β_k^1 with all the other parameters remaining at their original values. The arc gradient calculated in this way is not zero or undefined, and provides information on the direction of rise. Nevertheless, experience indicates that the AR simulated probability is still difficult to use.

5.6.2. Smoothed AR Simulators

One way to mitigate the difficulties with the AR simulator is to replace the 0–1 AR indicator with a smooth, strictly positive function. The simulation starts the same as with AR, by taking draws of the random terms and calculating the utility of each alternative for each draw: U_{nj}^r. Then, instead of determining whether alternative i has the highest utility (that is, instead of calculating the indicator function I^r), the simulated utilities $U_{nj}^r \ \forall j$ are entered into a function. Any function can be used for simulating P_{ni} as long as it rises when U_{ni}^r rises, declines when U_{nj}^r rises, is strictly positive, and has defined first and second derivatives with respect to $U_{nj}^r \ \forall j$. A function that is particularly convenient is the logit function, as suggested by McFadden (1989). Use of this function gives the *logit-smoothed AR simulator*.

The simulator is implemented in the following steps, which are the same as with the AR simulator except for step 3.

1. Draw a value of the J-dimensional vector of errors, ε_n, from a normal density with zero mean and covariance Ω. Label the draw ε_n^r with $r = 1$, and the elements of the draw as $\varepsilon_{n1}^r, \ldots, \varepsilon_{nJ}^r$.

2. Using these values of the errors, calculate the utility that each alternative obtains with these errors. That is, calculate $U_{nj}^r = V_{nj} + \varepsilon_{nj}^r \ \forall j$.
3. Put these utilities into the logit formula. That is, calculate

$$
S_r = \frac{e^{U_{ni}^r/\lambda}}{\sum_j e^{U_{nj}^r/\lambda}},
$$

where $\lambda > 0$ is a scale factor specified by the researcher and discussed in following text.

4. Repeat steps 1–3 many times. Label the number of repetitions (including the first) as R, so that r takes values of 1 through R.
5. The simulated probability is the number of accepts divided by the number of repetitions: $\check{P}_{ni} = \frac{1}{R} \sum_{r=1}^R S^r$.

Since $S^r > 0$ for all finite values of U_{nj}^r, the simulated probability is strictly positive for any draws of the errors. It rises with U_{ni}^r and declines when U_{nj}^r, $j \neq i$, rises. It is smooth (twice differentiable), since the logit formula itself is smooth.

The logit-smoothed AR simulator can be applied to any choice model, simply by simulating the utilities under any distributional assumptions about the errors and then inserting the utilities into the logit formula. When applied to probit, Ben-Akiva and Bolduc (1996) have called it "logit-kernel probit."

The scale factor λ determines the degree of smoothing. As $\lambda \to 0$, S^r approaches the indicator function I^r. Figure 5.2 illustrates the situation for a two-alternative case. For a given draw of ε_n^r, the utility of the two alternatives is calculated. Consider the simulated probability for alternative 1. With AR, the 0–1 indicator function is zero if U_{n1}^r is below U_{n2}^r, and one if U_{n1}^r exceeds U_{n2}^r. With logit smoothing, the step function is replaced by a smooth sigmoid curve. The factor λ determines the proximity of the sigmoid to the 0–1 indicator. Lowering λ increases the scale of the utilities when they enter the logit function (since the utilities are divided by λ). Increasing the scale of utility increases the absolute difference between the two utilities. The logit formula gives probabilities that are closer to zero or one when the difference in utilities is larger. The logit-smoothed S^r therefore becomes closer to the step function as λ becomes closer to zero.

The researcher needs to set the value of λ. A lower value of λ makes the logit smoother a better approximation to the indicator function. However, this fact is a double-edged sword: if the logit smoother approximates the indicator function too well, the numerical difficulties of using

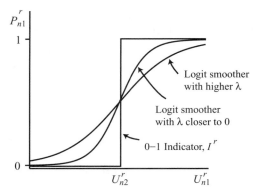

Figure 5.2. AR smoother.

the unsmoothed AR simulator will simply be reproduced in the logit-smoothed simulator. The researcher wants to set λ low enough to obtain a good approximation but not so low as to reintroduce numerical difficulties. There is little guidance on the appropriate level of λ. Perhaps the best approach is for the researcher to experiment with different λ's. The same draws of ε_n should be used with every λ, so as to assure that differences in results are due to the change in the λ rather than to differences in the draws.

McFadden (1989) describes other smoothing functions. For all of them, the researcher must specify the degree of smoothing. An advantage of the logit smoother is its simplicity. Also, we will see in Chapter 6 that the logit smoother applied to a probit or any other model constitutes a type of mixed logit specification. That is, instead of seeing the logit smoother as providing an approximation that has no behavioral relation to the model (simply serving a numerical purpose), we can see it as arising from a particular type of error structure in the behavioral model itself. Under this interpretation, the logit formula applied to simulated utilities is not an approximation but actually represents the true model.

5.6.3. GHK Simulator

The most widely used probit simulator is called GHK, after Geweke (1989, 1991), Hajivassiliou (as reported in Hajivassiliou and McFadden, 1998), and Keane (1990, 1994), who developed the procedure. In a comparison of numerous probit simulators, Hajivassiliou et al. (1996) found GHK to be the most accurate in the settings that they examined. Geweke et al. (1994) found the GHK simulator works better than smoothed AR. Experience has confirmed its usefulness and relative accuracy (e.g., Borsch-Supan and Hajivassiliou, 1993).

The GHK simulator operates on utility differences. The simulation of probability P_{ni} starts by subtracting the utility of alternative i from each other alternative's utility. Importantly, the utility of a different alternative is subtracted depending on which probability is being simulated: for P_{ni}, U_{ni} is subtracted from the other utilities, while for P_{nj}, U_{nj} is subtracted. This fact is critical to the implementation of the procedure.

I will explain the GHK procedure first in terms of a three-alternative case, since that situation can be depicted graphically in two dimensions for utility differences. I will then describe the procedure in general for any number of alternatives. Bolduc (1993, 1999) provides an excellent alternative description of the procedure, along with methods to simulate the analytic derivatives of the probit probabilities. Keane (1994) provides a description of the use of GHK for transition probabilities.

Three Alternatives

We start with a specification of the behavioral model in utilities: $U_{nj} = V_{nj} + \varepsilon_{nj}$, $j = 1, 2, 3$. The vector $\varepsilon'_n = \langle \varepsilon_{n1}, \varepsilon_{n2}, \varepsilon_{n3} \rangle \sim N(0, \Omega)$. We assume that the reseacher has normalized the model for scale and level, so that the parameters that enter Ω are identified. Also, Ω can be a parametric function of data, as with random taste variation, though we do not show this dependence in our notation.

Suppose we want to simulate the probability of the first alternative, P_{n1}. We reexpress the model in utility differences by subtracting the utility of alternative 1:

$$U_{nj} - U_{n1} = (V_{nj} - V_{n1}) + (\varepsilon_{nj} - \varepsilon_{n1}),$$
$$\tilde{U}_{nj1} = \tilde{V}_{nj1} + \tilde{\varepsilon}_{nj1},$$

for $j = 2, 3$. The vector $\tilde{\varepsilon}'_{n1} = \langle \tilde{\varepsilon}_{n21}, \tilde{\varepsilon}_{n31} \rangle$ is distributed $N(0, \tilde{\Omega}_1)$, where $\tilde{\Omega}_1$ is derived from Ω.

We take one more transformation to make the model more convenient for simulation. Namely, let L_1 be the Choleski factor of $\tilde{\Omega}_1$. Since $\tilde{\Omega}_1$ is 2×2 in our current illustration, L_1 is a lower-triangular matrix that takes the form

$$L_1 = \begin{pmatrix} c_{aa} & 0 \\ c_{ab} & c_{bb} \end{pmatrix}.$$

Using this Choleski factor, the original error differences, which are correlated, can be rewritten as linear functions of *uncorrelated* standard normal deviates:

$$\tilde{\varepsilon}_{n21} = c_{aa}\eta_1,$$
$$\tilde{\varepsilon}_{n31} = c_{ab}\eta_1 + c_{bb}\eta_2,$$

where η_1 and η_2 are iid $N(0, 1)$. The error differences $\tilde{\varepsilon}_{n21}$ and $\tilde{\varepsilon}_{n31}$ are correlated because both of them depend on η_1. With this way of expressing the error differences, the utility differences can be written

$$\tilde{U}_{n21} = \tilde{V}_{n21} + c_{aa}\eta_1,$$
$$\tilde{U}_{n31} = \tilde{V}_{n31} + c_{ab}\eta_1 + c_{bb}\eta_2.$$

The probability of alternative 1 is $P_{n1} = \text{Prob}(\tilde{U}_{n21} < 0 \text{ and } \tilde{U}_{n31} < 0) = \text{Prob}(\tilde{V}_{n21} + \tilde{\varepsilon}_{n21} < 0 \text{ and } \tilde{V}_{n31} + \tilde{\varepsilon}_{n31} < 0)$. This probability is hard to evaluate numerically in terms of the $\tilde{\varepsilon}$'s, because they are correlated. However, using the transformation based on the Choleski factor, the probability can be written in a way that involves independent random terms. The probability becomes a function of the one-dimensional standard cumulative normal distribution:

$$
\begin{aligned}
P_{n1} &= \text{Prob}(\tilde{V}_{n21} + c_{aa}\eta_1 < 0 \text{ and } \tilde{V}_{n31} + c_{ab}\eta_1 + c_{bb}\eta_2 < 0) \\
&= \text{Prob}(\tilde{V}_{n21} + c_{aa}\eta_1 < 0) \\
&\quad \times \text{Prob}(\tilde{V}_{n31} + c_{ab}\eta_1 + c_{bb}\eta_2 < 0 \mid \tilde{V}_{n21} + c_{aa}\eta_1 < 0) \\
&= \text{Prob}(\eta_1 < -\tilde{V}_{n21}/c_{aa}) \\
&\quad \times \text{Prob}(\eta_2 < -(\tilde{V}_{n31} + c_{ab}\eta_1)/c_{bb} \mid \eta_1 < -\tilde{V}_{n21}/c_{aa}) \\
&= \Phi\left(\frac{-\tilde{V}_{n21}}{c_{aa}}\right) \times \int_{\eta_1=-\infty}^{-\tilde{V}_{n21}/c_{aa}} \Phi\left(\frac{-(\tilde{V}_{n31} + c_{ab}\eta_1)}{c_{bb}}\right)\phi(\eta_1)\,d\eta_1,
\end{aligned}
$$

where $\Phi(\cdot)$ is the standard normal cumulative distribution evaluated at the point in the parentheses, and $\phi(\cdot)$ is the truncated normal density. The first factor, $\Phi(-\tilde{V}_{n21}/c_{aa})$, is easy to calculate: it is simply the cumulative standard normal evaluated at $-\tilde{V}_{n21}/c_{aa}$. Computer packages contain fast routines for calculating the cumulative standard normal. The second factor is an integral. As we know, computers cannot integrate, and we use simulation to approximate integrals. This is the heart of the GHK procedure: using simulation to approximate the integral in P_{n1}.

Let us examine this integral more closely. It is the integral over a truncated normal, namely, over η_1 up to $-\tilde{V}_{n21}/c_{aa}$. The simulation proceeds as follows. Draw a value of η_1 from a standard normal density truncated above at $-\tilde{V}_{n21}/c_{aa}$. For this draw, calculate the factor $\Phi(-(\tilde{V}_{n31} + c_{ab}\eta_1)/c_{bb})$. Repeat this process for many draws, and average the results. This average is a simulated approximation to $\int_{\eta_1=-\infty}^{-\tilde{V}_{n21}/c_{aa}} \Phi(-(\tilde{V}_{n31} + c_{ab}\eta_1)/c_{bb})\phi(\eta_1)\,d\eta_1$. The simulated probability is then obtained by multiplying this average by the value of $\Phi(-\tilde{V}_{n21}/c_{aa})$, which is calculated exactly. Simple enough!

The question arises: how do we take a draw from a truncated normal? We describe how to take draws from truncated univariate distributions in Section 9.2.4. The reader may want to jump ahead and quickly view

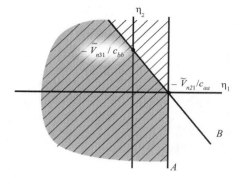

Figure 5.3. Probability of alternative 1.

that section. For truncated normals, the process is to take a draw from a standard uniform, labeled μ. Then calculate $\eta = \Phi^{-1}(\mu\Phi(-\tilde{V}_{n21}/c_{aa}))$. The resulting η is a draw from a normal density truncated from above at $-\tilde{V}_{n21}/c_{aa}$.

We can now put this all together to give the explicit steps that are used for the GHK simulator in our three-alternative case. The probability of alternative 1 is

$$P_{n1} = \Phi\left(\frac{-\tilde{V}_{n21}}{c_{aa}}\right) \times \int_{\eta_1=-\infty}^{-\tilde{V}_{n21}/c_{aa}} \Phi\left(\frac{-\left(\tilde{V}_{n31}+c_{ab}\eta_1\right)}{c_{bb}}\right)\phi(\eta_1)\,d\eta_1.$$

This probability is simulated as follows:

1. Calculate $k = \Phi(-\tilde{V}_{n21}/c_{aa})$.
2. Draw a value of η_1, labeled η_1^r, from a truncated standard normal truncated at $-\tilde{V}_{n21}/c_{aa}$. This is accomplished as follows:
   (a) Draw a standard uniform μ^r.
   (b) Calculate $\eta_1^r = \Phi^{-1}(\mu^r\Phi(-\tilde{V}_{n21}/c_{aa}))$.
3. Calculate $g^r = \Phi(-(\tilde{V}_{n31}+c_{ab}\eta_1^r)/c_{bb})$.
4. The simulated probability for this draw is $\check{P}_{n1}^r = k \times g^r$.
5. Repeat steps 1–4 R times, and average the results. This average is the simulated probability: $\check{P}_{n1} = (1/R)\sum \check{P}_{n1}^r$.

A graphical depiction is perhaps useful. Figure 5.3 shows the probability for alternative 1 in the space of independent errors η_1 and η_2. The x-axis is the value of η_1, and the y-axis is the value of η_2. The line labeled A is where η_1 is equal to $-\tilde{V}_{n21}/c_{aa}$. The condition that η_1 is below $-\tilde{V}_{n21}/c_{aa}$ is met in the striped area to the left of line A. The line labeled B is where $\eta_2 = -(\tilde{V}_{n31}+c_{ba}\eta_1)/c_{bb}$. Note that the y-intercept is where $\eta_1 = 0$, so that $\eta_2 = -\tilde{V}_{n31}/c_{bb}$ at this point. The slope of the line is $-c_{ba}/c_{bb}$. The condition that $\eta_2 < -(\tilde{V}_{n31}+c_{ba}\eta_1)/c_{bb}$ is satisfied below line B. The shaded area is where η_1 is to the left of line A and

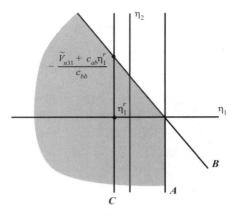

Figure 5.4. Probability that η_2 is in the correct range, given η_1^r.

η_2 is below line B. The mass of density in the shaded area is therefore the probability that alternative 1 is chosen.

The probability (i.e., the shaded mass) is the mass of the striped area times the proportion of this striped mass that is below line B. The striped area has mass $\Phi(-\tilde{V}_{n21}/c_{aa})$. This is easy to calculate. For any given value of η_1, the portion of the striped mass that is below line B is also easy to calculate. For example, in Figure 5.4, when η_1 takes the value η_1^r, then the probability that η_2 is below line B is the share of line C's mass that is below line B. This share is simply $\Phi(-(\tilde{V}_{n31} + c_{ab}\eta_1^r)/c_{bb})$. The portion of the striped mass that is below line B is therefore the average of $\Phi(-(\tilde{V}_{n31} + c_{ab}\eta_1^r)/c_{bb})$ over all values of η_1 that are to the left of line A. This average is simulated by taking draws of η_1 to the left of line A, calculating $\Phi(-(\tilde{V}_{n31} + c_{ab}\eta_1^r)/c_{bb})$ for each draw, and averaging the results. The probability is then this average times the mass of the striped area, $\Phi(-\tilde{V}_{n21}/c_{aa})$.

General Model

We can now describe the GHK simulator in general terms quickly, since the basic logic has already been discussed. This succinct expression serves to reinforce the concept that the GHK simulator is actually easier than it might at first appear.

Utility is expressed as

$$U_{nj} = V_{nj} + \varepsilon_{nj}, \qquad j = 1, \ldots, J,$$

$$\varepsilon_n' = \langle \varepsilon_{n1}, \ldots, \varepsilon_{nJ} \rangle, \qquad \varepsilon_n : J \times 1,$$

$$\varepsilon_n \sim N(0, \Omega).$$

Transform to utility differences against alternative i:

$$\tilde{U}_{nji} = \tilde{V}_{nji} + \tilde{\varepsilon}_{nji}, \qquad j \neq i,$$

$$\tilde{\varepsilon}'_{ni} = \langle \tilde{\varepsilon}_{n1}, \ldots, \tilde{\varepsilon}_{nJ} \rangle, \qquad \text{where} \ldots \text{is over all except } i,$$

$$\tilde{\varepsilon}_{ni} : (J-1) \times 1,$$

$$\tilde{\varepsilon}_{ni} \sim N(0, \tilde{\Omega}_i),$$

where $\tilde{\Omega}_i$ is derived from Ω.

Reexpress the errors as a Choleski transformation of iid standard normal deviates.

$$L_i \qquad \text{s.t.} \quad L_i L'_i = \tilde{\Omega}_i,$$

$$L_i = \begin{pmatrix} c_{11} & 0 & \cdots & \cdots & \cdots & 0 \\ c_{21} & c_{22} & 0 & \cdots & \cdots & 0 \\ c_{31} & c_{32} & c_{33} & 0 & \cdots & 0 \\ \vdots & \vdots & \vdots & \vdots & \vdots & \vdots \end{pmatrix}.$$

Then, stacking utilities $\tilde{U}'_{ni} = (\tilde{U}_{n1i}, \ldots, \tilde{U}_{nJ})$, we get the vector form of the model,

$$\tilde{U}_{ni} = \tilde{V}_{ni} + L_i \eta_n,$$

where $\eta'_n = \langle \eta_{1n}, \ldots, \eta_{J-1,n} \rangle$ is a vector of iid standard normal deviates: $\eta_{nj} \sim N(0, 1) \; \forall j$. Written explicitly, the model is

$$\tilde{U}_{n1i} = \tilde{V}_{n1i} + c_{11}\eta_1,$$

$$\tilde{U}_{n2i} = \tilde{V}_{n2i} + c_{21}\eta_1 + c_{22}\eta_2,$$

$$\tilde{U}_{n3i} = \tilde{V}_{n3i} + c_{31}\eta_1 + c_{32}\eta_2 + c_{33}\eta_3,$$

and so on. The choice probabilities are

$$P_{ni} = \text{Prob}(\tilde{U}_{nji} < 0 \; \forall j \neq i)$$

$$= \text{Prob}\left(\eta_1 < \frac{-\tilde{V}_{n1i}}{c_{11}} \right)$$

$$\times \text{Prob}\left(\eta_2 < \frac{-(\tilde{V}_{n2i} + c_{21}\eta_1)}{c_{22}} \,\bigg|\, \eta_1 < \frac{-\tilde{V}_{n1i}}{c_{11}} \right)$$

$$\times \text{Prob}\left(\eta_3 < \frac{-(\tilde{V}_{n3i} + c_{31}\eta_1 + c_{32}\eta_2)}{c_{33}} \,\bigg|\right.$$

$$\left. \eta_1 < \frac{-\tilde{V}_{n1i}}{c_{11}} \text{ and } \eta_2 < \frac{-(\tilde{V}_{n2i} + c_{21}\eta_1)}{c_{22}} \right).$$

$$\times \cdots.$$

The GHK simulator is calculated as follows:

1. Calculate

$$
\text{Prob}\left(\eta_1 < \frac{-\tilde{V}_{n1i}}{c_{11}}\right) = \Phi\left(\frac{-\tilde{V}_{n1i}}{c_{11}}\right).
$$

2. Draw a value of η_1, labeled η_1^r, from a truncated standard normal truncated at $-\tilde{V}_{1in}/c_{11}$. This draw is obtained as follows:
   (a) Draw a standard uniform μ_1^r.
   (b) Calculate $\eta_1^r = \Phi^{-1}(\mu_1^r \Phi(-\tilde{V}_{n1i}/c_{11}))$.

3. Calculate

$$
\text{Prob}\left(\eta_2 < \frac{-(\tilde{V}_{n2i} + c_{21}\eta_1)}{c_{22}}\,\Big|\,\eta_1 = \eta_1^r\right)
$$
$$
= \Phi\left(\frac{-\left(\tilde{V}_{n2i} + c_{21}\eta_1^r\right)}{c_{22}}\right).
$$

4. Draw a value of η_2, labeled η_2^r, from a truncated standard normal truncated at $-(\tilde{V}_{n2i} + c_{21}\eta_1^r)/c_{22}$. This draw is obtained as follows:
   (a) Draw a standard uniform μ_2^r.
   (b) Calculate $\eta_2^r = \Phi^{-1}(\mu_2^r \Phi(-(\tilde{V}_{n2i} + c_{21}\eta_1^r)/c_{22}))$.

5. Calculate

$$
\text{Prob}\left(\eta_3 < \frac{-(\tilde{V}_{n3i} + c_{31}\eta_1 + c_{32}\eta_2)}{c_{33}}\,\Big|\,\eta_1 = \eta_1^r\,,\ \eta_2 = \eta_2^r\right)
$$
$$
= \Phi\left(\frac{-\left(\tilde{V}_{n3i} + c_{31}\eta_1^r + c_{32}\eta_2^r\right)}{c_{33}}\right).
$$

6. And so on for all alternatives but i.

7. The simulated probability for this rth draw of $\eta_1, \eta_2, \ldots$ is calculated as

$$
\check{P}_{ni}^r = \Phi\left(\frac{-\tilde{V}_{n1i}}{c_{11}}\right)
$$
$$
\times \Phi\left(\frac{-\left(\tilde{V}_{n2i} + c_{21}\eta_1^r\right)}{c_{22}}\right)
$$
$$
\times \Phi\left(\frac{-\left(\tilde{V}_{n3i} + c_{31}\eta_1^r + c_{32}\eta_2^r\right)}{c_{33}}\right)
$$
$$
\times \cdots.
$$

8. Repeat steps 1–7 many times, for $r = 1, \ldots, R$.
9. The simulated probability is

$$\check{P}_{in} = \frac{1}{R} \sum_r \check{P}_{in}^r.$$

GHK Simulator with Maximum Likelihood Estimation

There are several issues that need to be addressed when using the GHK simulator in maximum likelihood estimation. First, in the log-likelihood function, we use the probability of the decision maker's chosen alternative. Since different decision makers choose different alternatives, P_{ni} must be calculated for different i's. The GHK simulator takes utility differences against the alternative for which the probability is being calculated, and so different utility differences must be taken for decision makers who chose different alternatives. Second, for a person who chose alternative i, the GHK simulator uses the covariance matrix $\tilde{\Omega}_i$, while for a person who chose alternative j, the matrix $\tilde{\Omega}_j$ is used. Both of these matrices are derived from the same covariance matrix Ω of the original errors. We must assure that the parameters in $\tilde{\Omega}_i$ are consistent with those in $\tilde{\Omega}_j$, in the sense that they both are derived from a common Ω. Third, we need to assure that the parameters that are estimated by maximum likelihood imply covariance matrices $\tilde{\Omega}_j \ \forall j$ that are positive definite, as a covariance matrix must be. Fourth, as always, we must make sure that the model is normalized for scale and level of utility, so that the parameters are identified.

Researchers use various procedures to address these issues. I will describe the procedure that I use.

To assure that the model is identified, I start with the covariance matrix of scaled utility differences with the differences taken against the first alternative. This is the matrix $\tilde{\Omega}_1$, which is $(J-1) \times (J-1)$. To assure that the covariance matrix is positive definite, I parameterize the model in terms of the Choleski factor of $\tilde{\Omega}_1$. That is, I start with a lower-triangular matrix that is $(J-1) \times (J-1)$ and whose top-left element is 1:

$$L_1 = \begin{pmatrix} 1 & 0 & \cdots & \cdots & \cdots & 0 \\ c_{21} & c_{22} & 0 & \cdots & \cdots & 0 \\ c_{31} & c_{32} & c_{33} & 0 & \cdots & 0 \\ \vdots & \vdots & \vdots & \vdots & & \vdots \end{pmatrix}.$$

The elements $c_{k\ell}$ of this Choleski factor are the parameters that are estimated in the model. Any matrix that is the product of a lower-triangular full-rank matrix multiplied by itself is positive definite. So by using the elements of L_1 as the parameters, I am assured that $\tilde{\Omega}_1$ is positive definite for any estimated values of these parameters.

The matrix Ω for the J nondifferenced errors is created from L_1. I create a $J \times J$ Choleski factor for Ω by adding a row of zeros at the top of L_1 and a column of zeros at the left. The resulting matrix is

$$
L = \begin{pmatrix}
0 & 0 & \cdots & \cdots & \cdots & \cdots & 0 \\
0 & 1 & 0 & \cdots & \cdots & \cdots & 0 \\
0 & c_{21} & c_{22} & 0 & \cdots & \cdots & 0 \\
0 & c_{31} & c_{32} & c_{33} & 0 & \cdots & 0 \\
\vdots & \vdots & \vdots & \vdots & \vdots & & \vdots
\end{pmatrix}.
$$

Then Ω is calculated as LL'. With this Ω, I can derive $\tilde{\Omega}_j$ for any j. Note that Ω constructed in this way is fully general (i.e., allows any substitution pattern), since it utilizes all the parameters in the normalized $\tilde{\Omega}_1$.

Utility is expressed in vector form stacked by alternatives: $U_n = V_n + \varepsilon_n$, $\varepsilon_n \sim N(0, \Omega)$. Consider a person who has chosen alternative i. For the log-likelihood function, we want to calculate P_{ni}. Recall the matrix M_i that we introduced in Section 5.1. Utility differences are taken using this matrix: $\tilde{U}_{ni} = M_i U_n$, $\tilde{V}_{ni} = M_i V_n$, and $\tilde{\varepsilon}_{ni} = M_i \varepsilon_n$. The covariance of the error differences $\tilde{\varepsilon}_{ni}$ is calculated as $\tilde{\Omega}_i = M_i \Omega M_i'$. The Choleski factor of $\tilde{\Omega}_i$ is taken and labeled L_i. (Note that L_1 obtained here will necessarily be the same as the L_1 that we used at the beginning to parameterize the model.) The person's utility is expressed as: $\tilde{U}_{ni} = \tilde{V}_{ni} + L_i \eta_n$, where η_n is a $(J - 1)$-vector of iid standard normal deviates. The GHK simulator is applied to this expression.

This procedure satisfies all of our requirements. The model is necessarily normalized for scale and level, since we parameterize it in terms of the Choleski factor L_1 of the covariance of *scaled* error *differences*, $\tilde{\Omega}_1$. Each $\tilde{\Omega}_i$ is consistent with each other $\tilde{\Omega}_j$ for $j \neq i$, because they are both derived from the same Ω (which is constructed from L_1). Each $\tilde{\Omega}_i$ is positive definite for any values of the parameters, because the parameters are the elements of L_1. As stated earlier, any matrix that is the product of a lower-triangular matrix multiplied by itself is positive definite, and so $\tilde{\Omega}_1 = LL'$ is positive definite. And each of the other $\tilde{\Omega}_j$'s, for $j = 2, \ldots, J$, is also positive definite, since they are constructed to be consistent with Ω_1, which is positive definite.

GHK as Importance Sampling

As I described in the three-alternative case, the GHK simulator provides a simulated approximation of the integral

$$\int_{\eta_1=-\infty}^{-\tilde{V}_{n21}/c_{aa}} \Phi\left(\frac{-\tilde{V}_{n31}+c_{ab}\eta_1}{c_{bb}}\right)\phi(\eta_1)\,d\eta_1.$$

The GHK simulator can be interpreted in another way that is often useful.

Importance sampling is a way of transforming an integral to be more convenient to simulate. The procedure is described in Section 9.2.7, and readers may find it useful to jump ahead to view that section. Importance sampling can be summarized as follows. Consider any integral $\bar{t}=\int t(\varepsilon)g(\varepsilon)\,d\varepsilon$ over a density g. Suppose that another density exists from which it is easy to draw. Label this other density $f(\varepsilon)$. The density g is called the target density, and f is the generating density. The integral can be rewritten as $\bar{t}=\int[t(\varepsilon)g(\varepsilon)/f(\varepsilon)]f(\varepsilon)\,d\varepsilon$. This integral is simulated by taking draws from f, calculating $t(\varepsilon)g(\varepsilon)/f(\varepsilon)$ for each draw, and averaging the results. This procedure is called importance sampling because each draw from f is weighted by g/f when taking the average of t; the weight g/f is the "importance" of the draw from f. This procedure is advantageous if (1) it is easier to draw from f than g, and/or (2) the simulator based on $t(\varepsilon)g(\varepsilon)/f(\varepsilon)$ has better properties (e.g., smoothness) than the simulator based on $t(\varepsilon)$.

The GHK simulator can be seen as making this type of transformation, and hence as being a type of importance sampling. Let η be a vector of $J-1$ iid standard normal deviates. The choice probability can be expressed as

$$(5.7)\quad P_{ni}=\int I(\eta\in B)g(\eta)\,d\eta,$$

where $B=\{\eta\text{ s.t. }\tilde{U}_{nji}<0\ \forall\ j\neq i\}$ is the set of η's that result in i being chosen; $g(\eta)=\phi(\eta_1)\cdots\phi(\eta_{J-1})$ is the density, where ϕ denotes the standard normal density; and the utilities are

$$\tilde{U}_{n1i}=\tilde{V}_{n1i}+c_{11}\eta_1,$$
$$\tilde{U}_{n2i}=\tilde{V}_{n2i}+c_{21}\eta_1+c_{22}\eta_2,$$
$$\tilde{U}_{n3i}=\tilde{V}_{n3i}+c_{31}\eta_1+c_{32}\eta_2+c_{33}\eta_3,$$

and so on.

The direct way to simulate this probability is to take draws of η, calculate $I(\eta\in B)$ for each draw, and average the results. This is the AR simulator. This simulator has the unfortunate properties that it can be zero and is not smooth.

For GHK we draw η from a different density, not from $g(\eta)$. Recall that for GHK, we draw η_1 from a standard normal density truncated at $-\tilde{V}_{n1i}/c_{11}$. The density of this truncated normal is $\phi(\eta_1)/\Phi(-\tilde{V}_{n1i}/c_{11})$, that is, the standard normal density normalized by the total probability below the truncation point. Draws of η_2, η_3, and so on are also taken from truncated densities, but with different truncation points. Each of these truncated densities takes the form $\phi(\eta_j)/\Phi(\cdot)$ for some truncation point in the denominator. The density from which we draw for the GHK simulator is therefore

$$(5.8) \quad f(\eta) = \begin{cases} \dfrac{\phi(\eta_1)}{\Phi(-\tilde{V}_{n1i}/c_{11})} \times \dfrac{\phi(\eta_2)}{\Phi(-(\tilde{V}_{n2i}+c_{21}\eta_1)/c_{22})} \times \cdots & \text{for } \eta \in B, \\ 0 & \text{for } \eta \notin B. \end{cases}$$

Note that we only take draws that are consistent with the person choosing alternative i (since we draw from the correctly truncated distributions). So $f(\eta) = 0$ for $\eta \notin B$.

Recall that for a draw of η within the GHK simulator, we calculate:

$$\check{P}_{in}(\eta) = \Phi\left(\frac{-\tilde{V}_{n1i}}{c_{11}}\right)$$
$$\times \Phi\left(\frac{-(\tilde{V}_{n2i} + c_{21}\eta_1)}{c_{22}}\right)$$
$$(5.9) \qquad \times \cdots.$$

Note that this expression is the denominator of $f(\eta)$ for $\eta \in B$, given in equation (5.8). Using this fact, we can rewrite the density $f(\eta)$ as

$$f(\eta) = \begin{cases} g(\eta)/\check{P}_{ni}(\eta) & \text{for } \eta \in B, \\ 0 & \text{for } \eta \notin B. \end{cases}$$

With this expression for $f(\eta)$, we can prove that the GHK simulator, $\check{P}_{in}(\eta)$, is unbiased for $P_{ni}(\eta)$:

$$E(\check{P}_{in}(\eta)) = \int \check{P}_{in}(\eta) f(\eta) \, d\eta$$
$$= \int_{\eta \in B} \check{P}_{in}(\eta) \frac{g(\eta)}{\check{P}_{in}(\eta)} \, d\eta \qquad \text{by (5.6.3)}$$
$$= \int_{\eta \in B} g(\eta) \, d\eta$$
$$= \int I(\eta \in B) g(\eta) \, d\eta$$
$$= P_{in}.$$

The interpretation of GHK as an importance sampler is also obtained from this expression:

$$
\begin{aligned}
P_{in} &= \int I(\eta \in B) g(\eta) \, d\eta \\
&= \int I(\eta \in B) g(\eta) \frac{f(\eta)}{f(\eta)} d\eta \\
&= \int I(\eta \in B) \frac{g(\eta)}{g(\eta)/\check{P}_{in}(\eta)} f(\eta) \, d\eta \qquad \text{by (5.6.3)} \\
&= \int I(\eta \in B) \check{P}_{in}(\eta) f(\eta) \, d\eta \\
&= \int \check{P}_{in}(\eta) f(\eta) \, d\eta,
\end{aligned}
$$

where the last equality is because $f(\eta) > 0$ only when $\eta \in B$. The GHK procedure takes draws from $f(\eta)$, calculates $\check{P}_{in}(\eta)$ for each draw, and averages the results. Essentially, GHK replaces the 0–1 $I(\eta \in B)$ with smooth $\check{P}_{in}(\eta)$ and makes the corresponding change in the density from $g(\eta)$ to $f(\eta)$.

6   Mixed Logit

6.1   Choice Probabilities

Mixed logit is a highly flexible model that can approximate any random utility model (McFadden and Train, 2000). It obviates the three limitations of standard logit by allowing for random taste variation, unrestricted substitution patterns, and correlation in unobserved factors over time. Unlike probit, it is not restricted to normal distributions. Its derivation is straightforward, and simulation of its choice probabilities is computationally simple.

Like probit, the mixed logit model has been known for many years but has only become fully applicable since the advent of simulation. The first application of mixed logit was apparently the automobile demand models created jointly by Boyd and Mellman (1980) and Cardell and Dunbar (1980). In these studies, the explanatory variables did not vary over decision makers, and the observed dependent variable was market shares rather than individual customers' choices. As a result, the computationally intensive integration that is inherent in mixed logit (as explained later) needed to be performed only once for the market as a whole, rather than for each decision maker in a sample. Early applications on customer-level data, such as Train *et al.* (1987a) and Ben-Akiva *et al.* (1993), included only one or two dimensions of integration, which could be calculated by quadrature. Improvements in computer speed and in our understanding of simulation methods have allowed the full power of mixed logits to be utilized. Among the studies to evidence this power are those by Bhat (1998a) and Brownstone and Train (1999) on cross-sectional data, and Erdem (1996), Revelt and Train (1998), and Bhat (2000) on panel data. The description in the current chapter draws heavily from Train (1999).

Mixed logit models can be derived under a variety of different behavioral specifications, and each derivation provides a particular interpretation. The mixed logit model is *defined* on the basis of the functional form for its choice probabilities. Any behavioral specification whose derived choice probabilities take this particular form is called a mixed logit model.

Mixed logit probabilities are the integrals of standard logit probabilities over a density of parameters. Stated more explicitly, a mixed logit model is any model whose choice probabilities can be expressed in the form

$$P_{ni} = \int L_{ni}(\beta) f(\beta) \, d\beta,$$

where $L_{ni}(\beta)$ is the logit probability evaluated at parameters β:

$$L_{ni}(\beta) = \frac{e^{V_{ni}(\beta)}}{\sum_{j=1}^{J} e^{V_{nj}(\beta)}}$$

and $f(\beta)$ is a density function. $V_{ni}(\beta)$ is the observed portion of the utility, which depends on the parameters β. If utility is linear in β, then $V_{ni}(\beta) = \beta' x_{ni}$. In this case, the mixed logit probability takes its usual form:

$$(6.1) \quad P_{ni} = \int \left(\frac{e^{\beta' x_{ni}}}{\sum_{j} e^{\beta' x_{nj}}} \right) f(\beta) \, d\beta.$$

The mixed logit probability is a weighted average of the logit formula evaluated at different values of β, with the weights given by the density $f(\beta)$. In the statistics literature, the weighted average of several functions is called a mixed function, and the density that provides the weights is called the mixing distribution. Mixed logit is a mixture of the logit function evaluated at different β's with $f(\beta)$ as the mixing distribution.

Standard logit is a special case where the mixing distribution $f(\beta)$ is degenerate at fixed parameters b: $f(\beta) = 1$ for $\beta = b$ and 0 for $\beta \neq b$. The choice probability (6.1) then becomes the simple logit formula

$$P_{ni} = \frac{e^{b' x_{ni}}}{\sum_{j} e^{b' x_{nj}}}.$$

The mixing distribution $f(\beta)$ can be discrete, with β taking a finite set of distinct values. Suppose β takes M possible values labeled $b_1, \ldots, b_M$, with probability s_m that $\beta = b_m$. In this case, the mixed logit becomes the *latent class model* that has long been popular in psychology and marketing; examples include Kamakura and Russell (1989) and Chintagunta *et al.* (1991). The choice probability is

$$P_{ni} = \sum_{m=1}^{M} s_m \left(\frac{e^{b'_m x_{ni}}}{\sum_{j} e^{b'_m x_{nj}}} \right).$$

This specification is useful if there are M segments in the population, each of which has its own choice behavior or preferences. The share of the population in segment m is s_m, which the researcher can estimate within the model along with the b's for each segment.

In most applications that have actually been called mixed logit (such as those cited in the introductory paragraphs in this chapter), $f(\beta)$ is specified to be continuous. For example, the density of β can be specified to be normal with mean b and covariance W. The choice probability under this density becomes

$$P_{ni} = \int \left(\frac{e^{\beta' x_{ni}}}{\sum_j e^{\beta' x_{nj}}} \right) \phi(\beta \mid b, W) \, d\beta,$$

where $\phi(\beta \mid b, W)$ is the normal density with mean b and covariance W. The researcher estimates b and W. The lognormal, uniform, triangular, gamma, or any other distribution can be used. As will be shown in Section 6.5, by specifying the explanatory variables and density appropriately, the researcher can represent any utility-maximizing behavior by a mixed logit model, as well as many forms of non-utility-maximizing behavior.

Tests for the need for a nondegenerate mixing distribution, as well as the adequacy of any given distribution, have been developed by McFadden and Train (2000) and Chesher and Santos-Silva (2002). Several studies have compared discrete and continuous mixing distributions within the context of mixed logit; see, for example, Wedel and Kamakura (2000) and Ainslie *et al.* (2001).

An issue of terminology arises with mixed logit models. There are two sets of parameters in a mixed logit model. First, we have the parameters β, which enter the logit formula. These parameters have density $f(\beta)$. The second set are parameters that describe this density. For example, if β is normally distributed with mean b and covariance W, then b and W are parameters that describe the density $f(\beta)$. Usually (though not always, as noted in the following text), the researcher is interested in estimating the parameters of f.

Denote the parameters that describe the density of β as θ. The more appropriate way to denote this density is $f(\beta \mid \theta)$. The mixed logit choice probabilities do not depend on the values of β. These probabilities are $P_{ni} = \int L_{ni}(\beta) f(\beta \mid \theta) \, d\beta$, which are functions of θ. The parameters β are integrated out. Thus, the β's are similar to the ε_{nj}'s, in that both are random terms that are integrated out to obtain the choice probability.

Under some derivations of the mixed logit model, the values of β have interpretable meaning as representing the tastes of individual decision makers. In these cases, the researcher might want to obtain information about the β's for each sampled decision maker, as well as the θ that describes the distribution of β's across decision makers. In Chapter 11, we describe how the researcher can obtain this information from estimates of θ and the observed choices of each decision maker. In the current chapter, we describe the estimation and interpretation of θ, using classical estimation procedures. In Chapter 12, we describe Bayesian procedures that provide information about θ and each decision maker's β simultaneously.

6.2   Random Coefficients

The mixed logit probability can be derived from utility-maximizing behavior in several ways that are formally equivalent but provide different interpretations. The most straightforward derivation, and most widely used in recent applications, is based on random coefficients. The decision maker faces a choice among J alternatives. The utility of person n from alternative j is specified as

$$U_{nj} = \beta_n' x_{nj} + \varepsilon_{nj},$$

where x_{nj} are observed variables that relate to the alternative and decision maker, β_n is a vector of coefficients of these variables for person n representing that person's tastes, and ε_{nj} is a random term that is iid extreme value. The coefficients vary over decision makers in the population with density $f(\beta)$. This density is a function of parameters θ that represent, for example, the mean and covariance of the β's in the population. This specification is the same as for standard logit except that β varies over decision makers rather than being fixed.

The decision maker knows the value of his own β_n and ε_{nj}'s for all j and chooses alternative i if and only if $U_{ni} > U_{nj} \, \forall j \neq i$. The researcher observes the x_{nj}'s but not β_n or the ε_{nj}'s. If the researcher observed β_n, then the choice probability would be standard logit, since the ε_{nj}'s are iid extreme value. That is, the probability *conditional* on β_n is

$$L_{ni}(\beta_n) = \frac{e^{\beta_n' x_{ni}}}{\sum_j e^{\beta_n' x_{nj}}}.$$

However, the researcher does not know β_n and therefore cannot condition on β. The unconditional choice probability is therefore the integral of

$L_{ni}(\beta_n)$ over all possible variables of β_n:

$$P_{ni} = \int \left(\frac{e^{\beta' x_{ni}}}{\sum_j e^{\beta' x_{nj}}} \right) f(\beta) \, d\beta,$$

which is the mixed logit probability (6.1).

The researcher specifies a distribution for the coefficients and estimates the parameters of that distribution. In most applications, such as Revelt and Train (1998), Mehndiratta (1996), and Ben-Akiva and Bolduc (1996), $f(\beta)$ has been specified to be normal or lognormal: $\beta \sim N(b, W)$ or $\ln \beta \sim N(b, W)$ with parameters b and W that are estimated. The lognormal distribution is useful when the coefficient is known to have the same sign for every decision maker, such as a price coefficient that is known to be negative for everyone. Revelt and Train (2000), Hensher and Greene (2001), and Train (2001) have used triangular and uniform distributions. With the uniform density, β is distributed uniformly between $b - s$ and $b + s$, where the mean b and spread s are estimated. The triangular distribution has positive density that starts at $b - s$, rises linearly to b, and then drops linearly to $b + s$, taking the form of a tent or triangle. The mean b and spread s are estimated, as with the uniform, but the density is peaked instead of flat. These densities have the advantage of being bounded on both sides, thereby avoiding the problem that can arise with normals and lognormals having unreasonably large coefficients for some share of decision makers. By constraining $s = b$, the researcher can assure that the coefficients have the same sign for all decision makers. Siikamaki (2001) and Siikamaki and Layton (2001) use the Rayleigh distribution (Johnson et al., 1994), which is on one side of zero like the lognormal but, as these researchers found, can be easier for estimation than the lognormal. Revelt (1999) used truncated normals. As these examples indicate, the researcher is free to specify a distribution that satisfies his expectations about behavior in his own application.

Variations in tastes that are related to observed attributes of the decision maker are captured through specification of the explanatory variables and/or the mixing distribution. For example, cost might be divided by the decision maker's income to allow the value or relative importance of cost to decline as income rises. The random coefficient of this variable then represents the variation over people with the same income in the value that they place on cost. The mean valuation of cost declines with increasing income while the variance around the mean is fixed. Observed attributes of the decision maker can also enter $f(\beta)$, so that higher-order moments of taste variation can also depend on attributes of the decision maker. For example, Bhat (1998a, 2000) specify $f(\beta)$ to be lognormal with mean and variance depending on decision maker characteristics.

6.3   Error Components

A mixed logit model can be used without a random-coefficients interpretation, as simply representing error components that create correlations among the utilities for different alternatives. Utility is specified as

$$U_{nj} = \alpha' x_{nj} + \mu_n' z_{nj} + \varepsilon_{nj},$$

where x_{nj} and z_{nj} are vectors of observed variables relating to alternative j, α is a vector of fixed coefficients, μ is a vector of random terms with zero mean, and ε_{nj} is iid extreme value. The terms in z_{nj} are error components that, along with ε_{nj}, define the stochastic portion of utility. That is, the unobserved (random) portion of utility is $\eta_{nj} = \mu_n' z_{nj} + \varepsilon_{nj}$, which can be correlated over alternatives depending on the specification of z_{nj}. For the standard logit model, z_{nj} is identically zero, so that there is no correlation in utility over alternatives. This lack of correlation gives rise to the IIA property and its restrictive substitution patterns. With nonzero error components, utility is correlated over alternatives: $\text{Cov}(\eta_{ni}, \eta_{nj}) = E(\mu_n' z_{ni} + \varepsilon_{ni})(\mu_n' z_{nj} + \varepsilon_{nj}) = z_{ni}' W z_{nj}$, where W is the covariance of μ_n. Utility is correlated over alternatives even when, as in most specifications, the error components are independent, such that W is diagonal.

Various correlation patterns, and hence substitution patterns, can be obtained by appropriate choice of variables to enter as error components. For example, an analog to nested logit is obtained by specifying a dummy variable for each nest that equals 1 for each alternative in the nest and zero for alternatives outside the nest. With K non-overlapping nests, the error components are $\mu_n' z_{nj} = \sum_{k=1}^{K} \mu_{nk} d_{jk}$, where $d_{jk} = 1$ if j is in nest k and zero otherwise. It is convenient in this situation to specify the error components to be independently normally distributed: μ_{nk} iid $N(0, \sigma_k)$. The random quantity μ_{nk} enters the utility of each alternative in nest k, inducing correlation among these alternatives. It does not enter any of the alternatives in other nests, thereby not inducing correlation between alternatives in the nest with those outside the nest. The variance σ_k captures the magnitude of the correlation. It plays an analogous role to the inclusive value coefficient of nested logit models.

To be more precise, the covariance between two alternatives in nest k is $\text{Cov}(\eta_{ni}, \eta_{nj}) = E(\mu_k + \varepsilon_{ni})(\mu_k + \varepsilon_{nj}) = \sigma_k$. The variance for each of the alternatives in nest k is $\text{Var}(\eta_{ni}) = E(\mu_k + \varepsilon_{ni})^2 = \sigma_k + \pi^2/6$, since the variance of the extreme value term, ε_{ni}, is $\pi^2/6$ (see Section 3.1). The correlation between any two alternatives within nest k is therefore $\sigma_k/(\sigma_k + \pi^2/6)$. Constraining the variance of each nest's error component to be the same for all nests (i.e., constraining $\sigma_k = \sigma$, $k = 1, \ldots, K$) is analogous to constraining the log-sum coefficient to be the same for all nests in a nested logit. This constraint also assures that the mixed logit model is normalized for scale and level.

Allowing different variances for the random quantities for different nests is analogous to allowing the inclusive value coefficient to differ across nests in a nested logit. An analog to overlapping nests is captured with dummies that identify overlapping sets of alternatives, as in Bhat (1998a). An analog to heteroskedastic logit (discussed in Section 4.5) is obtained by entering an error component for each alternative. Ben-Akiva *et al.* (2001) provide guidance on how to specify these variables appropriately.

Error-component and random-coefficient specifications are formally equivalent. Under the random-coefficient motivation, utility is specified as $U_{nj} = \beta'_n x_{nj} + \varepsilon_{nj}$ with random β_n. The coefficients β_n can be decomposed into their mean α and deviations μ_n, so that $U_{nj} = \alpha' x_{nj} + \mu'_n x_{nj} + \varepsilon_{nj}$, which has error components defined by $z_{nj} = x_{nj}$. Conversely, under an error-component motivation, utility is $U_{nj} = \alpha' x_{nj} + \mu'_n z_{nj} + \varepsilon_{nj}$, which is equivalent to a random-parameter model with fixed coefficients for variables x_{nj} and random coefficients with zero means for variables z_{nj}. If x_{nj} and z_{nj} overlap (in the sense that some of the same variables enter x_{nj} and z_{nj}), the coefficients of these variables can be considered to vary randomly with mean α and the same distribution as μ_n around their means.

Though random coefficients and error components are formally equivalent, the way a researcher thinks about the model affects the specification of the mixed logit. For example, when thinking in terms of random parameters, it is natural to allow each variable's coefficient to vary and perhaps even to allow correlations among the coefficients. This is the approach pursued by Revelt and Train (1998). However, when the primary goal is to represent substitution patterns appropriately through the use of error components, the emphasis is placed on specifying variables that can induce correlations over alternatives in a parsimonious fashion so as to provide sufficiently realistic substitution patterns. This is the approach taken by Brownstone and Train (1999). The goals differed in these studies, Revelt and Train being interested in the pattern of tastes, while Brownstone and Train were more concerned with prediction. The number of explanatory variables also differed, Revelt and Train examining 6 variables, so that estimating the joint distribution of their coefficients was a reasonable goal, while Brownstone and Train included

26 variables. Expecting to estimate the distribution of 26 coefficients is unreasonable, and yet thinking in terms of random parameters instead of error components can lead the researcher to such expectations. It is important to remember that the mixing distribution, whether motivated by random parameters or by error components, captures variance and correlations in unobserved factors. There is a natural limit on how much one can learn about things that are not seen.

6.4   Substitution Patterns

Mixed logit does not exhibit independence from irrelevant alternatives (IIA) or the restrictive substitution patterns of logit. The ratio of mixed logit probabilities, P_{ni}/P_{nj}, depends on all the data, including attributes of alternatives other than i or j. The denominators of the logit formula are inside the integrals and therefore do not cancel. The percentage change in the probability for one alternative given a change in the mth attribute of another alternative is

$$E_{ni\chi_{nj}^m} = -\frac{1}{P_{ni}} \int \beta^m L_{ni}(\beta) L_{nj}(\beta) f(\beta) d\beta$$

$$= -\int \beta^m L_{nj}(\beta) \left[\frac{L_{ni}(\beta)}{P_{ni}} \right] f(\beta) d\beta,$$

where β^m is the mth element of β. This elasticity is different for each alternative i. A ten-percent reduction for one alternative need not imply (as with logit) a ten-percent reduction in each other alternative. Rather, the substitution pattern depends on the specification of the variables and mixing distribution, which can be determined empirically.

Note that the percentage change in probability depends on the correlation between $L_{ni}(\beta)$ and $L_{nj}(\beta)$ over different values of β, which is determined by the researcher's specification of variables and mixing distribution. For example, to represent a situation where an improvement in alternative j draws proportionally more from alternative i than from alternative k, the researcher can specify an element of x that is positively correlated between i and j but uncorrelated or negatively correlated between k and j, with a mixing distribution that allows the coefficient of this variable to vary.

6.5   Approximation to Any Random Utility Model

McFadden & Train (2000) show that any random utility model (RUM) can be approximated to any degree of accuracy by a mixed logit with appropriate choice of variables and mixing distribution. This proof is analogous to the RUM-consistent approximations provided by Dagsvik

(1994). An intuitive explanation can easily be provided. Suppose the true model is $U_{nj} = \alpha'_n z_{nj}$, where z_{nj} are variables related to alternative j, and α follows any distribution $f(\alpha)$. Any RUM can be expressed in this form. (The more traditional notation $U_{nj} = \beta'_n x_{nj} + \varepsilon_{nj}$ is obtained by letting $z'_{nj} = \langle x'_{nj}, d_j \rangle$, $\alpha' = \langle \beta'_n, \varepsilon_{nj} \rangle$, and $f(\alpha)$ be the joint density of β_n and ε_{nj} $\forall j$.) Conditional on α, the person's choice is fully determined, since U_{nj} is then known for each j. The conditional probability is therefore

$$q_{ni}(\alpha) = I(\alpha'_n z_{ni} > \alpha'_n z_{nj} \ \forall j \neq i),$$

where $I(\cdot)$ is the 1–0 indicator of whether the event in parentheses occurs. This conditional probability is deterministic in the sense that the probability is either zero or one: conditional on all the unknown random terms, the decision maker's choice is completely determined. The unconditional choice probability is the integral of $q_{ni}(\alpha)$ over α:

$$Q_{ni} = \int I(\alpha'_n z_{ni} > \alpha'_n z_{ni} \ \forall j \neq i) f(\alpha) \, d\alpha.$$

We can approximate this probability with a mixed logit. Scale utility by λ, so that $U^*_{nj} = (\alpha/\lambda) z_{nj}$. This scaling does not change the model, since behavior is unaffected by the scale of utility. Then add an iid extreme value term: ε_{nj}. The addition of the extreme value term does change the model, since it changes the utility of each alternative. We add it because doing so gives us a mixed logit. And, as we will show (this is the purpose of the proof), adding the extreme value term is innocuous. The mixed logit probability based on this utility is

$$P_{ni} = \int \left(\frac{e^{(\alpha/\lambda)' z_{ni}}}{\sum_j e^{(\alpha/\lambda)' z_{nj}}} \right) f(\alpha) \, d\alpha.$$

As λ approaches zero, the coefficients α/λ in the logit formula grow large, and P_{ni} approaches a 1–0 indicator for the alternative with the highest utility. That is, the mixed logit probability P_{ni} approaches the true probability Q_{ni} as λ approaches zero. By scaling the coefficients upward sufficiently, the mixed logit based on these scaled coefficients is arbitrarily close to the true model. Srinivasan and Mahmassani (2000) use this concept of raising the scale of coefficients to show that a mixed logit can approximate a probit model; the concept applies generally to approximate any RUM.

Recall that we added an iid extreme value term to the true utility of each alternative. These terms change the model, because the alternative with highest utility before the terms are added may not have highest utility afterward (since a different amount is added to each utility). However, by raising the scale of utility sufficiently, we can be essentially sure that the addition of the extreme value terms has no effect. Consider a two-alternative example. Suppose, using the true model with its original scaling, that the utility of alternative 1 is 0.5 units higher than the utility of alternative 2, so that alternative 1 is chosen. Suppose we add an extreme value term to each alternative. There's a good chance, given the variance of these random terms, that the value obtained for alternative 2 will exceed that for alternative 1 by at least half a unit, so that alternative 2 now obtains the higher utility instead of 1. The addition of the extreme value terms thus changes the model, since it changes which alternative has the higher utility. Suppose, however, that we scale up the original utility by a factor of 10 (i.e., $\lambda = 0.10$). The utility for alternative 1 now exceeds the utility for alternative 2 by 5 units. It is highly unlikely that adding extreme value terms to these utilities will reverse this difference. That is, it is highly unlikely, in fact next to impossible, that the value of ε_{n2} that is added to the utility of alternative 2 is larger by 5 than the ε_{n1} that is added to the utility of alternative 1. If scaling up by 10 is not sufficient to assure that adding the extreme value term has no effect, then the original utilities can be scaled up by 100 or 1000. At some point, a scale will be found for which the addition of the extreme value terms has no effect. Stated succinctly, adding an extreme value term to true utility, which makes the model into a mixed logit, does not change utility in any meaningful way when the scale of the utility is sufficiently large. A mixed logit can approximate any RUM simply by scaling up utility sufficiently.

This demonstration is not intended to suggest that raising the scale of utility is actually how the researcher would proceed in specifying a mixed logit as an approximation to the true model. Rather, the demonstration simply indicates that if no other means for specifying a mixed logit to approximate the true model can be found, then this rescaling procedure can be used to attain the approximation. Usually, a mixed logit can be specified that adequately reflects the true model without needing to resort to an upward scaling of utility. For example, the true model will usually contain some iid term that is added to the utility of each alternative. Assuming an extreme value distribution for this term is perhaps close enough to reality to be empirically indistinguishable from other distributional assumptions for the iid term. In this case, the scale of utility is determined naturally by the variance of this iid term. The researcher's task is simply to find variables and a mixing distribution that capture the other parts of utility, namely, the parts that are correlated over alternatives or heteroskedastic.

6.6   Simulation

Mixed logit is well suited to simulation methods for estimation. Utility is $U_{nj} = \beta'_n x_{nj} + \varepsilon_{nj}$, where the coefficients β_n are distributed with density $f(\beta \mid \theta)$, where θ refers collectively to the parameters of this distribution (such as the mean and covariance of β). The researcher specifies the functional form $f(\cdot)$ and wants to estimate the parameters θ. The choice probabilities are

$$P_{ni} = \int L_{ni}(\beta) f(\beta \mid \theta) \, d\beta,$$

where

$$L_{ni}(\beta) = \frac{e^{\beta' x_{ni}}}{\sum_{j=1}^{J} e^{\beta' x_{nj}}}.$$

The probabilities are approximated through simulation for any given value of θ: (1) Draw a value of β from $f(\beta \mid \theta)$, and label it β^r with the superscript $r = 1$ referring to the first draw. (2) Calculate the logit formula $L_{ni}(\beta^r)$ with this draw. (3) Repeat steps 1 and 2 many times, and average the results. This average is the simulated probability:

$$\check{P}_{ni} = \frac{1}{R} \sum_{r=1}^{R} L_{ni}(\beta^r),$$

where R is the number of draws. $\check{P}_{ni}$ is an unbiased estimator of P_{ni} by construction. Its variance decreases as R increases. It is strictly positive, so that $\ln \check{P}_{ni}$ is defined, which is useful for approximating the log-likelihood function below. $\check{P}_{ni}$ is smooth (twice differentiable) in the parameters θ and the variables x, which facilitates the numerical search for the maximum likelihood function and the calculation of elasticities. And $\check{P}_{ni}$ sums to one over alternatives, which is useful in forecasting.

The simulated probabilities are inserted into the log-likelihood function to give a simulated log likelihood:

$$\text{SLL} = \sum_{n=1}^{N} \sum_{j=1}^{J} d_{nj} \ln \check{P}_{nj},$$

where $d_{nj} = 1$ if n chose j and zero otherwise. The maximum simulated likelihood estimator (MSLE) is the value of θ that maximizes SLL. The properties of this estimator are discussed in Chapter 10. Usually, different draws are taken for each observation. This procedure maintains independence over decision makers of the simulated probabilities that enter SLL. Lee (1992) describes the properties of MSLE when the same draws are used for all observations.

The simulated mixed logit probability can be related to accept–reject (AR) methods of simulation. AR simulation is described in Section 5.6 for probit models, but it is applicable more generally. For any random utility model, the AR simulator is constructed as follows: (1) A draw of the random terms is taken. (2) The utility of each alternative is calculated from this draw, and the alternative with the highest utility is identified. (3) Steps 1 and 2 are repeated many times. (4) The simulated probability for an alternative is calculated as the proportion of draws for which that alternative has the highest utility. The AR simulator is unbiased by construction. However, it is not strictly positive for any finite number of draws. It is also not smooth, but rather a step function: constant within ranges of parameters for which the identity of the alternative with the highest utility does not change for any draws, and with jumps where changes in the parameters change the identity of the alternative with the highest utility. Numerical methods for maximization based on the AR simulator are hampered by these characteristics. To address these numerical problems, the AR simulator can be smoothed by replacing the 0–1 indicator with the logit formula. As discussed in Section 5.6.2, the logit-smoothed AR simulator can approximate the AR simulator arbitrarily closely by scaling utility appropriately.

The mixed logit simulator can be seen as a logit-smoothed AR simulator of any RUM: draws of the random terms are taken, utility is calculated for these draws, the calculated utilities are inserted into the logit formula, and the results are averaged. The theorem that a mixed logit can approximate any random utility model (Section 6.5) can be viewed from this perspective. We know from Section 5.6.2 that the logit-smoothed AR simulator can be arbitrarily close to the AR simulator for any model, with sufficient scaling of utility. Since the mixed logit simulator is equivalent to a logit-smoothed AR simulator, the simulated mixed logit model can be arbitrarily close to the AR simulator of any model.

6.7   Panel Data

The specification is easily generalized to allow for repeated choices by each sampled decision maker. The simplest specification treats the coefficients that enter utility as varying over people but being constant over choice situations for each person. Utility from alternative j in choice situation t by person n is $U_{njt} = \beta_n x_{njt} + \varepsilon_{njt}$, with ε_{njt} being iid extreme value over time, people, and alternatives. Consider a sequence of alternatives, one for each time period, $\mathbf{i} = \{i_1, \ldots, i_T\}$. Conditional on β the probability that the person makes this sequence of choices is the product of logit formulas:

$$(6.2) \quad L_{ni}(\beta) = \prod_{t=1}^{T} \left[\frac{e^{\beta'_n x_{ni_t t}}}{\sum_j e^{\beta'_n x_{njt}}} \right]$$

since the ε_{njt}'s are independent over time. The unconditional probability is the integral of this product over all values of β:

$$(6.3) \quad P_{ni} = \int L_{ni}(\beta) f(\beta) \, d\beta.$$

The only difference between a mixed logit with repeated choices and one with only one choice per decision maker is that the integrand involves a *product* of logit formulas, one for each time period, rather than just one logit formula. The probability is simulated similarly to the probability with one choice period. A draw of β is taken from its distribution. The logit formula is calculated for each period, and the product of these logits is taken. This process is repeated for many draws, and the results are averaged.

Past and future exogenous variables can be added to the utility in a given period to represent lagged response and anticipatory behavior, as described in Section 5.5 in relation to probit with panel data. However, unlike probit, lagged dependent variables can be added in a mixed logit model without changing the estimation procedure. Conditional on β_n, the only remaining random terms in the mixed logit are the ε_{nj}'s, which are independent over time. A lagged dependent variable entering U_{njt} is uncorrelated with these remaining error terms for period t, since these terms are independent over time. The conditional probabilities (conditional on β) are therefore the same as in equation (6.2), but with the x's including lagged dependent variables. The unconditional probability is then the integral of this conditional probability over all values of β, which is just equation (6.3). In this regard, mixed logit is more convenient than probit for representing state dependence, since lagged dependent variables can be added to mixed logit without adjusting the probability formula or simulation method. Erdem (1996) and Johannesson and Lundin (2000) exploit this advantage to examine habit formation and variety seeking within a mixed logit that also captures random taste variation.

If choices and data are not observed from the start of the process (i.e., from the first choice situation that the person faces), the issue of initial conditions must be confronted, just as with probit. The researcher must somehow represent the probability of the first observed choice, which depends on the previous, unobserved choices. Heckman and Singer (1986) provide ways to handle this issue. However, when the researcher observes the choice process from the beginning, the initial conditions issue does not arise. In this case, the use of lagged dependent variables to capture inertia or other types of state dependence is straightforward with mixed logit. Stated-preference data (that is, answers to a series of choice situations posed to respondents in a survey) provide a prominent example of the researcher observing the entire sequence of choices.

In the specification so far and in nearly all applications, the coefficients β_n are assumed to be constant over choice situations for a given decision maker. This assumption is appropriate if the decision maker's tastes are stable over the time period that spans the repeated choices. However, the coefficients associated with each person can be specified to vary over time in a variety of ways. For example, each person's tastes might be serially correlated over choice situations, so that utility is

$$U_{njt} = \beta_{nt}x_{njt} + \varepsilon_{njt},$$
$$\beta_{nt} = b + \tilde{\beta}_{nt},$$
$$\tilde{\beta}_{nt} = \rho\tilde{\beta}_{nt-1} + \mu_{nt},$$

where b is fixed and μ_{nt} is iid over n and t. Simulation of the probability for the sequence of choices proceeds as follows:

1. Draw μ_{n1}^r for the initial period, and calculate the logit formula for this period using $\beta_{n1}^r = b + \mu_{n0}^r$.
2. Draw μ_{n2}^r for the second period, calculate $\beta_{n2} = b + \rho\mu_{n1}^r + \mu_{n2}^r$, and then calculate the logit formula based on this β_{n2}^r.
3. Continue for all T time periods.
4. Take the product of the T logits.
5. Repeat steps 1–4 for numerous sequences of draws.
6. Average the results.

The burden placed on simulation is greater than with coefficients being constant over time for each person, requiring T times as many draws.

6.8   Case Study

As illustration, consider a mixed logit of anglers' choices of fishing sites (Train, 1999). The specification takes a random-coefficients form. Utility is $U_{njt} = \beta_n x_{njt} + \varepsilon_{njt}$, with coefficients β_n varying over anglers but not over trips for each angler. The probability of the sequence of sites chosen by each angler is given by equation (6.3).

The sample consists of 962 river trips taken in Montana by 258 anglers during the period of July 1992 through August 1993. A total of 59 possible river sites were defined, based on geographical and other relevant factors. Each site contains one or more of the stream segments used in the Montana River Information System. The following variables enter as elements of x for each site:

1. Fish stock, measured in units of 100 fish per 1000 feet of river.
2. Aesthetics rating, measured on a scale of 0 to 3, with 3 being the highest.
3. Trip cost: cost of traveling from the angler's home to the site, including the variable cost of driving (gas, maintenance, tires, oil) and the value of time spent driving (with time valued at one-third the angler's wage.)
4. Indicator that the *Angler's Guide to Montana* lists the site as a major fishing site.
5. Number of campgrounds per U.S. Geological Survey (USGS) block in the site.
6. Number of state recreation access areas per USGS block in the site.
7. Number of restricted species at the site.
8. Log of the size of the site, in USGS blocks.

The coefficients of variables 4–7 can logically take either sign; for example, some anglers might like having campgrounds and others prefer the privacy that comes from not having nearby campgrounds. Each of these coefficients is given an independent normal distribution with mean and standard deviation that are estimated. The coefficients for trip cost, fish stock, and aesthetics rating of the site are expected to have the same sign for all anglers, with only their magnitudes differing over anglers. These coefficients are given independent lognormal distributions. The mean and standard deviation of the log of the coefficient are estimated, and the mean and standard deviation of the coefficient itself are calculated from these estimates. Since the lognormal distribution is defined over the positive range and trip cost is expected to have a negative coefficient for all anglers, the negative of trip cost enters the model. The coefficient for the log of size is assumed to be fixed. This variable allows for the fact that the probability of visiting a larger site is higher than that for a smaller site, all else equal. Having the coefficient of this variable vary over people, while possible, would not be particularly meaningful. A version of the model with correlated coefficients is given by Train (1998). The site choice model is part of an overall model, given by Desvousges *et al.* (1996), of the joint choice of trip frequency and site choice.

Table 6.1. *Mixed logit model of river fishing site choice*

Variable	Parameter	Value	Std. Error
Fish stock	Mean of ln(coefficient)	−2.876	0.6066
	Std. dev. of ln(coefficient)	1.016	0.2469
Aesthetics	Mean of ln(coefficient)	−0.794	0.2287
	Std. dev. of ln(coefficient)	0.849	0.1382
Total cost (neg.)	Mean of ln(coefficient)	−2.402	0.0631
	Std. dev. of ln(coefficient)	0.801	0.0781
Guide lists as major	Mean coefficient	1.018	0.2887
	Std. dev. of coefficient	2.195	0.3518
Campgrounds	Mean coefficient	0.116	0.3233
	Std. dev. of coefficient	1.655	0.4350
Access areas	Mean coefficient	−0.950	0.3610
	Std. dev. of coefficient	1.888	0.3511
Restricted species	Mean coefficient	−0.499	0.1310
	Std. dev. of coefficient	0.899	0.1640
Log(size)	Mean coefficient	0.984	0.1077
Likelihood ratio index		0.5018	
SLL at convergence		−1932.33	

Simulation was performed using one thousand random draws for each sampled angler. The results are given in Table 6.1. The standard deviation of each random coefficient is highly significant, indicating that these coefficients do indeed vary in the population.

Consider first the normally distributed coefficients. The estimated means and standard deviations of these coefficients provide information on the share of the population that places a positive value on the site attribute and the share that places a negative value. The distribution of the coefficient of the indicator that the *Angler's Guide to Montana* lists the site as a major site obtains an estimated mean of 1.018 and estimated standard deviation of 2.195, such that 68 percent of the distribution is above zero and 32 percent below. This implies that being listed as a major site in the *Angler's Guide to Montana* is a positive inducement for about two-thirds of anglers and a negative factor for the other third, who apparently prefer more solitude. Campgrounds are preferred by about half (53 percent) of anglers and avoided by the other half. And about one-third of anglers (31 percent) are estimated to prefer having numerous access areas, while the other two-thirds prefer there being fewer access areas.

Consider now the lognormal coefficients. Coefficient β^k follows a lognormal if the log of β^k is normally distributed. We parameterize the lognormal distribution in terms of the underlying normal. That is, we estimate parameters m and s that represent the mean and variance of the log of the coefficient: $\ln \beta^k \sim N(m, s)$. The mean and variance of β^k are then derived from the estimates of m and s. The median is $\exp(m)$, the mean is $\exp(m + s/2)$, and the variance is $\exp(2m + s)[\exp(s) - 1]$. The point estimates imply that the coefficients of fish stock, aesthetics, and trip cost have the following median, mean, and standard deviations:

Variable	Median	Mean	Std. Dev.
Fish stock	0.0563	0.0944	0.1270
Aesthetics	0.4519	0.6482	0.6665
Trip cost	0.0906	0.1249	0.1185

The ratio of an angler's fish stock coefficients to the trip cost coefficient is a measure of the amount that the angler is willing to pay to have additional fish in the river. Since the ratio of two independent lognormally distributed terms is also lognormally distributed, we can calculate moments for the distribution of willingness to pay. The log of the ratio of the fish stock coefficient to the trip cost coefficient has estimated mean -0.474 and standard deviation of 1.29. The ratio itself therefore has median 0.62, mean 1.44, and standard deviation 2.96. That is, the average willingness to pay to have the fish stock raised by 100 fish per 1000 feet of river is estimated to be \$1.44, and there is very wide variation in anglers' willingness to pay for additional fish stock. Similarly, \$9.87 is the estimated average willingness to pay for a site that has an aesthetics rating that is higher by 1, and again the variation is fairly large.

As this application illustrates, the mixed logit provides more information than a standard logit, in that the mixed logit estimates the extent to which anglers differ in their preferences for site attributes. The standard deviations of the coefficients enter significantly, indicating that a mixed logit provides a significantly better representation of the choice situation than standard logit, which assumes that coefficients are the same for all anglers. The mixed logit also allows for the fact that several trips are observed for each sampled angler and that each angler's preferences apply to each of the angler's trips.

7   Variations on a Theme

7.1   Introduction

Simulation gives the researcher the freedom to specify models that appropriately represent the choice situations under consideration, without being unduly hampered by purely mathematical concerns. This perspective has been the overarching theme of our book. The discrete choice models that we have discussed – namely, logit, nested logit, probit, and mixed logit – are used in the vast majority of applied work. However, readers should not feel themselves constrained to use these models. In the current chapter, we describe several models that are derived under somewhat different behavioral concepts. These models are variations on the ones already discussed, directed toward specific issues and data. The point is not simply to describe additional models. Rather, the discussion illustrates how the researcher might examine a choice situation and develop a model and estimation procedure that seem appropriate for that particular situation, drawing from, and yet adapting, the standard set of models and tools.

Each section of this chapter is motivated by a type of data, representing the outcome of a particular choice process. The arena in which such data might arise is described, and the limitations of the primary models for these data are identified. In each case, a new model is described that better represents the choice situation. Often this new model is only a slight change from one of the primary models. However, the slight change will often make the standard software unusable, so that the researcher will need to develop her own software, perhaps by modifying the codes that are available for standard models. The ability to revise code to represent new specifications enables the researcher to utilize the freedom that the field offers.

7.2   Stated-Preference and Revealed-Preference Data

Revealed-preference data relate to people's actual choices in real-world situations. These data are so called because people reveal their tastes, or preferences, though the choices they make in the world. *Stated-preference* data are data collected in experimental or survey situations where respondents are presented with hypothetical choice situations. The term refers to the fact that the respondents state what their choices would be in the hypothetical situations. For example, in a survey, a person might be presented with three cars with different prices and other attributes. The person is asked which of the three cars he would buy if offered only these three cars in the real world. The answer the person gives is the person's stated choice. A revealed-preference datum for the respondent is obtained by asking which car he bought when he last bought a car.

There are advantages and limitations to each type of data. Revealed-preference data have the advantage that they reflect actual choices. This, of course, is a very big advantage. However, such data are limited to the choice situations and attributes of alternatives that currently exist or have existed historically. Often a researcher will want to examine people's responses in situations that do not currently exist, such as the demand for a new product. Revealed-preference data are simply not available for these new situations. Even for choice situations that currently exist, there may be insufficient variation in relevant factors to allow estimation with revealed-preference data. For example, suppose the researcher wants to examine the factors that affect California households' choice of energy supplier. While residential customers have been able to choose among suppliers for many years, there has been practically no difference in price among the suppliers' offers. Customers' response to price cannot be estimated on data that contain little or no price variation. An interesting paradox arises in this regard. If customers were highly price-responsive, then suppliers, knowing this, would offer prices that met their competitors' prices; the well-known equilibrium in this situation is that all firms offer (essentially) the same price. If the data from this market were used in a choice model, the price coefficient would be found to be insignificant, since there is little price variation in the data. The researcher could erroneously conclude from this insignificance that price is unimportant to consumers. This paradox is inherent in revealed-preference data. Factors that are the most important to consumers will often exhibit the least variation due to the natural forces of market equilibrium. Their importance might therefore be difficult to detect with revealed-preference data.

Stated-preference data complement revealed-preference data. A questionnaire is designed in which the respondent is presented with one or more choice experiments. In each experiment, two or more options are described, and the respondent is asked which option he would choose if facing the choice in the real world. For example, in the data that we examine in Chapter 11, each surveyed respondent is presented with 12 experiments. In each experiment, four hypothetical energy suppliers were described, with the price, contract terms, and other attributes given for each supplier. The respondent is asked to state which of the four suppliers he would choose.

The advantage of stated-preference data is that the experiments can be designed to contain as much variation in each attribute as the researcher thinks is appropriate. While there may be little price variation over suppliers in the real world, the suppliers that are described in the experiments can be given sufficiently different prices to allow precise estimation. Attributes can be varied over respondents and over experiments for each respondent. This degree of variation contrasts with market data, where often the same products are available to all customers, such that there is no variation over customers in the attributes of products. Importantly, for products that have never been offered before, or for new attributes of old products, stated-preference data allow estimation of choice models when revealed-preference data do not exist. Louviere *et al.* (2000) describe the appropriate collection and analysis of stated-preference data.

The limitations of stated-preference data are obvious: what people say they will do is often not the same as what they actually do. People may not know what they would do if a hypothetical situation were real. Or they may not be willing to say what they would do. In fact, respondents' idea of what they would do might be influenced by factors that wouldn't arise in the real choice situations, such as their perception of what the interviewer expects or wants as answers.

By combining stated- and revealed-preference data, the advantages of each can be obtained while mitigating the limitations. The stated-preference data provide the needed variation in attributes, while the revealed-preference data ground the predicted shares in reality. To utilize these relative strengths, an estimation procedure is needed that (1) allows the ratios of coefficients (which represent the relative importance of the various attributes) to be estimated primarily from the stated-preference data (or more generally, from whatever variation in the attributes exists, which is usually from the stated-preference data), while (2) allowing the alternative-specific constants and overall scale of the parameters to be determined by the revealed preference data (since the constants and scale determine average shares in base conditions).

Procedures for estimating discrete choice models on a combination of stated- and revealed-preference data are described by Ben-Akiva and Morikawa (1990), Hensher and Bradley (1993), and Hensher *et al.* (1999) in the context of logit models, and by Bhat and Castelar (2002) and Brownstone *et al.* (2000) with mixed logit. These procedures constitute variations on the methods we have already examined. The most prevalent issue when combining stated- and revealed-preference data is that the unobserved factors are generally different for the two types of data. We describe in the following paragraphs how this issue can readily be addressed.

Let the utility that person n obtains from alternative j in situation t be specified as $U_{njt} = \beta' x_{njt} + e_{njt}$, where x_{njt} does not include alternative-specific constants and e_{njt} represents the effect of factors that are not observed by the researcher. These factors have a mean for each alternative (representing the average effect of all excluded factors on the utility of that alternative) and a distribution around this mean. The mean is captured by an alternative-specific constant, labeled c_j, and for a standard logit model the distribution around this mean is extreme value with variance $\lambda^2 \pi^2 / 6$. As described in Chapters 2 and 3, the scale of utility is set by normalizing the variance of the unobserved portion of utility. The utility function becomes $U_{njt} = (\beta/\lambda)' x_{njt} + c_j/\lambda + \varepsilon_{njt}$, where the normalized error $\varepsilon_{njt} = (e_{njt} - c_j)/\lambda$ is now iid extreme value with variance $\pi^2/6$. The choice probability is given by the logit formula based on $(\beta/\lambda)' x_{njt} + c_j/\lambda$. The parameters that are estimated are the original parameters divided by the scale factor λ.

This specification is reasonable for many kinds of data and choice situations. However, there is no reason to expect the alternative-specific constants and the scale factor to be the same for stated-preference data as for revealed-preference data. These parameters reflect the effects of unobserved factors, which are necessarily different in real choice situations than hypothetical survey situations. In real choices, a multitude of issues that affect a person but are not observed by the researcher come into play. In a stated-preference experiment, the respondent is (usually) asked to assume all alternatives to be the same on factors that are not explicitly mentioned in the experiment. If the respondent followed this instruction exactly, there would, by definition, be no unobserved factors in the stated-preference choices. Of course, respondents inevitably bring some outside concepts into the experiments, such that unobserved factors do enter. However, there is no reason to expect that these factors are the same, in mean or variance, as in real-world choices.

To account for these differences, separate constants and scale parameters are specified for stated-preference choice situations and for revealed-preference situations. Let c_j^s and c_j^r represent the mean effect of unobserved factors for alternative j in stated-preference experiments and revealed-preference choices, respectively. Similarly, let λ^s and λ^r represent the scales (proportional to the standard deviations) of the distributions of unobserved factors around these means in stated- and revealed-preference situations, respectively. To set the overall scale of utility, we normalize either of the scale parameters to 1, which makes the other scale parameter equal the ratio of the two original scale parameters. Let's normalize λ^r, so that λ^s reflects the variance of unobserved factors in stated-preference situations relative to that in revealed-preference situations. Utility then becomes

$$U_{njt} = (\beta/\lambda^s)'x_{njt} + c_j^s/\lambda^s + \varepsilon_{njt}$$

for each t that is a stated-preference situation, and

$$U_{njt} = \beta'x_{njt} + c_j^r + \varepsilon_{njt}$$

for each t that is a revealed-preference situation.

The model is estimated on the data from both the revealed- and stated-preference choices. Both groups of observations are "stacked" together as input to a logit estimation routine. A separate set of alternative-specific constants is estimated for the stated-preference and revealed-preference data. Importantly, the coefficients in the model are divided by a parameter $1/\lambda^s$ for the stated-preference observations. This separate scaling is not feasible in most standard logit estimation packages. However, the researcher can easily modify available codes (or her own code) to allow for this extra parameter. Hensher and Bradley (1993) show how to estimate this model on software for nested logits.

Note that, with this setup, the elements of β are estimated on both types of data. The estimates will necessarily reflect the amount of variation that each type of data contains for the attributes (that is, the elements of x). If there is little variance in the revealed-preference data, reflecting conditions in real-world markets, then the β's will be determined primarily by the stated-preference data, which contain whatever variation was built into the experiments. Insofar as the revealed-preference data contain usable variation, this information will be incorporated into the estimates.

The alternative-specific constants are estimated separately for the two types of data. This distinction allows the researcher to avoid many of the biases that stated-preference data might exhibit. For example, respondents often say that they will buy a product far more than they actually end up doing. The average probability of buying the product is captured in the alternative-specific constant for the product. If this bias is occurring, then the estimated constant for the stated-preference data will be greater than that for the revealed-preference data. When forecasting, the researcher can use the constant from the revealed-preference data, thereby grounding the forecast in a market-based reality. Similarly, the scale for the revealed-preference data (which is normalized to 1) can be used in forecasting instead of the scale from the stated-preference data, thereby incorporating correctly the real-world variance in unobserved factors.

7.3   Ranked Data

In stated-preference experiments, respondents may be asked to rank the alternatives instead of just identifying the one alternative that they would choose. This ranking can be requested in a variety of ways. The respondents can be asked to state which alternative they would choose, and then, after they have made this choice, can be asked which of the remaining alternatives they would choose, continuing through all the alternatives. Instead, respondents can simply be asked to rank the alternatives from best to worst. In any case, the data that the researcher obtains constitute a ranking of the alternatives that presumably reflects the utility that the respondent obtains from each alternative.

Ranked data can be handled in a standard logit or mixed logit model using currently available software without modification. All that is required is that the input data be constructed in a particular way, which we describe in the following text. For a probit model, the available software would need to be modified slightly to handle ranked data. However, the modification is straightforward. We consider standard and mixed logit first.

7.3.1. Standard and Mixed Logit

Under the assumptions for standard logit, the probability of any ranking of the alternatives from best to worst can be expressed as the product of logit formulas. Consider, for example, a respondent who was presented with four alternatives labeled A, B, C, and D. Suppose the person ranked the alternatives as follows: C, B, D, A, where C is the first choice. If the utility of each alternative is distributed iid extreme value (as for a logit model), then the probability of this ranking can be expressed as the logit probability of choosing alternative C from the set A, B, C, D, *times* the logit probability of choosing alternative B from the remaining alternatives A, B, D, *times* the probability of choosing alternative D from the remaining alternatives A and D.

Stated more explicitly, let $U_{nj} = \beta' x_{nj} + \varepsilon_{nj}$ for $j = A, \ldots, D$ with ε_{nj} iid extreme value. Then

Prob(ranking C, B, D, A)

$$(7.1) \quad = \frac{e^{\beta' x_{nC}}}{\sum_{j=A,B,C,D} e^{\beta' x_{nj}}} \frac{e^{\beta' x_{nB}}}{\sum_{j=A,B,D} e^{\beta' x_{nj}}} \frac{e^{\beta' x_{nD}}}{\sum_{j=A,D} e^{\beta' x_{nj}}}.$$

This simple expression for the ranking probability is an outcome of the particular form of the extreme value distribution, first shown by Luce and Suppes (1965). It does not apply in general; for example, it does not apply with probit models.

Equation (7.1) implies that the ranking of the four alternatives can be represented as being the same as three independent choices by the respondent. These three choices are called *pseudo-observations*, because each respondent's complete ranking, which constitutes an observation, is written as if it were multiple observations. In general, a ranking of J alternatives provides $J - 1$ pseudo-observations in a standard logit model. For the first pseudo-observation, all alternatives are considered available, and the dependent variable identifies the first-ranked alternative. For the second pseudo-observation, the first-ranked alternative is discarded. The remaining alternatives constitute the choice set, and the dependent variable identifies the second-ranked alternative, and so on. In creating the input file for logit estimation, the explanatory variables for each alternative are repeated $J - 1$ times, making that many pseudo-observations. The dependent variable for these pseudo-observations identifies, respectively, the first-ranked, second-ranked, and so on, alternatives. For each pseudo-observation, the alternatives that are ranked above the dependent variable for that pseudo-observation are omitted (i.e., censored out). Once the data are constructed in this way, the logit estimation proceeds as usual.

A logit model on ranked alternatives is often called an *exploded logit*, since each observation is exploded into several pseudo-observations for the purposes of estimation. Prominent applications include Beggs *et al.* (1981), Chapman and Staelin (1982), and Hausman and Ruud (1987).

A mixed logit model can be estimated on ranked data with the same explosion. Assume now that β is random with density $g(\beta \mid \theta)$, where θ are parameters of this distribution. Conditional on β, the probability of the person's ranking is a product of logits, as given in equation (7.1). The unconditional probability is then the integral of this product over the density of β:

$$
\text{Prob(ranking } C, B, A, D)
$$

$$
= \int \left(\frac{e^{\beta' x_{nC}}}{\sum_{j=A,B,C,D} e^{\beta' x_{nj}}} \frac{e^{\beta' x_{nB}}}{\sum_{j=A,B,D} e^{\beta' x_{nj}}} \frac{e^{\beta' x_{nD}}}{\sum_{j=A,D} e^{\beta' x_{nj}}} \right)
$$
$$
\times g(\beta \mid \theta) \, d\theta.
$$

The mixed logit model on ranked alternatives is estimated with regular mixed logit routines for panel data, using the input data setup as described previously for logit, where the $J - 1$ pseudo-observations for each ranking are treated as $J - 1$ choices in a panel. The mixed logit incorporates the fact that each respondent has his own coefficients and, importantly, that the respondent's coefficients affect his entire ranking, so that the pseudo-observations are correlated. A logit model on ranked data does not allow for this correlation.

7.3.2. Probit

Ranked data can also be utilized effectively in a probit model. Let the utility of the four alternatives be as just stated for a logit except that the error terms are jointly normal: $U_{nj} = \beta' x_{nj} + \varepsilon_{nj}$ for $j = A, B, C, D$, where $\varepsilon_n = \langle \varepsilon_{nA}, \ldots, \varepsilon_{nD} \rangle'$ is distributed $N(0, \Omega)$. As before, the probability of the person's ranking is Prob(ranking $C, B, D, A) = \text{Prob}(U_{nC} > U_{nB} > U_{nD} > U_{nA})$. Decomposing this joint probability into conditionals and a marginal does not help with a probit in the way that it does with logit, since the conditional probabilities do not collapse to unconditional probabilities as they do under independent errors. Another tack is taken instead. Recall that for probit models, we found that it is very convenient to work in utility differences rather than the utilities themselves. Denote $\tilde{U}_{njk} = U_{nj} - U_{nk}$, $\tilde{x}_{njk} = x_{nj} - x_{nk}$, and $\tilde{\varepsilon}_{njk} = \varepsilon_{nj} - \varepsilon_{nk}$. The probability of the ranking can then be expressed as Prob(ranking $C, B, D, A) = \text{Prob}(U_{nC} > U_{nB} > U_{nD} > U_{nA}) = \text{Prob}(\tilde{U}_{nBC} < 0, \tilde{U}_{nDB} < 0, \tilde{U}_{nAD} < 0)$.

To express this probability, we define a transformation matrix M that takes appropriate differences. The reader might want to review Section 5.6.3 on simulation of probit probabilities for one chosen alternative, which uses a similar transformation matrix. The same procedure is used for ranked data, but with a different transformation matrix.

Stack the alternatives A to D, so that utility is expressed in vector form as $U_n = V_n + \varepsilon_n$, where $\varepsilon_n \sim N(0, \Omega)$. Define the 3×4 matrix

$$
M = \begin{pmatrix} 0 & 1 & -1 & 0 \\ 0 & -1 & 0 & 1 \\ 1 & 0 & 0 & -1 \end{pmatrix}.
$$

This matrix has a row for each inequality in the argument of the probability $\text{Prob}(\tilde{U}_{nBC} < 0, \tilde{U}_{nDB} < 0, \tilde{U}_{nAD} < 0)$. Each row contains a 1 and a -1, along with zeros, where the 1 and -1 identify the alternatives that are being differenced for the inequality. With this matrix, the probability of the ranked alternatives becomes

$$
\begin{aligned}
\text{Prob(ranking } C, B, D, A) &= \text{Prob}(\tilde{U}_{nBC} < 0, \tilde{U}_{nDB} < 0, \tilde{U}_{nAD} < 0) \\
&= \text{Prob}(M U_n < 0) \\
&= \text{Prob}(M V_n + M \varepsilon_n < 0) \\
&= \text{Prob}(M \varepsilon_n < -M V_n).
\end{aligned}
$$

The error differences defined by $M \varepsilon_n$ are distributed jointly normal with zero mean and covariance $M \Omega M'$. The probability that these correlated error differences fall below $-M V_n$ is simulated by GHK in the manner given in Section 5.6.3. The procedure has been implemented by Hajivassiliou and Ruud (1994) and Schechter (2001).

7.4   Ordered Responses

In surveys, respondents are often asked to provide ratings of various kinds. Examples include:

How good a job do you think the president is doing? Check one:

1. very good job
2. good job
3. neither good nor bad
4. poor job
5. very poor job

How well do you like this book? Rate the book from 1 to 7, where 1 is the worst you have ever read (aside from *The Bridges of Madison County*, of course) and 7 is the best

       1   2   3   4   5   6   7

How likely are you to buy a new computer this year?

1. Not likely at all
2. Somewhat likely
3. Very likely

The main characteristic of these questions, from a modeling perspective, is that the potential responses are ordered. A book rating of 6 is higher than 5, which is higher than 4; and a presidential rating of "very poor" is worse than "poor," which is worse than "neither good nor bad." A standard logit model could be specified with each potential response as an alternative. However, the logit model's assumption of independent errors for each alternative is inconsistent with the fact that the alternatives are ordered: with ordered alternatives, one alternative is similar to those close to it and less similar to those further away. The ordered nature could be handled by specifying a nested logit, mixed logit, or probit model that accounts for the pattern of similarity and dissimilarily among the alternatives. For example, a probit model could be estimated with correlation among the alternatives, with the correlation between 2 and 3 being greater than that between 1 and 3, and the correlation between 1 and 2 also being greater than that between 1 and 3. However, such a specification, while it might provide fine results, does not actually fit the structure of the data. Recall that the traditional derivation for these models starts with a specification of the utility associated with each alternative. For the ratings question about the president's job, the derivation would assume that there are five utilities, one for each potential response, and that the person chooses the number 1 to 5 that has the greatest utility. While it is perhaps possible to think of the decision process in this way (and the resulting model will probably provide useful results), it is not a very natural way to think about the respondent's decision.

A more natural representation of the decision process is to think of the respondent as having some level of utility or opinion associated with the object of the question and answering the question on the basis of how great this utility is. For example, on the presidential question, the following derivation seems to better represent the decision process. Assume that the respondent has an opinion on how well the president is doing. This opinion is represented in a (unobservable) variable that we label U, where higher levels of U mean that the person thinks the president is doing a better job and lower levels mean he thinks the president is doing a poorer job. In answering the question, the person is asked to express this opinion in one of five categories: "very good job," "good job," and so on. That is, even though the person's opinion, U, can take many different levels representing various levels of liking or disliking the job the president is doing, the question allows only five possible responses. The person chooses a response on the basis of the level of his U. If U is above some cutoff, which we label k_1, the respondent chooses the answer "very good job." If U is below k_1 but above another cutoff, k_2, then he answers "good job." And so on. The decision is represented as

- "very good job" if $U > k_1$
- "good job" if $k_1 > U > k_2$
- "neither good or bad" if $k_2 > U > k_3$
- "poor job" if $k_3 > U > k_4$
- "very poor job" if $k_4 > U$.

The researcher observes some factors that relate to the respondent's opinion, such as the person's political affiliation, income, and so on.

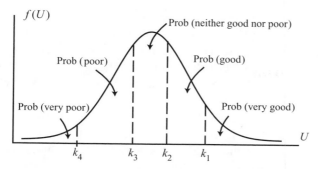

Figure 7.1. Distribution of opinion about president's job.

However, other factors that affect the person's opinion cannot be observed. Decompose U into observed and unobserved components: $U = \beta'x + \varepsilon$. As usual, the unobserved factors ε are considered random. Their distribution determines the probability for the five possible responses.

Figure 7.1 illustrates the situation. U is distributed around $\beta'x$ with the shape of the distribution following the distribution of ε. There are cutoff points for the possible responses: $k_1, \ldots, k_4$. The probability that the person answers with "very poor job" is the probability that U is less than k_4, which is the area in the left tail of the distribution. The probability that the person says "poor job" is the probability that U is above k_4, indicating that he doesn't think that the job is very poor, but is below k_3. This probability is the area between k_4 and k_3.

Once a distribution for ε is specified, the probabilities can be calculated exactly. For simplicity, assume that ε is distributed logistic, which means that the cumulative distribution of ε is $F(\varepsilon) = \exp(\varepsilon)/(1 + \exp(\varepsilon))$. The probability of the answer "very poor job" is then

$$
\begin{aligned}
\text{Prob("very poor job")} &= \text{Prob}(U < k_4) \\
&= \text{Prob}(\beta'x + \varepsilon < k_4) \\
&= \text{Prob}(\varepsilon < k_4 - \beta'x) \\
&= \frac{e^{k_4 - \beta'x}}{1 + e^{k_4 - \beta'x}}.
\end{aligned}
$$

The probability of "poor job" is

$$
\begin{aligned}
\text{Prob("poor job")} &= \text{Prob}(k_4 < U < k_3) \\
&= \text{Prob}(k_4 < \beta'x + \varepsilon < k_3) \\
&= \text{Prob}(k_4 - \beta'x < \varepsilon < k_3 - \beta'x) \\
&= \text{Prob}(\varepsilon < k_3 - \beta'x) - \text{Prob}(\varepsilon < k_4 - \beta'x) \\
&= \frac{e^{k_3 - \beta'x}}{1 + e^{k_3 - \beta'x}} - \frac{e^{k_4 - \beta'x}}{1 + e^{k_4 - \beta'x}}.
\end{aligned}
$$

Probabilities for the other answers are obtained analogously. The probabilities enter the log-likelihood function as usual, and maximization of the likelihood function provides estimates of the parameters. Note that the parameters consist of β, which gives the impact of the explanatory variables on people's opinion of the president, as well as the cutoff points $k_1, \ldots, k_4$.

The model is called *ordered logit*, since it uses the logistic distribution on ordered alternatives. Unfortunately, nested logit models have occasionally been called ordered logits; this nomenclature causes confusion and will hopefully be avoided in the future.

Note that the probabilities in the ordered logit model incorporate the binary logit formula. This similarity to binary logit is only incidental: the traditional derivation of a binary logit specifies two alternatives with utility for each, while the ordered logit model has one utility with multiple alternatives to represent the level of that utility. The similarity in formula arises from the fact that, if two random variables are iid extreme value, then their difference follows a logistic distribution. Therefore, assuming that both utilities in a binary logit are iid extreme value is equivalent to assuming that the difference in the utilities is distributed logistic, the same as the utility in the ordered logit model.

A similar model is obtained under the assumption that ε is distributed standard normal instead of logistic (Zavoina and McKelvey, 1975). The only difference arises in that the binary logit formula is replaced with the cumulative standard normal distribution. That is,

$$\text{Prob("very poor job")} = \text{Prob}(\varepsilon < k_4 - \beta'x)$$
$$= \Phi(k_4 - \beta'x)$$

and

$$\text{Prob("poor job")} = \text{Prob}(\varepsilon < k_3 - \beta'x) - \text{Prob}(\varepsilon < k_4 - \beta'x)$$
$$= \Phi(k_3 - \beta'x) - \Phi(k_4 - \beta'x),$$

where Φ is the standard cumulative normal function. This model is called *ordered probit*. Software for ordered logit and probit is available in many commercial packages.

The researcher might believe that the parameters vary randomly in the population. In that case, a mixed version of the model can be specified, as in Bhat (1999). Let the density of β be $g(\beta \mid \theta)$. Then the mixed ordered logit probabilities are simply the ordered logit probabilities integrated over the density $g(\cdot)$. For example,

$$\text{Prob("very poor job")} = \int \left(\frac{e^{k_4 - \beta'x}}{1 + e^{k_4 - \beta'x}} \right) g(\beta \mid \theta) \, d\beta$$

and

$$\text{Prob(``poor job'')} = \int \left(\frac{e^{k_3 - \beta'x}}{1 + e^{k_3 - \beta'x}} - \frac{e^{k_4 - \beta'x}}{1 + e^{k_4 - \beta'x}} \right) g(\beta \mid \theta) \, d\beta,$$

and so on. These probabilities are simulated in the same way as mixed logits, by drawing values of β from $g(\cdot)$, calculating the ordered logit probability for each draw, and averaging the results. Mixed ordered probit is derived similarly.

7.4.1. Multiple Ordered Responses

Respondents' answers to different questions are often related. For example, a person's rating of how well the president is doing is probably related to the person's rating of how well the economy is doing. The researcher might want to incorporate into the analysis the fact that the answers are related. To be concrete, suppose that respondents are asked to rate both the president and the economy on a five-point scale, like the rating given for the president. Let U be the respondent's opinion of the job the president is doing, and let W be the respondent's assessment of the economy. Each of these assessments can be decomposed into observed and unobserved factors: $U = \beta'x + \varepsilon$ and $W = \alpha'z + \mu$. Insofar as the assessments are related due to observed factors, the same variables can be included in x and z. To allow for the possibility that the assessments are related due to unobserved factors, we specify ε and μ to be jointly normal with correlation ρ (and unit variances by normalization). Let the cutoffs for U be denoted $k_1, \ldots, k_4$ as before, and the cutoffs for W be denoted $c_1, \ldots, c_4$. We want to derive the probability of each possible combination of responses to the two questions.

The probability that the person says the president is doing a "very poor job" and also that the economy is doing "very poorly" is derived as follows:

$$\begin{aligned}
&\text{Prob(President ``very poor'' and economy ``very poor'')} \\
&= \text{Prob}(U < k_4 \text{ and } W < c_4) \\
&= \text{Prob}(\varepsilon < k_4 - \beta'x \text{ and } \mu < c_4 - \alpha'z) \\
&= \text{Prob}(\varepsilon < k_4 - \beta'x) \\
&\quad \times \text{Prob}(\mu < c_4 - \alpha'z \mid \varepsilon < k_4 - \beta'x).
\end{aligned}$$

Similarly, the probability of a rating of "very poor" for the president and "good" for the economy is

$$\text{Prob(President "very poor" and economy "good")}$$
$$= \text{Prob}(U < k_4 \text{ and } c_2 < W < c_1)$$
$$= \text{Prob}(\varepsilon < k_4 - \beta'x \text{ and } c_2 - \alpha'z < \mu < c_1 - \alpha'z)$$
$$= \text{Prob}((\varepsilon < k_4 - \beta'x)$$
$$\times \text{Prob}(c_2 - \alpha'z < \mu < c_1 - \alpha'z \mid \varepsilon < k_4 - \beta'x).$$

The probabilities for other combinations are derived similarly, and generalization to more than two related questions is straightforward. The model is called multivariate (or multiresponse) ordered probit. The probabilities can be simulated by GHK in a manner similar to that described in Chapter 5. The explanation in Chapter 5 assumes that truncation of the joint normal is only on one side (since for a standard probit the probability that is being calculated is the probability that all utility differences are below zero, which is truncation from above), while the probabilities for multivariate ordered probit are truncated on two sides (as for the second probability listed earlier). However, the logic is the same, and interested readers can refer to Hajivassiliou and Ruud (1994) for an explicit treatment of GHK with two-sided truncation.

7.5   Contingent Valuation

In some surveys, respondents are asked to express their opinions or actions relative to a specific number that the interviewer states. For example, the interviewer might ask: "Consider a project that protected the fish in specific rivers in Montana. Would you be willing to spend $50 to know that the fish in these rivers are safe?" This question is sometimes followed by another question that depends on the respondent's answer to the first question. For example, if the person said "yes" to the above question, the interviewer might follow up by asking, "How about $75? Would you be willing to pay $75?" If the person answered "no" to the first question, indicating that he was not willing to pay $50, the interviewer would follow up with "Would you be willing to pay $25?"

These kinds of questions are used in environmental studies where the lack of markets for environmental quality prevent valuation of resources by revelation procedures; the papers edited by Hausman (1993) provide a review and critique of the procedure, which is often called "contingent valuation." When only one question is asked, such as whether the person is willing to pay $50, the method is called *single-bounded*, since the person's answer gives one bound on his true willingness to pay. If the person answers "yes," the researcher knows that his true willingness to pay is at least $50, but she does not know how *much* more. If the person answers "no," the researcher knows that the person's willingness to pay is less than $50. Examples of studies using single-bounded methods are Cameron and James (1987) and Cameron (1988).

When a follow-up question is asked, the method is called *double-bounded*. If the person says that he is willing to pay $50 but not $75, the researcher knows his true willingness to pay is between $50 and $75, that is, is bounded on both sides. If the person says he is not willing to pay $50 but is willing to pay $25, his willingness to pay is known to be between $25 and $50. Of course, even with a double-bounded method, some respondents' willingness to pay is only singly bounded, such as that of a person who says he is willing to pay $50 and also willing to pay $75. Examples of this approach include Hanemann *et al.* (1991), Cameron and Quiggin (1994), and Cai *et al.* (1998).

The figure that is used as the prompt (i.e., the $50 in our example) is varied over respondents. The answers from a sample of people are then used to estimate the distribution of willingness to pay. The estimation procedure is closely related to that just described for ordered logits and probits, except that the cutoff points are given by the questionnaire design rather than estimated as parameters. We describe the procedure as follows.

Let W_n represent the true willingness to pay of person n. W_n varies over people with distribution $f(W \mid \theta)$, where θ are the parameters of the distribution, such as the mean and variance. The researcher's goal is to estimate these population parameters. Suppose the researcher designs a questionnaire with a single-bounded approach, giving a different prompt (or reference value) for different respondents. Denote the prompt that is given to person n as k_n. The person answers the question with a "yes" if $W_n > k_n$ and "no" otherwise. The researcher assumes that W_n is distributed normally in the population with mean $\bar{W}$ and variance σ^2.

The probability of "yes" is $\text{Prob}(W_n > k_n) = 1 - \text{Prob}(W_n < k_n) = 1 - \Phi((k_n - \bar{W})/\sigma)$, and the probability of "no" is $\Phi((k_n - \bar{W})/\sigma)$, where $\Phi(\cdot)$ is the standard cumulative normal function. The log-likelihood function is then $\sum_n y_n \ln(1 - \Phi((k_n - \bar{W})/\sigma)) + (1 - y_n) \ln (\Phi((k_n - \bar{W})/\sigma))$, where $y_n = 1$ if person n said "yes" and 0 otherwise. Maximizing this function provides estimates of $\bar{W}$ and σ.

A similar procedure is used if the researcher designs a double-bounded questionnaire. Let the prompt for the second question be k_{nu} if the person answered "yes" to the first question, where $k_{nu} > k_n$, and let k_{nl} be the second prompt if the person initially answered "no," where $k_{nl} < k_n$. There are four possible sequences of answers to the two questions. The

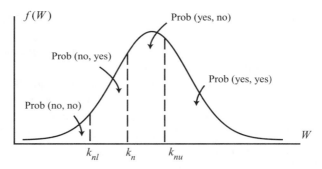

Figure 7.2. Distribution of willingness to pay.

probabilities for these sequences are illustrated in Figure 7.2 and given below:

- "no" then "no": $P = \text{Prob}(W_n < k_{nl}) = \Phi((k_{nl} - \bar{W})/\sigma)$
- "no" then "yes": $P = \text{Prob}(k_{nl} < W_n < k_n) = \Phi((k_n - \bar{W})/\sigma) - \Phi((k_{nl} - \bar{W})/\sigma)$
- "yes" then "no": $P = \text{Prob}(k_n < W_n < k_{nu}) = \Phi((k_{nu} - \bar{W})/\sigma) - \Phi((k_n - \bar{W})/\sigma)$
- "yes" then "yes": $P = \text{Prob}(W_n > k_{nu}) = 1 - \Phi((k_{nu} - \bar{W})/\sigma)$.

These probabilities enter the log-likelihood function, which is maximized to obtain estimates of $\bar{W}$ and σ. Other distributions can of course be used instead of normal. Lognormal is attractive if the researcher assumes that all people have a positive willingness to pay. Or the researcher might specify a distribution that has a mass at zero to represent the share of people who are not willing to pay anything, and a lognormal for the remaining share. Generalization to multiple dimensions is straightforward, to reflect, for example, that people's willingness to pay for one environmental package might also be related to their willingness to pay for another. As with multiresponse ordered probit, the GHK simulator comes in handy when the multiple values are assumed to be distributed jointly normal.

7.6   Mixed Models

We have discussed mixed logit and mixed ordered logit. Of course, mixed models of all kinds can be developed using the same logic. Any model whose probabilities can be written as a function of parameters can also be mixed by allowing the parameters to be random and integrating the function over the distribution of parameters (Greene, 2001). The probability is simulated by drawing from the distribution, calculating the function for each draw, and averaging the results. We give two examples in the following section, but researchers will inevitably develop others that meet the needs of their particular projects, such as Bhat's (1999) use of mixed ordered logit.

7.6.1. Mixed Nested Logit

The mixed logit model does not exhibit the independence from irrelevant alteratives property as logit does, and can approximate any substitution pattern by appropriate specification of variables and mixing distribution. This fact has led some people to feel that there is no further need for nested logit models. A mixed logit can be estimated that provides correlation–substitution patterns analogous to those of a nested logit. For example, consider a nested logit with two nests of alternatives labeled A and B. Provided the log-sum coefficients are between 0 and 1, substitution within each nest is greater than substitution across nests. This substitution pattern can be represented in a mixed logit model by specifying a dummy variable for each nest and allowing the coefficients on the dummies to be random (constraining, for identification purposes, the means to be zero if a full set of alternative-specific constants are included, and the two variances to be the same).

While a mixed logit can be specified in this way, doing so misses the point of simulation. As discussed in Chapter 1, simulation is used as a way to approximate integrals when a closed form does not exist. Analytic integration is always more accurate than simulation and should be used whenever feasible, unless there is a compelling reason to the contrary. Using a mixed logit to represent the substitution patterns of a nested logit, while feasible, replaces the closed-form integral of the nested logit with an integral that needs to be simulated. From a numerical perspective, this replacement can only reduce accuracy. The only possible advantages of mixed logit in this context are that (1) it might be easier for the researcher to test numerous nesting structures, including overlapping nests, within a mixed logit than a nested logit, and (2) the researcher might have specified other coefficients to be random, so that a mixed logit is already being used.

The second reason suggests a mixed nested logit. Suppose the researcher believes that some of the coefficients in the model are random and also that, conditional on these coefficients, the unobserved factors are correlated over alternatives in a way that can be represented by a nested logit. A mixed nested logit model can be specified to represent this situation. Conditional on the coefficients that enter utility, the choice probabilities are nested logit, which is a closed form and can be calculated exactly. The unconditional probability is the nested logit formula integrated over the distribution of the the random coefficients. Software for mixed logit can be modified by simply locating the logit formula within the code and changing it to the appropriate nested logit formula. Experience indicates that maximizing the likelihood function for unmixed nested logits is often difficult numerically, and mixing the model will compound this difficulty. Hierarchical Bayes estimation (Chapter 12) could prove particularly useful in this situation, since it does not involve maximizing the likelihood function.

7.6.2. Mixed Probit

A constraint of probit models, and in fact their defining characteristic, is that all random terms enter utility linearly and are randomly distributed in such a way that utility itself is normally distributed. This constraint can be removed by specifying a *mixed probit*. Suppose that some random terms enter nonlinearly or are not randomly distributed, but that *conditional* on these, utility is normally distributed. For example, a price coefficient might be lognormal to assure that it is negative for all people, and yet all other coefficients be either fixed or normal, and the final error terms jointly normal. A mixed probit model is appropriate for this specification. Conditional on the price coefficient, the choice probabilities follow the standard probit formula. The unconditional probabilities are the integral of this probit formula over the distribution of the price coefficient. Two layers of simulation are used to approximate the probabilities: (1) a draw of the price coefficient is taken, and (2) for this draw, the GHK or other probit simulator is used to approximate the conditional choice probability. This process is repeated many times, and the results are averaged.

Long run times can be expected for the mixed probit model, since the GHK simulator is calculated for each draw of the price coefficient. However, the number of draws in the GHK simulator can be reduced, since the averaging over draws of the price coefficient reduces the variance generated by the GHK simulator. In principle, the GHK simulator can be based on only one draw for each draw of the price coefficient. In practice, it may be advisable to use more than one draw, but far fewer than would be used in an unmixed probit.

The mixed probit model provides a way for the researcher to avoid some of the practical difficulties that can arise with a mixed logit model. For example, to represent pure heteroskedasticity (i.e., a different variance for each alternative's utility) or a fixed correlation pattern among alternatives (i.e., a covariance matrix that does not depend on the variables), it can often be easier to estimate a probit instead of specifying numerous error components within a mixed logit. As emphasized by Ben-Akiva *et al.* (2001), specification of covariance and heteroskedasticity can be more complex in a mixed logit model than in a probit, because iid extreme value terms are necessarily added to whatever other random elements the researcher specifies. Probit is a more natural specification in these situations. However, if the researcher wants to include some nonnormal random terms, an unmixed probit cannot be used. Mixing the probit allows the researcher to include nonnormal terms while still maintaining the simplicity of probit's representation of fixed covariance for additive errors. Conceptually, the specification and estimation procedure are straightforward. The cost comes only in extra computation time, which becomes less relevant as computers get faster.

7.7   Dynamic Optimization

In previous chapters we examined certain types of dynamics, by which choices in one period affect choices in another period. For example, we described how a lagged dependent variable can be included to capture inertia or variety-seeking behavior. These discussions suggest a much wider realm of dynamics than we had actually considered. In particular: if past choices affect current choices, then current choices affect future choices, and a decision maker who is aware of this fact will take these future effects into consideration. A link from the past to the present necessarily implies a link from the present to the future.

In many situations, the choices that a person makes at one point in his life have a profound influence on the options that are available to him in the future. Going to college, while expensive and sometimes irritating, enhances future job possibilities. Saving money now allows a person to buy things later that he otherwise would not be able to afford. Going to the gym today means that we can skip going tomorrow. Most of us take future effects like these into consideration when choosing among current alternatives.

The question is: how can behavior such as this be represented in discrete choice models? In general the situation can be described as follows. A person makes a series of choices over time. The alternative that is chosen in one period affects the attributes and availability of alternatives in the future. Sometimes the future effects are not fully known, or depend on factors that have not yet transpired (such as the future state of the economy). However, the person knows that he will, in the future, maximize utility among the alternatives that are available at that time under the conditions that prevail at that time. This knowledge enables him to choose the alternative in the current period that maximizes his expected utility over the current and future periods. The researcher recognizes that the decision maker acts in this way, but does not observe everything that the decision maker considers in the current and future periods. As usual, the choice probability is an integral of the decision maker's behavior over all possible values of the factors that the researcher does not observe.

In this section we specify models in which the future consequences of current decisions are incorporated. For these models, we will assume that the decision maker is fully rational in the sense that he optimizes perfectly in each time period given the information that is available to him at that point in time and given that he knows he will act optimally in the future when future information is revealed. The procedures for modeling these decisions were first developed for various applications by, for example, Wolpin (1984) on women's fertility, Pakes (1986) on patent options, Wolpin (1987) on job search, Rust (1987) on engine replacement, Berkovec and Stern (1991) on retirement, and others. Eckstein and Wolpin (1989) provide an excellent survey of these early contributions. The thrust of more recent work has primarily been toward solving some of the computational difficulties that can arise in these models, as discussed below.

Before embarking on this endeavor, it is important to keep the concept of rationality in perspective. A model of rational decision making over time does not necessarily represent behavior more accurately than a model of myopic behavior, where the decision maker ignores future consequences. In fact, the truth in a given situation might lie between these two extremes: decision makers might be acting in ways that are neither completely myopic nor completely rational. As we will see, the truly optimizing behavior is very complex. People might engage in behavior that is only approximately optimal simply because they (we) can't figure out the truly optimal way to proceed. Viewed in another light, one could argue that people always optimize when the realm of optimization is broadened sufficiently. For example, rules of thumb or other behavior that seem only to approximate optimality may actually turn out to be optimal when the costs of optimization are considered.

The concepts and procedures that are developed to examine optimizing behavior carry over, in modified form, to other types of behavior that recognize future effects of current choices. Furthermore, the researcher can often test alternative behavioral representations. Myopic behavior nearly always appears as a testable restriction on a fully rational model, namely, a zero coefficient for the variable that captures future effects.

Sometimes, the standard rational model is a restriction on a supposedly nonrational one. For example, O'Donoghue and Rabin (1999), among others, argue that people are time-inconsistent: when it is Monday, we weigh the benefits and costs that will come on, say, Wednesday only marginally more than those that will arrive on Thursday, and yet when Wednesday actually arrives, we weigh Wednesday's (today's) benefits and costs far more than Thursday's. Essentially, we have a bias for the present. The standard rational model, where the same discount rate is used between any two periods independent of whether the person is in one of the periods, constitutes a restriction on the time-inconsistent model.

The concepts in this area of analysis are more straightforward than the notation. To develop the concepts with a minimum of notation, we will start with a two-period model in which the decision maker knows the exact effect of first-period choices on the second-period alternatives and utilities. We will then expand the model to more periods and to situations where the decision maker faces uncertainty about future effects.

7.7.1. Two Periods, No Uncertainty about Future Effects

To make the explication concrete, consider a high school student's choice of whether or not to go to college. The choice can be examined in the context of two periods: the college years and the post-college years. In the first period, the student either goes to college or not. Even though these are called the college years, the student need not go to college but can take a job instead. In the second period the student chooses among the jobs that are available to him at that time. Going to college during the college years means less income during that period but better job options in the post-college years. U_{1C} is the utility that the student obtains in period 1 from going to college, and U_{1W} is the utility he obtains in the first period if he works in the first period instead of going to college. If the student were myopic, he would choose college only if $U_{1C} > U_{1W}$. However, we assume that he is not myopic. For the second period, let J denote the set of all possible jobs. The utility of job j in period 2 is U_{2j}^{C} if the student went to college and U_{2j}^{W} if he worked in the first period. The utility from a job depends on the wage that the person is paid as well as other factors. For many jobs, people with a college degree are paid higher wages and granted greater autonomy and responsibility. For these jobs, $U_{2j}^{C} > U_{2j}^{W}$. However, working in the first period provides on-the-job experience that commands higher wages and responsibility than a college degree for some jobs; for these, $U_{2j}^{W} > U_{2j}^{C}$.

A job not being available is represented as having a utility of negative infinity. For example, if job j is available only to college graduates, then $U_{2j}^W = -\infty$.

How will the high school student decide whether to go to college? We assume for now that the student knows U_{2j}^C and U_{2j}^W for all $j \in J$ when deciding whether to go to college in the first period. That is, the student has perfect knowledge of his future options under whatever choice he makes in the first period. We will later consider how the decision process changes when the student is uncertain about these future utilities. The student knows that when the second period arrives he will choose the job that provides the greatest utility. That is, he knows in the first period that the utility that he will obtain in the second period if he chooses college in the first period is the maximum of U_{2j}^C over all possible jobs. We label this utility as $U_2^C = \max_j(U_{2j}^C)$. The student therefore realizes that, if he chooses college in the first period, his total utility over both periods will be

$$
\begin{aligned}
\mathrm{TU}_C &= U_{1C} + \lambda U_2^C \\
&= U_{1C} + \lambda \max_j(U_{2j}^C),
\end{aligned}
$$

where λ reflects the relative weighting of the two periods' utilities in the student's decision process. Given the way we have defined time periods, λ incorporates the relative time spans of each period as well as the traditional discounting of future utility relative to current utility. Thus, λ can exceed one, even with discounting, if the second period represents say forty years while the first period is four years. Myopic behavior is represented as $\lambda = 0$.

The same logic is applied to the option of working in the first period instead of going to school. The student knows that he will choose the job that offers the greatest utility, so that $U_2^W = \max_j(U_{2j}^W)$ and the total utility over both period from choosing to work in the first period is

$$
\begin{aligned}
\mathrm{TU}_W &= U_{1W} + \lambda U_2^W \\
&= U_{1W} + \lambda \max_j(U_{2j}^W).
\end{aligned}
$$

The student chooses college if $\mathrm{TU}_C > \mathrm{TU}_W$ and otherwise chooses to work in the first period.

This completes the description of the decision maker's behavior. We now turn to the researcher. As always, the researcher observes only some of the factors that affect the student's utility. Each utility in each period is decomposed into an observed and unobserved component:

$$
\begin{aligned}
U_{1C} &= V_{1C} + \varepsilon_{1C}, \\
U_{1W} &= V_{1W} + \varepsilon_{1W}
\end{aligned}
$$

and

$$U_{2j}^C = V_{2j}^C + \varepsilon_{2j}^C,$$
$$U_{2j}^W = V_{2j}^W + \varepsilon_{2j}^W$$

for all $j \in J$. Collect the unobserved components into vector $\varepsilon = \langle \varepsilon_{1C}, \varepsilon_{1W}, \varepsilon_{2j}^C, \varepsilon_{2j}^W, \forall j \rangle$, and denote the density of these terms as $f(\varepsilon)$. The probability of the student choosing college is

$$\begin{aligned}
P_C &= \text{Prob}(\text{TU}_C > \text{TU}_W) \\
&= \text{Prob}\big[U_{1C} + \max_j(U_{2j}^C) > U_{1W} + \max_j(U_{2j}^W)\big] \\
&= \text{Prob}\big[V_{1C} + \varepsilon_{1C} + \max_j(V_{2j}^C + \varepsilon_{2j}^C) \\
&\qquad > V_{1W} + \varepsilon_{1W} + \max_j(V_{2j}^W + \varepsilon_{2j}^W)\big] \\
&= \int I\big[V_{1C} + \varepsilon_{1C} + \max_j(V_{2j}^C + \varepsilon_{2j}^C) \\
&\qquad > V_{1W} + \varepsilon_{1W} + \max_j(V_{2j}^W + \varepsilon_{2j}^W)\big] f(\varepsilon)\, d\varepsilon
\end{aligned}$$

where $I[\cdot]$ is an indicator of whether the statement in brackets is true.

The integral can be approximated through simulation. For an accept–reject simulator:

1. Take a draw from $f(\varepsilon)$, with its components labeled ε_{1C}^r, $\varepsilon_{2j}^{Cr}, \ldots$.
2. Calculate $U_{2j}^C = V_{2j}^C + \varepsilon_{2j}^{Cr}$ for all j, determine the highest one, and label it U_2^{Cr}. Similarly, calculate U_2^{Wr}.
3. Calculate the total utilities as $\text{TU}_C^r = V_{1C}^r + \varepsilon_{1C}^r + \lambda U_2^{Cr}$, and similarly for TU_W^r.
4. Determine whether $\text{TU}_C^r > \text{TU}_W^r$. If so, set $I^r = 1$. Otherwise, let $I^r = 0$.
5. Repeat steps 1–4 R times. The simulated probability of choosing college is $\tilde{P}_C = \sum_r I^r / R$.

Convenient error partitioning (as explained in Section 1.2) can be utilized to obtain a smooth and more accurate simulator than accept–reject, provided that the integral over the first-period errors has a closed form conditional on the second-period errors. Suppose for example that ε_{1C} and ε_{1W} are iid extreme value. Label the second-period errors collectively as ε_2 with any density $g(\varepsilon_2)$. Conditional on the second-period errors, the probability of the student going to college is given by a standard logit model with an extra explanatory variable that captures the future effect of the current choice. That is,

$$P_C(\varepsilon_2) = \frac{e^{V_{1C} + \lambda U_2^C(\varepsilon_2)}}{e^{V_{1C} + \lambda U_2^C(\varepsilon_2)} + e^{V_{1W} + \lambda U_2^W(\varepsilon_2)}},$$

where $U_2^C(\varepsilon_2)$ is calculated from the second-period errors as $U_2^C(\varepsilon_2) = \max_j(V_{2j}^C + \varepsilon_{2j}^C)$, and similarly for $U_2^W(\varepsilon_2)$. The unconditional probability is then the integral of this logit formula over all possible values of the second-period errors:

$$P_C = \int P_C(\varepsilon_2)g(\varepsilon_2)\,d\varepsilon_2.$$

The probability is simulated as follows: (1) Take a draw from density $g(\cdot)$ and label it ε_2^r . (2) Using this draw of the second-period errors, calculate the utility that would be obtained from each possible job if the person went to college. That is, calculate $U_{2j}^{Cr} = V_{2j}^C + \varepsilon_{2j}^{Cr}$ for all j. (3) Determine the maximum of these utilities, and label it $\check{U}_2^{Cr}$. This is the utility that the person would obtain in the second period if he went to college in the first period, based on this draw of the second-period errors. (4)–(5) Similarly, calculate $U_{2j}^{Wr}\ \forall j$, and then determine the maximum $\check{U}_2^{Wr}$. (6) Calculate the conditional choice probability for this draw as

$$P_C^r = \frac{e^{V_{1C}+\lambda \check{U}_2^{Cr}}}{e^{V_{1C}+\lambda \check{U}_2^{Cr}} + e^{V_{1W}+\lambda \check{U}_2^{Wr}}}.$$

(7) Repeat steps 1–6 many times, labeled $r = 1, \ldots, R$. (8) The simulated probability is $\tilde{P}_C = \sum_r P_C^r/R$.

If the second-period errors are also iid extreme value, then the probability of taking a particular job in the second period is standard logit. The probability of going to college and taking job j is

$$P_{Cj} = \left(\int \left[\frac{e^{V_{1C}+\lambda U_2^C(\varepsilon_2)}}{e^{V_{1C}+\lambda U_2^C(\varepsilon_2)} + e^{V_{1W}+\lambda U_2^W(\varepsilon_2)}}\right] g(\varepsilon_2)d\varepsilon_2\right)\left(\frac{e^{V_{2j}^C}}{\sum_k e^{V_{2k}^C}}\right).$$

The choice probabilities for the first period are simulated by taking draws of the second-period errors, as just described, with $g(\cdot)$ being the extreme value distribution. However, the probabilities for the second period are calculated exactly. The draws of the second-period errors are used only in calculating the first-period probabilities where they do not integrate out in closed form. The second-period errors integrate out of the second-period probabilities in closed form, which is used to calculate the second-period probabilities exactly. Application to other distributions that allow correlation over alternatives, such as GEV or normal, is straightforward. Allowing the errors to be correlated over time can be accomplished with a joint normal distribution and simulation of both periods' probabilities.

7.7.2. Multiple Periods

We first expand to three periods and then generalize to any number of periods. The model of college choice can be extended by considering retirement options. When a person reaches retirement age, there are usually several options available. He can continue working full time, or work part time and spend part of his retirement funds, or retire fully and collect social security and perhaps a pension. The person's income under these alternatives depends largely on the job that the person has held and the retirement plan that the job provided. Three periods are sufficient to capture the decision process. The person goes to college or not in the first period, chooses a job in the second period, and chooses among the available retirement-age options in the third period. The high school student knows, when deciding whether to go to college, that this decision will affect his job opportunities, which in turn will affect his retirement options. (This foreknowledge is starting to seem like a mighty big burden for a high school student.)

The set of retirement-age alternatives is labeled S, and its elements indexed by s. In the third period, the utility that the person obtains from alternative s if he went to college in the first period and had job j in the second period is U_{3s}^{Cj}. Conditional on these previous choices, the person chooses option s if $U_{3s}^{Cj} > U_{3t}^{Cj}$ for all $s \neq t$ and $s, t \in S$. Similar notation and behavior apply conditional on other choices in the first and second periods.

In the second period, the person recognizes that his job choice will affect his retirement-age options. He knows he will maximize among the available options when retirement age arrives. Suppose he chose college in the first period. In the second period, he knows that the utility he will obtain in the third period if he chooses job j is $\max_s U_{3s}^{Cj}$. The total utility of choosing job j in the second period, given that he chose college in the first period, is therefore $\mathrm{TU}_j^C = U_{2j}^C + \theta \max_s U_{3s}^{Cj}$, where θ weights period three relative to period two. He chooses job j if $\mathrm{TU}_j^C > \mathrm{TU}_k^C$ for all $k \neq j$ and $j, k \in J$. Similar notation and behavior occur if he chose to work in the first period.

Consider now the first period. He knows that, if he chooses college, he will choose the job that maximizes his utility from jobs conditional on going to college, and then will choose the retirement-age option that maximizes his utility conditional on that chosen job. The total utility from college is

$$\mathrm{TU}_C = U_{1c} + \lambda \max_j \mathrm{TU}_j^C$$
$$= U_{1c} + \lambda \max_j \left(U_{2j}^C + \theta \max_s U_{3s}^{Cj} \right).$$

This expression is similar to that in the two-period model except that it includes an additional layer of maximization: the maximization for the third period is contained in each maximization for the second period. A similar expression gives the total utility of working in the first period, TU_W. The person chooses college if $TU_C > TU_W$.

This completes the description of the person's behavior. The researcher observes a portion of each utility function: U_{1C}, U_{1W}, U_{2j}^C, and $U_{2j}^W \; \forall j \in J$, and U_{3s}^{Cj} and $U_{3s}^{Wj} \; \forall s \in S$, $j \in J$. The unobserved portions are collectively labeled by the vector ε with density $f(\varepsilon)$. The probability that the person chooses college is

$$P_C = \int I(\varepsilon) f(\varepsilon) \, d\varepsilon,$$

where

$$I(\varepsilon) = 1$$

if

$$V_{1C} + \varepsilon_{1C} + \lambda \max_j \left(V_{2j}^C + \varepsilon_{2j}^C + \theta \max_s \left(V_{3s}^{Cj} + \varepsilon_{3s}^{Cj} \right) \right)$$
$$> V_{1W} + \varepsilon_{1W} + \lambda \max_j \left(V_{2j}^W + \varepsilon_{2j}^W + \theta \max_s \left(V_{3s}^{Wj} + \varepsilon_{3s}^{Wj} \right) \right).$$

This expression is the same as in the two-period model except that now the term inside the indicator function has an extra level of maximization. An accept–reject simulator is obtained: (1) draw from $f(\varepsilon)$; (2) calculate the third-period utility U_{3s}^{Cj} for each s; (3) identify the maximum over s; (4) calculate TU_{2j}^C with this maximum; (5) repeat steps (2)–(5) for each j, and identify the maximum of TU_{2j}^C over j; (6) calculate TU_C using this maximum; (7) repeat steps (2)–(6) for TU_W; (8) determine whether $TU_C > TU_W$, and set $I = 1$ if it is; (9) repeat steps (1)–(8) many times, and average the results. Convenient error partitioning can also be used. For example if all errors are iid extreme value, then the first-period choice probabilities, conditional on draws of the second- and third-period errors, are logit; the second-period probabilities, conditional on the third-period errors, are logit; and the third-period probabilities are logit.

We can now generalize these concepts and introduce some widely used terminology. Note that the analysis of the person's behavior and the simulation of the choice probabilities by the researcher start with the last period and work backward in time to the first period. This process is called backwards recursion. Suppose there are J alternatives in each of T equal-length time periods. Let a sequence of choices up to period t be denoted $\{i_1, i_2, \ldots, i_t\}$. The utility that the person obtains in period t from alternative j is $U_{tj}(i_1, i_2, \ldots, i_{t-1})$, which depends on all previous choices. If the person chooses alternative j in period t, he will obtain this utility plus the future utility of choices conditioned on this choice. The total utility (current and future) that the person obtains from choosing alternative j in period t is $TU_{tj}(i_1, i_2, \ldots, i_{t-1})$. He chooses the alternative in the current period that provides the greatest total utility. Therefore the total utility he receives from his optimal choice in period t is $TU_t(i_1, i_2, \ldots, i_{t-1}) = \max_j TU_{tj}(i_1, i_2, \ldots, i_{t-1})$. This total utility from the optimal choice at time t, TU_t, is called the valuation function at time t.

The person chooses optimally in the current period with knowledge that he will choose optimally in the future. This fact establishes a convenient relation between the valuation function in successive periods. In particular,

$$TU_t(i_1, \ldots, i_{t-1}) = \max_j[U_{jt}(i_1, \ldots, i_{t-1}) + \delta TU_{t+1}(i_1, \ldots, i_t = j)],$$

where δ is a parameter that discounts the future. TU_{t+1} on the right-hand side is the total utility that the person will obtain from period $t+1$ onward if he chooses alternative j in period t (i.e., if $i_t = j$). The equation states that the total utility that the person obtains from optimizing behavior from period t onward, given previous choices, is the maximum over j of the utility from j in period t plus the discounted total utility from optimizing behavior from period $t+1$ onward conditional on choosing j in period t. This relation is Bellman's equation (1957) applied to discrete choice with perfect information.

$TU_{tj}(i_1, \ldots, i_{t-1})$ is sometimes called the conditional valuation function, conditional on choosing alternative j in period t. A Bellman equation also operates for this term:

$$\begin{aligned} TU_{tj}(i_1, \ldots, i_{t-1}) &= U_{jt}(i_1, \ldots, i_{t-1}) \\ &+ \delta \max_k[TU_{t+1,k}(i_1, \ldots, i_t = j)]. \end{aligned}$$

Since by definition $TU_t(i_1, \ldots, i_{t-1}) = \max_j[TU_{tj}(i_1, \ldots, i_{t-1})]$, the Bellman equation in terms of the conditional valuation function is equivalent to that in terms of the unconditional valuation function.

If T is finite, the Bellman equation can be applied with backward recursion to calculate TU_{tj} for each time period. At $t = T$, there is no future time period, and so $TU_{Tj}(i_1, \ldots, i_{T-1}) = U_{Tj}(i_1, \ldots, i_{T-1})$. Then $TU_{T-1,j}(i_1, \ldots, i_{T-2})$ is calculated from $TU_{Tj}(i_1, \ldots, i_{T-1})$ using Bellman's equation, and so on forward to $t = 1$. Note that $U_{tj}(i_1, \ldots, i_{t-1})$ must be calculated for each t, each j, and, importantly, each possible sequence of past choices, $i_1, \ldots, i_{t-1}$. With J alternatives in T time periods, the recursion requires calculation of $(J^T)T$ utilities (that is, J^T possible sequences of choices, with each sequence containing T one-period utilities). To simulate the probabilities, the researcher must calculate these utilities for each draw of unobserved factors. And these probabilities must be simulated for each value of the parameters in the numerical search for the estimates. This huge computational burden is called the *curse of dimensionality* and is the main stumbling block to application of the procedures with more than a few time periods and/or alternatives. We discuss in the next subsection procedures that have been suggested to avoid or mitigate this curse, after showing that the curse is even greater when uncertainty is considered.

7.7.3. Uncertainty about Future Effects

In the analysis so far we have assumed that the decision maker knows the utility for each alternative in each future time period and how this utility is affected by prior choices. Usually, the decision maker does not possess such foreknowledge. A degree of uncertainty shrouds the future effects of current choices.

The behavioral model can be adapted to incorporate uncertainty. For simplicity, return to the two-period model for our high school student. In the first period, the student does not know for sure the second-period utilities, U_{2j}^C and $U_{2j}^W \ \forall j$. For example, the student does not know, before going to college, how strong the economy, and hence his job possibilities, will be when he graduates. These utilities can be expressed as functions of unknown factors $U_{2j}^C(e)$, where e refers collectively to all factors in period two that are unknown in period one. These unknown factors will become known (that is, will be revealed) when the student reaches the second period, but are unknown to the person in the first period. The student has a subjective distribution on e that reflects the likelihood that he ascribes to the unknown factors taking a particular realization in the second period. This density is labeled $g(e)$. He knows that, whatever realization of e actually occurs, he will, in the second period, choose the job that gives him the maximum utility. That is, he will receive utility $\max_j U_{2j}^C(e)$ in the second period if he chooses college in the first period and the unknown factors end up being e. In the first period, when evaluating whether to go to college, he takes the expectation of this future utility over all possible realizations of the unknown factors, using his subjective distribution over these realizations. The expected utility that he will obtain in the second period if he chooses college in the first period is therefore $\int [\max_j U_{2j}^C(e)] g(e) \, de$. The total expected utility from choosing college in the first period is then

$$\text{TEU}_C = U_{1C} + \lambda \int \left[\max_j U_{2j}^C(e)\right] g(e)\, de.$$

TEU_W is defined similarly. The person chooses college if $\text{TEU}_C > \text{TEU}_W$. In the second period, the unknown factors become known, and the person chooses job j if he had chosen college if $U_{2j}^C(e^*) > U_{2k}^C(e^*)$ for all $k \neq j$, where e^* is the realization that actually occurred.

Turning to the researcher, we have an extra complication introduced by $g(e)$, the decision maker's subjective distribution for unknown factors. In addition to not knowing utilities in their entirety, the researcher has only partial knowledge of the decision maker's subjective probability $g(e)$. This lack of information is usually represented through parameterization. The researcher specifies a density, labeled $h(e \mid \theta)$, that depends on unknown parameters θ. The researcher then assumes that the person's subjective density is the specified density evaluated at the true parameters θ^*. That is, the researcher assumes $h(e \mid \theta^*) = g(e)$. Stated more persuasively and accurately: the true parameters are, by definition, the parameters for which the researcher's specified density $h(e \mid \theta)$ becomes the density $g(e)$ that the person actually used. With a sufficiently flexible h, any g can be represented as h evaluated at some parameters, which are called the true parameters. These parameters are estimated along with the parameters that enter utility. (Other ways of representing the researcher's lack of knowledge about $g(e)$ can be specified; however, they are generally more complex.)

Utilities are decomposed into their observed and unobserved portions, with the unobserved portions collectively called ε with density $f(\varepsilon)$. The probability that the person goes to college is

$$
\begin{aligned}
P_C &= \text{Prob}(\text{TEU}_C > \text{TEU}_W) \\
&= \int \left[I\left(V_{1c} + \varepsilon_{1C} + \lambda \int \left\{\max_j \left(V_{2j}^C(e) + \varepsilon_{2j}^C(e)\right)\right\} h(e \mid \theta)\, de \right) \right] \\
&\quad \times f(\varepsilon)\, d\varepsilon.
\end{aligned}
$$

The probability can be approximated by simulating the inside integral within the simulation of the outside integral: (1) Take a draw of ε. (2a) Take a draw of e from $h(e \mid \theta)$. (2b) Using this draw, calculate the term in braces. (2c) Repeat steps (2a–b) many times, and average the results. (3) Using the value from (2c), calculate the quantity in square brackets. (4) Repeat steps (1)–(3) many times, and average the results. As the reader can see, the curse of dimensionality grows worse.

Several authors have suggested ways to reduce the computational burden. Keane and Wolpin (1994) calculate the valuation function at selected realizations of the unknown factors and past choices; they then approximate the valuation function at other realizations and past choices through interpolating from the calculated valuations. Rust (1997) suggests simulating future paths and using the average over these simulated paths as an approximation in the valuation function. Hotz and Miller (1993) and Hotz *et al.* (1993) show that there is a correspondence between the valuation function in each time period and the choice probabilities in future periods. This correspondence allows the valuation functions to be calculated with these probabilities instead of backward recursion.

Each of these procedures has limitations and is applicable only in certain situations, which the authors themselves describe. As Rust (1994) has observed, it is unlikely that a general-purpose breakthrough will arise that makes estimation simple for all forms of dynamic optimization models. Inevitably the researcher will need to make trade-offs in specifying the model to assure feasibility, and the most appropriate specification and estimation method will depend on the particulars of the choice process and the goals of the research. In this regard, I have found that two simplifications are very powerful in that they often provide a large gain in computational feasibility for a relatively small loss (and sometimes a gain) in content.

The first suggestion is for the researcher to consider ways to capture the nature of the choice situation with as few time periods as possible. Sometimes, in fact usually, time periods will need to be defined not by the standard markers, such as the year or month, but rather in a way that is more structural with respect to the decision process. For example, for the high school student deciding whether to go to college, it might seem natural to say that he makes a choice each year among the jobs and schooling options that are available in that year, given his past choices. Indeed, this statement is true: the student does indeed make annual (or even monthly, weekly, daily) choices. However, such a model would clearly face the curse of dimensionality. In contrast, the specification that we discussed earlier involves only two time periods, or three if retirement is considered. Estimation is quite feasible for this specification. In fact, the two-period model might be more accurate than an annual model: students deciding on college probably think in terms of the college years and their post-college options, rather than trying to anticipate their future choices in each future year. McFadden and Train (1996) provide an example of how a dynamic optimization model with only a few well-considered periods can accurately capture the nature of the choice situation.

A second powerful simplification was first noted by Rust (1987). Suppose that the factors that the decision maker does not observe beforehand are also the factors that the researcher does not observe (either before or after), and that these factors are thought by the decision maker to be iid extreme value. Under this admittedly restrictive assumption, the choice probabilities take a closed form that is easy to calculate. The result can be readily derived for our model of college choice. Assume that the student, when in the first period, decomposes second-period utility into a known and unknown part, e.g., $U_{2j}^C(e) = V_{2j}^C + e_{2j}^C$, and assumes that e_{2j}^C follows an extreme value distribution independent of all else. This unknown factor becomes known to the student in the second period, so that second-period choice entails maximization over known $U_{2j}^C \forall j$. However, in the first period it is unknown. Recall from Section 3.5 that the expected maximum of utilities that are iid extreme value takes the familiar log-sum formula. In our context, this result means that

$$E\left(\max_j \left(V_{2j}^C + \varepsilon_{2j}^C\right)\right) = \alpha \ln\left(\sum_j e^{V_{2j}^C}\right),$$

which we can label LS_2^C. LS_2^W is derived similarly. The person chooses college if then

$$TEU_C > TEU_W,$$
$$U_{1C} + \lambda\, LS_2^C > U_{1W} + \lambda\, LS_2^W.$$

Note that this decision rule is in closed form: the integral over unknown future factors becomes the log-sum formula. Consider now the researcher. Each first-period utility is decomposed into an observed and an unobserved part ($U_{1C} = V_{1C} + \varepsilon_{1C}$, $U_{1W} = V_{1W} + \varepsilon_{1W}$), and we assume that the unobserved parts are iid extreme value. For the second-period utilities, we make a fairly restrictive assumption. We assume that the part of utility that the researcher does not observe is the same as the part that the student does not know beforehand. That is, we assume $U_{2j}^C = V_{2j}^C + \varepsilon_{2j}^C \forall j$, where the researcher's ε_{2j}^C is the same as the student's e_{2j}^C. Under this assumption, the researcher can calculate the log-sum terms for future utility, LC_2^C and LS_2^W, exactly, since these terms depend only on the observed portion of utility in the second period, $V_{2j}^C \forall j$, which is observed by the researcher and known beforehand by the decision maker. The probability of the student choosing college is then

$$\begin{aligned}
P_C &= Prob(TEU_C > TEU_W) \\
&= Prob\left(U_{1C} + \lambda\, LS_2^C > U_{1W} + \lambda\, LS_2^W\right) \\
&= Prob\left(V_{1C} + \varepsilon_{1C} + \lambda\, LS_2^C > V_{1W} + \varepsilon_{1W} + \lambda\, LS_2^W\right) \\
&= \frac{e^{V_{1C}+LS_2^C}}{e^{V_{1C}+\lambda\, LS_2^C} + e^{V_{1W}+\lambda\, LS_2^W}}.
\end{aligned}$$

The model takes the same form as the upper part of a nested logit model: the first-period choice probability is the logit formula with a log-sum term included as an extra explanatory variable. Multiple periods are handled the same way as multilevel nested logits.

It is doubtful that the researcher, in reality, observes everything that the decision maker knows beforehand. However, the simplification that arises from this assumption is so great, and the curse of dimensionality that would arise otherwise is so severe, that proceeding as if it were true is perhaps worthwhile in many situations.

Part II

Estimation

8   Numerical Maximization

8.1   Motivation

Most estimation involves maximization of some function, such as the likelihood function, the simulated likelihood function, or squared moment conditions. This chapter describes numerical procedures that are used to maximize a likelihood function. Analogous procedures apply when maximizing other functions.

Knowing and being able to apply these procedures is critical in our new age of discrete choice modeling. In the past, researchers adapted their specifications to the few convenient models that were available. These models were included in commercially available estimation packages, so that the researcher could estimate the models without knowing the details of how the estimation was actually performed from a numerical perspective. The thrust of the wave of discrete choice methods is to free the researcher to specify models that are tailor-made to her situation and issues. Exercising this freedom means that the researcher will often find herself specifying a model that is not exactly the same as any in commercial software. The researcher will need to write special code for her special model.

The purpose of this chapter is to assist in this exercise. Though not usually taught in econometrics courses, the procedures for maximization are fairly straightforward and easy to implement. Once learned, the freedom they allow is invaluable.

8.2   Notation

The log-likelihood function takes the form $LL(\beta) = \sum_{n=1}^{N} \ln P_n(\beta)/N$, where $P_n(\beta)$ is the probability of the observed outcome for decision maker n, N is the sample size, and β is a $K \times 1$ vector of parameters. In this chapter, we divide the log-likelihood function by N, so that LL is the average log-likelihood in the sample. Doing so does not affect the location of the maximum (since N is fixed for a given sample) and yet

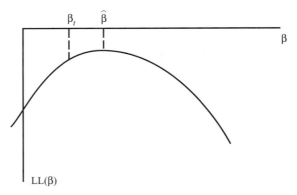

Figure 8.1. Maximum likelihood estimate.

facilitates interpretation of some of the procedures. All the procedures operate the same whether or not the log-likelihood is divided by N. The reader can verify this fact as we go along by observing that N cancels out of the relevant formulas.

The goal is to find the value of β that maximizes $LL(\beta)$. In terms of Figure 8.1, the goal is to locate $\hat{\beta}$. Note in this figure that LL is always negative, since the likelihood is a probability between 0 and 1 and the log of any number between 0 and 1 is negative. Numerically, the maximum can be found by "walking up" the likelihood function until no further increase can be found. The researcher specifies starting values β_0. Each iteration, or step, moves to a new value of the parameters at which $LL(\beta)$ is higher than at the previous value. Denote the current value of β as β_t, which is attained after t steps from the starting values. The question is: what is the best step we can take next, that is, what is the best value for β_{t+1}?

The gradient at β_t is the vector of first derivatives of $LL(\beta)$ evaluated at β_t:

$$g_t = \left(\frac{\partial LL(\beta)}{\partial \beta} \right)_{\beta_t}.$$

This vector tells us which way to step in order to go up the likelihood function. The Hessian is the matrix of second derivatives:

$$H_t = \left(\frac{\partial g_t}{\partial \beta'} \right)_{\beta_t} = \left(\frac{\partial^2 LL(\beta)}{\partial \beta\, \partial \beta'} \right)_{\beta_t}.$$

The gradient has dimension $K \times 1$, and the Hessian is $K \times K$. As we will see, the Hessian can help us to know *how far* to step, given that the gradient tells us *in which direction* to step.

insert linear case

8.3   Algorithms

Of the numerous maximization algorithms that have been developed over the years, I next describe only the most prominent, with an emphasis on the pedagogical value of the procedures as well as their practical use. Readers who are induced to explore further will find the treatments by Judge *et al.* (1985, Appendix B) and Ruud (2000) rewarding.

8.3.1. Newton–Raphson

To determine the best value of β_{t+1}, take a second-order Taylor's approximation of $LL(\beta_{t+1})$ around $LL(\beta_t)$:

(8.1)

$$LL(\beta_{t+1}) = LL(\beta_t) + (\beta_{t+1} - \beta_t)'g_t + \tfrac{1}{2}(\beta_{t+1} - \beta_t)'H_t(\beta_{t+1} - \beta_t).$$

Now find the value of β_{t+1} that maximizes this approximation to $LL(\beta_{t+1})$:

linear FOC

$$\frac{\partial LL(\beta_{t+1})}{\partial \beta_{t+1}} = g_t + H_t(\beta_{t+1} - \beta_t) = 0,$$

$$H_t(\beta_{t+1} - \beta_t) = -g_t,$$

$$\beta_{t+1} - \beta_t = -H_t^{-1}g_t,$$

$$\beta_{t+1} = \beta_t + (-H_t^{-1})g_t.$$

The Newton–Raphson (NR) procedure uses this formula. The step from the current value of β to the new value is $(-H_t^{-1})g_t$, that is, the gradient vector premultiplied by the negative of the inverse of the Hessian.

This formula is intuitively meaningful. Consider $K = 1$, as illustrated in Figure 8.2. The slope of the log-likelihood function is g_t. The second derivative is the Hessian H_t, which is negative for this graph, since the curve is drawn to be concave. The negative of this negative Hessian is positive and represents the degree of curvature. That is, $-H_t$ is the positive curvature. Each step of β is the slope of the log-likelihood function divided by its curvature. If the slope is positive, β is raised as in the first panel, and if the slope if negative, β is lowered as in the second panel. The curvature determines how large a step is made. If the curvature is great, meaning that the slope changes quickly as in the first panel of Figure 8.3, then the maximum is likely to be close, and so a small step is taken.

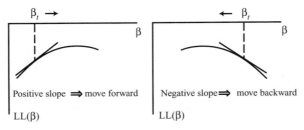

Figure 8.2. Direction of step follows the slope.

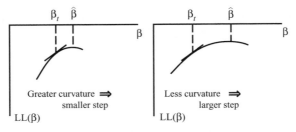

Figure 8.3. Step size is inversely related to curvature.

(Dividing the gradient by a large number gives a small number.) Conversely, if the curvature is small, meaning that the slope is not changing much, then the maximum seems to be further away and so a larger step is taken.

Three issues are relevant to the NR procedure.

Quadratics

If LL(β) were exactly quadratic in β, then the NR procedure would reach the maximum in one step from any starting value. This fact can easily be verified with $K = 1$. If LL(β) is quadratic, then it can be written as

$$LL(\beta) = a + b\beta + c\beta^2.$$

The maximum is

$$\frac{\partial LL(\beta)}{\partial \beta} = b + 2c\beta = 0,$$

$$\hat{\beta} = -\frac{b}{2c}.$$

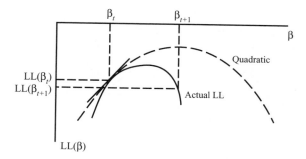

Figure 8.4. Step may go beyond maximum to lower LL.

The gradient and Hessian are $g_t = b + 2c\beta_t$ and $H_t = 2c$, and so NR gives us

$$
\begin{aligned}
\beta_{t+1} &= \beta_t - H_t^{-1} g_t \\
&= \beta_t - \frac{1}{2c}(b + 2c\beta_t) \\
&= \beta_t - \frac{b}{2c} - \beta_t \\
&= -\frac{b}{2c} = \hat{\beta}.
\end{aligned}
$$

Most log-likelihood functions are not quadratic, and so the NR procedure takes more than one step to reach the maximum. However, knowing how NR behaves in the quadratic case helps in understanding its behavior with nonquadratic LL, as we will see in the following discussion.

Step Size

It is possible for the NR procedure, as for other procedures discussed later, to step past the maximum and move to a lower LL(β). Figure 8.4 depicts the situation. The actual LL is given by the solid line. The dashed line is a quadratic function that has the slope and curvature that LL has at the point β_t. The NR procedure moves to the top of the quadratic, to β_{t+1}. However, LL(β_{t+1}) is lower than LL(β_t) in this case.

To allow for this possibility, the step is multiplied by a scalar λ in the NR formula:

$$
\beta_{t+1} = \beta_t + \lambda(-H_t)^{-1} g_t.
$$

The vector $(-H_t)^{-1} g_t$ is called the direction, and λ is called the step size. (This terminology is standard even though $(-H_t)^{-1} g_t$ contains step-size

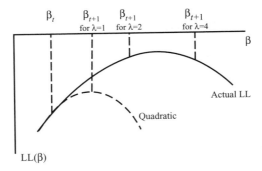

Figure 8.5. Double λ as long as LL rises.

information through H_t, as already explained in relation to Figure 8.3.) The step size λ is reduced to assure that each step of the NR procedure provides an increase in LL(β). The adjustment is performed separately in each iteration, as follows.

Start with $\lambda = 1$. If LL(β_{t+1}) > LL(β_t), move to β_{t+1} and start a new iteration. If LL(β_{t+1}) < LL(β_t), then set $\lambda = \frac{1}{2}$ and try again. If, with $\lambda = \frac{1}{2}$, LL(β_{t+1}) is still below LL(β_t), then set $\lambda = \frac{1}{4}$ and try again. Continue this process until a λ is found for which LL(β_{t+1}) > LL(β_t). If this process results in a tiny λ, then little progress is made in finding the maximum. This can be taken as a signal to the researcher that a different iteration procedure may be needed.

An analogous step-size adjustment can be made in the other direction, that is, by increasing λ when appropriate. A case is shown in Figure 8.5. The top of the quadratic is obtained with a step size of $\lambda = 1$. However, the LL(β) is not quadratic, and its maximum is further away. The step size can be adjusted upward as long as LL(β) continues to rise. That is, calculate β_{t+1} with $\lambda = 1$ at β_{t+1}. If LL(β_{t+1}) > LL(β_t), then try $\lambda = 2$. If the β_{t+1} based on $\lambda = 2$ gives a higher value of the log-likelihood function than with $\lambda = 1$, then try $\lambda = 4$, and so on, doubling λ as long as doing so further raises the likelihood function. Each time, LL(β_{t+1}) with a doubled λ is compared with its value at the previously tried λ, rather than with $\lambda = 1$, in order to assure that each doubling raises the likelihood function further than it had previously been raised with smaller λ's. In Figure 8.5, a final step size of 2 is used, since the likelihood function with $\lambda = 4$ is lower than when $\lambda = 2$, even though it is higher than with $\lambda = 1$.

The advantage of this approach of raising λ is that it usually reduces the number of iterations that are needed to reach the maximum. New values of λ can be tried without recalculating g_t and H_t, while each new iteration requires calculation of these terms. Adjusting λ can therefore quicken the search for the maximum.

Concavity

If the log-likelihood function is globally concave, then the NR procedure is guaranteed to provide an increase in the likelihood function at each iteration. This fact is demonstrated as follows. $LL(\beta)$ being concave means that its Hessian is negative definite at all values of β. (In one dimension, the slope of $LL(\beta)$ is declining, so that the second derivative is negative.) If H is negative definite, then H^{-1} is also negative definite, and $-H^{-1}$ is positive definite. By definition, a symmetric matrix M is positive definite if $x'Mx > 0$ for any $x \neq 0$. Consider a first-order Taylor's approximation of $LL(\beta_{t+1})$ around $LL(\beta_t)$:

$$LL(\beta_{t+1}) = LL(\beta_t) + (\beta_{t+1} - \beta_t)'g_t.$$

Under the NR procedure, $\beta_{t+1} - \beta_t = \lambda(-H_t^{-1})g_t$. Substituting gives

$$LL(\beta_{t+1}) = LL(\beta_t) + \left(\lambda\left(-H_t^{-1}\right)g_t\right)'g_t$$
$$= LL(\beta_t) + \lambda g_t'\left(-H_t^{-1}\right)g_t.$$

Since $-H^{-1}$ is positive definite, we have $g_t'(-H_t^{-1})g_t > 0$ and $LL(\beta_{t+1}) > LL(\beta_t)$. Note that since this comparison is based on a first-order approximation, an increase in $LL(\beta)$ may only be obtained in a small neighborhood of β_t. That is, the value of λ that provides an increase might be small. However, an increase is indeed guaranteed at each iteration if $LL(\beta)$ is globally concave.

Suppose the log-likelihood function has regions that are not concave. In these areas, the NR procedure can fail to find an increase. If the function is convex at β_t, then the NR procedure moves in the opposite direction to the slope of the log-likelihood function. The situation is illustrated in Figure 8.6 for $K = 1$. The NR step with one parameter is $LL'(\beta)/(-LL''(\beta))$, where the prime denotes derivatives. The second derivative is positive at β_t, since the slope is rising. Therefore, $-LL''(\beta)$ is negative, and the step is in the opposite direction to the slope. With $K > 1$, if the Hessian is positive definite at β_t, then $-H_t^{-1}$ is negative definite, and NR steps in the opposite direction to g_t.

The sign of the Hessian can be reversed in these situations. However, there is no reason for using the Hessian where the function is not concave, since the Hessian in convex regions does not provide any useful information on where the maximum might be. There are easier ways to find

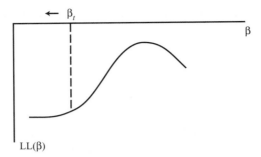

Figure 8.6. NR in the convex portion of LL.

an increase in these situations than calculating the Hessian and reversing
its sign. This issue is part of the motivation for other procedures.

The NR procedure has two drawbacks. First, calculation of the Hessian
is usually computation-intensive. Procedures that avoid calculating the
Hessian at every iteration can be much faster. Second, as we have just
shown, the NR procedure does not guarantee an increase in each step if
the log-likelihood function is not globally concave. When $-H_t^{-1}$ is not
positive definite, an increase is not guaranteed.

Other approaches use approximations to the Hessian that address these
two issues. The methods differ in the form of the approximation. Each
procedure defines a step as

$$\beta_{t+1} = \beta_t + \lambda M_t g_t,$$

where M_t is a $K \times K$ matrix. For NR, $M_t = -H^{-1}$. Other procedures
use M_t's that are easier to calculate than the Hessian and are necessarily
positive definite, so as to guarantee an increase at each iteration even in
convex regions of the log-likelihood function.

8.3.2. BHHH

The NR procedure does not utilize the fact that the function being maximized is actually the sum of log likelihoods over a sample of
observations. The gradient and Hessian are calculated just as one would
do in maximizing any function. This characteristic of NR provides generality, in that the NR procedure can be used to maximize any function,
not just a log likelihood. However, as we will see, maximization can be
faster if we utilize the fact that the function being maximized is a sum
of terms in a sample.

We need some additional notation to reflect the fact that the log-
likelihood function is a sum over observations. The *score* of an

observation is the derivative of that observation's log likelihood with respect to the parameters: $s_n(\beta_t) = \partial \ln P_n(\beta)/\partial \beta$ evaluated at β_t. The gradient, which we defined earlier and used for the NR procedure, is the average score: $g_t = \sum_n s_n(\beta_t)/N$. The outer product of observation n's score is the $K \times K$ matrix

$$
s_n(\beta_t)s_n(\beta_t)' = \begin{pmatrix} s_n^1 s_n^1 & s_n^1 s_n^2 & \cdots & s_n^1 s_n^K \\ s_n^1 s_n^2 & s_n^2 s_n^2 & \cdots & s_n^2 s_n^K \\ \vdots & \vdots & & \vdots \\ s_n^1 s_n^K & s_n^2 s_n^K & \cdots & s_n^K s_n^K \end{pmatrix},
$$

where s_n^k is the kth element of $s_n(\beta_t)$ with the dependence on β_t omitted for convenience. The average outer product in the sample is $B_t = \sum_n s_n(\beta_t)s_n(\beta_t)'/N$. This average is related to the covariance matrix: if the average score were zero, then B would be the covariance matrix of scores in the sample. Often B_t is called the "outer product of the gradient." This term can be confusing, since B_t is not the outer product of g_t. However, it does reflect the fact that the score is an observation-specific gradient and B_t is the average outer product of these observation-specific gradients.

At the parameters that maximize the likelihood function, the average score is indeed zero. The maximum occurs where the slope is zero, which means that the gradient, that is, the average score, is zero. Since the average score is zero, the outer product of the scores, B_t, becomes the variance of the scores. That is, at the maximizing values of the parameters, B_t is the variance of scores in the sample.

The variance of the scores provides important information for locating the maximum of the likelihood function. In particular, this variance provides a measure of the curvature of the log-likelihood function, similar to the Hessian. Suppose that all the people in the sample have similar scores. Then the sample contains very little information. The log-likelihood function is fairly flat in this situation, reflecting the fact that different values of the parameters fit the data about the same. The first panel of Figure 8.7 depicts this situation: with a fairly flat log likelihood, different values of β give similar values of $LL(\beta)$. The curvature is small when the variance of the scores is small. Conversely, scores differing greatly over observations mean that the observations are quite different and the sample provides a considerable amount of information. The log-likelihood function is highly peaked, reflecting the fact that the sample provides good information on the values of β. Moving away from the maximizing values of β causes a large loss of fit. The second panel

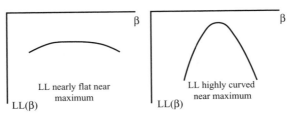

Figure 8.7. Shape of log-likelihood function near maximum.

of Figure 8.7 illustrates this situation. The curvature is great when the variance of the scores is high.

These ideas about the variance of the scores and their relation to the curvature of the log-likelihood function are formalized in the famous *information identity*. This identity states that the covariance of the scores at the true parameters is equal to the negative of the expected Hessian. We demonstrate this identity in the last section of this chapter; Theil (1971) and Ruud (2000) also provide useful and heuristic proofs. However, even without proof, it makes intuitive sense that the variance of the scores provides information on the curvature of the log-likelihood function.

Berndt, Hall, Hall, and Hausman (1974), hereafter referred to as BHHH (and commonly pronounced B-triple H), proposed using this relationship in the numerical search for the maximum of the log-likelihood function. In particular, the BHHH procedure uses B_t in the optimization routine in place of $-H_t$. Each iteration is defined by

$$\beta_{t+1} = \beta_t + \lambda B_t^{-1} g_t.$$

This step is the same as for NR except that B_t is used in place of $-H_t$. Given the preceding discussion about the variance of the scores indicating the curvature of the log-likelihood function, replacing $-H_t$ with B_t makes sense.

There are two advantages to the BHHH procedure over NR:

1. B_t is far faster to calculate that H_t. The scores must be calculated to obtain the gradient for the NR procedure anyway, and so calculating B_t as the average outer product of the scores takes hardly any extra computer time. In contrast, calculating H_t requires calculating the second derivatives of the log-likelihood function.
2. B_t is necessarily positive definite. The BHHH procedure is therefore guaranteed to provide an increase in LL(β) in each iteration, even in convex portions of the function. Using the proof given previously for NR when $-H_t$ is positive definite, the BHHH step $\lambda B_t^{-1} g_t$ raises LL(β) for a small enough λ.

Our discussion about the relation of the variance of the scores to the curvature of the log-likelihood function can be stated a bit more precisely. For a correctly specified model at the true parameters, $B \rightarrow -H$ as $N \rightarrow \infty$. This relation between the two matrices is an implication of the information identity, discussed at greater length in the last section. This convergence suggests that B_t can be considered an approximation to $-H_t$. The approximation is expected to be better as the sample size rises. And the approximation can be expected to be better close to the true parameters, where the expected score is zero and the information identity holds, than for values of β that are farther from the true values. That is, B_t can be expected to be a better approximation close to the maximum of the LL(β) than farther from the maximum.

There are some drawbacks of BHHH. The procedure can give small steps that raise LL(β) very little, especially when the iterative process is far from the maximum. This behavior can arise because B_t is not a good approximation to $-H_t$ far from the true value, or because LL(β) is highly nonquadratic in the area where the problem is occurring. If the function is highly nonquadratic, NR does not perform well, as explained earlier; since BHHH is an approximation to NR, BHHH would not perform well even if B_t were a good approximation to $-H_t$.

8.3.3. BHHH-2

The BHHH procedure relies on the matrix B_t, which, as we have described, captures the covariance of the scores when the average score is zero (i.e., at the maximizing value of β). When the iterative process is not at the maximum, the average score is not zero and B_t does not represent the covariance of the scores.

A variant on the BHHH procedure is obtained by subtracting out the mean score before taking the outer product. For any level of the average score, the covariance of the scores over the sampled decision makers is

$$W_t = \sum_n \frac{(s_n(\beta_t) - g_t)(s_n(\beta_t) - g_t)'}{N},$$

where the gradient g_t is the average score. W_t is the covariance of the scores around their mean, and B_t is the average outer product of the scores. W_t and B_t are the same when the mean gradient is zero (i.e., at the maximizing value of β), but differ otherwise.

The maximization procedure can use W_t instead of B_t:

$$\beta_{t+1} = \beta_t + \lambda W_t^{-1} g_t.$$

This procedure, which I call BHHH-2, has the same advantages as BHHH. W_t is necessarily positive definite, since it is a covariance matrix, and so the procedure is guaranteed to provide an increase in $LL(\beta)$ at every iteration. Also, for a correctly specified model at the true parameters, $W \to -H$ as $N \to \infty$, so that W_t can be considered an approximation to $-H_t$. The information identity establishes this equivalence, as it does for B.

For β's that are close to the maximizing value, BHHH and BHHH-2 give nearly the same results. They can differ greatly at values far from the maximum. Experience indicates, however, that the two methods are fairly similar in that either both of them work effectively for a given likelihood function, or neither of them does. The main value of BHHH-2 is pedagogical, to elucidate the relation between the covariance of the scores and the average outer product of the scores. This relation is critical in the analysis of the information identity in Section 8.7.

8.3.4. Steepest Ascent

This procedure is defined by the iteration formula

$$\beta_{t+1} = \beta_t + \lambda g_t.$$

The defining matrix for this procedure is the identity matrix I. Since I is positive definite, the method guarantees an increase in each iteration. It is called "steepest ascent" because it provides the greatest possible increase in $LL(\beta)$ for the distance between β_t and β_{t+1}, at least for small enough distance. Any other step of the same distance provides less increase. This fact is demonstrated as follows. Take a first-order Taylor's expansion of $LL(\beta_{t+1})$ around $LL(\beta_t)$: $LL(\beta_{t+1}) = LL(\beta_t) + (\beta_{t+1} - \beta_t)g_t$. Maximize this expression for $LL(\beta_{t+1})$ subject to the Euclidian distance from β_t to β_{t+1} being $\sqrt{k}$. That is, maximize subject to $(\beta_{t+1} - \beta_t)'(\beta_{t+1} - \beta_t) = k$. The Lagrangian is

$$\mathcal{L} = LL(\beta_t) + (\beta_{t+1} - \beta_t)g_t - \frac{1}{2\lambda}[(\beta_{t+1} - \beta_t)'(\beta_{t+1} - \beta_t) - k],$$

and we have

$$\frac{\partial \mathcal{L}}{\partial \beta_{t+1}} = g_t - \frac{1}{\lambda}(\beta_{t+1} - \beta_t) = 0,$$
$$\beta_{t+1} - \beta_t = \lambda g_t,$$
$$\beta_{t+1} = \beta_t + \lambda g_t,$$

which is the formula for steepest ascent.

At first encounter, one might think that the method of steepest ascent is the best possible procedure, since it gives the greatest possible increase in the log-likelihood function at each step. However, the method's property is actually less grand than this statement implies. Note that the derivation relies on a first-order approximation that is only accurate in a neighborhood of β_t. The correct statement of the result is that there is some sufficiently small distance for which the method of steepest ascent gives the greatest increase for that distance. This distinction is critical. Experience indicates that the step sizes are often very small with this method. The fact that the ascent is greater than for any other step of the same distance is not particularly comforting when the steps are so small. Usually, BHHH and BHHH-2 converge more quickly than the method of steepest ascent.

8.3.5. DFP and BFGS

The Davidon–Fletcher–Powell (DFP) and Broyden–Fletcher–Goldfarb–Shanno (BFGS) methods calculate the approximate Hessian in a way that uses information at more than one point on the likelihood function. Recall that NR uses the actual Hessian at β_t to determine the step to β_{t+1}, and BHHH and BHHH-2 use the scores at β_t to approximate the Hessian. Only information at β_t is being used to determine the step in these procedures. If the function is quadratic, then information at one point on the function provides all the information that is needed about the shape of the function. These methods work well, therefore, when the log-likelihood function is close to quadratic. In contrast, the DFP and BFGS procedures use information at several points to obtain a sense of the curvature of the log-likelihood function.

The Hessian is the matrix of second derivatives. As such, it gives the amount by which the slope of the curve changes as one moves along the curve. The Hessian is defined for infinitesimally small movements. Since we are interested in making large steps, understanding how the slope changes for noninfinitesimal movements is useful. An *arc* Hessian can be defined on the basis of how the gradient changes from one point to another. For example, for function $f(x)$, suppose the slope at $x = 3$ is 25 and at $x = 4$ the slope is 19. The change in slope for a one unit change in x is -6. In this case, the arc Hessian is -6, representing the change in the slope as a step is taken from $x = 3$ to $x = 4$.

The DFP and BFGS procedures use these concepts to approximate the Hessian. The gradient is calculated at each step in the iteration process. The difference in the gradient between the various points that have been reached is used to calculate an arc Hessian over these points. This arc Hessian reflects the change in gradient that occurs for actual movement on the curve, as opposed to the Hessian, which simply reflects the change in slope for infinitesimally small steps around that point. When the log-likelihood function is nonquadratic, the Hessian at any point provides little information about the shape of the function. The arc Hessian provides better information.

At each iteration, the DFP and BFGS procedures update the arc Hessian using information that is obtained at the new point, that is, using the new gradient. The two procedures differ in how the updating is performed; see Greene (2000) for details. Both methods are extremely effective – usually far more efficient that NR, BHHH, BHHH-2, or steepest ascent. BFGS refines DFP, and my experience indicates that it nearly always works better. BFGS is the default algorithm in the optimization routines of many commercial software packages.

8.4   Convergence Criterion

In theory the maximum of $LL(\beta)$ occurs when the gradient vector is zero. In practice, the calculated gradient vector is never exactly zero: it can be very close, but a series of calculations on a computer cannot produce a result of exactly zero (unless, of course, the result is set to zero through a Boolean operator or by multiplication by zero, neither of which arises in calculation of the gradient). The question arises: when are we sufficiently close to the maximum to justify stopping the iterative process?

The statistic $m_t = g_t'(-H_t^{-1})g_t$ is often used to evaluate convergence. The researcher specifies a small value for m, such as $\check{m} = 0.0001$, and determines in each iteration whether $g_t'(-H_t^{-1})g_t < \check{m}$. If this inequality is satisfied, the iterative process stops and the parameters at that iteration are considered the converged values, that is, the estimates. For procedures other than NR that use an approximate Hessian in the iterative process, the approximation is used in the convergence statistic to avoid calculating the actual Hessian. Close to the maximum, where the criterion becomes relevant, each form of approximate Hessian that we have discussed is expected to be similar to the actual Hessian.

The statistic m_t is the test statistic for the hypothesis that all elements of the gradient vector are zero. The statistic is distributed chi-squared with K degrees of freedom. However, the convergence criterion $\check{m}$ is usually set far more stringently (that is, lower) than the critical value of a chi-squared at standard levels of significance, so as to assure that the estimated parameters are very close to the maximizing values. Usually, the hypothesis that the gradient elements are zero cannot be rejected for a fairly wide area around the maximum. The distinction can be illustrated for an estimated coefficient that has a t-statistic of 1.96. The hypothesis cannot be rejected if this coefficient has any value between zero and twice its estimated value. However, we would not want convergence to be defined as having reached any parameter value within this range.

It is tempting to view small changes in β_t from one iteration to the next, and correspondingly small increases in $LL(\beta_t)$, as evidence that convergence has been achieved. However, as stated earlier, the iterative procedures may produce small steps because the likelihood function is not close to a quadratic rather than because of nearing the maximum. Small changes in β_t and $LL(\beta_t)$ accompanied by a gradient vector that is not close to zero indicate that the numerical routine is not effective at finding the maximum.

Convergence is sometimes assessed on the basis of the gradient vector itself rather than through the test statistic m_t. There are two procedures: (1) determine whether each element of the gradient vector is smaller in magnitude than some value that the researcher specifies, and (2) divide each element of the gradient vector by the corresponding element of β, and determine whether each of these quotients is smaller in magnitude than some value specified by the researcher. The second approach normalizes for the units of the parameters, which are determined by the units of the variables that enter the model.

8.5   Local versus Global Maximum

All of the methods that we have discussed are susceptible to converging at a local maximum that is not the global maximum, as shown in Figure 8.8. When the log-likelihood function is globally concave, as for logit with linear-in-parameters utility, then there is only one maximum and the issue doesn't arise. However, most discrete choice models are not globally concave.

A way to investigate the issue is to use a variety of starting values and observe whether convergence occurs at the same parameter values. For example, in Figure 8.8, starting at β_0 will lead to convergence at β_1. Unless other starting values were tried, the researcher would mistakenly believe that the maximum of $LL(\beta)$ had been achieved. Starting at β_2, convergence is achieved at $\hat{\beta}$. By comparing $LL(\hat{\beta})$ with $LL(\beta_1)$, the researcher finds that β_1 is not the maximizing value. Liu and Mahmassani (2000) propose a way to select starting values that involves the researcher setting upper and lower bounds on each parameter and randomly choosing values within those bounds.

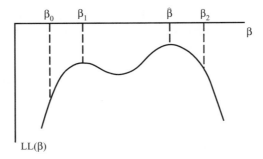

Figure 8.8. Local versus global maximum.

8.6   Variance of the Estimates

In standard econometric courses, it is shown that, for a correctly specified model,

$$\sqrt{N}(\hat{\beta} - \beta^*) \xrightarrow{d} N(0, (-\mathbf{H})^{-1})$$

as $N \to \infty$, where β^* is the true parameter vector, $\hat{\beta}$ is the maximum likelihood estimator, and $\mathbf{H}$ is the expected Hessian in the population. The negative of the expected Hessian, $-\mathbf{H}$, is often called the information matrix. Stated in words, the sampling distribution of the difference between the estimator and the true value, normalized for sample size, converges asymptotically to a normal distribution centered on zero and with covariance equal to the inverse of the information matrix, $-\mathbf{H}^{-1}$. Since the asymptotic covariance of $\sqrt{N}(\hat{\beta} - \beta^*)$ is $-\mathbf{H}^{-1}$, the asymptotic covariance of $\hat{\beta}$ itself is $-\mathbf{H}^{-1}/N$.

The boldface type in these expressions indicates that $\mathbf{H}$ is the average in the population, as opposed to H, which is the average Hessian in the sample. The researcher calculates the asymptotic covariance by using H as an estimate of $\mathbf{H}$. That is, the asymptotic covariance of $\hat{\beta}$ is calculated as $-H^{-1}/N$, where H is evaluated at $\hat{\beta}$.

Recall that W is the covariance of the scores in the sample. At the maximizing values of β, B is also the covariance of the scores. By the information identity just discussed and explained in the last section, $-H$, which is the (negative of the) average Hessian in the sample, converges to the covariance of the scores for a correctly specified model at the true parameters. In calculating the asymptotic covariance of the estimates $\hat{\beta}$, any of these three matrices can be used as an estimate of $-\mathbf{H}$. The asymptotic variance of $\hat{\beta}$ is calculated as W^{-1}/N, B^{-1}/N, or $-H^{-1}/N$, where each of these matrices is evaluated at $\hat{\beta}$.

If the model is not correctly specified, then the asymptotic covariance of $\hat{\beta}$ is more complicated. In particular, for any model for which the expected score is zero at the true parameters,

$$\sqrt{N}(\hat{\beta} - \beta^*) \overset{d}{\to} N(0, \mathbf{H}^{-1}\mathbf{V}\mathbf{H}^{-1}),$$

where $\mathbf{V}$ is the variance of the scores in the population. When the model is correctly specified, the matrix $-\mathbf{H} = \mathbf{V}$ by the information identity, such that $\mathbf{H}^{-1}\mathbf{V}\mathbf{H}^{-1} = -\mathbf{H}^{-1}$ and we get the formula for a correctly specified model. However, if the model is not correctly specified, this simplification does not occur. The asymptotic varlance of $\hat{\beta}$ is $\mathbf{H}^{-1}\mathbf{V}\mathbf{H}^{-1}/N$. This matrix is called the *robust covariance matrix*, since it is valid whether or not the model is correctly specified.

To estimate the robust covariance matrix, the researcher must calculate the Hessian H. If a procedure other than NR is being used to reach convergence, the Hessian need not be calculated at each iteration; however, it must be calculated at the final iteration. Then the asymptotic covariance is calculated as $H^{-1}WH^{-1}$, or with B instead of W. This formula is sometimes called the "sandwich" estimator of the covariance, since the Hessian inverse appears on both sides.

8.7   Information Identity

The information identity states that, for a correctly specified model at the true parameters, $\mathbf{V} = -\mathbf{H}$, where $\mathbf{V}$ is the covariance matrix of the scores in the population and $\mathbf{H}$ is the average Hessian in the population. The score for a person is the vector of first derivatives of that person's $\ln P(\beta)$ with respect to the parameters, and the Hessian is the matrix of second derivatives. The information identity states that, in the population, the covariance matrix of the first derivatives equals the average matrix of second derivatives (actually, the negative of that matrix). This is a startling fact, not something that would be expected or even believed if there were not proof. It has implications throughout econometrics. The implications that we have used in the previous sections of this chapter are easily derivable from the identity. In particular:

(1) *At the maximizing value of β, $W \to -H$ as $N \to \infty$, where W is the sample covariance of the scores and H is the sample average of each observation's Hessian.* As sample size rises, the sample covariance approaches the population covariance: $W \to \mathbf{V}$. Similarly, the sample average of the Hessian approaches the population average: $H \to \mathbf{H}$. Since $\mathbf{V} = -\mathbf{H}$ by the information identity, W approaches the same matrix that $-H$ approaches, and so they approach each other.

(2) *At the maximizing value of* β, *B* $\rightarrow$ $-H$ *as* $N \rightarrow \infty$, *where B is the sample average of the outer product of the scores.* At $\hat{\beta}$, the average score in the sample is zero, so that *B* is the same as *W*. The result for *W* applies for *B*.

We now demonstrate the information identity. We need to expand our notation to encompass the population instead of simply the sample. Let $P_i(x, \beta)$ be the probability that a person who faces explanatory variables x chooses alternative i given the parameters β. Of the people in the population who face variables x, the share who choose alternative i is this probability calculated at the true parameters: $S_i(x) = P_i(x, \beta^*)$ where β^* are the true parameters. Consider now the gradient of $\ln P_i(x, \beta)$ with respect to β. The average gradient in the population is

$$(8.2) \quad \mathbf{g} = \int \sum_i \frac{\partial \ln P_i(x, \beta)}{\partial \beta} S_i(x) f(x) \, dx,$$

where $f(x)$ is the density of explanatory variables in the population. This expression can be explained as follows. The gradient for people who face x and choose i is $\partial \ln P_{ni}(\beta)/\partial \beta$. The average gradient is the average of this term over all values of x and all alternatives i. The share of people who face a given value of x is given by $f(x)$, and the share of people who face this x that choose i is $S_i(x)$. So $S_i(x) f(x)$ is the share of the population who face x and choose i and therefore have gradient $\partial \ln P_i(x, \beta)/\partial \beta$. Summing this term over all values of i and integrating over all values of x (assuming the x's are continuous) gives the average gradient, as expressed in (8.2).

The average gradient in the population is equal to zero at the true parameters. This fact can be considered either the definition of the true parameters or the result of a correctly specified model. Also, we know that $S_i(x) = P_i(x, \beta^*)$. Substituting these facts into (8.2), we have

$$0 = \int \sum_i \frac{\partial \ln P_i(x, \beta)}{\partial \beta} P_i(x, \beta) f(x) \, dx,$$

where all functions are evaluated at β^*. We now take the derivative of this equation with respect to the parameters:

$$0 = \int \sum_i \left(\frac{\partial^2 \ln P_i(x, \beta)}{\partial \beta \, \partial \beta'} P_i(x, \beta) + \frac{\partial \ln P_i(x, \beta)}{\partial \beta} \frac{\partial P_i(x, \beta)}{\partial \beta'} \right) f(x) \, dx.$$

Since $\partial \ln P/\partial \beta = (1/P)\partial P/\partial \beta$ by the rules of derivatives, we can substitute $[\partial \ln P_i(x, \beta)/\partial \beta'] P_i(x, \beta)$ for $\partial P_i(x, \beta)/\partial \beta'$ in the last term in parentheses:

$$0 = \int \sum_i \left(\frac{\partial^2 \ln P_i(x, \beta)}{\partial \beta \, \partial \beta'} P_i(x, \beta) \right.$$
$$+ \left. \frac{\partial \ln P_i(x, \beta)}{\partial \beta} \frac{\partial \ln P_i(x, \beta)}{\partial \beta'} P_i(x, \beta) \right) f(x) \, dx.$$

Rearranging,

$$- \int \sum_i \frac{\partial^2 \ln P_i(x, \beta)}{\partial \beta \, \partial \beta'} P_i(x, \beta) f(x) \, dx$$
$$= \int \sum_i \frac{\partial \ln P_i(x, \beta)}{\partial \beta} \frac{\partial \ln P_i(x, \beta)}{\partial \beta'} P_i(x, \beta) f(x) \, dx.$$

Since all terms are evaluated at the true parameters, we can replace $P_i(x, \beta)$ with $S_i(x)$ to obtain

$$- \int \sum_i \frac{\partial^2 \ln P_i(x, \beta)}{\partial \beta \, \partial \beta'} S_i(x) f(x) \, dx$$
$$= \int \sum_i \frac{\partial \ln P_i(x, \beta)}{\partial \beta} \frac{\partial \ln P_i(x, \beta)}{\partial \beta'} S_i(x) f(x) \, dx.$$

The left-hand side is the negative of the average Hessian in the population, $-\mathbf{H}$. The right-hand side is the average outer product of the gradient, which is the covariance of the gradient, $\mathbf{V}$, since the average gradient is zero. Therefore, $-\mathbf{H} = \mathbf{V}$, the information identity. As stated, the matrix $-\mathbf{H}$ is often called the information matrix.

9   Drawing from Densities

9.1   Introduction

Simulation consists of drawing from a density, calculating a statistic for each draw, and averaging the results. In all cases, the researcher wants to calculate an average of the form $\bar{t} = \int t(\varepsilon) f(\varepsilon)\, d\varepsilon$, where $t(\cdot)$ is a statistic of interest and $f(\cdot)$ is a density. To approximate this average through simulation, the researcher must be able to take draws from the density $f(\cdot)$. For some densities, this task is simple. However, in many situations, it is not immediately clear how to draw from the relevant density. Furthermore, even with simple densities, there may be ways of taking draws that provide a better approximation to the integral than a sequence of purely random draws.

    We explore these issues in this chapter. In the first sections, we describe the most prominent methods that have been developed for taking purely random draws from various kinds of densities. These methods are presented in a progressive sequence, starting with simple procedures that work with a few convenient densities and moving to ever more complex methods that work with less convenient densities. The discussion culminates with the Metropolis–Hastings algorithm, which can be used with (practically) any density. The chapter then turns to the question of whether and how a sequence of draws can be taken that provides a better approximation to the relevant integral than a purely random sequence. We discuss antithetics, systematic sampling, and Halton sequences and show the value that these types of draws provide in estimation of model parameters.

9.2   Random Draws

9.2.1. Standard Normal and Uniform

    If the researcher wants to take a draw from a standard normal density (that is, a normal with zero mean and unit variance) or a standard uniform density (uniform between 0 and 1), the process from a programming perspective is very easy. Most statistical packages contain random number generators for these densities. The researcher simply calls these routines to obtain a sequence of random draws. In the sections below, we refer to a draw of a standard normal as η and a draw of a standard uniform as μ.

The draws from these routines are actually *pseudo-random* numbers, because nothing that a computer does is truly random. There are many issues involved in the design of these routines. The intent in their design is to produce numbers that exhibit the properties of random draws. The extent to which this intent is realized depends, of course, on how one defines the properties of "random" draws. These properties are difficult to define precisely, since randomness is a theoretical concept that has no operational counterpart in the real world. From a practical perspective, my advice is the following: unless one is willing to spend considerable time investigating and resolving (literally, re-solving) these issues, it is probably better to use the available routines rather than write a new one.

9.2.2. Transformations of Standard Normal

Some random variables are transformations of a standard normal. For example, a draw from a normal density with mean b and variance s^2 is obtained as $\varepsilon = b + s\eta$. A draw from a lognormal density is obtained by exponentiating a draw from a normal density: $\varepsilon = e^{b+s\eta}$. The moments of the lognormal are functions of the mean and variance of the normal that is exponentiated. In particular, the mean of ε is $\exp(b + (s^2/2))$, and its variance is $\exp(2b + s^2) \cdot (\exp(s^2) - 1)$. Given values for the mean and variance of the lognormal, the appropriate values of b and s to use in the transformation can be calculated. It is more common, however, to treat b and s as the parameters of the lognormal and calculate its mean and variance from these parameters.

9.2.3. Inverse Cumulative for Univariate Densities

Consider a random variable with density $f(\varepsilon)$ and corresponding cumulative distribution $F(\varepsilon)$. If F is invertible (that is, if F^{-1} can be calculated), then draws of ε can be obtained from draws of a standard uniform. By definition, $F(\varepsilon) = k$ means that the probability of obtaining a draw equal to or below ε is k, where k is between zero and one. A draw μ from the standard uniform provides a number between zero and one. We can set $F(\varepsilon) = \mu$ and solve for the corresponding ε: $\varepsilon = F^{-1}(\mu)$.

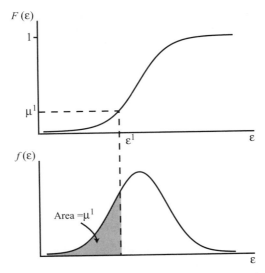

Figure 9.1. Draw of μ^1 from uniform and create $\varepsilon^1 = F^{-1}(\mu)$.

When ε is drawn in this way, the cumulative distribution of the draws is equal to F, such that the draws are equivalent to draws directly from F. An illustration is provided in Figure 9.1. A draw μ^1 from a standard uniform translates into the value of ε labeled ε^1, at which $F(\varepsilon^1) = \mu^1$.

The extreme value distribution, which is the basis for multinomial logit models, provides an example. The density is $f(\varepsilon) = \exp(-\varepsilon) \cdot \exp(-\exp(-\varepsilon))$ with cumulative distribution $F(\varepsilon) = \exp(-\exp(-\varepsilon))$. A draw from this density is obtained as $\varepsilon = -\ln(-\ln \mu)$.

Note that this procedure works only for univariate distributions. If there are two or more elements of ε, then $F^{-1}(\mu)$ is not unique, since various combinations of the elements of ε have the same cumulative probability.

9.2.4. Truncated Univariate Densities

Consider a random variable that ranges from a to b with density proportional to $f(\varepsilon)$ within this range. That is, the density is $(1/k)f(\varepsilon)$ for $a \leq \varepsilon \leq b$, and 0 otherwise, where k is the normalizing constant that insures that the density integrates to 1: $k = \int_a^b f(\varepsilon)\,d\varepsilon = F(b) - F(a)$. A draw from this density can be obtained by applying the procedure in Section 9.2.3 while assuring that the draw is within the appropriate range.

Draw μ from a standard uniform density. Calculate the weighted average of $F(a)$ and $F(b)$ as $\bar{\mu} = (1 - \mu)F(a) + \mu F(b)$. Then calculate

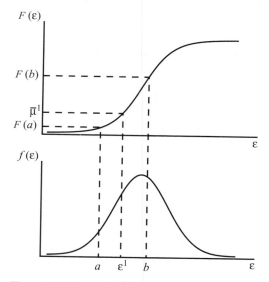

Figure 9.2. Draw of $\bar{\mu}^1$ between $F(a)$ and $F(b)$ gives draw ε^1 from $f(\varepsilon)$ between a and b.

$\varepsilon = F^{-1}(\bar{\mu})$. Since $\bar{\mu}$ is between $F(a)$ and $F(b)$, ε is necessarily between a and b. Essentially, the draw of μ determines how far to go between a and b. Note that the normalizing constant k is not used in the calculations and therefore need not be calculated. Figure 9.2 illustrates the process.

9.2.5. Choleski Transformation for Multivariate Normals

As described in Section 9.2.2, a univariate normal with mean b and variance s^2 is obtained as $\varepsilon = b + s\mu$, where μ is standard normal. An analogous procedure can be used to draw from a multivariate normal. Let ε be a vector with K elements distributed $N(b, \Omega)$. A Choleski factor of Ω is defined as a lower-triangular matrix L such that $LL' = \Omega$. It is often called the generalized square root of Ω or generalized standard deviation of ε. With $K = 1$ and variance s^2, the Choleski factor is s, which is just the standard deviation of ε. Most statistical and matrix manipulation packages have routines to calculate a Choleski factor for any positive definite, symmetric matrix.

A draw of ε from $N(b, \Omega)$ is obtained as follows. Take K draws from a standard normal, and label the vector of these draws $\eta = \langle \eta_1, \ldots, \eta_K \rangle'$. Calculate $\varepsilon = b + L\eta$. We can verify the properties of ε. It is normally distributed, since the sum of normals is normal. Its mean is b: $E(\varepsilon) = b + LE(\eta) = b$. And its covariance is Ω: $\mathrm{Var}(\varepsilon) = E(L\eta(\eta L)') = LE(\eta\eta')L' = L\mathrm{Var}(\eta)L' = LIL' = LL' = \Omega$.

To be concrete, consider a three-dimensional ε with zero mean. A draw of ε is calculated as

$$\begin{pmatrix} \varepsilon_1 \\ \varepsilon_2 \\ \varepsilon_3 \end{pmatrix} = \begin{pmatrix} s_{11} & 0 & 0 \\ s_{21} & s_{22} & 0 \\ s_{31} & s_{32} & s_{33} \end{pmatrix} \begin{pmatrix} \eta_1 \\ \eta_2 \\ \eta_3 \end{pmatrix},$$

or

$$\varepsilon_1 = s_{11}\eta_1,$$
$$\varepsilon_2 = s_{21}\eta_1 + s_{22}\eta_2,$$
$$\varepsilon_3 = s_{31}\eta_1 + s_{32}\eta_2 + s_{33}\eta_3.$$

From this we see that $\mathrm{Var}(\varepsilon_1) = s_{11}^2$, $\mathrm{Var}(\varepsilon_2) = s_{21}^2 + s_{22}^2$, and $\mathrm{Var}(\varepsilon_3) = s_{31}^2 + s_{32}^2 + s_{33}^2$. Also, $\mathrm{Cov}(\varepsilon_1, \varepsilon_2) = s_{11}s_{21}$, and so on. The elements ε_1 and ε_2 are correlated because of the common influence of η_1 on both of them. They are not perfectly correlated because η_2 enters ε_2 without affecting ε_1. Similar analysis applies to ε_1 and ε_3, and ε_2 and ε_3. Essentially, the Choleski factor expresses K correlated terms as arising from K independent components, with each component *loading* differently onto each term. For any pattern of covariance, there is some set of loadings from independent components that reproduces that covariance.

9.2.6. Accept–Reject for Truncated Multivariate Densities

The procedure in Section 9.2.4 for drawing from truncated densities applies only to univariate distributions. With multivariate densities, drawing from a truncated support is more difficult. We describe an accept–reject procedure that can always be applied. However, as we will see, there are disadvantages of the approach that might cause a researcher to choose another approach when possible.

Suppose we want to draw from multivariate density $g(\varepsilon)$ within the range $a \leq \varepsilon \leq b$ where a and b are vectors with the same length as ε. That is, we want to draw from $f(\varepsilon) = \frac{1}{k}g(\varepsilon)$ if $a \leq \varepsilon \leq b$, and equal zero otherwise, where k is the normalizing constant. We can obtain draws from f by simply drawing from g and retaining ("accepting") the draws that are within the relevant range and discarding ("rejecting") the draws that are outside the range. The advantage of this procedure is that it can be applied whenever it is possible to draw from the untruncated density. Importantly, the normalizing constant, k, does not need to be known for the truncated density. This fact is useful because the normalizing constant is usually difficult to calculate.

The disadvantage of the procedure is that the number of draws that are accepted (that is, the number of draws from f that are obtained) is not fixed but rather is itself random. If R draws are taken from g, then the expected number of accepts is kR. This expected number is not known without knowing k, which, as stated, is usually difficult to calculate. It is therefore hard to determine an appropriate number of draws to take from g. More importantly, the actual number of accepted draws will generally differ from the expected number. In fact, there is a positive probability of obtaining no accepts from a fixed number of draws. When the truncation space is small (or, more precisely, when k is small), obtaining no accepts, and hence no draws from the truncated density, is a likely event.

This difficulty can be circumvented by drawing from g until a certain number of accepted draws is obtained. That is, instead of setting in advance the number of draws from g that will be taken, the researcher can set the number of draws from f that are obtained. Of course, the researcher will not know how long it will take to attain the set number.

In most situations, other procedures can be applied more easily to draw from a multivariate truncated density. Nevertheless, it is important to remember that, when nothing else seems possible with a truncated distribution, the accept–reject procedure can be applied.

9.2.7. Importance Sampling

Suppose ε has a density $f(\varepsilon)$ that cannot be easily drawn from by the other procedures. Suppose further that there is another density, $g(\varepsilon)$, that can easily be drawn from. Draws from $f(\varepsilon)$ can be obtained as follows. Take a draw from $g(\varepsilon)$ and label it ε^1. Weight the draw by $f(\varepsilon^1)/g(\varepsilon^1)$. Repeat this process many times. The set of weighted draws is equivalent to a set of draws from f.

To verify this fact, we show that the cumulative distribution of the weighted draws from g is the same as the cumulative distribution of draws from f. Consider the share of draws from g that are below some value m, with each draw weighted by f/g. This share is

$$\int \frac{f(\varepsilon)}{g(\varepsilon)} I(\varepsilon < m) g(\varepsilon) \, d\varepsilon = \int_{-\infty}^{m} \frac{f(\varepsilon)}{g(\varepsilon)} g(\varepsilon) \, d\varepsilon$$

$$= \int_{-\infty}^{m} f(\varepsilon) \, d\varepsilon = F(m).$$

In simulation, draws from a density are used to calculate the average of a statistic over that density. Importance sampling can be seen as a change in the statistic and a corresponding change in the density that makes the density easy to draw from. Suppose we want to calculate $\int t(\varepsilon)f(\varepsilon)\,d\varepsilon$, but find it hard to draw from f. We can multiply the integrand by $g \div g$ without changing its value, so that the integral is $\int t(\varepsilon)[f(\varepsilon)/g(\varepsilon)]g(\varepsilon)\,d\varepsilon$. To simulate the integral, we take draws from g, calculate $t(\varepsilon)[f(\varepsilon)/g(\varepsilon)]$ for each draw, and average the results. We have simply transformed the integral so that it is easier to simulate.

The density f is called the target density, and g is called the proposal density. The requirements for importance sampling are that (1) the support of $g(\varepsilon)$ needs to cover the support of f, so that any ε that could arise with f can also arise with g, and (2) the ratio $f(\varepsilon)/g(\varepsilon)$ must be finite for all values of ε, so that this ratio can always be calculated.

A useful illustration of importance sampling arises with multivariate truncated normals. Suppose we want to draw from $N(0, \Omega)$ but with each element being positive (i.e., truncated below at zero). The density is

$$f(\varepsilon) = \frac{1}{k(2\pi)^{\frac{1}{2}K}|\Omega|^{1/2}} e^{-\frac{1}{2}\varepsilon'\Omega^{-1}\varepsilon}$$

for $\varepsilon \geq 0$, and 0 otherwise, where K is the dimension of ε and k is the normalizing constant. (We assume for the purposes of this example that k is known. In reality, calculating k might itself take simulation.) Drawing from this density is difficult, because the elements of ε are correlated as well as truncated. However, we can use the procedure in Section 9.2.4 to draw independent truncated normals and then apply importance sampling to create the correlation. Draw K univariate normals truncated below at zero, using the procedure in Section 9.2.4. These draws collectively constitute a draw of a K-dimensional vector ε from the positive quadrant support with density

$$g(\varepsilon) = \frac{1}{m(2\pi)^{\frac{1}{2}K}} e^{-\frac{1}{2}\varepsilon'\varepsilon},$$

where $m = 1/2^K$. For each draw, assign the weight

$$\frac{f(\varepsilon)}{g(\varepsilon)} = \frac{m}{k}|\Omega|^{-1/2} e^{\varepsilon'(\Omega^{-1}-I)\varepsilon}.$$

The weighted draws are equivalent to draws from $N(0, \Omega)$ truncated below at zero.

As a sidelight, note that the accept–reject procedure in Section 9.2.6 is a type of importance sampling. The truncated distribution is the target, and the untruncated distribution is the proposal density. Each draw from the untruncated density is weighted by a constant if the draw is within the truncation space and weighted by zero if the draw is outside the truncation space. Weighting by a constant or zero is equivalent to weighting by one (accept) or zero (reject).

9.2.8. Gibbs Sampling

For multinomial distributions, it is sometimes difficult to draw directly from the joint density and yet easy to draw from the conditional density of each element given the values of the other elements. Gibbs sampling (the term was apparently introduced by Geman and Geman, 1984) can be used in these situations. A general explanation is provided by Casella and George, (1992), which the reader can use to supplement the more concise description that I give in the following.

Consider two random variables ε_1 and ε_2. Generalization to higher dimension is obvious. The joint density is $f(\varepsilon_1, \varepsilon_2)$, and the conditional densities are $f(\varepsilon_1|\varepsilon_2)$ and $f(\varepsilon_2|\varepsilon_1)$. Gibbs sampling proceeds by drawing iteratively from the conditional densities: drawing ε_1 conditional on a value of ε_2, drawing ε_2 conditional on this draw of ε_1, drawing a new ε_1 conditional on the new value of ε_2, and so on. This process converges to draws from the joint density.

To be more precise: (1) Choose an initial value for ε_1, called ε_1^0. Any value with nonzero density can be chosen. (2) Draw a value of ε_2, called ε_2^0, from $f(\varepsilon_2|\varepsilon_1^0)$. (3) Draw a value of ε_1, called ε_1^1, from $f(\varepsilon_1|\varepsilon_2^0)$. (4) Draw ε_2^1 from $f(\varepsilon_2|\varepsilon_1^1)$, and so on. The values of ε_1^t from $f(\varepsilon_1|\varepsilon_2^{t-1})$ and the values of ε_2^t from $f(\varepsilon_2|\varepsilon_1^t)$ constitute a sequence in t. For sufficiently large t (that is, for sufficiently many iterations), the sequence converges to draws from the joint density $f(\varepsilon_1, \varepsilon_2)$.

As an example, consider two standard normal deviates that are independent except that they are truncated on the basis of their sum: $\varepsilon_1 + \varepsilon_2 \leq m$. Figure 9.3 depicts the truncated density. The circles are contours of the untruncated density, and the shaded area represents the truncated density. To derive the conditional densities, consider first the untruncated normals. Since the two deviates are independent, the conditional density of each is the same as its unconditional density. That is, ignoring truncation, $\varepsilon_1|\varepsilon_2 \sim N(0, 1)$. The truncation rule is $\varepsilon_1 + \varepsilon_2 \leq m$ which can be re-expressed as $\varepsilon_1 \leq m - \varepsilon_2$. Therefore, $\varepsilon_1|\varepsilon_2$ is distributed as a univariate standard normal truncated from above at $m - \varepsilon_2$. Given ε_2, a draw of ε_1 is obtained with the procedure in Section 9.2.4: $\varepsilon_1 = \Phi^{-1}(\mu\Phi(m - \varepsilon_2))$, where μ is a standard uniform draw and $\Phi(\cdot)$ is the cumulative standard normal distribution. Draws from ε_2 conditional on ε_1 are obtained analogously. Drawing sequentially from these conditional densities eventually provides draws from the joint truncated density.

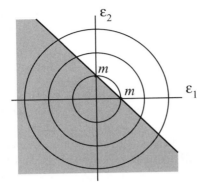

Figure 9.3. Truncated normal density.

9.2.9. Metropolis–Hastings Algorithm

If all else fails, the Metropolis–Hastings (MH) algorithm can be used to obtain draws from a density. Initially developed by Metropolis *et al.* (1953) and generalized by Hastings (1970), the MH algorithm operates as follows. The goal is to obtain draws from $f(\varepsilon)$.

1. Start with a value of the vector ε, labeled ε^0.
2. Choose a trial value of ε^1 as $\tilde{\varepsilon}^1 = \varepsilon^0 + \eta$, where η is drawn from a distribution $g(\eta)$ that has zero mean. Usually a normal distribution is specified for $g(\eta)$.
3. Calculate the density at the trial value $\tilde{\varepsilon}^1$, and compare it with the density at the original value ε^0. That is, compare $f(\tilde{\varepsilon}^1)$ with $f(\varepsilon^0)$. If $f(\tilde{\varepsilon}^1) > f(\varepsilon^0)$, then accept $\tilde{\varepsilon}^1$, label it ε^1, and move to step 4. If $f(\tilde{\varepsilon}^1) \leq f(\varepsilon^0)$, then accept $\tilde{\varepsilon}^1$ with probability $f(\tilde{\varepsilon}^1)/f(\varepsilon^0)$, and reject it with probability $1 - f(\tilde{\varepsilon}^1)/f(\varepsilon^0)$. To determine whether to accept or reject $\tilde{\varepsilon}^1$ in this case, draw a standard uniform μ. If $\mu \leq f(\tilde{\varepsilon}^1)/f(\varepsilon^0)$, then keep $\tilde{\varepsilon}^1$. Otherwise, reject $\tilde{\varepsilon}^1$. If $\tilde{\varepsilon}^1$ is accepted, then label it ε^1. If $\tilde{\varepsilon}^1$ is rejected, then use ε^0 as ε^1.
4. Choose a trial value of ε^2 as $\tilde{\varepsilon}^2 = \varepsilon^1 + \eta$, where η is a new draw from $g(\eta)$.
5. Apply the rule in step 3 to either accept $\tilde{\varepsilon}^2$ as ε^2 or reject $\tilde{\varepsilon}^2$ and use ε^1 as ε^2.
6. Continue this process for many iterations. The sequence ε^t becomes equivalent to draws from $f(\varepsilon)$ for sufficiently large t.

The draws are serially correlated, since each draw depends on the previous draw. In fact, when a trial value is rejected, the current draw is the same as the previous draw. This serial correlation needs to be considered when using these draws.

The MH algorithm can be applied with any density that can be calculated. The algorithm is particularly useful when the normalizing constant for a density is not known or cannot be easily calculated. Suppose that we know that ε is distributed proportional to $f^*(\varepsilon)$. This means that the density of ε is $f(\varepsilon) = \frac{1}{k}f^*(\varepsilon)$, where the normalizing constant $k = \int f^*(\varepsilon)\,d\varepsilon$ assures that f integrates to 1. Usually k cannot be calculated analytically, for the same reason that we need to simulate integrals in other settings. Luckily, the MH algorithm does not utilize k. A trial value of ε^t is tested by first determining whether $f(\tilde{\varepsilon}^t) > f(\varepsilon^{t-1})$. This comparison is unaffected by the normalizing constant, since the constant enters the denominator on both sides. Then, if $f(\tilde{\varepsilon}^t) \leq f(\varepsilon^{t-1})$, we accept the trial value with probability $f(\tilde{\varepsilon}^t)/f(\varepsilon^{t-1})$. The normalizing constant drops out of this ratio.

The MH algorithm is actually more general than I describe here, though in practice it is usually applied as I describe. Chib and Greenberg, (1995) provide an excellent description of the more general algorithm as well as an explanation of why it works. Under the more general definition, Gibbs sampling is a special case of the MH algorithm, as Gelman, (1992) pointed out. The MH algorithm and Gibbs sampling are often called Markov chain Monte Carlo (MCMC, or MC-squared) methods; a description of their use in econometrics is provided by Chib and Greenberg (1996). The draws are Markov chains because each value depends only on the immediately preceding one, and the methods are Monte Carlo because random draws are taken. We explore further issues about the MH algorithm, such as how to choose $g(\varepsilon)$, in the context of its use with hierarchical Bayes procedures (in Chapter 12).

9.3   Variance Reduction

The use of independent random draws in simulation is appealing because it is conceptually straightforward and the statistical properties of the resulting simulator are easy to derive. However, there are other ways to take draws that can provide greater accuracy for a given number of draws. We examine these alternative methods in the following sections.

Recall that the objective is to approximate an integral of the form $\int t(\varepsilon)f(\varepsilon)\,d\varepsilon$. In taking a sequence of draws from the density $f(\cdot)$, two issues are at stake: coverage and covariance. Consider coverage first. The integral is over the entire density f. It seems reasonable that a more accurate approximation would be obtained by evaluating $t(\varepsilon)$ at values of

ε that are spread throughout the domain of f. With independent random draws, it is possible that the draws will be clumped together, with no draws from large areas of the domain. Procedures that guarantee better coverage can be expected to provide a better approximation.

Covariance is another issue. With independent draws, the covariance over draws is zero. The variance of a simulator based on R independent draws is therefore the variance based on one draw divided by R. If the draws are negatively correlated instead of independent, then the variance of the simulator is lower. Consider $R = 2$. The variance of $\check{t} = [t(\varepsilon_1) + t(\varepsilon_2)]/2$ is $[V(t(\varepsilon_1)) + V(t(\varepsilon_2)) + 2\operatorname{Cov}(t(\varepsilon_1), t(\varepsilon_2))]/4$. If the draws are independent, then the variance is $V(t(\varepsilon_r))/2$. If the two draws are negatively correlated with each other, the covariance term is negative and the variance becomes less than $V(t(\varepsilon_r))/2$. Essentially, when the draws are negatively correlated within an unbiased simulator, a value above $\bar{t} = E_r(t(\varepsilon))$ for one draw will tend to be associated with a value for the next draw that is below $E_r(t(\varepsilon))$, such that their average is closer to the true value $\bar{t}$.

The same concept arises when simulators are summed over observations. For example, the simulated log-likelihood function is a sum over observations of the log of simulated probabilities. If the draws for each observation's simulation are independent of the draws for the other observations, then the variance of the sum is simply the sum of the variances. If the draws are taken in a way that creates negative correlation over observations, then the variance of the sum is lower.

For a given observation, the issue of covariance is related to coverage. By inducing a negative correlation between draws, better coverage is usually assured. With $R = 2$, if the two draws are taken independently, then both could end up being at the low side of the distribution. If negative correlation is induced, then the second draw will tend to be high if the first draw is low, which provides better coverage.

We describe below methods to attain better coverage for each observation's integral and to induce negative correlation over the draws for each observation as well as over observations. We assume for the sake of discussion that the integral is a choice probability and that the sum over observations is the simulated log-likelihood function. However, the concepts apply to other integrals, such as scores, and to other sums, such as moment conditions and market shares. Also, unless otherwise noted, we illustrate the methods with only two random terms so that the draws can be depicted graphically. The random terms are labeled ε^a and ε^b, and collectively as $\varepsilon = \langle \varepsilon^a, \varepsilon^b \rangle'$. A draw of ε from its density $f(\varepsilon)$ is denoted $\varepsilon_r = \langle \varepsilon_r^a, \varepsilon_r^b \rangle'$ for $r = 1, \ldots, R$. Thus, ε_3^a, for example, is the third draw of the first random term.

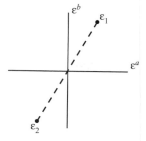

Figure 9.4. Reverse sign of both elements.

9.3.1. Antithetics

Antithetic draws, suggested by Hammersley and Morton (1956), are obtained by creating various types of mirror images of a random draw. For a symmetric density that is centered on zero, the simplest antithetic variate is created by reversing the sign of all elements of a draw. Figure 9.4 illustrates. Suppose a random draw is taken from $f(\varepsilon)$ and the value $\varepsilon_1 = \langle \varepsilon_1^a, \varepsilon_1^b \rangle'$ is obtained. The second "draw," which is called the antithetic of the first draw, is created as $\varepsilon_2 = \langle -\varepsilon_1^a, -\varepsilon_1^b \rangle'$. Each draw from f creates a pair of "draws," the original draw and its mirror image (mirrored through the origin). To obtain a total of R draws, $R/2$ draws are taken independently from f and the other $R/2$ are created as the negative of the original draws.

When the density is not centered on zero, the same concept is applied but through a different process. For example, the standard uniform density is between 0 and 1, centered on 0.5. A draw is taken, labeled μ_1, and its antithetic variate is created as $\mu_2 = 1 - \mu_1$. The variate is the same distance from 0.5 as the original draw, but on the other side of 0.5. In general, for any univariate density with cumulative function $F(\varepsilon)$, the antithetic of a draw ε is created as $F^{-1}(1 - F(\varepsilon))$. In the case of a symmetric density centered on zero, this general formula is equivalent to simply reversing the sign. In the remaining discussion we assume that the density is symmetric and centered on zero, which makes the concepts easier to express and visualize.

The correlation between a draw and its antithetic variate is exactly -1, so that the variance of their sum is zero: $V(\varepsilon_1 + \varepsilon_2) = V(\varepsilon_1) + V(\varepsilon_2) + 2\,\mathrm{Cov}(\varepsilon_1, \varepsilon_2) = 0$. This fact does not mean that there is no variance in the simulated probability that is based on these draws. The simulated probability is a nonlinear function of the random terms, and so the correlation between $P(\varepsilon_1)$ and $P(\varepsilon_2)$ is less than one. The variance of the simulated probability $\check{P} = \frac{1}{2}[P(\varepsilon_1) + P(\varepsilon_2)]$ is greater than zero. However, the

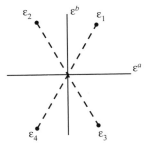

Figure 9.5. Reverse sign of each element, then of both.

variance of the simulated probabilities is less than $\frac{1}{2}V_r(P(\varepsilon_r))$, which is the variance with two independent draws.

As shown in Figure 9.4, reversing the sign of a draw gives evaluation points in opposite quadrants. The concept can be extended to obtain draws in each quadrant. A draw is taken, and then antithetic draws are created by reversing the sign of each element alone (leaving the sign of the other elements unchanged), reversing the sign of each pair of elements, each triplet of elements, and so on. For ε with two elements, this process creates three antithetic draws for each independent draw. For $\varepsilon_1 = \langle \varepsilon_1^a, \varepsilon_1^b \rangle'$, the antithetic draws are

$$\varepsilon_2 = \langle -\varepsilon_1^a, \varepsilon_1^b \rangle',$$
$$\varepsilon_3 = \langle \varepsilon_1^a, -\varepsilon_1^b \rangle',$$
$$\varepsilon_4 = \langle -\varepsilon_1^a, -\varepsilon_1^b \rangle'.$$

These draws are shown in Figure 9.5. Each quadrant contains a draw.

Better coverage and higher negative correlation can be obtained by shifting the position of each element as well as reversing their signs. In Figure 9.5, ε_1 and ε_2 are fairly close together, as are ε_3 and ε_4. This placement leaves large uncovered areas between ε_1 and ε_3 and between ε_2 and ε_4. Orthogonal draws with even placement can be obtained by switching element ε_1^a with ε_1^b while also reversing the signs. The antithetic draws are

$$\varepsilon_2 = \langle -\varepsilon_1^b, \varepsilon_1^a \rangle',$$
$$\varepsilon_3 = \langle \varepsilon_1^b, -\varepsilon_1^a \rangle',$$
$$\varepsilon_4 = \langle -\varepsilon_1^a, -\varepsilon_1^b \rangle',$$

which are illustrated in Figure 9.6. These concepts can, of course, be extended to any number of dimensions. For M-dimensional ε, each random draw creates 2^M antithetic draws (including the original one), with one in each quadrant.

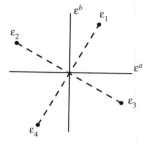

Figure 9.6. Switch positions and reverse signs.

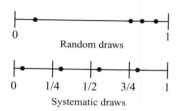

Figure 9.7. Draws from standard uniform.

Comparisons performed by Vijverberg (1997) and Sándor and András (2001) show that antithetics substantially improve the estimation of probit models. Similarly, Geweke (1988) has shown their value when calculating statistics based on Bayesian posteriors.

9.3.2. Systematic Sampling

Coverage can also be improved through systematic sampling (McGrath, 1970), which creates a grid of points over the support of the density and randomly shifts the entire grid. Consider draws from a uniform distribution between 0 and 1. If four draws are taken independently, the points may look like those in the top part of Figure 9.7, which provide fairly poor coverage. Instead, the unit interval is divided into four segments and draws taken in a way that assures one draw in each segment with equal distance between the draws. Take a draw from a uniform between 0 and 0.25 (by drawing from a standard uniform and dividing the result by 4). Label the draw ε_1. Three other draws are created as

$$\varepsilon_2 = 0.25 + \varepsilon_1,$$
$$\varepsilon_3 = 0.50 + \varepsilon_1,$$
$$\varepsilon_4 = 0.75 + \varepsilon_1.$$

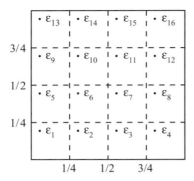

Figure 9.8. Systematic draws in two dimensions.

These draws look like those in the bottom part of Figure 9.7, which provide better coverage than independent draws.

The issue arises of how finely to segment the interval. For example, to obtain a total of 100 draws, the unit interval can be divided into 100 segments. A draw between 0 and 0.01 is taken, and then the other 99 draws are created from this one draw. Instead, the unit interval can be divided into fewer than 100 draws and more independent draws taken. If the interval is divided into four segments, then 25 independent draws are taken between 0 and 0.25, and three draws in the other segments are created for each of the independent draws. There is a tradeoff that the researcher must consider in deciding how fine a grid to use in systematic sampling. More segments provide more even coverage for a given total number of draws. However, fewer segments provide more randomness to the process. In our example with $R = 100$, there is only one random draw when 100 segments are used, whereas there are 25 random draws when four segments are used.

The randomness of simulation draws is a necessary component in the derivation of the asymptotic properties of the simulation-based estimators, as described in Chapter 10. Many of the asymptotic properties rely on the concept that the number of random draws increases without bound with sample size. The asymptotic distributions become relatively accurate only when enough random draws have been taken. Therefore, for a given total number of draws, the goal of better coverage, which is attained with a more finely defined segmentation, needs to be traded off against the goal of having enough randomness for the asymptotic formulas to apply, which is attained with a more coarsely defined segmentation. The same issue applies to the antithetics discussed earlier.

Systematic sampling can be performed in multiple dimensions. Consider a two-dimensional uniform on the unit square. A grid is created by dividing each dimension into segments. As shown in Figure 9.8,

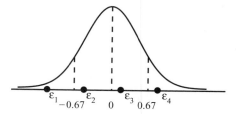

Figure 9.9. Systematic draws for univariate normal.

when each dimension is divided into four segments, the unit square is partitioned into 16 areas. A draw between 0 and 0.25 is taken for each element, giving $\varepsilon_1 = \langle \varepsilon_1^a, \varepsilon_1^b \rangle'$, where $0 < \varepsilon_1^a < 0.25$ and $0 < \varepsilon_1^b < 0.25$. This draw falls somewhere in the bottom-left area in Figure 9.8. Fifteen other draws are then created as the "origin" of each area, plus $\langle \varepsilon_1^a, \varepsilon_1^b \rangle'$. For example, the point that is created for the bottom-right area is $\varepsilon_4 = \langle (0.75 + \varepsilon_1^a), (0 + \varepsilon_1^b) \rangle'$.

These draws are defined for a uniform distribution. When f represents another density, the points are transformed using the method described in Section 9.2.3. In particular, let F be the cumulative distribution associated with univariate density f. Systematic draws from f are created by transforming each systematic draw from a uniform by F^{-1}. For example, for a standard normal, four equal-sized segments of the density are created with breakpoints: $\Phi^{-1}(0.25) = -0.67$, $\Phi^{-1}(0.5) = 0$, and $\Phi^{-1}(0.75) = 0.67$. As shown in Figure 9.9, these segments are equal-sized in the sense that each contains the same mass. The draws for the standard normal are created by taking a draw from a uniform between 0 and 0.25, labeled μ_1. The corresponding point on the normal is $\varepsilon_1 = \Phi^{-1}(\mu_1)$, which falls in the first segment. The points for the other three segments are created as $\varepsilon_2 = \Phi^{-1}(0.25 + \mu_1)$, $\varepsilon_3 = \Phi^{-1}(0.5 + \mu_1)$, and $\varepsilon_4 = \Phi^{-1}(0.75 + \mu_1)$.

Draws of multidimensional random terms are obtained similarly, provided that the elements are independent. For example, if ε consists of two elements each of which is standard normal, then draws analogous to those in Figure 9.8 are obtained as follows: Draw μ_1^a and μ_1^b from a uniform between 0 and 0.25. Calculate ε_1 as $\langle \Phi^{-1}(\mu_1^a), \Phi^{-1}(\mu_1^b) \rangle'$. Calculate the other 15 points as ε_r as $\langle \Phi^{-1}(x_r + \mu_1^a), \Phi^{-1}(y_r + \mu_1^b) \rangle'$, where $\langle x_r, y_r \rangle'$ is the origin of area r in the unit square.

The requirement that the elements of ε be independent is not restrictive. Correlated random elements are created through transformations of independent elements, such as the Choleski transformation. The independent elements are drawn from their density, and then the correlation is created inside the model.

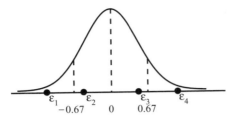

Figure 9.10. Symmetric systematic draws.

Obviously, numerous sets of systematically sampled draws can be obtained to gain more randomization. In two dimensions with four segments in each dimension, 64 draws are obtained by taking 4 independent draws in the 0-to-$\frac{1}{4}$ square and creating 15 other draws from each. This procedure provides greater randomization but less fine coverage than defining the draws in terms of eight segments in each dimension such that each random draw in the 0 to $\frac{1}{8}$ square translates into 64 systematic draws.

The draws for the normal distribution that are created as just described are not symmetric around zero. An alternative approach can be used to assure such symmetry. For a unidimensional normal, 4 draws that are symmetric around zero are obtained as follows. Draw a uniform between 0 and 0.25, labeled μ_1. Create the draw from the normal as $\varepsilon_1 = \Phi^{-1}(\mu_1)$. Create the draw for the second segment as $\varepsilon_2 = \Phi^{-1}(0.25 + \mu_1)$. Then create the draws for the third and fourth segments as the negative of these draws: $\varepsilon_3 = -\varepsilon_2$ and $\varepsilon_4 = -\varepsilon_1$. Figure 9.10 illustrates the draws using the same μ_1 as for Figure 9.9. This procedure combines systematic sampling with antithetics. It can be extended to multiple dimensions by creating systematic draws for the positive quadrant and then creating antithetic variates for the other quadrants.

9.3.3. Halton Sequences

Halton sequences (Halton, 1960) provide coverage and, unlike the other methods we have discussed, induce a negative correlation over observations. A Halton sequence is defined in terms of a given number, usually a prime. The sequence is most easily understood though an example. Consider the prime 3. The Halton sequence for 3 is created by dividing the unit interval into three parts with breaks at $\frac{1}{3}$ and $\frac{2}{3}$, as shown in the top panel of Figure 9.11. The first terms in the sequence are these breakpoints: $\frac{1}{3}$, $\frac{2}{3}$. Then each of the three segments is divided into thirds, and the breakpoints for these segments are added to the sequences in a

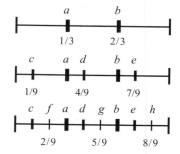

Figure 9.11. Halton sequence for prime 3.

particular way. The sequence becomes $\frac{1}{3}, \frac{2}{3}, \frac{1}{9}, \frac{4}{9}, \frac{7}{9}, \frac{2}{9}, \frac{5}{9}, \frac{8}{9}$. Note that the lower breakpoints in all three segments $(\frac{1}{9}, \frac{4}{9}, \frac{7}{9})$ are entered in the sequence before the higher breakpoints $(\frac{2}{9}, \frac{5}{9}, \frac{8}{9}.)$ Then each of the nine segments is divided into thirds, with the breakpoints added to the sequences. The sequence becomes $\frac{1}{3}, \frac{2}{3}, \frac{1}{9}, \frac{4}{9}, \frac{7}{9}, \frac{2}{9}, \frac{5}{9}, \frac{8}{9}, \frac{1}{27}, \frac{10}{27}, \frac{19}{27}, \frac{4}{27}, \frac{13}{27},$ and so on. This process is continued for as many points as the researcher wants to obtain.

From a programming perspective, it is easy to create a Halton sequence. The sequence is created iteratively. At each iteration t, the sequence is denoted s_t, which is a series of numbers. The sequence is extended in each iteration with the new sequence being $s_{t+1} = \{s_t, s_t + 1/3^t, s_t + 2/3^t\}$. Start with 0 as the initial sequence: $s_0 = \{0\}$. The number zero is not actually part of a Halton sequence, but considering it to be the first element facilitates creation of the sequence, as we will see. It can be dropped after the entire sequence is created. In the first iteration, add $1/3^1$ $(= \frac{1}{3})$ and then $2/3^1$ $(= \frac{2}{3})$ to this element and append the results, to get $\{0, \frac{1}{3}, \frac{2}{3}\}$. The sequence has three elements. In the second iteration, add $1/3^2$ $(= \frac{1}{9})$ and then $2/3^2$ $(= \frac{2}{9})$ to each element of the sequence and append the results:

$$
\begin{aligned}
0 &= 0, \\
1/3 &= 1/3, \\
2/3 &= 2/3, \\
0 + 1/9 &= 1/9, \\
1/3 + 1/9 &= 4/9, \\
2/3 + 1/9 &= 7/9, \\
0 + 2/9 &= 2/9, \\
1/3 + 2/9 &= 5/9, \\
2/3 + 2/9 &= 8/9.
\end{aligned}
$$

The new sequence consists of nine elements.

In the third iteration, add $1/3^3$ ($= \frac{1}{27}$) and then $2/3^3$ ($= \frac{1}{27}$) to each element of this sequence and append the results:

$$0 = 0,$$
$$1/3 = 1/3,$$
$$2/3 = 2/3,$$
$$1/9 = 1/9,$$
$$4/9 = 4/9,$$
$$7/9 = 7/9,$$
$$2/9 = 2/9,$$
$$5/9 = 5/9,$$
$$8/9 = 8/9,$$
$$0 + 1/27 = 1/27,$$
$$1/3 + 1/27 = 10/27,$$
$$2/3 + 1/27 = 19/27,$$
$$1/9 + 1/27 = 4/27,$$
$$4/9 + 1/27 = 13/27,$$
$$7/9 + 1/27 = 22/27,$$
$$2/9 + 1/27 = 7/27,$$
$$5/9 + 1/27 = 16/27,$$
$$8/9 + 1/27 = 25/27,$$
$$0 + 2/27 = 2/27,$$
$$1/3 + 2/27 = 11/27,$$
$$2/3 + 2/27 = 20/27,$$
$$1/9 + 2/27 = 5/27,$$
$$4/9 + 2/27 = 14/27,$$
$$7/9 + 2/27 = 23/27,$$
$$2/9 + 2/27 = 8/27,$$
$$5/9 + 2/27 = 17/27,$$
$$8/9 + 2/27 = 26/27.$$

The sequence now consists of 27 elements. In the fourth iteration, add $1/3^4$ ($= \frac{1}{81}$) and then $2/3^4$ ($= \frac{2}{81}$) to each element of the sequence and append the results, and so on.

Note that the sequence cycles over the unit interval every three numbers:

0	1/3	2/3
1/9	4/9	7/9
2/9	5/9	8/9
1/27	10/27	19/27
4/27	13/27	22/27
7/27	16/27	25/27

2/27	11/27	20/27
5/27	14/27	23/27
8/27	17/27	26/27

Within each cycle the numbers are ascending.

Halton sequences for other prime numbers are created similarly. The sequence for 2 is $\{\frac{1}{2}, \frac{1}{4}, \frac{3}{4}, \frac{1}{8}, \frac{5}{8}, \frac{3}{8}, \frac{7}{8}, \frac{1}{16}, \frac{9}{16}, \ldots\}$. In general, the sequence for prime k is created iteratively, with the sequence at iteration $t + 1$ being $s_{t+1} = \{s_t, s_t + 1/k^t, s_t + 2/k^t, \ldots, s_t + (k - 1)/k^t\}$. The sequence contains cycles of length k, where each cycle consists of k ascending points on the unit interval equidistant from each other.

Since a Halton sequence is defined on the unit interval, its elements can be considered as well-placed "draws" from a standard uniform density. The Halton draws provide better coverage than random draws, on average, because they are created to progressively fill in the unit interval evenly and ever more densely. The elements in each cycle are equidistant apart, and each cycle covers the unit interval in the areas not covered by previous cycles.

When using Halton draws for a sample of observations, one long Halton sequence is usually created and then part of the sequence is used for each observation. The initial elements of the sequence are discarded for reasons we will discuss. The remaining elements are then used in groups, with each group of elements constituting the "draws" for one observation. For example, suppose there are two observations, and the researcher wants $R = 5$ draws for each. If the prime 3 is used, and the researcher decides to discard the first 10 elements, then a sequence of length 20 is created. This sequence is

0	1/3	2/3
1/9	4/9	7/9
2/9	5/9	8/9
1/27	10/27	19/27
4/27	13/27	22/27
7/27	16/27	25/27
2/27	11/27.	

After eliminating the first 10 elements, the Halton draws for the first observation are $\{\frac{10}{27}, \frac{19}{27}, \frac{4}{27}, \frac{13}{27}, \frac{22}{27}\}$ and the Halton draws for the second observation are $\{\frac{7}{27}, \frac{16}{27}, \frac{25}{27}, \frac{2}{27}, \frac{11}{27}\}$. These draws are illustrated in Figure 9.12. Note that the gaps in coverage for the first observation are filled by the draws for the second observation. For example, the large gap between $\frac{4}{27}$ and $\frac{10}{27}$ for the first observation is filled in by the midpoint of this gap, $\frac{7}{27}$, for the second observation. The gap between $\frac{13}{27}$ and $\frac{19}{27}$ is

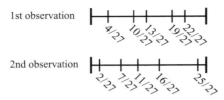

Figure 9.12. Halton draws for two observations.

filled in by its midpoint, $\frac{16}{27}$, for the second observation, and so on. The pattern by which Halton sequences are created makes them such that each subsequence fills in the gaps of the previous subsequences.

Because of this filling-in property, simulated probabilities based on Halton draws tend to be self-correcting over observations. The draws for one observation tend to be negatively correlated with those for the previous observation. In our example, the average of the first observation's draws is above 0.5, while the average of the draws for the second observation is below 0.5. This negative correlation reduces error in the simulated log-likelihood function.

When the number of draws used for each observation rises, the coverage for each observation improves. The negative covariance across observations diminishes, since there are fewer gaps in each observation's coverage to be filled in by the next observation. The self-correcting aspect of Halton draws over observations is greatest when few draws are used for each observation so that the correction is most needed. However, accuracy improves with more Halton draws, since coverage is better for each observation.

As described so far, the Halton draws are for a uniform density. To obtain a sequence of points for other univariate densities, the inverse cumulative distribution is evaluated at each element of the Halton sequence. For example, suppose the researcher wants draws from a standard normal density. A Halton sequence is created for, say, prime 3, and the inverse cumulative normal is taken for each element. The resulting sequence is

$$\Phi^{-1}\left(\tfrac{1}{3}\right) = -0.43,$$
$$\Phi^{-1}\left(\tfrac{2}{3}\right) = 0.43,$$
$$\Phi^{-1}\left(\tfrac{1}{9}\right) = -1.2,$$
$$\Phi^{-1}\left(\tfrac{4}{9}\right) = -0.14,$$
$$\Phi^{-1}\left(\tfrac{7}{9}\right) = 0.76,$$
$$\vdots$$

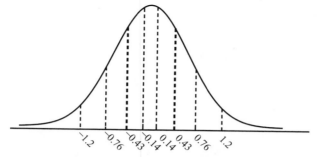

Figure 9.13. Halton draws for a standard normal.

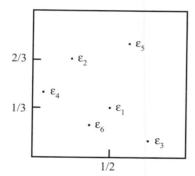

Figure 9.14. Halton sequence in two dimensions for primes 2 and 3.

This sequence is depicted in Figure 9.13. It can be considered the same as for the unit interval, as dividing the density into three segments of equal mass, with breakpoints at -0.43 and $+0.43$, and then dividing each segment into three subsegments of equal mass, and so on.

Halton sequences in multiple dimensions are obtained by creating a Halton sequence for each dimension with a different prime for each dimension. For example, a sequence in two dimensions is obtained by creating pairs from the Halton sequence for primes 2 and 3. The points are

$$\varepsilon_1 = \left\langle \tfrac{1}{2}, \tfrac{1}{3} \right\rangle,$$
$$\varepsilon_2 = \left\langle \tfrac{1}{4}, \tfrac{2}{3} \right\rangle,$$
$$\varepsilon_3 = \left\langle \tfrac{3}{4}, \tfrac{1}{9} \right\rangle,$$
$$\varepsilon_4 = \left\langle \tfrac{1}{8}, \tfrac{4}{9} \right\rangle,$$
$$\varepsilon_5 = \left\langle \tfrac{5}{8}, \tfrac{7}{9} \right\rangle,$$
$$\varepsilon_6 = \left\langle \tfrac{3}{8}, \tfrac{2}{9} \right\rangle,$$
$$\vdots$$

This sequence is depicted in Figure 9.14. To obtain draws for a

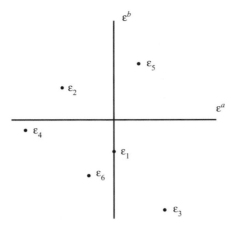

Figure 9.15. Halton sequence for two-dimensional standard normal.

two-dimensional independent standard normal, the inverse cumulative normal is taken of each element of these pairs. The draws are

$$\varepsilon_1 = \langle 0, -0.43 \rangle,$$
$$\varepsilon_2 = \langle -0.67, 0.43 \rangle,$$
$$\varepsilon_3 = \langle 0.67, -1.2 \rangle,$$
$$\varepsilon_4 = \langle -1.15, -0.14 \rangle,$$
$$\varepsilon_5 = \langle 0.32, 0.76 \rangle,$$
$$\varepsilon_6 = \langle -.32, -0.76 \rangle,$$
$$\vdots$$

which are shown in Figure 9.15.

When creating sequences in several dimensions, it is customary to eliminate the initial part of the series. The initial terms of two Halton sequences are highly correlated, through at least the first cycle of each sequence. For example, the sequences for 7 and 11 begin with $\{\frac{1}{7}, \frac{2}{7}, \frac{3}{7}, \frac{4}{7}, \frac{5}{7}, \frac{6}{7}\}$ and $\{\frac{1}{11}, \frac{2}{11}, \frac{3}{11}, \frac{4}{11}, \frac{5}{11}, \frac{6}{11}\}$. These first elements fall on a line in two dimensions, as shown in Figure 9.16. The correlation dissipates after each sequence has cycled through the unit interval, since sequences with different primes cycle at different rates. Discarding the initial part of the sequence eliminates the correlation. The number of initial elements to discard needs to be at least as large as the largest prime that is used in creating the sequences.

The potential for correlation is the reason that prime numbers are used to create the Halton sequences instead of nonprimes. If a nonprime is used, then there is a possibility that the cycles will coincide throughout the entire sequence, rather than for just the initial elements. For example,

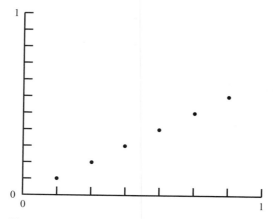

Figure 9.16. First six elements of Halton sequence for primes 7 and 11.

if Halton sequences are created for 3 and 6, the sequence for 3 cycles twice for every one cycle of the sequence for 6. Since the elements within a cycle are ascending, the elements in each cycle of the sequence for 3 are correlated with the elements in the cycle of the sequence for 6. Using only prime numbers avoids this overlapping of cycles.

The superior coverage and the negative correlation over observations that are obtained with Halton draws combine to make Halton draws far more effective than random draws for simulation. Spanier and Maize (1991) have shown that a small number of Halton draws provide relatively good integration. In the context of discrete choice models, Bhat (2001) found that 100 Halton draws provided more precise results for his mixed logit than 1000 random draws. In fact, the simulation error with 125 Halton draws was half as large as with 1000 random draws and somewhat smaller than with 2000 random draws. Train (2000), Munizaga and Alvarez-Daziano (2001), and Hensher (2001) confirm these results on other datasets.

As illustration, consider the mixed logit model that is described extensively in Chapter 11. Briefly, the model is for households' choice of electricity supplier. In a stated-preference survey, respondents were presented with a series of hypothetical choice situations. In each situation, four energy suppliers were described and the respondent was asked which company he would choose. The suppliers were differentiated on the basis of their price, whether the company required the customer to sign a long-term contract, whether the supplier was the local energy utility, whether the supplier was a well-known company, and whether the supplier offered time-of-day (TOD) or seasonal rates. A mixed logit model was estimated with these six characteristics as explanatory

Table 9.1. *Means of parameter estimates*

	1000 Random Draws	100 Halton Draws
Price	−0.8607	−0.8588
Contract length:		
Mean	−0.1955	−0.1965
Std. dev.	0.3092	0.3158
Local utility:		
Mean	2.0967	2.1142
Std. dev.	1.0535	1.0236
Known company:		
Mean	1.4310	1.4419
Std. dev.	0.8208	0.6894
TOD rates:		
Mean	−8.3760	−8.4149
Std. dev.	2.4647	2.5466
Seasonal rates:		
Mean	−8.6286	−8.6381
Std. dev.	1.8492	1.8977

variables. The coefficient of each variable was assumed to be normally distributed, except for the price coefficient, which was assumed to be fixed. The model therefore contained five random terms for simulation. A complete description of the data, the estimated model, and its implications are given in Chapter 11, where the content of the model is relevant to the topic of the chapter. For now, we are concerned only with the issue of Halton draws compared to random draws.

To investigate this issue, the model was estimated with 1000 random draws and then with 100 Halton draws. More specifically, the model was estimated five times using five different sets of 1000 random draws. The mean and standard deviation of the estimated parameters from these five runs were calculated. The model was then estimated five times with Halton sequences. The first model used the primes 2, 3, 5, 7, 11 for the five dimensions of simulation. The order of the primes was switched for the other models, so that the dimension for which each prime was used changed in the five runs. The average and standard deviation of the five sets of estimates were then calculated.

The means of the parameter estimates over the five runs are given in Table 9.1. The mean for the runs based on random draws are given in the first column, and the means for the runs based on Halton draws are given in the second column. The two sets of means are very similar. This result indicates that the Halton draws provide the same estimates, *on average*, as random draws.

Table 9.2. *Standard deviations of parameter estimates*

	1000 Random Draws	100 Halton Draws
Price	0.0310	0.0169
Contract length:		
Mean	0.0093	0.0045
Std. dev.	0.0222	0.0108
Local utility:		
Mean	0.0844	0.0361
Std. dev.	0.1584	0.1180
Known company:		
Mean	0.0580	0.0242
Std. dev.	0.0738	0.1753
TOD rates:		
Mean	0.3372	0.1650
Std. dev.	0.1578	0.0696
Seasonal rates:		
Mean	0.4134	0.1789
Std. dev.	0.2418	0.0679

The standard deviations of the parameter estimates are given in Table 9.2. For all but one of the 11 parameters, the standard deviations are lower with 100 Halton draws than with 1000 random draws. For eight of the parameters, the standard deviations are half as large. Given that both sets of draws give essentially the same means, the lower standard deviations with the Halton draws indicate that a researcher can expect to be closer to the expected values of the estimates using 100 Halton draws than 1000 random draws.

These results show the value of Halton draws. Computer time can be reduced by a factor of ten by using Halton draws instead of random draws, without reducing, and in fact increasing, accuracy.

These results need to be viewed with caution, however. The use of Halton draws and other quasi-random numbers in simulation-based estimation is fairly new and not completely understood. For example, an anomaly arose in the analysis that serves as a warning. The model was reestimated with 125 Halton draws instead of 100. It was estimated five times under each of the five orderings of the prime numbers as described earlier. Four of the five runs provided very similar estimates. However, the fifth run gave estimates that were noticeably different from the others. For example, the estimated price coefficient for the first four runs was −0.862, −0.865, −0.863, and −0.864, respectively, while the fifth gave −0.911. The standard deviations over the five sets of estimates were lower than with 1000 random draws, confirming the value of the Halton draws. However, the standard deviations were greater with 125 Halton draws than with 100 Halton draws, due to the last run with 125 draws providing such different results. The reason for this anomaly has not been determined. Its occurrence indicates the need for further investigation of the properties of Halton sequences in simulation-based estimation.

9.3.4. Randomized Halton Draws

Halton sequences are systematic rather than random. However, the asymptotic properties of simulation-based estimators are derived under the assumption that the draws are random. There are two ways that this issue can be addressed. First, one can realize that draws from a random number generator are not actually random either. They are systematic, like anything done by a computer. A random number generator creates draws that have many of the characteristics of truly random draws, but in fact they are only pseudorandom. In this regard, therefore, Halton draws can be seen as a systematic way of approximating integration that is more precise than using pseudorandom draws, which are also systematic. Neither matches the theoretical concept of randomness, and, in fact, it is not clear that the theoretical concept actually has a real-world counterpart. Both meet the basic underlying goal of approximating an integral over a density.

Second, Halton sequences can be transformed in a way that makes them random, at least in the same way that pseudorandom numbers are random. Bhat (forthcoming) describes the process, based on procedures introduced by Tuffin (1996):

1. Take a draw from a standard uniform density. Label this random draw μ.
2. Add μ to each element of the Halton sequence. If the resulting element exceeds 1, subtract 1 from it. Otherwise, keep the resulting element as is (without subtracting 1).

The formula for this transformation is $s_n = \text{mod}(s_o + \mu)$, where s_o is the original element of the Halton sequence, s_n is the transformed element, and mod takes the fractional part of the argument in parentheses.

The transformation is depicted in Figure 9.17. Suppose the draw of μ from the uniform density is 0.40. The number 0.33 is the first element of the Halton sequence for prime 3. This element is transformed, as shown in the top panel, to $0.33 + 0.40 = 0.73$, which is just a 0.40 move up

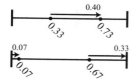

Figure 9.17. Random transformation of Halton draws with $\mu = 0.40$.

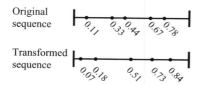

Figure 9.18. Randomization of Halton sequence in one dimension.

the line. The number 0.67 is the second element of the sequence. It is transformed by adding 0.4 and then, since the result exceeds 1, by subtracting 1 to get 0.07 $(0.67 + 0.40 - 1 = 0.07)$. As shown in the bottom panel, this transformation is visualized as moving the original point up by a distance 0.40, but wrapping around when the end of the unit interval is reached. The point moves up 0.33 to where the line ends, and then wraps to the start of the line and continues to move up another 0.07, for a total movement of 0.40.

Figure 9.18 depicts the transformation for the first five elements of the sequence. The relation between the points and the degree of coverage are the same before and after the transformation. However, since the transformation is based on the random draw of μ, the numerical values of the transformed sequence are random. The resulting sequence is called a randomized Halton sequence. It has the same properties of coverage and negative correlation over observations as the original Halton draws, since the relative placement of the elements is the same; however, it is now random.

With multiple dimensions, the sequence used for each dimension is transformed separately based on its own draw from the standard uniform density. Figure 9.19 represents a transformation of a two-dimensional sequence of length 3 defined for primes 2 and 3. The sequence for prime 3 is given by the x-axis and obtains a random draw of 0.40. The sequence for prime 2 obtains a draw of 0.35. Each point in the original two-dimensional sequence is moved to the right by 0.40 and up by 0.35, wrapping as needed. The relation between the points in each dimension is maintained, and yet the sequence is now random.

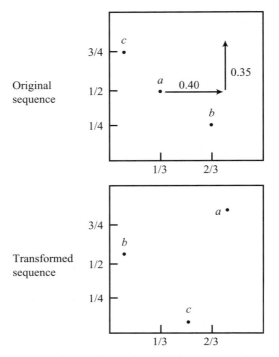

Figure 9.19. Randomization of Halton sequence in two dimensions.

9.3.5. Scrambled Halton Draws

Another issue with Halton draws arises when they are used in high dimensions. For simulation of high-dimensional integrals, Halton sequences based on large primes are necessary. For example, with 15 dimensions, the primes up to 47 are needed. However, Halton draws defined by large primes can be highly correlated with each other over large portions of the sequence. The correlation is not confined to the initial elements as described earlier, and so cannot be eliminated by discarding these elements. Two sequences defined by large and similar primes periodically become synchronized with each other and stay that way for many cycles.

Bhat (forthcoming) describes the problem and an effective solution. Figure 9.20 reproduces a graph from his paper that depicts the Halton sequence for primes 43 and 47. Clearly, these sequences are highly correlated.

This correlation can be removed while retaining the desirable coverage of Halton sequences by *scrambling* the digits of each element of the

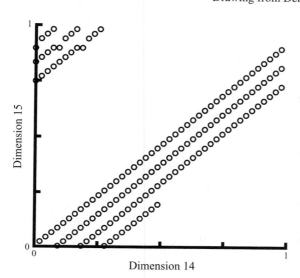

Figure 9.20. Standard Halton sequence.

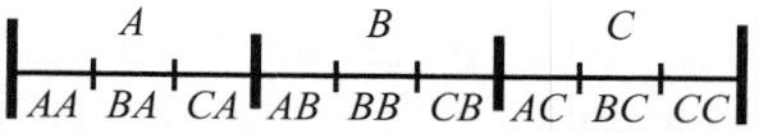

Figure 9.21. Segments for scrambling the Halton sequence.

sequences. The scrambling can be done in various ways. Braatan and Weller (1979) describe a procedure that is most easily explained through an example. Consider the Halton sequence for prime 3:

$$\frac{1}{3}, \frac{2}{3}, \frac{1}{9}, \frac{4}{9}, \frac{7}{9}, \frac{2}{9}, \frac{5}{9}, \frac{8}{9}, \ldots$$

Recall that the sequence is created by dividing the unit interval into three segments, which we label A, B, and C in Figure 9.21. Each segment is divided into three subsegments, labeled AA (for subsegment A of segment A), BA (subsegment B of segment A), CA, AB, BB, CB, AC, BC, and CC. The Halton sequence is the starting point of each segment arranged alphabetically and ignoring A (i.e., ignore A, $\frac{1}{3}$ for B, $\frac{2}{3}$ for C), followed by the starting point of each subsegment arranged alphabetically and ignoring A (i.e., ignore AA, AB, and AC, $\frac{1}{9}$ for BA, $\frac{4}{9}$ for BB, $\frac{7}{9}$ for BC, $\frac{2}{9}$ for CA, $\frac{5}{9}$ for CB, and $\frac{8}{9}$ for CC.) Note that the segments and subsegments starting with A are ignored because their starting points either are 0 (for segment A) or are already included in the sequence (e.g., the starting point of subsegment AB is the same as the starting point of segment B).

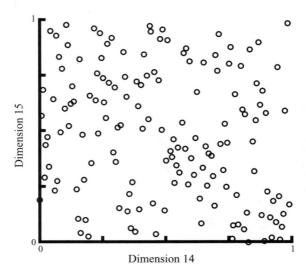

Figure 9.22. Scrambled Halton sequence.

The scrambled sequence is obtained by reversing B and C, that is, by considering C to be before B in the alphabet. The alphabetical listing is now: segments $A\ C\ B$, subsegments $AA\ AC\ AB\ CA\ CC\ CB\ BA\ BC\ BB$. The sequence is then created the same way as before but with this new alphabetical ordering: ignore A, $\frac{2}{3}$ for C, $\frac{1}{3}$ for B; ignore AA, AC, and AB, $\frac{2}{9}$ for CA, $\frac{8}{9}$ for CC, $\frac{5}{9}$ for CB, $\frac{1}{9}$ for BA, $\frac{7}{9}$ for BC, $\frac{4}{9}$ for BB. The orginal and scrambled sequences are:

Original	Scrambled
1/3	2/3
2/3	1/3
1/9	2/9
4/9	8/9
7/9	5/9
2/9	1/9
5/9	7/9
8/9	4/9

Different permutations of the letters are used for different primes. Figure 9.22, from Bhat (forthcoming), shows the scrambled sequence for primes 43 and 47. The points are not correlated as they are in the original sequence. Bhat demonstrates that scrambled sequences perform well for high-dimensional integrals in the same way that unscrambled ones do for low-dimensional integrals.

9.3.6. Other Procedures

We have described only a few of the most prominent and straightforward antithetic and quasi-random procedures. More complex procedures, with desirable theoretical properties, are described by Niederreiter (1978, 1988), Morokoff and Caflisch (1995), Joe and Sloan (1993), and Sloan and Wozniakowski (1998), to name only a few in this burgeoning area of research. As we have seen with Halton sequences, fairly simple procedures can provide large improvements over random draws. Comparisons performed by Sándor and András (2001) on probit and Sándor and Train (2002) on mixed logit indicate that the accuracy of simulation-based estimation of discrete choice models can be improved even further with the more complex procedures. It is important to remember, however, in the excitement of these methods, that accuracy can always be improved by simply using more draws. The researcher needs to decide whether learning and coding new methods of taking draws is more expedient, given her time constraints, than simply running her model with more draws.

10 Simulation-Assisted Estimation

10.1 Motivation

So far we have examined how to simulate choice probabilities but have not investigated the properties of the parameter estimators that are based on these simulated probabilities. In the applications we have presented, we simply inserted the simulated probabilities into the log-likelihood function and maximized this function, the same as if the probabilities were exact. This procedure seems intuitively reasonable. However, we have not actually shown, at least so far, that the resulting estimator has any desirable properties, such as consistency, asymptotic normality, or efficiency. We have also not explored the possibility that other forms of estimation might perhaps be preferable when simulation is used rather than exact probabilities.

The purpose of this chapter is to examine various methods of estimation in the context of simulation. We derive the properties of these estimators and show the conditions under which each estimator is consistent and asymptotically equivalent to the estimator that would arise with exact values rather than simulation. These conditions provide guidance to the researcher on how the simulation needs to be performed to obtain desirable properties of the resultant estimator. The analysis also illuminates the advantages and limitations of each form of estimation, thereby facilitating the researcher's choice among methods.

We consider three methods of estimation:

1. *Maximum Simulated Likelihood: MSL.* This procedure is the same as maximum likelihood (ML) except that simulated probabilities are used in lieu of the exact probabilities. The properties of MSL have been derived by, for example, Gourieroux and Monfort,(1993), Lee (1995), and Hajivassiliou and Ruud (1994).
2. *Method of Simulated Moments: MSM.* This procedure, suggested by McFadden (1989), is a simulated analog to the traditional method of moments (MOM). Under traditional MOM for discrete choice, residuals are defined as the difference between

the 0–1 dependent variable that identifies the chosen alternative and the probability of the alternative. Exogenous variables are identified that are uncorrelated with the model residuals in the population. The estimates are the parameter values that make the variables and residuals uncorrelated in the sample. The simulated version of this procedure calculates residuals with the simulated probabilities rather than the exact probabilities.

3. *Method of Simulated Scores: MSS.* As discussed in Chapter 8, the gradient of the log likelihood of an observation is called the score of the observation. The method of scores finds the parameter values that set the average score to zero. When exact probabilities are used, the method of scores is the same as maximum likelihood, since the log-likelihood function is maximized when the average score is zero. Hajivassiliou and McFadden (1998) suggested using simulated scores instead of the exact ones. They showed that, depending on how the scores are simulated, MSS can differ from MSL and, importantly, can attain consistency and efficiency under more relaxed conditions.

In the next section we define these estimators more formally and relate them to their nonsimulated counterparts. We then describe the properties of each estimator in two stages. First, we derive the properties of the traditional estimator based on exact values. Second, we show how the derivation changes when simulated values are used rather than exact values. We show that the simulation adds extra elements to the sampling distribution of the estimator. The analysis allows us to identify the conditions under which these extra elements disappear asymptotically so that the estimator is asymptotically equivalent to its nonsimulated analog. We also identify more relaxed conditions under which the estimator, though not asymptotically equivalent to its nonsimulated counterpart, is nevertheless consistent.

10.2   Definition of Estimators

10.2.1. Maximum Simulated Likelihood

The log-likelihood function is

$$LL(\theta) = \sum_n \ln P_n(\theta),$$

where θ is a vector of parameters, $P_n(\theta)$ is the (exact) probability of the observed choice of observation n, and the summation is over a sample of N independent observations. The ML estimator is the value of θ that maximizes LL(θ). Since the gradient of LL(θ) is zero at the maximum, the ML estimator can also be defined as the value of θ at which

$$\sum_n s_n(\theta) = 0,$$

where $s_n(\theta) = \partial \ln P_n(\theta)/\partial\theta$ is the score for observation n.

Let $\check{P}_n(\theta)$ be a simulated approximation to $P_n(\theta)$. The simulated log-likelihood function is SLL(θ) = $\sum_n \ln \check{P}_n(\theta)$, and the MSL estimator is the value of θ that maximizes SLL(θ). Stated equivalently, the estimator is the value of θ at which $\sum_n \check{s}_n(\theta) = 0$, where $\check{s}_n(\theta) = \partial \ln \check{P}_n(\theta)/\partial\theta$.

A preview of the properties of MSL can be given now, with a full explanation reserved for the next section. The main issue with MSL arises because of the log transformation. Suppose $\check{P}_n(\theta)$ is an unbiased simulator of $P_n(\theta)$, so that $E_r\check{P}_n(\theta) = P_n(\theta)$, where the expectation is over draws used in the simulation. All of the simulators that we have considered are unbiased for the true probability. However, since the log operation is a nonlinear transformation, $\ln \check{P}_n(\theta)$ is not unbiased for $\ln P_n(\theta)$ even though $\check{P}_n(\theta)$ is unbiased for $P_n(\theta)$. The bias in the simulator of $\ln P_n(\theta)$ translates into bias in the MSL estimator. This bias diminishes as more draws are used in the simulation.

To determine the asymptotic properties of the MSL estimator, the question arises of how the simulation bias behaves when the sample size rises. The answer depends critically on the relationship between the number of draws that are used in the simulation, labeled R, and the sample size, N. If R is considered fixed, then the MSL estimator does not converge to the true parameters, because of the simulation bias in $\ln \check{P}_n(\theta)$. Suppose instead that R rises with N; that is, the number of draws rises with sample size. In this case, the simulation bias disappears as N (and hence R) rises without bound. MSL is consistent in this case. As we will see, if R rises faster than $\sqrt{N}$, MSL is not only consistent but also efficient, asymptotically equivalent to maximum likelihood on the exact probabilities.

In summary, if R is fixed, then MSL is inconsistent. If R rises at any rate with N, then MSL is consistent. If R rises faster than $\sqrt{N}$, then MSL is asymptotically equivalent to ML.

The primary limitation of MSL is that it is inconsistent for fixed R. The other estimators that we consider are motivated by the desire for a simulation-based estimator that is consistent for fixed R. Both MSM and MSS, if structured appropriately, attain this goal. This benefit comes at a price, however, as we see in the following discussion.

10.2.2. Method of Simulated Moments

The traditional MOM is motivated by the recognition that the residuals of a model are necessarily uncorrelated in the population with factors that are exogenous to the behavior being modeled. The MOM estimator is the value of the parameters that make the residuals in the *sample* uncorrelated with the exogenous variables. For discrete choice models, MOM is defined as the parameters that solve the equation

$$(10.1) \quad \sum_n \sum_j [d_{nj} - P_{nj}(\theta)] z_{nj} = 0,$$

where

d_{nj} is the dependent variable that identifies the chosen alternative: $d_{nj} = 1$ if n chose j, and $= 0$ otherwise, and

z_{nj} is a vector of exogenous variables called instruments.

The residuals are $d_{nj} - P_{nj}(\theta)$, and the MOM estimator is the parameter values at which the residuals are uncorrelated with the instruments in the sample.

This MOM estimator is analogous to MOM estimators for standard regression models. A regression model takes the form $y_n = x_n' \beta + \varepsilon_n$. The MOM estimator for this regression is the β at which

$$\sum_n (y_n - x_n' \beta) z_n = 0$$

for a vector of exogenous instruments z_n. When the explanatory variables in the model are exogenous, then they serve as the instruments. The MOM estimator in this case becomes the ordinary least squares estimator:

$$\sum_n (y_n - x_n' \beta) x_n = 0,$$

$$\sum_n x_n y_n = \sum_n x_n x_n' \beta,$$

$$\hat{\beta} = \left(\sum_n x_n x_n' \right)^{-1} \left(\sum_n x_n y_n \right),$$

which is the formula for the least squares estimator. When instruments are specified to be something other than the explanatory variables, the

MOM estimator becomes the standard instrumental variables estimator:

$$\sum_n (y_n - x_n'\beta)z_n = 0,$$

$$\sum_n z_n y_n = \sum_n z_n x_n'\beta,$$

$$\hat{\beta} = \left(\sum_n z_n x_n'\right)^{-1}\left(\sum_n z_n y_n\right),$$

which is the formula for the instrumental variables estimator. This estimator is consistent if the instruments are independent of ε in the population. The estimator is more efficient the more highly correlated the instruments are with the explanatory variables in the model. When the explanatory variables, x_n, are themselves exogenous, then the ideal instruments (i.e., those that give the highest efficiency) are the explanatory variables themselves, $z_n = x_n$.

For discrete choice models, MOM is defined analogously and has a similar relation to other estimators, especially ML. The researcher identifies instruments z_{nj} that are exogenous and hence independent in the population of the residuals $[d_{nj} - P_{nj}(\theta)]$. The MOM estimator is the value of θ at which the sample correlation between instruments and residuals is zero. Unlike the linear case, equation (10.1) cannot be solved explicitly for $\hat{\theta}$. Instead, numerical procedures are used to find the value of θ that solves this equation.

As with regression, ML for a discrete choice model is a special case of MOM. Let the instruments be the scores: $z_{nj} = \partial \ln P_{nj}(\theta)/\partial\theta$. With these instruments, MOM is the same as ML:

$$\sum_n \sum_j [d_{nj} - P_{nj}(\theta)]z_{nj} = 0,$$

$$\sum_n \left\{ \left(\sum_j d_{nj}\frac{\partial \ln P_{nj}(\theta)}{\partial\theta}\right) - \left(\sum_j P_{nj}(\theta)\frac{\partial \ln P_{nj}(\theta)}{\partial\theta}\right) \right\} = 0,$$

$$\sum_n \frac{\partial \ln P_{ni}(\theta)}{\partial\theta} - \sum_n \sum_j P_{nj}(\theta)\frac{1}{P_{nj}(\theta)}\frac{\partial P_{nj}(\theta)}{\partial\theta} = 0,$$

$$\sum_n s_n(\theta) - \sum_n \sum_j \frac{\partial P_{nj}(\theta)}{\partial\theta} = 0,$$

$$\sum_n s_n(\theta) = 0,$$

which is the defining condition for ML. In the third line, i is the chosen alternative, recognizing that $d_{nj} = 0$ for all $j \neq i$. The fourth line uses the fact that the sum of $\partial P_{nj}/\partial \theta$ over alternatives is zero, since the probabilities must sum to 1 before and after the change in θ.

Since MOM becomes ML and hence is fully efficient when the instruments are the scores, the scores are called the ideal instruments. MOM is consistent whenever the instruments are independent of the model residuals. It is more efficient the higher the correlation between the instruments and the ideal instruments.

An interesting simplification arises with standard logit. For the standard logit model, the ideal instruments are the explanatory variables themselves. As shown in Section 3.7.1, the ML estimator for standard logit is the value of θ that solves $\sum_n \sum_j [d_{nj} - P_{nj}(\theta)]x_{nj} = 0$, where x_{nj} are the explanatory variables. This is a MOM estimator with the explanatory variables as instruments.

A simulated version of MOM, called the method of simulated moments (MSM), is obtained by replacing the exact probabilities $P_{nj}(\theta)$ with simulated probabilities $\check{P}_{nj}(\theta)$. The MSM estimator is the value of θ that solves

$$\sum_n \sum_j [d_{nj} - \check{P}_{nj}(\theta)]z_{nj} = 0$$

for instruments z_{nj}. As with its nonsimulated analog, MSM is consistent if z_{nj} is independent of $d_{nj} - \check{P}_{nj}(\theta)$.

The important feature of this estimator is that $\check{P}_{nj}(\theta)$ enters the equation linearly. As a result, if $\check{P}_{nj}(\theta)$ is unbiased for $P_{nj}(\theta)$, then $[d_{nj} - \check{P}_{nj}(\theta)]z_{nj}$ is unbiased for $[d_{nj} - P_{nj}(\theta)]z_{nj}$. Since there is no simulation bias in the estimation condition, the MSM estimator is consistent, even when the number of draws R is fixed. In contrast, MSL contains simulation bias due to the log transformation of the simulated probabilities. By not taking a nonlinear transformation of the simulated probabilities, MSM avoids simulation bias.

MSM still contains simulation noise (variance due to simulation). This noise becomes smaller as R rises and disappears when R rises without bound. As a result, MSM is asymptotically equivalent to MOM if R rises with N.

Just like its unsimulated analog, MSM is less efficient than MSL unless the ideal instruments are used. However, the ideal instruments are functions of $\ln P_{nj}$. They cannot be calculated exactly for any but the simplest models, and, if they are simulated using the simulated probability, simulation bias is introduced by the log operation. MSM is usually applied with nonideal weights, which means that there is a loss of efficiency. MSM with ideal weights that are simulated without bias becomes MSS, which we discuss in the next section.

In summary, MSM has the advantage over MSL of being consistent with a fixed number of draws. However, there is no free lunch, and the cost of this advantage is a loss of efficiency when nonideal weights are used.

10.2.3. Method of Simulated Scores

MSS provides a possibility of attaining consistency without a loss of efficiency. The cost of this double advantage is numerical: the versions of MSS that provide efficiency have fairly poor numerical properties such that calculation of the estimator can be difficult.

The method of scores is defined by the condition

$$\sum_n s_n(\theta) = 0,$$

where $s_n(\theta) = \partial \ln P_n(\theta)/\partial\theta$ is the score for observation n. This is the same defining condition as ML: when exact probabilities are used, the method of scores is simply ML.

The method of simulated scores replaces the exact score with a simulated counterpart. The MSS estimator is the value of θ that solves

$$\sum_n \check{s}_n(\theta) = 0,$$

where $\check{s}_n(\theta)$ is a simulator of the score. If $\check{s}_n(\theta)$ is calculated as the derivative of the log of the simulated probability; that is, $\check{s}_n(\theta) = \partial \ln \check{P}_n(\theta)/\partial\theta$, then MSS is the same as MSL. However, the score can be simulated in other ways. When the score is simulated in other ways, MSS differs from MSL and has different properties.

Suppose that an unbiased simulator of the score can be constructed. With this simulator, the defining equation $\sum_n \check{s}_n(\theta) = 0$ does not incorporate any simulation bias, since the simulator enters the equation linearly. MSS is therefore consistent with a fixed R. The simulation noise decreases as R rises, such that MSS is asymptotically efficient, equivalent to MSL, when R rises with N. In contrast, MSL uses the biased score simulator $\check{s}_n(\theta) = \partial \ln \check{P}_n(\theta)/\partial\theta$, which is biased due to the log operator. MSS with an unbiased score simulator is therefore better than MSL with its biased score simulator in two regards: it is consistent under less stringent conditions (with fixed R rather than R rising with N) and is efficient under less stringent conditions (R rising at any rate with N rather than R rising faster than $\sqrt{N}$).

The difficulty with MSS comes in finding an unbiased score simulator. The score can be rewritten as

$$s_n(\theta) = \frac{\partial \ln P_{nj}(\theta)}{\partial \theta} = \frac{1}{P_{nj}(\theta)} \frac{\partial P_{nj}}{\partial \theta}.$$

An unbiased simulator for the second term $\partial P_{nj}/\partial \theta$ is easily obtained by taking the derivative of the simulated probability. Since differentiation is a linear operation, $\partial \check{P}_{nj}/\partial \theta$ is unbiased for $\partial P_{nj}/\partial \theta$ if $\check{P}_{nj}(\theta)$ is unbiased for $P_{nj}(\theta)$. Since the second term in the score can be simulated without bias, the difficulty arises in finding an unbiased simulator for the first term $1/P_{nj}(\theta)$. Of course, simply taking the inverse of the simulated probability does not provide an unbiased simulator, since $E_r(1/\check{P}_{nj}(\theta)) \neq 1/P_{nj}(\theta)$. Like the log operation, an inverse introduces bias.

One proposal is based on the recognition that $1/P_{nj}(\theta)$ is the expected number of draws of the random terms that are needed before an "accept" is obtained. Consider drawing balls from an urn that contains many balls of different colors. Suppose the probability of obtaining a red ball is 0.20. That is, one-fifth of the balls are red. How many draws would it take, on average, to obtain a red ball? The answer is $1/0.2 = 5$. The same idea can be applied to choice probabilities. $P_{nj}(\theta)$ is the probability that a draw of the random terms of the model will result in alternative j having the highest utility. The inverse $1/P_{nj}(\theta)$ can be simulated as follows:

1. Take a draw of the random terms from their density.
2. Calculate the utility of each alternative with this draw.
3. Determine whether alternative j has the highest utility.
4. If so, call the draw an *accept*. If not, then call the draw a *reject* and repeat steps 1 to 3 with a new draw. Define B^r as the number of draws that are taken until the first *accept* is obtained.
5. Perform steps 1 to 4 R times, obtaining B^r for $r = 1, \ldots, R$. The simulator of $1/P_{nj}(\theta)$ is $(1/R) \sum_{r=1}^{R} B^r$.

This simulator is unbiased for $1/P_{nj}(\theta)$. The product of this simulator with the simulator $\partial \check{P}_{nj}/\partial \theta$ provides an unbiased simulator of the score. MSS based on this unbiased score simulator is consistent for fixed R and asymptotically efficient when R rises with N.

Unfortunately, the simulator of $1/P_{nj}(\theta)$ has the same difficulties as the accept–reject simulators that we discussed in Section 5.6. There is no guarantee than an accept will be obtained within any given number of draws. Also, the simulator is not continuous in parameters. The discontinuity hinders the numerical procedures that are used to locate the parameters that solve the MSS equation.

In summary, there are advantages and disadvantages of MSS relative to MSL, just as there are of MSM. Understanding the capabilities of each estimator allows the researcher to make an informed choice among them.

10.3   The Central Limit Theorem

Prior to deriving the properties of our estimators, it is useful to review the central limit theorem. This theorem provides the basis for the distributions of the estimators.

One of the most basic results in statistics is that, if we take draws from a distribution with mean μ and variance σ, the mean of these draws will be normally distributed with mean μ and variance σ/N, where N is a large number of draws. This result is the central limit theorem, stated intuitively rather than precisely. We will provide a more complete and precise expression of these ideas.

Let $t = (1/N) \sum_n t_n$, where each t_n is a draw from a distribution with mean μ and variance σ. The realization of the draws are called the sample, and t is the sample mean. If we take a different sample (i.e., obtain different values for the draws of each t_n), then we will get a different value for the statistic t. Our goal is to derive the sampling distribution of t.

For most statistics, we cannot determine the sampling distribution exactly for a given sample size. Instead, we examine how the sampling distribution behaves as sample size rises without bound. A distinction is made between the limiting distribution and the asymptotic distribution of a statistic. Suppose that, as sample size rises, the sampling distribution of statistic t converges to a fixed distribution. For example, the sampling distribution of t might become arbitrarily close to a normal with mean t^* and variance σ. In this case, we say that $N(t^*, \sigma)$ is the limiting distribution of t and that t converges in distribution to $N(t^*, \sigma)$. We denote this situation as $t \xrightarrow{d} N(t^*, \sigma)$.

In many cases, a statistic will not have a limiting distribution. As N rises, the sampling distribution keeps changing. The mean of a sample of draws is an example of a statistic without a limiting distribution. As stated, if t is the mean of a sample of draws from a distribution with mean μ and variance σ, then t is normally distributed with mean μ and variance σ/N. The variance decreases as N rises. The distribution changes as N rises, becoming more and more tightly dispersed around the mean. If a limiting distribution were to be defined in this case, it would have to be the degenerate distribution at μ: as N rises without bound, the distribution of t collapses on μ. This limiting distribution is useless in understanding the variance of the statistic, since the variance of this limiting distribution is zero. What do we do in this case to understand the properties of the statistic?

If our original statistic does not have a limiting distribution, then we often can transform the statistic in such a way that the transformed statistic has a limiting distribution. Suppose, as in our example of a sample mean, that the statistic we are interested in does not have a limiting distribution because its variance decreases as N rises. In that case, we can consider a transformation of the statistic that normalizes for sample size. In particular, we can consider $\sqrt{N}(t - \mu)$. Suppose that this statistic does indeed have a limiting distribution, for example $\sqrt{N}(t - \mu) \xrightarrow{d} N(0, \sigma)$. In this case, we can derive the properties of our original statistic from the limiting distribution of the transformed statistic. Recall from basic principles of probabilities that, for fixed a and b, if $a(t - b)$ is distributed normal with zero mean and variance σ, then t itself is distributed normal with mean b and variance σ/a^2. This statement can be applied to our limiting distribution. For large enough N, $\sqrt{N}(t - \mu)$ is distributed approximately $N(0, \sigma)$. Therefore, for large enough N, t is distributed approximately $N(\mu, \sigma/N)$. We denote this as $t \overset{a}{\sim} N(\mu, \sigma/N)$. Note that this is not the limiting distribution of t, since t has no nondegenerate limiting distribution. Rather, it is called the asymptotic distribution of t, derived from the limiting distribution of $\sqrt{N}(t - \mu)$.

We can now restate precisely our concepts about the sampling distribution of a sample mean. The central limit theorem states the following. Suppose t is the mean of a sample of N draws from a distribution with mean μ and variance σ. Then $\sqrt{N}(t - \mu) \xrightarrow{d} N(0, \sigma)$. With this limiting distribution, we can say that $t \overset{a}{\sim} N(\mu, \sigma/N)$.

There is another, more general version of the central limit theorem. In the version just stated, each t_n is a draw from the same distribution. Suppose t_n is a draw from a distribution with mean μ and variance σ_n, for $n = 1, \ldots, N$. That is, each t_n is from a different distribution; the distributions have the same mean but different variances. The generalized version of the central limit theorem states that $\sqrt{N}(t - \mu) \xrightarrow{d} N(0, \sigma)$, where σ is now the average variance: $\sigma = (1/N) \sum_n \sigma_n$. Given this limiting distribution, we can say that $t \overset{a}{\sim} N(\mu, \sigma/N)$. We will use both versions of the central limit theorem when deriving the distributions of our estimators.

10.4   Properties of Traditional Estimators

In this section, we review the procedure for deriving the properties of estimators and apply that procedure to the traditional, non-simulation-based estimators. This discussion provides the basis for analyzing the properties of the simulation-based estimators in the next section.

The true value of the parameters is denoted θ^*. The ML and MOM estimators are roots of an equation that takes the form

$$(10.2)\quad \sum_n g_n(\hat{\theta})/N = 0.$$

That is, the estimator $\hat{\theta}$ is the value of the parameters that solve this equation. We divide by N, even though this division does not affect the root of the equation, because doing so facilitates our derivation of the properties of the estimators. The condition states that the average value of $g_n(\theta)$ in the sample is zero at the parameter estimates. For ML, $g_n(\theta)$ is the score $\partial \ln P_n(\theta)/\partial\theta$. For MOM, $g_n(\theta)$ is the set of first moments of residuals with a vector of instruments, $\sum_j (d_{nj} - P_{nj})z_{nj}$. Equation (10.2) is often called the moment condition. In its nonsimulated form, the method of scores is the same as ML and therefore need not be considered separately in this section. Note that we call (10.2) an equation even though it is actually a set of equations, since $g_n(\theta)$ is a vector. The parameters that solve these equations are the estimators.

At any particular value of θ, the mean and variance of $g_n(\theta)$ can be calculated for the sample. Label the mean as $g(\theta)$ and the variance as $W(\theta)$. We are particularly interested in the sample mean and variance of $g_n(\theta)$ at the true parameters, θ^*, since our goal is to estimate these parameters.

The key to understanding the properties of an estimator comes in realizing that each $g_n(\theta^*)$ is a draw from a distribution of $g_n(\theta^*)$'s in the population. We do not know the true parameters, but we know that each observation has a value of $g_n(\theta^*)$ at the true parameters. The value of $g_n(\theta^*)$ varies over people in the population. So, by drawing a person into our sample, we are essentially drawing a value of $g_n(\theta^*)$ from its distribution in the population.

The distribution of $g_n(\theta^*)$ in the population has a mean and variance. Label the mean of $g_n(\theta^*)$ in the population as **g** and its variance in the population as **W**. The sample mean and variance at the true parameters, $g(\theta^*)$ and $W(\theta^*)$, are the sample counterparts to the population mean and variance, **g** and **W**.

We assume that $\mathbf{g} = 0$. That is, we assume that the average of $g_n(\theta^*)$ in the population is zero at the true parameters. Under this assumption, the estimator provides a sample analog to this population expectation: $\hat{\theta}$ is the value of the parameters at which the sample average of $g_n(\theta)$ equals zero, as given in the defining condition (10.2). For ML, the assumption that $\mathbf{g} = 0$ simply states that the average score in the population is zero, when evaluated at the true parameters. In a sense, this can be considered the definition of the true parameters, namely, θ^* are the parameters at which the log-likelihood function for the entire population obtains its maximum and hence has zero slope. The estimated parameters are the values that make the slope of the likelihood function in the sample zero. For MOM, the assumption is satisfied if the instruments are independent of the residuals. In a sense, the assumption with MOM is simply a reiteration that the instruments are exogenous. The estimated parameters are the values that make the instruments and residuals uncorrelated in the sample.

We now consider the population variance of $g_n(\theta^*)$, which we have denoted $\mathbf{W}$. When $g_n(\theta)$ is the score, as in ML, this variance takes a special meaning. As shown in Section 8.7, the information identity states that $\mathbf{V} = -\mathbf{H}$, where

$$-\mathbf{H} = -E\left(\frac{\partial^2 \ln P_n(\theta^*)}{\partial\theta\,\partial\theta'}\right)$$

is the information matrix and $\mathbf{V}$ is the variance of the scores evaluated at the true parameters: $\mathbf{V} = \text{Var}(\partial \ln P_n(\theta^*)/\partial\theta)$. When $g_n(\theta)$ is the score, we have $\mathbf{W} = \mathbf{V}$ by definition and hence $\mathbf{W} = -\mathbf{H}$ by the information identity. That is, when $g_n(\theta)$ is the score, $\mathbf{W}$ is the information matrix. For MOM with nonideal instruments, $\mathbf{W} \neq -\mathbf{H}$, so that $\mathbf{W}$ does not equal the information matrix.

Why does this distinction matter? We will see that knowing whether $\mathbf{W}$ equals the information matrix allows us to determine whether the estimator is efficient. The lowest variance that any estimator can achieve is $-\mathbf{H}^{-1}/N$. For a proof, see, for example, Greene (2000) or Ruud (2000). An estimator is efficient if its variance attains this lower bound. As we will see, this lower bound is achieved when $\mathbf{W} = -\mathbf{H}$ but not when $\mathbf{W} \neq -\mathbf{H}$.

Our goal is to determine the properties of $\hat{\theta}$. We derive these properties in a two-step process. First, we examine the distribution of $g(\theta^*)$, which, as stated earlier, is the sample mean of $g_n(\theta^*)$. Second, the distribution of $\hat{\theta}$ is derived from the distribution of $g(\theta^*)$. This two-step process is not necessarily the most direct way of examining traditional estimators.

However, as we will see in the next section, it provides a very convenient way for generalizing to simulation-based estimators.

Step 1: The Distribution of $g(\theta^*)$

Recall that the value of $g_n(\theta^*)$ varies over decision makers in the population. When taking a sample, the researcher is drawing values of $g_n(\theta^*)$ from its distribution in the population. This distribution has zero mean by assumption and variance denoted $\mathbf{W}$. The researcher calculates the sample mean of these draws, $g(\theta^*)$. By the central limit theorem, $\sqrt{N}(g(\theta^*) - 0) \xrightarrow{d} N(0, \mathbf{W})$ such that the sample mean has distribution $g(\theta^*) \overset{a}{\sim} N(0, \mathbf{W}/N)$.

Step 2: Derive the Distribution of $\hat{\theta}$ from the Distribution of $g(\theta^*)$

We can relate the estimator $\hat{\theta}$ to its defining term $g(\theta)$ as follows. Take a first-order Taylor's expansion of $g(\hat{\theta})$ around $g(\theta^*)$:

$$(10.3) \quad g(\hat{\theta}) = g(\theta^*) + D[\hat{\theta} - \theta^*],$$

where $D = \partial g(\theta^*)/\partial\theta'$. By definition of $\hat{\theta}$ (that is, by defining condition (10.2)), $g(\hat{\theta}) = 0$ so that the right-hand side of this expansion is 0. Then

$$0 = g(\theta^*) + D[\hat{\theta} - \theta^*],$$
$$\hat{\theta} - \theta^* = -D^{-1}g(\theta^*),$$
$$(10.4) \quad \sqrt{N}(\hat{\theta} - \theta^*) = \sqrt{N}(-D^{-1})g(\theta^*).$$

Denote the mean of $\partial g_n(\theta^*)/\partial\theta'$ in the population as $\mathbf{D}$. The sample mean of $\partial g_n(\theta^*)/\partial\theta'$ is D, as defined for equation (10.3). The sample mean D converges to the population mean $\mathbf{D}$ as the sample size rises. We know from step 1 that $\sqrt{N}g(\theta^*) \xrightarrow{d} N(0, \mathbf{W})$. Using this fact in (10.4), we have

$$(10.5) \quad \sqrt{N}(\hat{\theta} - \theta^*) \xrightarrow{d} N(0, \mathbf{D}^{-1}\mathbf{W}\mathbf{D}^{-1}).$$

This limiting distribution tells us that $\hat{\theta} \overset{a}{\sim} N(\theta^*, \mathbf{D}^{-1}\mathbf{W}\mathbf{D}^{-1}/N)$.

We can now observe the properties of the estimator. The asymptotic distribution of $\hat{\theta}$ is centered on the true value, and its variance decreases as the sample size rises. As a result, $\hat{\theta}$ converges in probability to θ^* as the sample sise rises without bound: $\hat{\theta} \xrightarrow{p} \theta$. The estimator is therefore consistent. The estimator is asymptotically normal. And its variance is $\mathbf{D}^{-1}\mathbf{W}\mathbf{D}^{-1}/N$, which can be compared with the lowest possible variance, $-\mathbf{H}^{-1}/N$, to determine whether it is efficient.

For ML, $g_n(\cdot)$ is the score, so that the variance of $g_n(\theta^*)$ is the variance of the scores: $\mathbf{W} = \mathbf{V}$. Also, the mean derivative of $g_n(\theta^*)$

is the mean derivative of the scores: $\mathbf{D} = \mathbf{H} = E(\partial^2 \ln P_n(\theta^*)/\partial\theta\,\partial\theta')$, where the expectation is over the population. By the information identity, $\mathbf{V} = -\mathbf{H}$. The asymptotic variance of $\hat{\theta}$ becomes $\mathbf{D}^{-1}\mathbf{W}\mathbf{D}^{-1}/N = \mathbf{H}^{-1}\mathbf{V}\mathbf{H}^{-1}/N = \mathbf{H}^{-1}(-\mathbf{H})\mathbf{H}^{-1}/N = -\mathbf{H}^{-1}/N$, which is the lowest possible variance of any estimator. ML is therefore efficient. Since $\mathbf{V} = -\mathbf{H}$, the variance of the ML estimator can also be expressed as $\mathbf{V}^{-1}/N$, which has a readily interpretable meaning: the variance of the estimator is equal to the inverse of the variance of the scores evaluated at the true parameters, divided by sample size.

For MOM, $g_n(\cdot)$ is a set of moments. If the ideal instruments are used, then MOM becomes ML and is efficient. If any other instruments are used, then MOM is not ML. In this case, $\mathbf{W}$ is the population variance of the moments and $\mathbf{D}$ is the mean derivatives of the moments, rather than the variance and mean derivatives of the scores. The asymptotic variance of $\hat{\theta}$ does not equal $-\mathbf{H}^{-1}/N$. MOM without ideal weights is therefore not efficient.

10.5   Properties of Simulation-Based Estimators

Suppose that the terms that enter the defining equation for an estimator are simulated rather than calculated exactly. Let $\check{g}_n(\theta)$ denote the simulated value of $g_n(\theta)$, and $\check{g}(\theta)$ the sample mean of these simulated values, so that $\check{g}(\theta)$ is the simulated version of $g(\theta)$. Denote the number of draws used in simulation for each n as R, and assume that independent draws are used for each n (e.g., separate draws are taken for each n). Assume further that the same draws are used for each value of θ when calculating $\check{g}_n(\theta)$. This procedure prevents *chatter* in the simulation: the difference between $\check{g}(\theta_1)$ and $\check{g}(\theta_2)$ for two different values of θ is not due to different draws.

These assumptions on the simulation draws are easy for the researcher to implement and simplify our analysis considerably. For interested readers, Lee (1992) examines the situation when the same draws are used for all observations. Pakes and Pollard (1989) provide a way to characterize an equicontinuity condition that, when satisfied, facilitates analysis of simulation-based estimators. McFadden (1989) characterizes this condition in a different way and shows that it can be met by using the same draws for each value of θ, which is the assumption that we make. McFadden (1996) provides a helpful synthesis that includes a discussion of the need to prevent chatter.

The estimator is defined by the condition $\check{g}(\hat{\theta}) = 0$. We derive the properties of $\hat{\theta}$ in the same two steps as for the traditional estimators.

Step 1: The Distribution of $\check{g}(\theta^*)$

To identify the various components of this distribution, let us reexpress $\check{g}(\theta^*)$ by adding and subtracting some terms and rearranging:

$$\check{g}(\theta^*) = \check{g}(\theta^*) + g(\theta^*) - g(\theta^*) + E_r\check{g}(\theta^*) - E_r\check{g}(\theta^*)$$
$$= g(\theta^*) + [E_r\check{g}(\theta^*) - g(\theta^*)] + [\check{g}(\theta^*) - E_r\check{g}(\theta^*)],$$

where $g(\theta^*)$ is the nonsimulated value and $E_r\check{g}(\theta^*)$ is the expectation of the simulated value over the draws used in the simulation. Adding and subtracting terms obviously does not change $\check{g}(\theta^*)$. Yet, the subsequent rearrangement of the terms allows us to identify components that have intuitive meaning.

The first term $g(\theta^*)$ is the same as arises for the traditional estimator. The other two terms are extra elements that arise because of the simulation. The term $E_r\check{g}(\theta^*) - g(\theta^*)$ captures the bias, if any, in the simulator of $g(\theta^*)$. It is the difference between the true value of $g(\theta^*)$ and the expectation of the simulated value. If the simulator is unbiased for $g(\theta^*)$, then $E_r\check{g}(\theta^*) = g(\theta^*)$ and this term drops out. Often, however, the simulator will not be unbiased for $g(\theta^*)$. For example, with MSL, $\check{g}_n(\theta) = \partial \ln \check{P}_n(\theta)/\partial\theta$, where $\check{P}_n(\theta)$ is an unbiased simulator of $P_n(\theta)$. Since $\check{P}_n(\theta)$ enters nonlinearly via the log operator, $\check{g}_n(\theta)$ is not unbiased. The third term, $\check{g}(\theta^*) - E_r\check{g}(\theta^*)$, captures simulation noise, that is, the deviation of the simulator for given draws from its expectation over all possible draws.

Combining these concepts, we have

(10.6) $\check{g}(\theta) = A + B + C,$

where

A is the same as in the traditional estimator,
B is simulation bias,
C is simulation noise.

To see how the simulation-based estimators differ from their traditional counterparts, we examine the simulation bias B and noise C.

Consider first the noise. This term can be reexpressed as

$$C = \check{g}(\theta^*) - E_r\check{g}(\theta^*)$$
$$= \frac{1}{N}\sum_n [\check{g}_n(\theta^*) - E_r\check{g}_n(\theta^*)]$$
$$= \sum_n d_n/N,$$

where d_n is the deviation of the simulated value for observation n from its expectation. The key to understanding the behavior of the simulation noise comes in noting that d_n is simply a statistic for observation n. The sample constitutes N draws of this statistic, one for each observation: $d_n, n = 1, \ldots, N$. The simulation noise C is the average of these N draws. Thus, the central limit theorem gives us the distribution of C.

In particular, for a given observation, the draws that are used in simulation provide a particular value of d_n. If different draws had been obtained, then a different value of d_n would have been obtained. There is a distribution of values of d_n over the possible realizations of the draws used in simulation. The distribution has zero mean, since the expectation over draws is subtracted out when creating d_n. Label the variance of the distribution as S_n/R, where S_n is the variance when one draw is used in simulation. There are two things to note about this variance. First, S_n/R is inversely related to R, the number of draws that are used in simulation. Second, the variance is different for different n. Since $g_n(\theta^*)$ is different for different n, the variance of the simulation deviation also differs.

We take a draw of d_n for each of N observations; the overall simulation noise, C, is the average of these N draws of observation-specific simulation noise. As just stated, each d_n is a draw from a distribution with zero mean and variance S_n/R. The generalized version of the central limit theorem tells us the distribution of a sample average of draws from distributions that have the same mean but different variances. In our case,

$$\sqrt{N} C \xrightarrow{d} N(0, \mathbf{S}/R),$$

where $\mathbf{S}$ is the population mean of S_n. Then $C \overset{a}{\sim} N(0, \mathbf{S}/NR)$.

The most relevant characteristic of the asymptotic variance of C is that it decreases as N increases, even when R is fixed. Simulation noise disappears as sample size increases, even without increasing the number of draws used in simulation. This is a very important and powerful fact. It means that increasing the sample size is a way to decrease the effects of simulation on the estimator. The result is intuitively meaningful. Essentially, simulation noise cancels out over observations. The simulation for one observation might, by chance, make that observation's $\breve{g}_n(\theta)$ too large. However, the simulation for another observation is likely, by chance, to be too small. By averaging the simulations over observations, the errors tend to cancel each other. As sample size rises, this canceling out property becomes more powerful until, with large enough samples, simulation noise is negligible.

Consider now the bias. If the simulator $\breve{g}(\theta)$ is unbiased for $g(\theta)$, then the bias term B in (10.6) is zero. However, if the simulator is biased, as with MSL, then the effect of this bias on the distribution of $\breve{g}(\theta^*)$ must be considered.

Usually, the defining term $g_n(\theta)$ is a function of a statistic, ℓ_n, that can be simulated without bias. For example, with MSL, $g_n(\theta)$ is a function of the choice probability, which can be simulated without bias; in this case ℓ_n is the probability. More generally, ℓ_n can be any statistic that is simulated without bias and serves to define $g_n(\theta)$. We can write the dependence in general as $g_n(\theta) = g(\ell_n(\theta))$ and the unbiased simulator of $\ell_n(\theta)$ as $\breve{\ell}_n(\theta)$ where $E_r \breve{\ell}_n(\theta) = \ell_n(\theta)$.

We can now reexpress $\breve{g}_n(\theta)$ by taking a Taylor's expansion around the unsimulated value $g_n(\theta)$:

$$
\breve{g}_n(\theta) = g_n(\theta) + \frac{\partial g(\ell_n(\theta))}{\partial \ell_n}[\breve{\ell}_n(\theta) - \ell_n(\theta)]
$$
$$
+ \frac{1}{2}\frac{\partial^2 g(\ell_n(\theta))}{\partial \ell_n^2}[\breve{\ell}_n(\theta) - \ell_n(\theta)]^2,
$$

$$
\breve{g}_n(\theta) - g_n(\theta) = g_n'[\breve{\ell}_n(\theta) - \ell_n(\theta)] + \frac{1}{2}g_n''[\breve{\ell}_n(\theta) - \ell_n(\theta)]^2,
$$

where g_n' and g_n'' are simply shorthand ways to denote the first and second derivatives of $g_n(\ell(\cdot))$ with respect to ℓ. Since $\breve{\ell}_n(\theta)$ is unbiased for $\ell_n(\theta)$, we know $E_r g_n'[\breve{\ell}_n(\theta) - \ell_n(\theta)] = g_n'[E_r \breve{\ell}_n(\theta) - \ell_n(\theta)] = 0$. As a result, only the variance term remains in the expectation:

$$
E_r \breve{g}_n(\theta) - g_n(\theta) = \frac{1}{2}g_n'' E_r[\breve{\ell}_n(\theta) - \ell_n(\theta)]^2
$$
$$
= \frac{1}{2}g_n'' \operatorname{Var}_r \breve{\ell}_n(\theta).
$$

Denote $\operatorname{Var}_r \breve{\ell}_n(\theta) = Q_n/R$ to reflect the fact that the variance is inversely proportional to the number of draws used in the simulation. The simulation bias is then

$$
E_r \breve{g}(\theta) - g(\theta) = \frac{1}{N}\sum_n E_r \breve{g}_n(\theta) - g_n(\theta)
$$
$$
= \frac{1}{N}\sum_n g_n'' \frac{Q_n}{2R}
$$
$$
= \frac{Z}{R},
$$

where Z is the sample average of $g_n'' Q_n/2$.

Since $B = \mathcal{Z}/R$, the value of this statistic normalized for sample size is

(10.7) $\sqrt{N}B = \dfrac{\sqrt{N}}{R}\mathcal{Z}.$

If R is fixed, then B is nonzero. Even worse, $\sqrt{N}B$ rises with N, in such a way that it has no limiting value. Suppose that R is considered to rise with N. The bias term then disappears asymptotically: $B = \mathcal{Z}/R \xrightarrow{p} 0$. However, the normalized bias term does not necessarily disappear. Since $\sqrt{N}$ enters the numerator of this term, $\sqrt{N}B = (\sqrt{N}/R)\mathcal{Z} \xrightarrow{p} 0$ only if R rises faster than $\sqrt{N}$, so that the ratio $\sqrt{N}/R$ approaches zero as N increases. If R rises slower than $\sqrt{N}$, the ratio $\sqrt{N}/R$ rises, such that the normalized bias term does not disappear but in fact gets larger and larger as sample size increases.

We can now collect our results for the distribution of the defining term normalized by sample size:

(10.8) $\sqrt{N}\breve{g}(\theta^*) = \sqrt{N}(A + B + C),$

where

$\sqrt{N}A \xrightarrow{d} N(0, \mathbf{W}),$ the same as in the traditional estimator,

$\sqrt{N}B = \dfrac{\sqrt{N}}{R}\mathcal{Z},$ capturing simulation bias,

$\sqrt{N}C \xrightarrow{d} N(0, \mathbf{S}/R),$ capturing simulation noise.

Step 2: Derive Distribution of $\hat{\theta}$ from Distribution of $\breve{g}(\theta^*)$

As with the traditional estimators, the distribution of $\hat{\theta}$ is directly related to the distribution of $\breve{g}(\theta^*)$. Using the same Taylor's expansion as in (10.3), we have

(10.9) $\sqrt{N}(\hat{\theta} - \theta^*) = -\breve{D}^{-1}\sqrt{N}\breve{g}(\theta^*) = -\breve{D}^{-1}\sqrt{N}(A + B + C),$

where $\breve{D}$ is the derivative of $\breve{g}(\theta^*)$ with respect to the parameters, which converges to its expectation $\breve{\mathbf{D}}$ as sample size rises. The estimator itself is expressed as

(10.10) $\hat{\theta} = \theta^* - \breve{D}^{-1}(A + B + C).$

We can now examine the properties of our estimators.

10.5.1. Maximum Simulated Likelihood

For MSL, $\breve{g}_n(\theta)$ is not unbiased for $g_n(\theta)$. The bias term in (10.9) is $\sqrt{N}B = (\sqrt{N}/R)\mathcal{Z}$. Suppose R rises with N. If R rises faster than $\sqrt{N}$, then

$$\sqrt{N}B = (\sqrt{N}/R)\mathcal{Z} \xrightarrow{p} 0,$$

since the ratio $\sqrt{N}/R$ falls to zero. Consider now the third term in (10.9), which captures simulation noise: $\sqrt{N}C \xrightarrow{d} N(0, \mathbf{S}/R)$. Since $\mathbf{S}/R$ decreases as R rises, we have $\mathbf{S}/R \xrightarrow{p} 0$ as $N \to \infty$ when R rises with N. The second and third terms disappear, leaving only the first term. This first term is the same as appears for the nonsimulated estimator. We have

$$\sqrt{N}(\hat{\theta} - \theta^*) = -\mathbf{D}^{-1}\sqrt{N}A \xrightarrow{d} N(0, \mathbf{D}^{-1}\mathbf{W}\mathbf{D}^{-1})$$
$$= N(0, \mathbf{H}^{-1}\mathbf{V}\mathbf{H}^{-1})$$
$$= N(0, -\mathbf{H}^{-1}),$$

where the next-to-last equality occurs because $g_n(\theta)$ is the score, and the last equality is due to the information identity. The estimator is distributed

$$\hat{\theta} \overset{a}{\sim} N(\theta^*, -\mathbf{H}^{-1}/N).$$

This is the same asymptotic distribution as ML. When R rises faster than $\sqrt{N}$, MSL is consistent, asymptotically normal and efficient, and asymptotically equivalent to ML.

Suppose that R rises with N but at a rate that is slower than $\sqrt{N}$. In this case, the ratio $\sqrt{N}/R$ grows larger as N rises. There is no limiting distribution for $\sqrt{N}(\hat{\theta} - \theta^*)$, because the bias term, $(\sqrt{N}/R)\mathcal{Z}$, rises with N. However, the estimator itself converges on the true value. $\hat{\theta}$ depends on $(1/R)\mathcal{Z}$, not multiplied by $\sqrt{N}$. This bias term disappears when R rises at any rate. Therefore, the estimator converges on the true value, just like its nonsimulated counterpart, which means that $\hat{\theta}$ is consistent. However, the estimator is not asymptotically normal, since $\sqrt{N}(\hat{\theta} - \theta^*)$ has no limiting distribution. Standard errors cannot be calculated, and confidence intervals cannot be constructed.

When R is fixed, the bias rises as N rises. $\sqrt{N}(\hat{\theta} - \theta^*)$ does not have a limiting distribution. Moreover, the estimator itself, $\hat{\theta}$, contains a bias $B = (1/R)\mathcal{Z}$ that does not disappear as sample size rises with fixed R. The MSL estimator is neither consistent nor asymptotically normal when R is fixed.

The properties of MSL can be summarized as follows:

1. If R is fixed, MSL is inconsistent.
2. If R rises slower than $\sqrt{N}$, MSL is consistent but not asymptotically normal.
3. If R rises faster than $\sqrt{N}$, MSL is consistent, asymptotically normal and efficient, and equivalent to ML.

10.5.2. Method of Simulated Moments

For MSM with fixed instruments, $\check{g}_n(\theta) = \sum_j [d_{nj} - \check{P}_{nj}(\theta)] z_{nj}$, which is unbiased for $g_n(\theta)$, since the simulated probability enters linearly. The bias term is zero. The distribution of the estimator is determined only by term A, which is the same as in the traditional MOM without simulation, and term C, which reflects simulation noise:

$$\sqrt{N}(\hat{\theta} - \theta^*) = -\check{D}^{-1}\sqrt{N}(A + C).$$

Suppose that R is fixed. Since $\check{D}$ converges to its expectation $\mathbf{D}$, we have $-\sqrt{N}\check{D}^{-1}A \xrightarrow{d} N(0, \mathbf{D}^{-1}\mathbf{W}\mathbf{D}^{-1})$ and $-\sqrt{N}\check{D}^{-1}C \xrightarrow{d} N(0, \mathbf{D}^{-1}(\mathbf{S}/R)\mathbf{D}^{-1})$, so that

$$\sqrt{N}(\hat{\theta} - \theta^*) \xrightarrow{d} N(0, \mathbf{D}^{-1}[\mathbf{W} + \mathbf{S}/R]\mathbf{D}^{-1}).$$

The asymptotic distribution of the estimator is then

$$\hat{\theta} \overset{a}{\sim} N(\theta^*, \mathbf{D}^{-1}[\mathbf{W} + \mathbf{S}/R]\mathbf{D}^{-1}/N).$$

The estimator is consistent and asymptotically normal. Its variance is greater than its nonsimulated counterpart by $\mathbf{D}^{-1}\mathbf{S}\mathbf{D}^{-1}/RN$, reflecting simulation noise.

Suppose now that R rises with N at any rate. The extra variance due to simulation noise disappears, so that $\hat{\theta} \overset{a}{\sim} N(\theta^*, \mathbf{D}^{-1}\mathbf{W}\mathbf{D}^{-1}/N)$, the same as its nonsimulated counterpart. When nonideal instruments are used, $\mathbf{D}^{-1}\mathbf{W}\mathbf{D}^{-1} \neq -\mathbf{H}^{-1}$ and so the estimator (in either its simulated or nonsimulated form) is less efficient than ML.

If simulated instruments are used in MSM, then the properties of the estimator depend on how the instruments are simulated. If the instruments are simulated without bias and independently of the probability that enters the residual, then this MSM has the same properties as MSM with fixed weights. If the instruments are simulated with bias and the instruments are not ideal, then the estimator has the same properties as MSL except that it is not asymptotically efficient, since the information identity does not apply. MSM with simulated ideal instruments is MSS, which we discuss next.

10.5.3. Method of Simulated Scores

With MSS using unbiased score simulators, $\check{g}_n(\theta)$ is unbiased for $g_n(\theta)$, and, moreover, $g_n(\theta)$ is the score such that the information identity applies. The analysis is the same as for MSM except that the information identity makes the estimator efficient when R rises with N. As with MSM, we have

$$\hat{\theta} \overset{a}{\sim} N(\theta^*, \mathbf{D}^{-1}[\mathbf{W} + \mathbf{S}/R]\mathbf{D}^{-1}/N),$$

which, since $g_n(\theta)$ is the score, becomes

$$\hat{\theta} \overset{a}{\sim} N\left(\theta^*, \frac{\mathbf{H}^{-1}[\mathbf{V} + \mathbf{S}/R]\mathbf{H}^{-1}}{N}\right) = N\left(\theta^*, -\frac{\mathbf{H}^{-1}}{N} + \frac{\mathbf{H}^{-1}\mathbf{S}\mathbf{H}^{-1}}{RN}\right).$$

When R is fixed, the estimator is consistent and asymptotically normal, but its covariance is larger than with ML because of simulation noise. If R rises at any rate with N, then we have

$$\hat{\theta} \overset{a}{\sim} N(\theta^*, -\mathbf{H}^{-1}/N).$$

MSS with unbiased score simulators is asymptotically equivalent to ML when R rises at any rate with N.

This analysis shows that MSS with unbiased score simulators has better properties than MSL in two regards. First, for fixed R, MSS is consistent and asymptotically normal, while MSL is neither. Second, for R rising with N, MSS is equivalent to ML no matter how fast R is rising, while MSL is equivalent to ML only if the rate is faster than $\sqrt{N}$.

As we discussed in Section 10.2.3, finding unbiased score simulators with good numerical properties is difficult. MSS is sometimes applied with biased score simulators. In this case, the properties of the estimator are the same as with MSL: the bias in the simulated scores translates into bias in the estimator, which disappears from the limiting distribution only if R rises faster than $\sqrt{N}$.

10.6   Numerical Solution

The estimators are defined as the value of θ that solves $\check{g}(\theta) = 0$, where $\check{g}(\theta) = \sum_n \check{g}_n(\theta)/N$ is the sample average of a simulated statistic $\check{g}_n(\theta)$. Since $\check{g}_n(\theta)$ is a vector, we need to solve the set of equations for the parameters. The question arises: how are these equations solved numerically to obtain the estimates?

Chapter 8 describes numerical methods for maximizing a function. These procedures can also be used for solving a set of equations. Let T be the negative of the inner product of the defining term for an estimator: $T = -\check{g}(\theta)'\check{g}(\theta) = -(\sum_n \check{g}_n(\theta))'(\sum_n \check{g}_n(\theta))/N^2$. T is necessarily less than or equal to zero, since it is the negative of a sum of squares. T has a highest value of 0, which is attained only when the squared terms that compose it are all 0. That is, the maximum of T is attained when $\check{g}(\theta) = 0$. Maximizing T is equivalent to solving the equation $\check{g}(\theta) = 0$. The approaches described in Chapter 8, with the exception of BHHH, can be used for this maximization. BHHH cannot be used, because that method assumes that the function being maximized is a sum of observation-specific terms, whereas T takes the square of each sum of observation-specific terms. The other approaches, especially BFGS and DFP, have proven very effective at locating the parameters at which $\check{g}(\theta) = 0$.

With MSL, it is usually easier to maximize the simulated likelihood function rather than T. BHHH can be used in this case, as well as the other methods.

11 Individual-Level Parameters

11.1 Introduction

Mixed logit and probit models allow random coefficients whose distribution in the population is estimated. Consider, for example, the model in Chapter 6, of anglers' choice among fishing sites. The sites are differentiated on the basis of whether campgrounds are available at the site. Some anglers like having campgrounds at the fishing sites, since they can use the grounds for overnight stays. Other anglers dislike the crowds and noise that are associated with campgrounds and prefer fishing at more isolated spots. To capture these differences in tastes, a mixed logit model was specified that included random coefficients for the campground variable and other site attributes. The distribution of coefficients in the population was estimated. Figure 11.1 gives the estimated distribution of the campground coefficient. The distribution was specified to be normal. The mean was estimated as 0.116, and the standard deviation was estimated as 1.655. This distribution provides useful information about the population. For example, the estimates imply that 47 percent of the population dislike having campgrounds at their fishing sites, while the other 53 percent like having them.

The question arises: where in the distribution of tastes does a particular angler lie? Is there a way to determine whether a given person tends to like or dislike having campgrounds at fishing sites?

A person's choices reveal something about his tastes, which the researcher can, in principle, discover. If the researcher observes that a particular angler consistently chooses sites without campgrounds, even when the cost of driving to these sites is higher, then the researcher can reasonably infer that this angler dislikes campgrounds. There is a precise way for performing this type of inference, given by Revelt and Train (2000).

We explain the procedure in the context of a mixed logit model; however, any behavioral model that incorporates random coefficients can

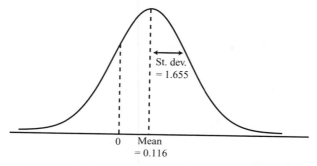

St. dev.
= 1.655

0   Mean
= 0.116

Figure 11.1. Distribution of coefficient of campgrounds in population of all anglers.

be used, including probit. The central concept is a distinction between two distributions: the distribution of tastes in the population, and the distribution of tastes in the subpopulation of people who make particular choices. Denote the random coefficients as vector β. The distribution of β in the population of all people is denoted $g(\beta \mid \theta)$, where θ are the parameters of this distribution, such as the mean and variance.

A choice situation consists of several alternatives described collectively by variables x. Consider the following thought experiment. Suppose everyone in the population faces the same choice situation described by the same variables x. Some portion of the population will choose each alternative. Consider the people who choose alternative i. The tastes of these people are not all the same: there is a distribution of coefficients among these people. Let $h(\beta \mid i, x, \theta)$ denote the distribution of β in the subpopulation of people who, when faced with the choice situation described by variables x, would choose alternative i. Now $g(\beta \mid \theta)$ is the distribution of β in the entire population. $h(\beta \mid i, x, \theta)$ is the distribution of β in the subpopulation of people who would choose alternative i when facing a choice situation described by x.

We can generalize the notation to allow for repeated choices. Let y denote a sequence of choices in a series of situations described collectively by variables x. The distribution of coefficients in the subpopulation of people who would make the sequences of choices y when facing situations described by x is denoted $h(\beta \mid y, x, \theta)$.

Note that $h(\cdot)$ conditions on y, while $g(\cdot)$ does not. It is sometimes useful to call h the conditional distribution and g the unconditional distribution. Two such distributions are depicted in Figure 11.2. If we knew nothing about a person's past choices, then the best we can do in describing his tastes is to say that his coefficients lie somewhere in

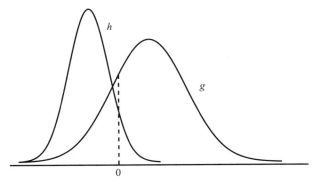

Figure 11.2. Unconditional (population) distribution g and conditional (sub-population) distribution h for subpopulation of anglers who chose sites without campgrounds.

$g(\beta \mid \theta)$. However, if we have observed that the person made choices y when facing situations described by x, then we know that that person's coefficients are in the distribution $h(\beta \mid y, x, \theta)$. Since h is tighter than g, we have better information about the person's tastes by conditioning on his past choices.

Inference of this form has long been conducted with linear regression models, where the dependent variable and the distribution of coefficients are both continuous (Griffiths, 1972; Judge et al., 1988). Regime-switching models, particularly in macroeconomics, have used an analogous procedure to assess the probability that an observation is within a given regime (Hamilton and Susmel, 1994; Hamilton, 1996). In these models, the dependent variable is continuous and the distribution of coefficients is discrete (representing one set of coefficients for each regime.) In contrast to both of these traditions, our models have discrete dependent variables. DeSarbo et al. (1995) developed an approach in the context of a discrete choice model with a discrete distribution of coefficients (that is, a latent class model). They used maximum likelihood procedures to estimate the coefficients for each segment, and then calculated the probability that an observation is within each segment based on the observed choices of the observation. The approach that we describe here applies to discrete choice models with continuous or discrete distributions of coefficients and uses maximum likelihood (or other classical methods) for estimation. The model of DeSarbo et al. (1995) is a special case of this more general method. Bayesian procedures have been also developed to perform this inference within discrete choice models (Rossi et al. 1996; Allenby and Rossi 1999). We describe the Bayesian methods in Chapter 12.

11.2   Derivation of Conditional Distribution

The relation between h and g can be established precisely. Consider a choice among alternatives $j = 1, \ldots, J$ in choice situations $t = 1, \ldots, T$. The utility that person n obtains from alternative j in situation t is

$$U_{njt} = \beta_n' x_{njt} + \varepsilon_{njt},$$

where $\varepsilon_{njt} \sim$ iid extreme value, and $\beta_n \sim g(\beta \mid \theta)$ in the population. The variables x_{njt} can be denoted collectively for all alternatives and choice situations as x_n. Let $y_n = \langle y_{n1}, \ldots, y_{nT} \rangle$ denote the person's sequence of chosen alternatives. If we knew β_n, then the probability of the person's sequence of choices would be a product of logits:

$$P(y_n \mid x_n, \beta) = \prod_{t=1}^{T} L_{nt}(y_{nt} \mid \beta),$$

where

$$L_{nt}(y_{nt} \mid \beta) = \frac{e^{\beta' x_{ny_{nt}t}}}{\sum_j e^{\beta' x_{njt}}}.$$

Since we do not know β_n, the probability of the person's sequence of choices is the integral of $P(y_n \mid x_n, \beta)$ over the distribution of β:

$$(11.1) \quad P(y_n \mid x_n, \theta) = \int P(y_n \mid x_n, \beta) g(\beta \mid \theta) \, d\beta.$$

This is the mixed logit probability that we discussed in Chapter 6.

We can now derive $h(\beta \mid y_n, x_n, \theta)$. By Bayes' rule,

$$h(\beta \mid y_n, x_n, \theta) \times P(y_n \mid x_n, \theta) = P(y_n \mid x_n, \beta) \times g(\beta \mid \theta).$$

This equation simply states that the joint density of β and y_n can be expressed as the probability of y_n times the probability of β conditional on y_n (which is the left-hand side), or with the other direction of conditioning, as the probability of β times the probability of y_n conditional on β (which is the right-hand side.) Rearranging,

$$(11.2) \quad h(\beta \mid y_n, x_n, \theta) = \frac{P(y_n \mid x_n, \beta) g(\beta \mid \theta)}{P(y_n \mid x_n, \theta)}.$$

We know all the quantities on the right-hand side. From these, we can calculate h.

Equation (11.2) also provides a way to interpret h intuitively. Note that the denominator $P(y_n \mid x_n, \theta)$ is the integral of the numerator, as given by the definition in (11.1). As such, the denominator is a constant that makes h integrate to 1, as required for any density. Since the denominator is a constant, h is proportional to the numerator, $P(y_n \mid x_n, \beta)g(\beta \mid y_n, x_n, \theta)$. This relation makes interpretation of h relatively easy. Stated in words, the density of β in the subpopulation of people who would choose sequence y_n when facing x_n is proportional to the density of β in the entire population *times* the probability that y_n would be chosen if the person's coefficients were β.

Using (11.2), various statistics can be derived conditional on y_n. The mean β in the subpopulation of people who would choose y_n when facing x_n is

$$\bar{\beta}_n = \int \beta \cdot h(\beta \mid y_n, x_n, \theta)\, d\beta.$$

This mean generally differs from the mean β in the entire population. Substituting the formula for h,

$$\bar{\beta}_n = \frac{\int \beta \cdot P(y_n \mid x_n, \beta)g(\beta \mid \theta)\, d\beta}{P(y_n \mid x_n, \theta)}$$

(11.3)
$$= \frac{\int \beta \cdot P(y_n \mid x_n, \beta)g(\beta \mid \theta)\, d\beta}{\int P(y_n \mid x_n, \beta)g(\beta \mid \theta)\, d\beta}.$$

The integrals in this equation do not have a closed form; however, they can be readily simulated. Take draws of β from the population density $g(\beta \mid \theta)$. Calculate the weighted average of these draws, with the weight for draw β^r being proportional to $P(y_n \mid x_n, \beta^r)$. The simulated subpopulation mean is

$$\check{\beta}_n = \sum_r w^r \beta^r,$$

where the weights are

(11.4) $w^r = \dfrac{P(y_n \mid x_n, \beta^r)}{\sum_r P(y_n \mid x_n, \beta^r)}.$

Other statistics can also be calculated. Suppose the person faces a new choice situation described by variables $x_{njT+1} \; \forall j$. If we had no information on the person's past choices, then we would assign the following probability to his choosing alternative i:

(11.5) $P(i \mid x_{nT+1}, \theta) = \displaystyle\int L_{nT+1}(i \mid \beta)g(\beta \mid \theta)\, d\beta$

where

$$L_{n\,T+1}(i \mid \beta) = \frac{e^{\beta' x_{ni\,T+1}}}{\sum_j e^{\beta' x_{nj\,T+1}}}.$$

This is just the mixed logit probability using the population distribution of β. If we observed the past choices of the person, then the probability can be conditioned on these choices. The probability becomes

$$(11.6) \quad P(i \mid x_{n\,T+1}, y_n, x_n, \theta) = \int L_{n\,T+1}(i \mid \beta) h(\beta \mid y_n, x_n, \theta) \, d\beta.$$

This is also a mixed logit probability, but using the conditional distribution h instead of the unconditional distribution g. When we do not know the person's previous choices, we mix the logit formula over density of β in the entire population. However, when we know the person's previous choices, we can improve our prediction by mixing over the density of β in the subpopulation who would have made the same choices as this person.

To calculate this probability, we substitute the formula for h from (11.2):

$$P(i \mid x_{n\,T+1}, y_n, x_n, \theta) = \frac{\int L_{n\,T+1}(i \mid \beta) P(y_n \mid x_n, \beta) g(\beta \mid \theta) \, d\beta}{\int P(y_n \mid x_n, \beta) g(\beta \mid \theta) \, d\beta}.$$

The probability is simulated by taking draws of β from the population distribution g, calculating the logit formula for each draw, and taking a weighted average of the results:

$$\check{P}_{ni\,T+1}(y_n, x_n, \theta) = \sum_r w^r L_{n\,T+1}(i \mid \beta^r),$$

where the weights are given by (11.4).

11.3   Implications of Estimation of θ

The population parameters θ are estimated in any of the ways described in Chapter 10. The most common approach is maximum simulated likelihood, with the simulated value of $P(y_n \mid x_n, \theta)$ entering the log-likelihood function. An estimate of θ, labeled $\hat{\theta}$, is obtained. We know that there is sampling variance in the estimator. The asymptotic co-variance of the estimator is also estimated, which we label $\hat{W}$. The asymptotic distribution is therefore estimated to be $N(\hat{\theta}, \hat{W})$.

The parameter θ describes the distribution of β in the population, giving, for example, the mean and variance of β over all decision makers. For any value of θ, equation (11.2) gives the conditional distribution of β

in the subpopulation of people who would make choices y_n when faced with situations described by x_n. This relation is exact in the sense that there is no sampling or other variance associated with it. Similarly, any statistic based on h is exact given a value of θ. For example, the mean of the conditional distribution, $\bar{\beta}_n$, is exactly equation (11.3) for a given value of θ.

Given this correspondence between θ and h, the fact that θ is estimated can be handled in two different ways. The first approach is to use the point estimate of θ to calculate statistics associated with the conditional distribution h. Under this approach, the mean of the condition distribution, $\bar{\beta}_n$, is calculated by inserting $\hat{\theta}$ into (11.3). The probability in a new choice situation is calculated by inserting $\hat{\theta}$ into (11.6). If the estimator of θ is consistent, then this approach is consistent for statistics based on θ.

The second approach is to take the sampling distribution of $\hat{\theta}$ into consideration. Each possible value of θ implies a value of h, and hence a value of any statistic associated with h, such as $\bar{\beta}_n$. The sampling variance in the estimator of θ induces sampling variance in the statistics that are calculated on the basis of θ. This sampling variance can be calculated through simulation, by taking draws of θ from its estimated sampling distribution and calculating the corresponding statistic for each of these draws.

For example, to represent the sampling distribution of $\hat{\theta}$ in the calculation of $\bar{\beta}_n$, the following steps are taken:

1. Take a draw from $N(\hat{\theta}, \hat{W})$, which is the estimated sampling distribution of $\hat{\theta}$. This step is accomplished as follows. Take K draws from a standard normal density, and label the vector of these draws η^r, where K is the length of θ. Then create $\theta^r = \hat{\theta} + L\eta^r$, where L is the Choleski factor of $\hat{W}$.
2. Calculate $\bar{\beta}_n^r$ based on this θ^r. Since the formula for $\bar{\beta}_n$ involves integration, we simulate it using formula (11.3).
3. Repeat steps 1 and 2 many times, with the number of times labeled R.

The resulting values are draws from the sampling distribution of $\bar{\beta}_n$ induced by the sampling distribution of $\hat{\theta}$. The average of $\bar{\beta}_n^r$ over the R draws of θ^r is the mean of the sampling distribution of $\bar{\beta}_n$. The standard deviation of the draws gives the asymptotic standard error of $\bar{\beta}_n$ that is induced by the sampling variance of $\hat{\theta}$.

Note that this process involves simulation within simulation. For each draw of θ^r, the statistic $\bar{\beta}_n^r$ is simulated with multiple draws of β from the population density $g(\beta \mid \theta^r)$.

Suppose either of these approaches is used to estimate $\bar{\beta}_n$. The question arises: can the estimate of $\bar{\beta}_n$ be considered an estimate of β_n? That is: is the estimated mean of the conditional distribution $h(\beta \mid y_n, x_n, \theta)$, which is conditioned on person n's past choices, an estimate of person n's coefficients?

There are two possible answers, depending on how the researcher views the data-generation process. If the number of choice situations that the researcher can observe for each decision maker is fixed, then the estimate of $\bar{\beta}_n$ is not a consistent estimate of β_n. When T is fixed, consistency requires that the estimate converge to the true value when sample size rises without bound. If sample size rises, but the choice situations faced by person n are fixed, then the conditional distribution and its mean do not change. Insofar as person n's coefficients do not happen to coincide with the mean of the conditional distribution (an essentially impossible event), the mean of the conditional distribution will never equal the person's coefficients no matter how large the sample is. Raising the sample size improves the estimate of θ and hence provides a better estimate of the mean of the conditional distribution, since this mean depends only on θ. However, raising the sample size does not make the conditional mean equal to the person's coefficients.

When the number of choice situations is fixed, then the conditional mean has the same interpretation as the population mean, but for a different, and less diverse, group of people. When predicting the future behavior of the person, one can expect to obtain better predictions using the conditional distribution, as in (11.6), than the population distribution. In the case study presented in the next section, we show that the improvement can be large.

If the number of choice situations that a person faces can be considered to rise, then the estimate of $\bar{\beta}_n$ can be considered to be an estimate of β_n. Let T be the number of choice situations that person n faces. If we observe more choices by the person (i.e., T rises), then we are better able to identify the person's coefficients. Figure 11.3 gives the conditional distribution $h(\beta \mid y_n, x_n, \theta)$ for three different values of T. The conditional distribution tends to move toward the person's own β_n as T rises, and to become more concentrated. As T rises without bound, the conditional distribution collapses onto β_n. The mean of the conditional distribution converges to the true value of β_n as the number of choice situations rises without bound. The estimate of $\bar{\beta}_n$ is therefore consistent for β_n.

In Chapter 12, we describe the Bernstein–von Mises theorem. This theorem states that, under fairly mild conditions, the mean of a posterior distribution for a parameter is asymptotically equivalent to the maximum

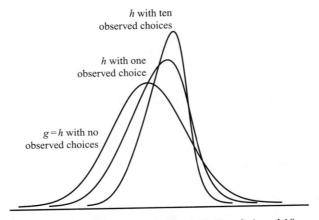

Figure 11.3. Conditional distribution with $T = 0, 1$, and 10.

of the likelihood function. The conditional distribution h is a posterior distribution: by (11.2) h is proportional to a density g, which can be interpreted as a prior distribution on β_n, *times* the likelihood of person n's T choices given β_n, which is $P(y_n \mid x_n, \beta_n)$. By the Bernstein–von Mises theorem, the mean of h is therefore an estimator of β_n that is asymptotically equivalent to the maximum likelihood estimator of β_n, where the asymptotics are defined as T rising. These concepts are described more fully in Chapter 12; we mention them now simply to provide another interpretation of the mean of the conditional distribution.

11.4   Monte Carlo Illustration

To illustrate the concepts, I constructed a hypothetical data set where the true population parameters θ are known as well as the true β_n for each decision maker. These data allow us to compare the mean of the conditional distribution for each decision maker's choices, $\bar{\beta}_n$, with the β_n for that decision maker. It also allows us to investigate the impact of increasing the number of choice situations on the conditional distribution. For this experiment, I constructed data sets consisting of 300 "customers" each facing $T = 1, 10, 20$, and 50 choice situations. There are three alternatives and four variables in each data set. The coefficients for the first two variables are held fixed for the entire population at 1.0, and the coefficients for the last two variables are distributed normal with a mean and variance of 1.0. Utility is specified to include these variables plus a final iid term that is distributed extreme value, so that the model is a mixed logit. The dependent variable for each customer was created by taking a draw from the density of the random terms, calculating the

Table 11.1. *Monte Carlo illustration*

	1st Coef.	2nd Coef.
1 choice situation:		
Standard deviation of $\bar{\beta}_n$	0.413	0.416
Absolute difference between $\bar{\beta}_n$ and β_n	0.726	0.718
10 choice situations:		
Standard deviation of $\bar{\beta}_n$	0.826	0.826
Absolute difference between $\bar{\beta}_n$ and β_n	0.422	0.448
20 choice situations:		
Standard deviation of $\bar{\beta}_n$	0.894	0.886
Absolute difference between $\bar{\beta}_n$ and β_n	0.354	0.350
50 choice situations:		
Standard deviation of $\bar{\beta}_n$	0.951	0.953
Absolute difference between $\bar{\beta}_n$ and β_n	0.243	0.243

utility of each alternative with this draw, and determining which alternative had the highest utility. To minimize the effect of simulation noise in the creation of the data, I constructed 50 datasets for each level of T. The results that are reported are the average over these 50 datasets.

The mean of the conditional distribution for each customer, $\bar{\beta}_n$, was calculated. The standard deviation of $\bar{\beta}_n$ over the 300 customers was calculated, as well as the average absolute deviation of $\bar{\beta}_n$ from the customer's β_n (i.e., the average over n of $|\bar{\beta}_n - \beta_n|$). Table 11.1 presents these statistics. Consider first the standard deviation. If there were no observed choice situations on which to condition ($T = 0$), then the conditional distribution for each customer would be the unconditional (population) distribution. Each customer would have the same $\bar{\beta}_n$ equal to the population mean of β. In this case, the standard deviation of $\bar{\beta}_n$ would be zero, since all customers have the same $\bar{\beta}_n$. At the other extreme, if we observed an unboundedly large number of choice situations ($T \to \infty$), then the conditional distribution for each customer would collapse to their own β_n. In this case, the standard deviation of $\bar{\beta}_n$ would equal the standard deviation of the population distribution of β_n, which is 1 in this experiment. For T between 0 and ∞, the standard deviation of $\bar{\beta}_n$ is between 0 and the standard deviation of β_n in the population.

In Table 11.1, we see that conditioning on only a few choice situations captures a large share of the variation in β's over customers. With only one choice situation, the standard deviation of $\bar{\beta}_n$ is over 0.4. Since the standard deviation of β_n in the population is 1 in this experiment, which means that conditioning on one choice situation captures over 40 percent of the variation in β_n. With 10 choice situations, over 80 percent of the variation is captured. There are strongly decreasing returns to observing more choice situations. Doubling from $T = 10$ to $T = 20$ only increases the proportion of variation captured from about .83 to about .89. Increasing T to 50 increases it to about .95.

Consider now the absolute difference between the mean of the customer's conditional distribution, $\bar{\beta}_n$, and the customer's actual β_n. With no conditioning ($T = 0$), the average absolute difference would be 0.8, which is the expected absolute difference for deviates that follow a standard normal as we have in our experiment. With perfect conditioning ($T \to \infty$), $\bar{\beta}_n = \beta_n$ for each customer, and so the absolute difference is 0. With only one choice situation, the average absolute deviation drops from 0.8 (without conditioning) to about 0.72, for a 10 percent improvement. The absolute deviation drops further as the number of choice situations rises.

Notice that the drop in the absolute deviation is smaller than the increase in the standard deviation. For example, with one choice situation the absolute deviation moves 10 percent of the way from no conditioning to perfect knowledge (from .80 with $T = 0$ to .72 with $T = 1$, which is 10 percent of the way to 0 with $T \to \infty$). Yet the standard deviation moves about 40 percent of the way from no conditioning to perfect knowledge (.4 with $T = 1$ is 40 percent of the distance from 0 with $T = 0$ to 1 with $T \to \infty$). This difference is due to the fact that the standard deviation incorporates movement of $\bar{\beta}_n$ away from β_n as well as movement toward β_n. This fact is important to recognize when evaluating the standard deviation of $\bar{\beta}_n$ in empirical applications, where the absolute difference cannot be calculated since β_n is not known. That is, the standard deviation of $\bar{\beta}_n$ expressed as a percentage of the estimated standard deviation in the population is an overestimate of the amount of information that is contained in the $\bar{\beta}_n$'s. With ten choice situations, the average standard deviation in $\bar{\beta}_n$ is over 80 percent of the value that it would have with perfect knowledge, and yet the absolute deviation is less than half as high as would be attained without conditioning.

11.5   Average Conditional Distribution

For a correctly specified model at the true population parameters, the conditional distribution of tastes, aggregated over all customers, equals the population distribution of tastes. Given a series of choice situations described by x_n, there is a set of possible sequences of choices. Label these possible sequences as y_s for $s = 1, \ldots, S$. Denote the true frequency of y_s as $m(y_s \mid x_n, \theta^*)$, expressing its dependence on the true parameters θ^*. If the model is correctly specified and consistently estimated, then $P(y_s \mid x_n, \hat{\theta})$ approaches $m(y_s \mid x_n, \theta^*)$ asymptotically. Conditional on the explanatory variables, the expected value of $h(\beta \mid y_s, x_n, \hat{\theta})$ is then

$$
\begin{aligned}
E_y h(\beta \mid y, x_n, \hat{\theta}) &= \sum_s \frac{P(y_s \mid x_n, \beta) g(\beta \mid x_n, \hat{\theta})}{P(y_s \mid x_n, \hat{\theta})} m(y_s \mid x_n, \theta^*) \\
&\to \sum_s P(y_s \mid x_n, \beta) g(\beta \mid x_n, \hat{\theta}) \\
&= g(\beta \mid x_n, \hat{\theta}).
\end{aligned}
$$

This relation provides a diagnostic tool (Allenby and Rossi 1999). If the average of the sampled customers' conditional taste distributions is similar to the estimated population distribution, the model is correctly specified and accurately estimated. If they are not similar, the difference could be due to (1) specification error, (2) an insufficient number of draws in simulation, (3) an inadequate sample size, and/or (4) the maximum likelihood routine converging at a local rather than global maximum.

11.6   Case Study: Choice of Energy Supplier

11.6.1. Population Distribution

We obtained stated-preference data on residential customers' choice of electricity supplier. Surveyed customers were presented with 8–12 hypothetical choice situations called *experiments*. In each experiment, the customer was presented with four alternative suppliers with different prices and other characteristics. The suppliers differed in price (fixed price given in cents per kilowatthour (c/kWh), TOD prices with stated prices in each time period, or seasonal prices with stated prices in each time period), the length of the contract (during which the supplier is required to provide service at the stated price and the customer would need to pay a penalty for leaving the supplier), and whether the supplier was their local utility, a well-known company other than their local utility, or an unfamiliar company. The data were collected by Research Triangle Institute (1997) for the Electric Power Research Institute and have been used by Goett (1998) to estimate mixed logits. We utilize a specification similar to Goett's, but we eliminate or combine variables that he found to be insignificant.

Two mixed logit models were estimated on these data, based on different specifications for the distribution of the random coefficients. All choices except the last situation for each customer are used to estimate

Table 11.2. *Mixed logit model of energy supplier choice*

	Model 1	Model 2
Price, kWh	−0.8574	−0.8827
	(0.0488)	(0.0497)
Contract length, years		
m	−0.1833	−0.2125
	(0.0289)	(0.0261)
s	0.3786	0.3865
	(0.0291)	(0.0278)
Local utility		
m	2.0977	2.2297
	(0.1370)	(0.1266)
s	1.5585	1.7514
	(0.1264)	(0.1371)
Known company		
m	1.5247	1.5906
	(0.1018)	(0.0999)
s	0.9520	0.9621
	(0.0998)	(0.0977)
TOD rate[a]		
m	−8.2857	2.1328
	(0.4577)	(0.0543)
s	2.5742	0.4113
	(0.1676)	(0.0397)
Seasonal rate[b]		
m	−8.5303	2.1577
	(0.4468)	(0.0509)
s	2.1259	0.2812
	(0.1604)	(0.0217)
Log likelihood at convergence	−3646.51	−3618.92

Standard errors in parentheses.
[a] TOD rates: 11c/kWh, 8 A.M.–8 P.M., 5c/kWh, 8 P.M.–8 A.M.
[b] Seasonal rates: 10c/kWh, summer; 8c/kWh, winter, 6c/kWh, spring and fall.

the parameters of the population distribution, and the customer's last choice situation was retained for use in comparing the predictive ability of different models and methods.

Table 11.2 gives the estimated population parameters. The price coefficient in both models is fixed across the population in such a way that the distribution of willingness to pay for each nonprice attribute (which is the ratio of the attribute's coefficient to the price coefficient) has the same distribution as the attribute's coefficient. For model 1, all of the nonprice coefficients are specified to be normally distributed in the population. The mean m and standard deviation s of each coefficient are estimated. For model 2, the first three nonprice coefficients are specified to be normal, and the fourth and fifth are log-normal. The fourth and fifth variables are indicators of TOD and seasonal rates, and their coefficients must logically be negative for all customers. The lognormal distribution (with the signs of the variables reversed) provides for this necessity. The log of these coefficients is distributed normal with mean m and standard deviation s, which are the parameters that are estimated. The coefficients themselves have mean $\exp(m + (s^2/2))$ and standard deviation equal to the mean times $\sqrt{\exp(s^2) - 1}$.

The estimates provide the following qualitative results:

- The average customer is willing to pay about $\frac{1}{5}$ to $\frac{1}{4}$ c/kWh in higher price, depending on the model, in order to have a contract that is shorter by one year. Stated conversely, a supplier that requires customers to sign a four- to five-year contract must discount its price by 1 c/kWh to attract the average customer.

- There is considerable variation in customers' attitudes toward contract length, with a sizable share of customers preferring a longer to a shorter contract. A long-term contract constitutes insurance for the customer against price increases, the supplier being locked into the stated price for the length of the contract. Such contracts, however, prevent the customer from taking advantage of lower prices that might arise during the term of the contract. Apparently, many customers value the insurance against higher prices more than they mind losing the option to take advantage of lower prices. The degree of customer heterogeneity implies that the market can sustain contracts of different lengths with suppliers making profits by writing contracts that appeal to different segments of the population.

- The average customer is willing to pay a whopping 2.5 c/kWh more for its local supplier than for an unknown supplier. Only a small share of customers prefer an unknown supplier to their local utility. This finding has important implications for competition. It implies that entry in the residential market by previously unknown suppliers will be very difficult, particularly since the price discounts that entrants can offer in most markets are fairly small. The experience in California, where only 1 percent of residential customers have switched away from their local utility after several years of open access, is consistent with this finding.

- The average customer is willing to pay 1.8 c/kWh more for a known supplier than for an unknown one. The estimated values of s imply that a sizable share of customers would be willing to pay more for a known supplier than for their local utility, presumably because of a bad experience or a negative attitude toward the local utility. These results imply that companies that are known to customers, such as their long-distance carriers, local telecommunications carriers, local cable companies, and even retailers like Sears and Home Depot, may be more successful in attracting customers for electricity supply than companies that were unknown prior to their entry as an energy supplier.

• The average customer evaluates the TOD rates in a way that is fairly consistent with TOD usage patterns. In model 1, the mean coefficient of the dummy variable for the TOD rates implies that the average customer considers these rates to be equivalent to a fixed price of 9.7 c/kWh. In model 2, the estimated mean and standard deviation of the log of the coefficient imply a median willingness to pay of 8.4 and a mean of 10.4 c/kWh, which span the mean from model 1. Here 9.5 c/kWh is the average price that a customer would pay under the TOD rates if 75 percent of its consumption occurred during the day (between 8 A.M. and 8 P.M.) and the other 25 percent occurred at night. These shares, while perhaps slightly high for the day, are not unreasonable. The estimated values of s are highly significant, reflecting heterogeneity in usage patterns and perhaps in customers' ability to shift consumption in response to TOD prices. These values are larger than reasonable, implying that a nonnegligible share of customers treat the TOD prices as being equivalent to a fixed price that is higher than the highest TOD price or lower than the lowest TOD price.

• The average customer seems to avoid seasonal rates for reasons beyond the prices themselves. The average customer treats the seasonal rates as being equivalent to a fixed 10 c/kWh, which is the highest seasonal price. A possible explanation for this result relates to the seasonal variation in customers' bills. In many areas, electricity consumption is highest in the summer, when air conditioners are being run, and energy bills are therefore higher in the summer than in other seasons, even under fixed rates. The variation in bills over months without commensurate variation in income makes it more difficult for customers to pay their summer bills. In fact, nonpayment for most energy utilities is most frequent in the summer. Seasonal rates, which apply the highest price in the summer, increase the seasonal variation in bills. Customers would rationally avoid a rate plan that exacerbates an already existing difficulty. If this interpretation is correct, then seasonal rates combined with bill smoothing (by which the supplier carries a portion of the summer bills over to the winter) could provide an attractive arrangement for customers and suppliers alike.

Model 2 attains a higher log-likelihood value than model 1, presumably because the lognormal distribution assures negative coefficients for the TOD and seasonal variables.

11.6.2. Conditional Distributions

We now use the estimated models to calculate customers' conditional distributions and the means of these distributions. We calculate $\bar{\beta}_n$ for each customer in two ways. First, we calculate $\bar{\beta}_n$ using equation (11.3) with the point estimates of the population parameters, $\hat{\theta}$. Second, we use the procedure in Section 11.3 to integrate over the sampling distribution of the estimated population parameters.

The means and standard deviations of $\bar{\beta}_n$ over the sampled customers calculated by these two methods are given in Tables 11.3 and 11.4, respectively. The price coefficient is not listed in Table 11.3, since it is fixed across the population. Table 11.4 incorporates the sampling distribution of the population parameters, which includes variance in the price coefficient.

Consider the results in Table 11.3 first. The mean of $\bar{\beta}_n$ is very close to the estimated population mean given in Table 11.2. This similarity is expected for a correctly specified and consistently estimated model. The standard deviation of $\bar{\beta}_n$ would be zero if there were no conditioning and would equal the population standard deviation if each customer's coefficient were known exactly. The standard deviations in Table 11.3 are considerably above zero and are fairly close to the estimated population standard deviations in Table 11.2. For example, in model 1, the conditional mean of the coefficient of contract length has a standard deviation of 0.318 over customers, and the point estimate of the standard deviation in the population is 0.379. Thus, variation in $\bar{\beta}_n$ captures more than 70 percent of the total estimated variation in this coefficient. Similar results are obtained for other coefficients. This result implies that the mean of a customer's conditional distribution captures a fairly large share of the variation in coefficients across customers and has the potential to be useful in distinguishing customers.

As discussed in Section 11.5, a diagnostic check on the specification and estimation of the model is obtained by comparing the sample average

Table 11.3. *Average $\bar{\beta}_n$ using point estimate $\hat{\theta}$*

	Model 1	Model 2
Contract length		
Mean	−0.2028	−0.2149
Std. dev.	0.3175	0.3262
Local utility		
Mean	2.1205	2.2146
Std. dev.	1.2472	1.3836
Known company		
Mean	1.5360	1.5997
Std. dev.	0.6676	0.6818
TOD rate		
Mean	−8.3194	−9.2584
Std. dev.	2.2725	3.1051
Seasonal rate		
Mean	−8.6394	−9.1344
Std. dev.	1.7072	2.0560

Table 11.4. *Average $\bar{\beta}_n$ with sampling distribution of $\hat{\theta}$*

	Model 1	Model 2
Price		
Mean	−0.8753	−0.8836
Std. dev.	0.5461	0.0922
Contract length		
Mean	−0.2004	−0.2111
Std. dev.	0.3655	0.3720
Local utility		
Mean	2.1121	2.1921
Std. dev.	1.5312	1.6815
Known company		
Mean	1.5413	1.5832
Std. dev.	0.9364	0.9527
TOD rate		
Mean	−9.1615	−9.0216
Std. dev.	2.4309	3.8785
Seasonal rate		
Mean	−9.4528	−8.9408
Std. dev.	1.9222	2.5615

of the conditional distributions with the estimated population distribution. The means in Table 11.3 represent the means of the sample average of the conditional distributions. The standard deviation of the sample-average conditional distribution depends on the standard deviation of $\bar{\beta}_n$, which is given in Table 11.3, plus the standard deviation of $\beta_n - \bar{\beta}_n$. When this latter portion is added, the standard deviation of each coefficient matches very closely the estimated population standard deviation. This equivalence suggests that there is no significant specification error and that the estimated population parameters are fairly accurate. This suggestion is somewhat tempered, however, by the results in Table 11.4.

Table 11.4 gives the sample mean and standard deviation of the mean of the sampling distribution of $\bar{\beta}_n$ that is induced by the sampling distribution of $\hat{\theta}$. The means in Table 11.4 are the means of the sample average of $h(\beta \mid y_n, x_n, \hat{\theta})$ integrated over the sampling distribution of $\hat{\theta}$. For model 1, a discrepancy occurs that indicates possible misspecification. In particular, the means of the TOD and seasonal rates coefficients in Table 11.4 exceed their estimated population means in Table 11.2. Interestingly, the means for these coefficients in Table 11.4 for model 1 are closer to the analogous means for model 2 than to the estimated population means for model 1 in Table 11.2. Model 2 has the more reasonably shaped lognormal distribution for these coefficients and obtains a considerably better fit than model 1. The conditioning in model 1 appears to be moving the coefficients closer to the values in the better-specified model 2 and away from its own misspecified population distributions. This is an example of how a comparison of the estimated population distribution with the sample average of the conditional distribution can reveal information about specification and estimation.

The standard deviations in Table 11.4 are larger than those in Table 11.3. This difference is due to the fact that the sampling variance in the estimated population parameters is included in the calculations for Table 11.4 but not for Table 11.3. The larger standard deviations do not mean that the portion of total variance in β_n that is captured by variation in $\bar{\beta}_n$ is larger when the sampling distribution is considered than when not.

Useful marketing information can be obtained by examining the $\bar{\beta}_n$ of each customer. The value of this information for targeted marketing has been emphasized by Rossi et al. (1996). Table 11.5 gives the calculated $\bar{\beta}_n$ for the first three customers in the data set, along with the population mean of β_n.

The first customer wants to enter a long-term contract, in contrast with the vast majority of customers who dislike long-term contracts. He is willing to pay a higher energy price if the price is guaranteed through a long term contract. He evaluates TOD and seasonal rates very

Table 11.5. *Condition means for three customers*

	Population	Customer 1	Customer 2	Customer 3
Contract length	-0.213	0.198	-0.208	-0.401
Local utility	2.23	2.91	2.17	0.677
Known company	1.59	1.79	2.15	1.24
TOD rates	-9.19	-5.59	-8.92	-12.8
Seasonal rates	-9.02	-5.86	-11.1	-10.9

generously, as if all of his consumption were in the lowest-priced period (note that the lowest price under TOD rates is 5 c/kWh and the lowest price under seasonal rates is 6 c/kWh). That is, the first customer is willing to pay, to be on TOD or seasonal rates, probably more than the rates are actually worth in terms of reduced energy bills. Finally, this customer is willing to pay more than the average customer to stay with the local utility. From a marketing perspective, the local utility can easily retain and make extra profits from this customer by offering a long-term contract under TOD or seasonal rates.

The third customer dislikes seasonal and TOD rates, evaluating them as if all of his consumption were in the highest-priced periods. He dislikes long-term contracts far more than the average customer, and yet, unlike most customers, prefers to receive service from a known company that is not his local utility. This customer is a prime target for capture by a well-known company if the company offers him a fixed price without requiring a commitment.

The second customer is less clearly a marketing opportunity. A well-known company is on about an equal footing with the local utility in competing for this customer. This in itself might make the customer a target of well-known suppliers, since he is less tied to the local utility than most customers. However, beyond this information, there is little beyond low prices (which all customers value) that would seem to attract the customer. His evaluation of TOD and seasonal rates is sufficiently negative that it is unlikely that a supplier could attract and make a profit from the customer by offering these rates. The customer is willing to pay to avoid a long-term contract, and so a supplier could attract this customer by not requiring a contract if other suppliers were requiring contracts. However, if other suppliers were not requiring contracts either, there seems to be little leverage that any supplier would have over its competitors. This customer will apparently be won by the supplier that offers the lowest fixed price.

The discussion of these three customers illustrates the type of information that can be obtained by conditioning on customer's choices, and how the information translates readily into characterizing each customer and identifying profitable marketing opportunities.

11.6.3. Conditional Probability for the Last Choice

Recall that the last choice situation faced by each customer was not included in the estimation. It can therefore be considered a new choice situation and used to assess the effect of conditioning on past choices. We identified which alternative each customer chose in the new choice situation and calculated the probability of this alternative. The probability was first calculated without conditioning on previous choices. This calculation uses the mixed logit formula (11.5) with the population distribution of β_n and the point estimates of the population parameters. The average of this unconditional probability over customers is 0.353. The probability was then calculated conditioned on previous choices. Four different ways of calculating this probability were used:

1. Based on formula (11.6) using the point estimates of the population parameters.
2. Based on formula (11.6) along with the procedure in Section 11.3 that takes account of the sampling variance of the estimates of the population parameters.
3–4. With the logit formula

$$\frac{e^{\beta_n' x_{niT+1}}}{\sum_j e^{\beta_n' x_{njT+1}}},$$

with the conditional mean $\bar{\beta}_n$ being used for β_n. This method is equivalent to using the customer's $\bar{\beta}_n$ as if it were an estimate of the customer's true coefficients, β_n. The two versions differ in whether $\bar{\beta}_n$ is calculated on the basis of the point estimate of the population parameters (method 3) or takes the sampling distribution into account (method 4).

Results are given in Table 11.6 for model 2. The most prominent result is that conditioning on each customer's previous choices improves the forecasts for the last choice situation considerably. The average probability of the chosen alternative increases from 0.35 without conditioning to over 0.50 with conditioning. For nearly three-quarters of the 361 sampled customers, the prediction of their last choice situation is better with conditioning than without, with the average probability rising by more than 0.25. For the other customers, the conditioning makes the prediction

Table 11.6. *Probability of chosen alternative in last choice situation*

	Method 1	Method 2	Method 3	Method 4
Average probability	0.5213	0.5041	0.5565	0.5487
Number of customers whose probability rises with conditioning	266	260	268	264
Average rise in probability for customers with a rise	0.2725	0.2576	0.3240	0.3204
Number of customers whose probability drops with conditioning	95	101	93	97
Average fall in probability for customers with a drop	0.1235	0.1182	0.1436	0.1391

in the last choice situations less accurate, with the average probability for these customers dropping.

There are several reasons why the predicted probability after conditioning is not always greater. First, the choice experiments were constructed so that each situation would be fairly different from the other situations, so as to obtain as much variation as possible. If the last situation involves new trade-offs, the previous choices will not be useful and may in fact be detrimental to predicting the last choice. A more appropriate test might be to design a series of choice situations that elicited information on the relevant trade-offs and then design an extra "holdout" situation that is within the range of trade-offs of the previous ones.

Second, we did not include in our model all of the attributes of the alternatives that were presented to customers. In particular, we omitted attributes that did not enter significantly in the estimation of the population parameters. Some customers might respond to these omitted attributes, even though they are insignificant for the population as a whole. Insofar as the last choice situation involves trade-offs of these attributes, the conditional distributions of tastes would be misleading, since the relevant tastes are excluded. This explanation suggests that, if a mixed logit is going to be used for obtaining conditional densities for each customer, the researcher might include attributes that could be important for some individuals even though they are insignificant for the population as a whole.

Third, regardless of how the survey and model are designed, some customers might respond to choice situations in a quixotic manner, such that the tastes that are evidenced in previous choices are not applied by the customer in the last choice situation.

Last, random factors can cause the probability for some customers to drop with conditioning even when the first three reasons do not.

While at least one of these reasons may be contributing to the lower choice probabilities for some of the customers in our sample, the gain in predictive accuracy for the customers with an increase in probability after conditioning is over twice as great as the loss in accuracy for those with a decrease, and the number of customers with a gain is almost three times as great as the number with a loss.

The third and easiest method, which simply calculates the standard logit formula using the customers' $\bar{\beta}_n$ based on the point estimate of the population parameters, gives the highest probability. This procedure does not allow for the distribution of β_n around $\bar{\beta}_n$ or for the sampling distribution of $\hat{\theta}$. Allowing for either variance reduces the average probability: using the conditional distribution of β_n rather than just the mean $\bar{\beta}_n$ (methods 1 and 2 compared with methods 3 and 4, respectively) reduces the average probability, and allowing for the sampling distribution of $\hat{\theta}$ rather than the point estimate (methods 2 and 4 compared with methods 1 and 3, respectively) also reduces the average probability. This result does not mean that method 3, which incorporates the least variance, is superior to the others. Methods 3 and 4 are consistent only if the number of choice situations is able to rise without bound, so that $\bar{\beta}_n$ can be considered to be an estimate of β_n. With fixed T, methods 1 and 2 are more appropriate, since they incorporate the entire conditional density.

11.7   Discussion

This chapter demonstrates how the distribution of coefficients conditioned on the customer's observed choices are obtained from the distribution of coefficients in the population. While these conditional distributions can be useful in several ways, it is important to recognize the limitations of the concept. First, the use of conditional distributions in forecasting is limited to those customers whose previous choices are observed. Second, while the conditional distribution of each customer can be used in cluster analysis and for other identification purposes, the researcher will often want to relate preferences to observable demographics of the customers. Yet, these observable demographics of the customers could be entered directly into the model itself, so that the population parameters vary with the observed characteristics of the customers in the population. In fact, entering demographics into the model is more direct and more accessible to hypothesis testing than estimating a model without these characteristics, calculating the conditional distribution for each customer, and then doing cluster and other analyses on the moments of the conditional distributions.

Given these issues, there are three main reasons that a researcher might benefit from calculating customers' conditional distributions. First, information on the past choices of customers is becoming more and more widely available. Examples include scanner data for customers with club cards at grocery stores, frequent flier programs for airlines, and purchases from internet retailers. In these situations, conditioning on previous choices allows for effective targeted marketing and the development of new products and services that match the revealed preferences of subgroups of customers.

Second, the demographic characteristics that differentiate customers with different preferences might be more evident through cluster analysis on the conditional distributions than through specification testing in the model itself. Cluster analysis has its own unique way of identifying patterns, which might in some cases be more effective than specification testing within a discrete choice model.

Third, examination of customers' conditional distributions can often identify patterns that cannot be related to observed characteristics of customers but are nevertheless useful to know. For instance, knowing that a product or marketing campaign will appeal to a share of the population because of their particular preferences is often sufficient, without needing to identify the people on the basis of their demographics. The conditional densities can greatly facilitate analyses that have these goals.

12   Bayesian Procedures

12.1   Introduction

A powerful set of procedures for estimating discrete choice models has been developed within the Bayesian tradition. The breakthough concepts were introduced by Albert and Chib (1993) and McCulloch and Rossi (1994) in the context of probit, and by Allenby and Lenk (1994) and Allenby (1997) for mixed logits with normally distributed coefficients. These authors showed how the parameters of the model can be estimated without needing to calculate the choice probabilities. Their procedures provide an alternative to the classical estimation methods described in Chapter 10. Rossi *et al.* (1996), Allenby (1997), and Allenby and Rossi (1999) showed how the procedures can also be used to obtain information on individual-level parameters within a model with random taste variation. By this means, they provide a Bayesian analog to the classical procedures that we describe in Chapter 11. Variations of these procedures to accommodate other aspects of behavior have been numerous. For example, Arora *et al.* (1998) generalized the mixed logit procedure to take account of the quantity of purchases as well as brand choice in each purchase occasion. Bradlow and Fader (2001) showed how similar methods can be used to examine rankings data at an aggregate level rather than choice data at the individual level. Chib and Greenberg (1998) and Wang *et al.* (2001) developed methods for interrelated discrete responses. Chiang *et al.* (1999) examined situations where the choice set that the decision maker considers is unknown to the researcher. Train (2001) extended the Bayesian procedure for mixed logit to nonnormal distributions of coefficients, including lognormal, uniform, and triangular distributions.

The Bayesian procedures avoid two of the most prominent difficulties associated with classical procedures. First, the Bayesian procedures do not require maximization of any function. With probit and some mixed logit models (especially those with lognormal distributions), maximization of the simulated likelihood function can be difficult numerically.

Often the algorithm fails to converge for various reasons. The choice of starting values is often critical, with the algorithm converging from starting values that are close to the maximum but not from other starting values. The issue of local versus global maxima complicates the maximization further, since convergence does not guarantee that the global maximum has been attained. Second, desirable estimation properties, such as consistency and efficiency, can be attained under more relaxed conditions with Bayesian procedures than classical ones. As shown in Chapter 10, maximum simulated likelihood is consistent only if the number of draws used in simulation is considered to rise with sample size; and efficiency is attained only if the number of draws rises faster than the square root of sample size. In contrast, the Bayesian estimators that we describe are consistent for a fixed number of draws used in simulation and are efficient if the number of draws rises at any rate with sample size.

These advantages come at a price, of course. For researchers who are trained in a classical perspective, the learning curve can be steep. Numerous interrelated techniques and concepts must be assimilated before the power of them becomes clear. I can assure the reader, however, that the effort is worthwhile. Another cost of the Bayesian procedures is more fundamental. To simulate relevant statistics that are defined over a distribution, the Bayesian procedures use an iterative process that converges, with a sufficient number of iterations, to draws from that distribution. This convergence is different from the convergence to a maximum that is needed for classical procedures and involves its own set of difficulties. The researcher cannot easily determine whether convergence has actually been achieved. Thus, the Bayesian procedures trade the difficulties of convergence to a maximum for the difficulties associated with this different kind of convergence. The researcher will need to decide, in a particular setting, which type of convergence is less burdensome.

For some behavioral models and distributional specifications, Bayesian procedures are far faster and, after the initial learning that a classicist needs, are more straightforward from a programming perspective than classical procedures. For other models, the classical procedures are easier. We will explore the relative speed of Bayesian and classical procedures in the sections to follow. The differences can be readily categorized, through an understanding of how the two sets of procedures operate. The researcher can use this understanding in deciding which procedure to use in a particular setting.

Two important notes are required before proceeding. First, the Bayesian procedures, and the term "hierarchical Bayes" that is often used in the context of discrete choice models, refer to an estimation method, not a behavioral model. Probit, mixed logit, or any other model that the researcher specifies can, in principle, be estimated by either classical or Bayesian procedures. Second, the Bayesian perspective from which these procedures arise provides a rich and intellectually satisfying paradigm for inference and decision making. Nevertheless, a researcher who is uninterested in the Bayesian perspective can still benefit from Bayesian procedures: the use of Bayesian procedures does not necessitate that the researcher adopt a Bayesian perspective on statistics. As we will show, the Bayesian procedures provide an estimator whose properties can be examined and interpreted in purely classical ways. Under certain conditions, the estimator that results from the Bayesian procedures is asymptotically equivalent to the maximum likelihood estimator. The researcher can therefore use Bayesian procedures to obtain parameter estimates and then interpret them the same as if they were maximum likelihood estimates. A highlight of the Bayesian procedures is that the results can be interpreted from both perspectives simultaneously, drawing on the insights afforded by each tradition. This dual interpretation parallels that of the classical procedures, whose results can be transformed for Bayesian interpretation as described by Geweke (1989). In short, the researcher's statistical perspective need not dictate her choice of procedure.

In the sections that follow, we provide an overview of Bayesian concepts in general, introducing the prior and posterior distributions. We then show how the mean of the posterior distribution can be interpreted from a classical perspective as being asymptotically equivalent to the maximum of the likelihood function. Next we address the numerical issue of how to calculate the mean of the posterior distribution. Gibbs sampling and, more generally, the Metropolis–Hastings algorithm can be used to obtain draws from practically any posterior distribution, no matter how complex. The mean of these draws simulates the mean of the posterior and thereby constitutes the parameter estimates. The standard deviation of the draws provides the classical standard errors of the estimates. We apply the method to a mixed logit model and compare the numerical difficulty and speed of the Bayesian and classical procedures under various specifications.

12.2   Overview of Bayesian Concepts

Consider a model with parameters θ. The researcher has some initial ideas about the value of these parameters and collects data to improve this understanding. Under Bayesian analysis, the researcher's ideas about the parameters are represented by a probability distribution over all possible values that the parameters can take, where the probability represents how likely the researcher thinks it is for the parameters to take a particular value. Prior to collecting data, the researcher's ideas are based on logic, intuition, or past analyses. These ideas are represented by a density on θ, called the prior distribution and denoted $k(\theta)$. The researcher collects data in order to improve her ideas about the value of θ. Suppose the researcher observes a sample of N independent decision makers. Let y_n denote the observed choice (or choices) of decision maker n, and let the set of observed choices for the entire sample be labeled collectively as $Y = \{y_1, \ldots, y_N\}$. Based on this sample information, the researcher changes, or updates, her ideas about θ. The updated ideas are represented by a new density on θ, labeled $K(\theta \mid Y)$ and called the posterior distribution. This posterior distribution depends on Y, since it incorporates the information that is contained in the observed sample.

The question arises: how exactly do the researcher's ideas about θ change from observing Y? That is, how does the posterior distribution $K(\theta \mid Y)$ differ from the prior distribution $k(\theta)$? There is a precise relationship between the prior and posterior distribution, established by Bayes' rule. Let $P(y_n \mid \theta)$ be the probability of outcome y_n for decision maker n. This probability is the behavioral model that relates the explanatory variables and parameters to the outcome, though the notation for the explanatory variables is omitted for simplicity. The probability of observing the sample outcomes Y is

$$L(Y \mid \theta) = \prod_{n=1}^{N} P(y_n \mid \theta).$$

This is the likelihood function (not logged) of the observed choices. Note that it is a function of the parameters θ.

Bayes' rule provides the mechanism by which the researcher improves her ideas about θ. By the rules of conditioning,

(12.1) $K(\theta \mid Y)L(Y) = L(Y \mid \theta)k(\theta),$

where $L(Y)$ is the marginal probability of Y, marginal over θ:

$$L(Y) = \int L(Y \mid \theta)k(\theta)\,d\theta.$$

Both sides of equation (12.1) represent the joint probability of Y and θ, with the conditioning in opposite directions. The left-hand side is the probability of Y times the probability of θ given Y, while the right-hand side is the probability of θ times the probability of Y given θ. Rearranging, we have

(12.2) $K(\theta \mid Y) = \dfrac{L(Y \mid \theta)k(\theta)}{L(Y)}.$

This equation is Bayes' rule applied to prior and posterior distributions. In general, Bayes rule links conditional and unconditional probabilities in any setting and does not imply a Bayesian perspective on statistics. Bayesian statistics arises when the unconditional probability is the prior distribution (which reflects the researcher's ideas about θ *not* conditioned on the sample information) and the conditional probability is the posterior distribution (which gives the researcher's ideas about θ conditioned on the sample information).

We can express equation (12.2) in a more compact and convenient form. The marginal probability of Y, $L(Y)$, is constant with respect to θ and, more specifically, is the integral of the numerator of (12.2). As such, $L(Y)$ is simply the normalizing constant that assures that the posterior distribution integrates to 1, as required for any proper density. Using this fact, equation (12.2) can be stated more succinctly by saying simply that the posterior distribution is proportional to the prior distribution times the likelihood function:

$$K(\theta \mid Y) \propto L(Y \mid \theta)k(\theta).$$

Intuitively, the probability that the researcher ascribes to a given value for the parameters *after* seeing the sample is the probability that she ascribes *before* seeing the sample times the probability (i.e., *likelihood*) that those parameter values would result in the observed choices.

The mean of the posterior distribution is

$$(12.3) \quad \bar{\theta} = \int \theta K(\theta \mid Y)\,d\theta.$$

This mean has importance from both a Bayesian and a classical perspective. From a Bayesian perspective, $\bar{\theta}$ is the value of θ that minimizes the expected cost of the researcher being wrong about θ, if the cost of error is quadratic in the size of the error. From a classical perspective, $\bar{\theta}$ is an estimator that has the same asymptotic sampling distribution as the maximum likelihood estimator. We explain both of these concepts in the following sections.

12.2.1. Bayesian Properties of $\bar{\theta}$

The researcher's views about θ are represented by the posterior $K(\theta \mid Y)$ after observing the sample. Suppose that the researcher were required to guess the true value of θ and would be levied a penalty for the extent to which her guess differed from the true value. More realistically, suppose that some action must be taken that depends on the value of θ, such as a manufacturer setting the price of a good when the revenues at any price depend on the price elasticity of demand. There is a cost to taking the wrong action, such as setting price based on the belief that the price elasticity is -0.2 when the true elasticity is actually -0.3. The question becomes: what value of θ should the researcher use in these decisions in order to minimize her expected cost of being wrong, given her beliefs about θ as represented in the posterior distribution?

If the cost of being wrong is quadratic in the distance between the θ that is used in the decision and the true θ, then the optimal value of θ to use in the decision is $\bar{\theta}$. This fact can be demonstrated as follows. If the researcher uses θ_0 in her decisions when the true value is θ^*, the cost of being wrong is

$$C(\theta_0, \theta^*) = (\theta_0 - \theta^*)' B(\theta_0 - \theta^*),$$

where B is a matrix of constants. The researcher doesn't know the true value of θ, but has beliefs about its value as represented in $K(\theta \mid Y)$. The researcher can therefore calculate the expected cost of being wrong when using the value θ_0. This expected cost is

$$\mathrm{EC}(\theta_0) = \int C(\theta_0, \theta) K(\theta \mid Y) \, d\theta$$

$$= \int (\theta_0 - \theta)' B(\theta_0 - \theta) K(\theta \mid Y) \, d\theta.$$

The value of θ_0 that minimizes this expected cost is determined by differentiating $\mathrm{EC}(\theta^0)$, setting the derivative equal to zero, and solving for θ^0. The derivative is

$$\frac{\partial \mathrm{EC}(\theta_0)}{\partial \theta_0} = \int \frac{\partial [(\theta_0 - \theta)' B(\theta_0 - \theta)]}{\partial \theta_0} K(\theta \mid Y) \, d\theta$$

$$= \int 2(\theta_0 - \theta)' B K(\theta \mid Y) \, d\theta$$

$$= 2\theta_0' B \int K(\theta \mid Y) \, d\theta - 2 \left(\int \theta K(\theta \mid Y) \, d\theta \right)' B$$

$$= 2\theta_0' B - 2\bar{\theta}' B.$$

Setting this expression to equal zero and solving for θ_0, we have

$$2\theta_0' B - 2\bar{\theta}' B = 0,$$
$$\theta_0' B = \bar{\theta}' B,$$
$$\theta_0 = \bar{\theta}.$$

The mean of the posterior, $\bar{\theta}$, is the value of θ that a Bayesian researcher would optimally act upon if the cost of being wrong about θ rises quadratically with the distance to the true θ.

Zellner (1971) describes the optimal Bayesian estimator under other loss functions. While the loss function is usually assumed to be symmetric and unbounded like the quadratic, it need not be either; see, for example, Wen and Levy (2001). Importantly, Bickel and Doksum (2000) show that the correspondence that we describe in the next section between the mean of the posterior and the maximum likelihood estimator also applies to Bayesian estimators that are optimal under many other loss functions.

12.2.2. Classical Properties of $\bar{\theta}$:
The Bernstein–von Mises Theorem

Classical statistics is not concerned with the researcher's beliefs and contains no notion of prior and posterior distributions. The concern of classical statistics is to determine the sampling distribution of an estimator. This distribution reflects the fact that a different sample would produce a different point estimate. The sampling distribution is the distribution of point estimates that would be obtained if many different samples were taken. Usually, the sampling distribution for an estimator cannot be derived for small samples. However, the asymptotic sampling distribution can usually be derived, which approximates the actual sampling distribution when the sample size is large enough. In classical statistics, the asymptotic sampling distribution determines the properties of the estimator, such as whether the estimator is consistent, asymptotically normal, and efficient. The variance of the asymptotic distribution provides the standard errors of the estimates and allows for hypothesis testing, the accuracy of which rises with sample size.

From a classical perspective, $\bar{\theta}$ is simply a statistic like any other statistic. Its formula, given in (12.3), exists and can be applied even if the researcher does not interpret the formula as representing the mean of a posterior distribution. The researcher can consider $K(\theta \mid Y)$ to be a function defined by equation (12.2) for any arbitrarily defined $k(\theta)$ that meets the requirements of a density. The relevant question for the classical researcher is the same as with any statistic: what is the sampling distribution of $\bar{\theta}$?

The answer to this question is given by the Bernstein–von Mises theorem. This theorem has a long provenance and takes many forms. In the nineteenth century, Laplace (1820) observed that posterior distributions start to look more and more like normal distributions as the sample size increases. Over the years, numerous versions of the observation have been demonstrated under various conditions, and its implications have been more fully explicated. See Rao (1987), Le Cam and Yang (1990), Lehmann and Casella (1998), and Bickel and Doksum (2000) for modern treatments with historical notes. The theorem is named after Bernstein (1917) and von Mises (1931) because they seem to have been the first to provide a formal proof of Laplace's observation, though under restrictive assumptions that others later relaxed.

I describe the theorem as three related statements. In these statements, the information matrix, which we used extensively in Chapters 8 and 10, is important. Recall that the score of an observation is the gradient of that observation's log likelihood with respect to the parameters: $s_n = \partial \ln P(y_n \mid \theta)/\partial\theta$, where $P(y_n \mid \theta)$ is the probability of decision maker n's observed choices. The information matrix, $-\mathbf{H}$, is the negative expected derivative of the score, evaluated at the true parameters:

$$-\mathbf{H} = -E\left(\frac{\partial^2 \ln P(y_n \mid \theta^*)}{\partial\theta\,\partial\theta'}\right),$$

where the expectation is over the population. (The negative is taken so that the information matrix can be positive definite, like a covariance matrix.) Recall also that the maximum likelihood estimator has an asymptotic variance equal to $(-\mathbf{H})^{-1}/N$. That is, $\sqrt{N}(\theta^* - \hat\theta) \xrightarrow{d} N(0, (-\mathbf{H})^{-1})$, so that $\hat\theta \overset{a}{\sim} N(\theta^*, (-\mathbf{H})^{-1}/N)$, where $\hat\theta$ is the maximum likelihood estimator.

We can now give the three statements that collectively constitute the Bernstein–von Mises theorem:

1. $\sqrt{N}(\theta - \bar\theta) \xrightarrow{d} N(0, (-\mathbf{H})^{-1})$.

   Stated intuitively, the posterior distribution of θ converges to a normal distribution with variance $(-\mathbf{H})^{-1}/N$ as the sample size rises. In using the expression $\xrightarrow{d}$ in this context, it is important to note that the distribution that is converging is the posterior distribution of $\sqrt{N}(\theta - \bar\theta)$ rather than the sampling distribution. In classical analysis of estimators, as in Chapter 10, the notation $\xrightarrow{d}$ is used to indicate that the sampling distribution is converging. Bayesian analysis examines the posterior rather than the sampling distribution, and the notation indicates that the posterior distribution is converging.

   The important points to recognize in this first statement are that, as sample size rises, (i) the posterior becomes normal and (ii) the variance of the posterior becomes the same as the sampling variance of the maximum likelihood estimator. These two points are relevant for the next two statements.

2. $\sqrt{N}(\bar\theta - \hat\theta) \xrightarrow{p} 0$.

   The mean of the posterior converges to the maximum of the likelihood function. An even stronger statement is being made.

The difference between the mean of the posterior and the maximum of the likelihood function disappears asymptotically, *even when* the difference is scaled up by $\sqrt{N}$.

This result makes intuitive sense, given the first result. Since the posterior eventually becomes normal, and the mean and maximum are the same for a normal distribution, the mean of the posterior eventually becomes the same as the maximum of the posterior. Also, the effect of the prior distribution on the posterior disappears as the sample size rises (provided of course that the prior is not zero in the neighborhood of the true value). The posterior is therefore proportional to the likelihood function for large enough sample sizes. The maximum of the likelihood function becomes the same as the maximum of the posterior, which, as stated, is also the mean. Stated succinctly: since the posterior is asymptotically normal so that its mean equals its maximum, and the posterior is proportional to the likelihood function asymptotically, the difference between $\bar{\theta}$ and $\hat{\theta}$ eventually disappears.

3. $\sqrt{N}(\bar{\theta} - \theta^*) \overset{d}{\to} N(0, (-\mathbf{H})^{-1})$.

The mean of the posterior, considered as a classical estimator, is asymptotically equivalent to the maximum likelihood estimator. That is, $\bar{\theta} \overset{a}{\sim} N(\theta^*, (-\mathbf{H})^{-1}/N)$, just like the maximum likelihood estimator. Note that since we are now talking in classical terms, the notation refers to the sampling distribution of $\bar{\theta}$, the same as it would for any estimator.

This third statement is an implication of the first two. The statistic $\sqrt{N}(\bar{\theta} - \theta^*)$ can be rewritten as

$$\sqrt{N}(\bar{\theta} - \theta^*) = \sqrt{N}(\hat{\theta} - \theta^*) + \sqrt{N}(\bar{\theta} - \hat{\theta}).$$

From statement 2, we know that $\sqrt{N}(\bar{\theta} - \hat{\theta}) \overset{p}{\to} 0$, so that the second term disappears asymptotically. Only the first term affects the asymptotic distribution. This first term is the defining statistic for the maximum likelihood estimator $\hat{\theta}$. We showed in Chapter 10 that $\sqrt{N}(\hat{\theta} - \theta^*) \overset{d}{\to} N(0, (-\mathbf{H})^{-1})$. The statistic $\sqrt{N}(\bar{\theta} - \theta^*)$ therefore follows the same distribution asymptotically. Essentially, since $\bar{\theta}$ and $\hat{\theta}$ converge, their asymptotic sampling distributions are the same.

The Bernstein–von Mises theorem establishes that $\bar{\theta}$ is on the same footing, in classical terms, as $\hat{\theta}$. Instead of maximizing the likelihood function, the researcher can calculate the mean of the posterior distribution and know that the resulting estimator is as good in classical terms as maximum likelihood.

The theorem also provides a procedure for obtaining the standard errors of the estimates. Statement 1 says that asymptotically the variance of the posterior distribution is $(-\mathbf{H})^{-1}/N$, which, by statement 3, is the asymptotic sampling variance of the estimator $\bar{\theta}$. The variance of the posterior is the asymptotic variance of the estimates. The researcher can perform estimation entirely by using moments of the posterior: the mean of the posterior provides the point estimates, and the standard deviation of the posterior provides the standard errors.

In applications, the posterior mean and the maximum of the likelihood function can differ when sample size is insufficient for the asymptotic convergence. Huber and Train (2001) found the two to be remarkably similar in their application, while Ainslie *et al.* (2001) found them to be sufficiently different to warrant consideration. When the two estimates are not similar, other grounds must be used to choose between them (if indeed a choice is necessary), since their asymptotic properties are the same.

12.3   Simulation of the Posterior Mean

To calculate the mean of the posterior distribution, simulation procedures are generally required. As stated previously, the mean is

$$\bar{\theta} = \int \theta K(\theta \mid Y)\, d\theta.$$

A simulated approximation of this integral is obtained by taking draws of θ from the posterior distribution and averaging the results. The simulated mean is

$$\check{\theta} = \frac{1}{R} \sum_{r=1}^{R} \theta^r,$$

where θ^r is the rth draw from $K(\theta \mid Y)$. The standard deviation of the posterior, which serves as the standard error of the estimates, is simulated by taking the standard deviation of the R draws.

As stated, $\bar{\theta}$ has the same asymptotic properties as the maximum likelihood estimator $\hat{\theta}$. How does the use of simulation to approximate $\bar{\theta}$ affect its properties as an estimator? For maximum simulated likelihood (MSL), we found that the number of draws used in simulation must rise faster than the square root of the sample size in order for the estimator to be asymptotically equivalent to maximum likelihood. With a fixed number of draws, the MSL estimator is inconsistent. If the number of draws rises with sample size but at a slower rate than the square root of the sample size, then MSL is consistent but not asymptotically normal or efficient. As we will see, desirable properties of the simulated mean of the posterior (SMP) are attained with more relaxed conditions on the number of draws. In particular, the SMP estimator is consistent and asymptotically normal for a fixed number of draws and becomes efficient and equivalent to maximum likelihood if the number of draws rises at any rate with sample size.

To demonstrate these properties, we examine the normalized statistic $\sqrt{N}(\check{\theta} - \theta^*)$. This statistic can be rewritten as

$$\sqrt{N}(\check{\theta} - \theta^*) = \sqrt{N}(\bar{\theta} - \theta^*) + \sqrt{N}(\check{\theta} - \bar{\theta}).$$

From statement 3 of the Bernstein–von Mises theorem, we know the limiting distribution of the first term: $\sqrt{N}(\bar{\theta} - \theta^*) \overset{d}{\to} N(0, (-\mathbf{H})^{-1})$. The central limit theorem gives us the limiting distribution of the second term. $\check{\theta}$ is the average of R draws from a distribution with mean $\bar{\theta}$ and variance $(-\mathbf{H}^{-1})/N$. Assuming the draws are independent, the central limit theorem states that the average of these R draws is distributed with mean $\bar{\theta}$ and variance $(-\mathbf{H})^{-1}/RN$. Plugging this information into the second term, we have $\sqrt{N}(\check{\theta} - \bar{\theta}) \overset{d}{\to} N(0, (-\mathbf{H})^{-1}/R)$. The two terms are independent by construction, and so

$$\sqrt{N}(\check{\theta} - \theta^*) \overset{d}{\to} N\left(0, \left(1 + \frac{1}{R}\right)(-\mathbf{H})^{-1}\right).$$

The simulated mean of the posterior is consistent and asymptotically normal for fixed R. The covariance is inflated by a factor of $1/R$ due to the simulation; however, the covariance matrix can be calculated, and so standard errors and hypothesis testing can be conducted that take into account the simulation noise.

If R rises at any rate with N, then the second term disappears asymptotically. We have

$$\sqrt{N}(\check{\theta} - \theta^*) \overset{d}{\to} N(0, (-\mathbf{H})^{-1}),$$

which is the same as for the actual (unsimulated) mean $\bar{\theta}$ and the maximum likelihood estimator $\hat{\theta}$. When R rises with N, $\check{\theta}$ is asymptotically efficient and equivalent to maximum likelihood.

Two notes are required regarding this derivation. First, we have assumed that the draws from the posterior distribution are independent. In the sections to follow, we describe methods for drawing from the posterior that result in draws that exhibit a type of serial correlation. When draws of this type are used, the variance of the simulated mean is inflated by more than a factor of $1/R$. The estimator is still consistent and asymptotically normal with a fixed number of nonindependent draws; its covariance is simply greater. And, if R rises with N, the extra covariance due to simulation disappears asymptotically even with nonindependent draws, such that the simulated mean is asymptotically equivalent to maximum likelihood.

Second, we have assumed that draws from the posterior distribution can be taken without needing to simulate the choice probabilities. For some models, taking a draw from the posterior requires simulating the choice probabilities on which the posterior is based. In this case, the simulated mean of the posterior involves simulation within simulation, and the formula for its asymptotic distribution is more complex. As we will see, however, for most models, including all the models that we consider in this book, draws from the posterior can be taken without simulating the choice probabilities. One of the advantages of the Bayesian procedures is that they usually avoid the need to simulate choice probabilities.

12.4   Drawing from the Posterior

Usually, the posterior distribution does not have a convenient form from which to take draws. For example, we know how to take draws easily from a joint untruncated normal distribution; however, it is rare that the posterior takes this form for the entire parameter vector. Importance sampling, which we describe in Section 9.2.7 in relation to any density, can be useful for simulating statistics over the posterior. Geweke (1992, 1997) describes the approach with respect to posteriors and provides practical guidance on appropriate selection of a proposal density. Two other methods that we described in Chapter 9 are particularly useful for taking draws from a posterior distribution: Gibbs sampling and the Metropolis–Hasting algorithm. These methods are often called Monte Carlo Markov chain, or MCMC, methods. Formally, Gibbs sampling is a special type of Metropolis–Hasting algorithm (Gelman, 1992). However, the case is so special, and so conceptually straightforward, that the term Metropolis–Hasting (MH) is usually reserved for versions that are more complex than Gibbs sampling. That is, when the MH algorithm is Gibbs sampling, it is referred to as Gibbs sampling, and when it is more complex than Gibbs sampling, it is referred to as the MH algorithm. I maintain this convention hereafter.

It will be useful for the reader to review Sections 9.2.8 and 9.2.9, which describe Gibbs sampling and the MH algorithm, since we will be using these procedures extensively in the remainder of this chapter. As stated, the mean of the posterior is simulated by taking draws from the posterior and averaging the draws. Instead of taking draws from the multidimensional posterior for all the parameters, Gibbs sampling allows the researcher to take draws of one parameter at a time (or a subset of parameters), conditional on values of the other parameters (Casella and George, 1992). Drawing from the posterior for one parameter conditional on the others is usually much easier than drawing from the posterior for all parameters simultaneously.

In some cases, the MH algorithm is needed in conjunction with Gibbs sampling. Suppose, for example, that the posterior for one parameter conditional on the other parameters does not take a simple form. In this case, the MH algorithm can be utilized, since it is applicable to (practically) any distribution (Chib and Greenberg, 1995).

The MH algorithm is particularly useful in the context of posterior distributions because the normalizing constant for the posterior need not be calculated. Recall that the posterior is the prior times the likelihood function, divided by a normalizing constant that assures that the posterior integrates to one:

$$K(\theta \mid Y) = \frac{L(Y \mid \theta)k(\theta)}{L(Y)},$$

where $L(Y)$ is the normalizing constant

$$L(Y) = \int L(Y \mid \theta)k(\theta)\,d\theta.$$

This constant can be difficult to calculate, since it involves integration. As described in Section 9.2.9, the MH algorithm can be applied without knowing or calculating the normalizing constant of the posterior.

In summary, Gibbs sampling, combined if necessary with the MH algorithm, allows draws to be taken from the posterior of a parameter vector for essentially any model. These procedures are applied to a mixed logit model in Section 12.6. First, however, we will derive the posterior distribution for some very simple models. As we will see, these results often apply in complex models for a subset of the parameters. This fact facilitates the Gibbs sampling of these parameters.

12.5 Posteriors for the Mean and Variance of a Normal Distribution

The posterior distribution takes a very convenient form for some simple inference processes. We describe two of these situations, which, as we will see, often arise within more complex models for a subset of the parameters. Both results relate to the normal distribution. We first consider the situation where the variance of a normal distribution is known, but the mean is not. We then turn the tables and consider the mean to be known but not the variance. Finally, combining these two situations with Gibbs sampling, we consider the situation where both the mean and variance are unknown.

12.5.1. Result A: Unknown Mean, Known Variance

We discuss the one-dimensional case first, and then generalize to multiple dimensions. Consider a random variable β that is distributed normal with unknown mean b and known variance σ. The researcher observes a sample of N realizations of the random variable, labeled β_n, $n = 1, \ldots, N$. The sample mean is $\bar{\beta} = (1/N) \sum_n \beta_n$. Suppose the researcher's prior on b is $N(b_0, s_0)$; that is, the researcher's prior beliefs are represented by a normal distribution with mean b_0 and variance s_0. Note that we now have two normal distributions: the distribution of β, which has mean b, and the prior distribution on this unknown mean, which has mean β_0. The prior indicates that the researcher thinks it is most likely that $b = \beta_0$ and also thinks there is a 95 percent chance that b is somewhere between $\beta_0 - 1.96\sqrt{s_0}$ and $\beta_0 + 1.96\sqrt{s_0}$. Under this prior, the posterior on b is $N(b_1, s_1)$ where

$$b_1 = \frac{\frac{1}{s_0}b_0 + \frac{N}{\sigma}\bar{\beta}}{\frac{1}{s_0} + \frac{N}{\sigma}}$$

and

$$s_1 = \frac{1}{\frac{1}{s_0} + \frac{N}{\sigma}}.$$

The posterior mean b_1 is the weighted average of the sample mean and the prior mean.

Proof: The prior is

$$k(b) = \frac{1}{\sqrt{2\pi s_0}} e^{-(b-b_0)^2/2s_0}.$$

The probability of drawing β_n from $N(b, \sigma)$ is

$$\frac{1}{\sqrt{2\pi\sigma}} e^{-(b-\beta_n)^2/2\sigma},$$

and so the likelihood of the N draws is

$$L(\beta_n \; \forall n \mid b) = \prod_n \frac{1}{\sqrt{2\pi\sigma}} e^{-(b-\beta_n)^2/2\sigma}$$

$$= \frac{1}{(2\pi\sigma)^{N/2}} e^{-\sum(b-\beta_n)^2/2\sigma}$$

$$= \frac{1}{(2\pi\sigma)^{N/2}} e^{(-N\bar{s}-N(b-\bar{\beta})^2)/2\sigma}$$

$$= \frac{1}{(2\pi\sigma)^{N/2}} e^{-N\bar{s}/2\sigma} \cdot e^{-N(b-\bar{\beta})^2/2\sigma},$$

where $\bar{s} = (1/N)\sum(\beta_n - \bar{\beta})^2$ is the sample variance of the β_n's. The posterior is therefore

$$K(b \mid \beta_n \; \forall n) \propto L(\beta_n \; \forall n \mid b)k(b)$$

$$= \frac{1}{(2\pi\sigma)^{N/2}} e^{-N\bar{s}/2\sigma} \cdot e^{-N(b-\bar{\beta})^2/2\sigma} \times \frac{1}{\sqrt{2\pi s_0}} e^{-(b-b_0)^2/2s_0}$$

$$= m_1 e^{-[N(b-\bar{\beta})^2/2\sigma]-[(b-b_0)^2/2s_0]},$$

where m_1 is a constant that contains all the multiplicative terms that do not depend on b. With some algebraic manipulation, we have

$$K(b \mid \beta_n \; \forall n) \propto e^{-[N(b-\bar{\beta})^2/2\sigma]-[(b-b_0)^2/2s_0)]}$$

$$\propto e^{(b^2-2b_1 b)/2s_1}$$

$$\propto e^{(b-b_1)^2/2s_1}.$$

The second $\propto$ removes $\bar{\beta}^2$ and b_0^2 from the exponential, since they do not depend on b and thereby only affect the normalizing constant. (Recall that $\exp(a+b) = \exp(a)\exp(b)$, so that adding and removing terms from the exponential has a multiplicative effect on $K(b \mid \beta_n \; \forall n)$.) The third $\propto$ adds $b_1\bar{\beta}$ to the exponential, which also does not depend on b. The posterior is therefore

$$K(b \mid \beta_n \; \forall n) = m e^{(b-b_1)^2/2s_1},$$

where m is the normalizing constant. This formula is the normal density with mean b_1 and variance s_1.

As stated, the mean of the posterior is a weighted average of the sample mean and the prior mean. The weight on the sample mean rises as sample size rises, so that for large enough N, the prior mean becomes irrelevant.

Often a researcher will want to specify a prior that represents very little knowledge about the parameters before taking the sample. In general, the researcher's uncertainty is reflected in the variance of the prior. A large variance means that the researcher has little idea about the value of the parameter. Stated equivalently, a prior that is nearly flat means that the researcher considers all possible values of the parameters to be equally likely. A prior that represents little information is called *diffuse*.

We can examine the effect of a diffuse prior on the posterior of b. By raising the variance of the prior, s_0, the normal prior becomes more spread out and flat. As $s_0 \to \infty$, representing an increasingly diffuse prior, the posterior approaches $N(\bar{\beta}, \sigma/N)$.

The multivariate versions of this result are similar. Consider a K-dimensional random vector $\beta \sim N(b, W)$ with known W and unknown b. The researcher observes a sample β_n, $n = 1, \ldots, N$, whose sample mean is $\bar{\beta}$. If the researcher's prior on b is diffuse (normal with an unboundedly large variance), then the posterior is $N(\bar{\beta}, W/N)$.

Taking draws from this posterior is easy. Let L be the Choleski factor of W/N. Draw K iid standard normal deviates, η_i, $i = 1, \ldots, K$, and stack them into a vector $\eta = \langle \eta_1, \ldots, \eta_K \rangle'$. Calculate $\tilde{b} = \bar{\beta} + L\eta$. The resulting vector $\tilde{b}$ is a draw from $N(\bar{\beta}, W/N)$.

12.5.2. Result B: Unknown Variance, Known Mean

Consider a (one-dimensional) random variable that is distributed normal with known mean b and unknown variance σ. The researcher observes a sample of N realizations, labeled β_n, $n = 1, \ldots, N$. The sample variance *around the known mean* is $\bar{s} = (1/N) \sum_n (\beta_n - b)^2$. Suppose the researcher's prior on σ is inverted gamma with degrees of freedom v_0 and scale s_0. This prior is denoted IG(v_0, s_0). The density is zero for any negative value for σ, reflecting the fact that a variance must be positive. The mode of the inverted gamma prior is $s_0 v_0/(1 + v_0)$. Under the inverted gamma prior, the posterior on σ is also inverted gamma IG(v_1, s_1), where

$$v_1 = v_0 + N,$$
$$s_1 = \frac{v_0 s_0 + N\bar{s}}{v_0 + N}.$$

Proof: An inverted gamma with v_0 degrees of freedom and scale s_0 has density

$$k(\sigma) = \frac{1}{m_0 \sigma^{(v_0/2)+1}} e^{-v_0 s_0/2\sigma},$$

where m_0 is the normalizing constant. The likelihood of the sample, treated as a function of σ, is

$$L(\beta_n \; \forall n \mid \sigma) = \frac{1}{(2\pi\sigma)^{N/2}}e^{-\sum(b-\beta_n)^2/2\sigma} = \frac{1}{(2\pi\sigma)^{N/2}}e^{-N\bar{s}/2\sigma}.$$

The posterior is then

$$K(\sigma \mid \beta_n \; \forall n) \propto L(\beta_n \; \forall n \mid \sigma)k(\sigma)$$

$$\propto \frac{1}{\sigma^{N/2}}e^{-N\bar{s}/2\sigma} \times \frac{1}{\sigma^{(v_0/2)+1}}e^{-v_0 s_0/2\sigma}$$

$$= \frac{1}{\sigma^{(N+v_0/2)+1}}e^{-(N\bar{s}+v_0 s_0)/2\sigma}$$

$$= \frac{1}{\sigma^{(v_1/2)+1}}e^{-v_1 s_1/2\sigma},$$

which is the inverted gamma density with v_1 degrees of freedom and scale s_1.

The inverted gamma prior becomes more diffuse with lower v_0. For the density to integrate to one and have a mean, v_0 must exceed 1. It is customary to set $s_0 = 1$ when specifying $v_0 \to 1$. Under this diffuse prior, the posterior becomes $IG(1 + N, (1 + N\bar{s})/(1 + N))$. The mode of this posterior is $(1 + N\bar{s})/(2 + N)$, which is approximately the sample variance $\bar{s}$ for large N.

The multivariate case is similar. The multivariate generalization of an inverted gamma distribution is the inverted Wishart distribution. The result in the multivariate case is the same as with one random variable except that the inverted gamma is replaced by the inverted Wishart.

A K-dimensional random vector $\beta \sim N(b, W)$ has known b but unknown W. A sample of size N from this distribution has variance around the known mean of $\bar{S} = (1/N)\sum_n(\beta_n - b)(\beta_n - b)'$. If the researcher's prior on W is inverted Wishart with v_0 degrees of freedom and scale matrix S_0, labeled $IW(v_0, S_0)$, then the posterior on W is $IW(v_1, S_1)$ where

$$v_1 = v_0 + N,$$
$$S_1 = \frac{v_0 S_0 + N\bar{S}}{v_0 + N}.$$

The prior becomes more diffuse with lower v_0, though v_0 must exceed K in order for the prior to integrate to one and have means. With $S_0 = I$, where I is the K-dimensional identity matrix, the posterior under a diffuse prior becomes $IW(K + N, (KI + N\bar{S})/(K + N))$. Conceptually, the prior is equivalent to the researcher having a previous sample of K observations whose sample variance was I. As N rises without bound, the influence of the prior on the posterior eventually disappears.

It is easy to take draws from inverted gamma and inverted Wishart distributions. Consider first an inverted gamma $IG(v_1, s_1)$. Draws are taken as follows:

1. Take v_1 draws from a standard normal, and label the draws η_i, $i = 1, \ldots, v_1$.
2. Divide each draw by $\sqrt{s_1}$, square the result, and take the average. That is, calculate $r = (1/v_1) \sum_i (\sqrt{1/s_1} \eta_i)^2$, which is the sample variance of v_1 draws from a normal distribution whose variance is $1/s_1$.
3. Take the inverse of r: $\tilde{s} = 1/r$ is a draw from the inverted gamma.

Draws from a K-dimensional inverted Wishart $IW(v_1, S_1)$ are obtained as follows:

1. Take v_1 draws of K-dimensional vectors whose elements are independent standard normal deviates. Label these draws η_i, $i = 1, \ldots, v_1$.
2. Calculate the Choleski factor of the inverse of S_1, labeled L, where $LL' = S_1^{-1}$.
3. Create $R = (1/v_1) \sum_i (L\eta_i)(L\eta_i)'$. Note that R is the variance of draws from a distribution with variance S_1^{-1}.
4. Take the inverse of R. The matrix $\tilde{S} = R^{-1}$ is a draw from $IW(v_1, S_1)$.

12.5.3. Unknown Mean and Variance

Suppose that both the mean b and variance W are unknown. For neither of these parameters does the posterior take a convenient form. However, draws can easily be obtained using Gibbs sampling and results A and B. A draw of b is taken conditional on W, and then a draw of W is taken conditional on b. Result A says that the posterior for b conditional on W is normal, which is easy to draw from. Result B says that the posterior for W conditional on b is inverted Wishart, which is also easy to draw from. Iterating through numerous cycles of draws from the conditional posteriors provides, eventually, draws from the joint posterior.

12.6   Hierarchical Bayes for Mixed Logit

In this section we show how the Bayesian procedures can be used to estimate the parameters of a mixed logit model. We utilize the approach developed by Allenby (1997), implemented by SawtoothSoftware (1999), and generalized by Train (2001). Let the utility that person n obtains from alternative j in time period t be

$$U_{njt} = \beta'_n x_{njt} + \varepsilon_{njt},$$

where ε_{njt} is iid extreme value and $\beta_n \sim N(b, W)$. Giving β_n a normal distribution allows us to use results A and B, which speeds estimation considerably. In the following section, we discuss the use of nonnormal distributions.

The researcher has priors on b and W. Suppose the prior on b is normal with an unboundedly large variance. Suppose that the prior on W is inverted Wishart with K degrees of freedom and scale matrix I, the K-dimensional identity matrix. Note that these are the priors used for results A and B. More flexible priors can be specified for W, using the procedures of, for example, McCulloch and Rossi (2000), though doing so makes the Gibbs sampling more complex.

A sample of N people is observed. The chosen alternatives in all time periods for person n are denoted $y'_n = \langle y_{n1}, \ldots, y_{nT} \rangle$, and the choices of the entire sample are labeled $Y = \langle y_1, \ldots, y_N \rangle$. The probability of person n's observed choices, conditional on β, is

$$L(y_n \mid \beta) = \prod_t \left(\frac{e^{\beta' x_{ny_{nt}t}}}{\sum_j e^{\beta' x_{njt}}} \right).$$

The probability *not* conditional on β is the integral of $L(y_n \mid \beta)$ over all β:

$$L(y_n \mid b, W) = \int L(y_n \mid \beta) \phi(\beta \mid b, W) \, d\beta,$$

where $\phi(\beta \mid b, W)$ is the normal density with mean b and variance W. This $L(y_n \mid b, W)$ is the mixed logit probability.

The posterior distribution of b and W is, by definition,

$$(12.4) \quad K(b, W \mid Y) \propto \prod_n L(y_n \mid b, W) k(b, W),$$

where $k(b, W)$ is the prior on b and W described earlier (i.e., normal for b times inverted Wishart for W).

It would be *possible* to draw directly from $K(b, W \mid Y)$ with the MH algorithm. However, doing so would be computationally very slow. For each iteration of the MH algorithm, it would be necessary to calculate the right-hand side of (12.4). However, the choice probability $L(y_n \mid b, W)$ is an integral without a closed form and must be approximated through simulation. Each iteration of the MH algorithm would therefore require simulation of $L(y_n \mid b, W)$ for each n. That would be very time-consuming, and the properties of the resulting estimator would be affected by it. Recall that the properties of the simulated mean of the posterior were derived under the assumption that draws can be taken from the posterior without needing to simulate the choice probabilities. MH applied to (12.3) violates this assumption.

Drawing from $K(b, W \mid Y)$ becomes fast and simple if each β_n is considered to be a parameter along with b and W, and Gibbs sampling is used for the three sets of parameters b, W, and β_n $\forall n$. The posterior for b, W, and β_n $\forall n$ is

$$K(b, W, \beta_n \; \forall n \mid Y) \propto \prod_n L(y_n \mid \beta_n) \phi(\beta_n \mid b, W) k(b, W).$$

Draws from this posterior are obtained through Gibbs sampling. A draw of each parameter is taken, conditional on the other parameters: (1) Take a draw of b conditional on values of W and β_n $\forall n$. (2) Take a draw of W conditional on values of b and β_n $\forall n$. (3) Take a draw of $\beta_n \forall n$ conditional on values of b and W. Each of these steps is easy, as we will see. Step 1 uses result A, which gives the posterior of the mean given the variance. Step 2 uses result B, which gives the posterior of the variance given the mean. Step 3 uses an MH algorithm, but in a way that does not involve simulation within the algorithm. Each step is described in the following.

1. $b \mid W, \beta_n \; \forall n$. We condition on W and each person's β_n in this step, which means that we treat these parameters as if they were known. Result A gives us the posterior distribution of b under these conditions. The β_n's constitute a sample of N realizations from a normal distribution with unknown mean b and known variance W. Given our diffuse prior on b, the posterior on b is $N(\bar{\beta}, W/N)$, where $\bar{\beta}$ is the sample mean of the β_n's. A draw from this posterior is obtained as described in Section 12.5.1.

2. $W \mid b, \beta_n \; \forall n$. Result B gives us the posterior for W conditional on b and the β_n's. The β_n's constitute a sample from a normal distribution with known mean b and unknown variance W. Under our prior on W, the posterior on W is inverted Wishart with $K + N$ degrees of freedom and scale matrix $(KI + NS_1)/(K + N)$, where $S_1 = (1/N) \sum_n (\beta_n - b)(\beta_n - b)'$ is the sample variance of the β_n's around the known mean b. A draw from the inverted Wishart is obtained as described in Section 12.5.2.

3. $\beta_n \mid b, W$. The posterior for each person's β_n, conditional on their choices and the population mean and variance of β_n, is

(12.5) $K(\beta_n \mid b, W, y_n) \propto L(y_n \mid \beta_n) \phi(\beta_n \mid b, W).$

There is no simple way to draw from this posterior, and so the MH algorithm is used. Note that the right-hand side of (12.5) is easy to calculate: $L(y_n \mid \beta_n)$ is a product of logits, and $\phi(\beta_n \mid b, W)$ is the normal density. The MH algorithm operates as follows:

(a) Start with a value β_n^0.
(b) Draw K independent values from a standard normal density, and stack the draws into a vector labeled η^1.
(c) Create a trial value of β_n^1 as $\tilde{\beta}_n^1 = \beta_n^0 + \rho L \eta^1$, where ρ is a scalar specified by the researcher and L is the Choleski factor of W. Note that the proposal distribution (which is labeled $g(\cdot)$ in Section 9.2.9) is specified to be normal with zero mean and variance $\rho^2 W$.
(d) Draw a standard uniform variable μ^1.
(e) Calculate the ratio

$$F = \frac{L(y_n \mid \tilde{\beta}_n^1)\phi(\tilde{\beta}_n^1 \mid b, W)}{L(y_n \mid \beta_n^0)\phi(\beta_n^0 \mid b, W)}.$$

(f) If $\mu^1 \leq F$, accept $\tilde{\beta}_n^1$ and let $\beta_n^1 = \tilde{\beta}_n^1$. If $\mu^1 > F$, reject $\tilde{\beta}_n^1$ and let $\beta_n^1 = \beta_n^0$.
(g) Repeat the process many times. For high enough t, β_n^t is a draw from the posterior.

We now know how to draw from the posterior for each parameter conditional on the other parameters. We combine the procedures into a Gibbs sampler for the three sets of parameters. Start with any initial values b^0, W^0, and $\beta_n^0 \, \forall n$. The tth iteration of the Gibbs sampler consists of these steps:

1. Draw b^t from $N(\bar{\beta}^{t-1}, W^{t-1}/N)$, where $\bar{\beta}^{t-1}$ is the mean of the β_n^{t-1}'s.
2. Draw W_t from $IW(K + N, (KI + NS^{t-1})/(K + N))$, where $S^{t-1} = \sum_n (\beta_n^{t-1} - b^t)(\beta_n^{t-1} - b^t)'/N$.
3. For each n, draw β_n^t using one iteration of the MH algorithm previously described, starting from β_n^{t-1} and using the normal density $\phi(\beta_n \mid b^t, W^t)$.

These three steps are repeated for many iterations. The resulting values converge to draws from the joint posterior of b, W, and $\beta_n \forall n$. Once the converged draws from the posterior are obtained, the mean and standard deviation of the draws can be calculated to obtain estimates and standard errors of the parameters. Note that this procedure provides information about β_n for each n, similar to the procedure described in Chapter 11 using classical estimation.

As stated, the Gibbs sampler converges, with enough iterations, to draws from the joint posterior of all the parameters. The iterations prior to convergence are often called *burn-in*. Unfortunately, it is not always easy to determine when convergence has been achieved, as emphasized by Kass *et al.* (1998). Cowles and Carlin (1996) provide a description of the various tests and diagnostics that have been proposed. For example, Gelman and Rubin (1992) suggest starting the Gibbs sampler from several different points and testing the hypothesis that the statistic of interest (in our case, the posterior mean) is the same when calculated from each of the presumably converged sequences. Sometimes convergence is fairly obvious, so that formal testing is unnecessary. During burn-in, the researcher will usually be able to see the draws trending, that is, moving toward the mass of the posterior. After convergence has been achieved, the draws tend to move around ("traverse") the posterior.

The draws from Gibbs sampling are correlated over iterations even after convergence has been achieved, since each iteration builds on the previous one. This correlation does not prevent the draws from being used for calculating the posterior mean and standard deviation, or other statistics. However, the researcher can reduce the amount of correlation among the draws by using only a portion of the draws that are obtained after convergence. For example, the researcher might retain every tenth draw and discard the others, thereby reducing the correlation among the retained draws by an order of 10. A researcher might therefore specify a total of 20,000 iterations in order to obtain 1000 draws: 10,000 for burn-in and 10,000 after convergence, of which every tenth is retained.

One issue remains. In the MH algorithm, the scalar ρ is specified by the researcher. This scalar determines the size of each jump. Usually, smaller jumps translate into more accepts, and larger jumps result in fewer accepts. However, smaller jumps mean that the MH algorithm takes more iterations to converge and embodies more serial correlation in the draws after convergence. Gelman *et al.* (1995, p. 335) have examined the optimal acceptance rate in the MH algorithm. They found that the optimal rate is about 0.44 when $K = 1$ and drops toward 0.23 as K rises. The value of ρ can be set by the researcher to achieve an acceptance rate in this neighborhood, lowering ρ to obtain a higher acceptance rate and raising it to get a lower acceptance rate.

In fact, ρ can be adjusted within the iterative process. The researcher sets the initial value of ρ. In each iteration, a trial β_n is accepted or rejected for each sampled n. If in an iteration, the acceptance rate among the N observations is above a given value (say, 0.33), then ρ is raised. If the acceptance rate is below this value, ρ is lowered. The value of ρ then moves during the iteration process to attain the specified acceptance level.

12.6.1. Succinct Restatement

Now that the Bayesian procedures have been fully described, the model and the Gibbs sampling can be stated succinctly, in the form that is used in most publications. The model is as follows. Utility:

$$U_{njt} = \beta_n' x_{njt} + \varepsilon_{njt},$$
$$\varepsilon_{njt} \text{ iid extreme value,}$$
$$\beta_n \sim N(b, W).$$

Observed choice:

$$y_{nt} = i \quad \text{if and only if} \quad U_{nit} > U_{njt} \, \forall j \neq i.$$

Priors:

$$k(b, W) = k(b)k(W),$$

where

$$k(b) \text{ is } N(b_0, S_0) \text{ with extremely large variance,}$$
$$k(W) \text{ is IW}(K, I).$$

Conditional posteriors:

$$K(\beta_n \mid b, W, y_n) \propto \prod_t \frac{e^{\beta_n' x_{nyntt}}}{\sum_j e^{\beta_n' x_{njt}}} \phi(\beta_n \mid b, W) \, \forall n,$$

$$K(b \mid W, \beta_n \, \forall n) \text{ is } N(\bar{\beta}, W/N)), \qquad \text{where } \bar{\beta} = \sum_n \beta_n / N,$$

$$K(W \mid b, \beta_n \, \forall n) \text{ is IW}\left(K + N, \frac{KI + N\bar{S}}{K + N}\right),$$

where $\bar{S} = \sum_n (\beta_n - b)(\beta_n - b)' / N$.

The three conditional posteriors are called *layers* of the Gibbs sampling. The first layer for each n depends only on data for that person, rather than for the entire sample. The second and third layers do not depend on the data directly, only on the draws of β_n, which themselves depend on the data.

The Gibbs sampling for this model is fast for two reasons. First, none of the layers requires integration. In particular, the first layer utilizes a product of logit formulas for a given value of β_n. The Bayesian procedure avoids the need to calculate the mixed logit probability, utilizing instead the simple logits conditional on β_n. Second, layers 2 and 3 do not utilize the data at all, since they depend only on the draws of $\beta_n \, \forall n$. Only the mean and variance of the β_n's need be calculated in these layers.

The procedure is often called *hierarchical Bayes* (HB), because there is a hierarchy of parameters. β_n are the *individual-level parameters* for person n, which describe the tastes of that person. The β_n's are distributed in the population with mean b and variance W. The parameters b and W are often called the *population-level parameters* or *hyper-parameters*. There is also a hierarchy of priors. The prior on each person's β_n is the density of β_n in the population. This prior has parameters (hyper-parameters), namely its mean b and variance W, which themselves have priors.

12.7   Case Study: Choice of Energy Supplier

We apply the Bayesian procedures to the data that were described in Chapter 11 regarding customers' choice among energy suppliers. The Bayesian estimates are compared with estimates obtained through maximum simulated likelihood (MSL).

Each of 361 customers was presented with up to 12 hypothetical choice situations. In each choice situation, four energy suppliers were described, and the respondent was asked which one he would choose if facing the choice in the real world. The suppliers were differentiated on the basis of six factors: (1) whether the supplier charged fixed prices, and if so the rate in cents per kilowatthour, (2) the length of contract in years, during which the rates were guaranteed and the customer would be required a penalty to switch to another supplier, (3) whether the supplier was the local utility, (4) whether the supplier was a well-known company other than the local utility, (5) whether the supplier charged time-of-day (TOD) rates (specified prices in each period), and (6) whether the supplier charged seasonal rates (specified prices in each season). In the experimental design, the fixed rates varied over situations, but the same prices were specified in all experiments whenever a supplier was said to charge TOD or seasonal rates. The coefficient of the dummies for TOD and seasonal rates therefore reflect the value of these rates at the specified prices. The coefficient of the fixed price indicates the value of each cent per kilowatthour.

12.7.1. Independent Normal Coefficients

A mixed logit model was estimated under the initial assumption that the coefficients are independently normally distributed in the population. That is, $\beta_n \sim N(b, W)$ with diagonal W. The population parameters are the mean and standard deviation of each coefficient. Table 12.1 gives the simulated mean of the posterior (SMP) for these parameters, along with the MSL estimates. For the Bayesian procedure, 20,000

Table 12.1. *Mixed logit model of choice among energy suppliers*

Estimates[a]		MSL	SMP	Scaled MSL
Price coeff.:	Mean	−0.976	−1.04	−1.04
		(.0370)	(.0374)	(.0396)
	St. dev.	0.230	0.253	0.246
		(.0195)	(.0169)	(.0209)
Contract coeff.:	Mean	−0.194	−0.240	−0.208
		(.0224)	(.0269)	(.0240)
	St. dev.	0.405	0.426	0.434
		(.0238)	(.0245)	(.0255)
Local coeff.:	Mean	2.24	2.41	2.40
		(.118)	(.140)	(.127)
	St. dev.	1.72	1.93	1.85
		(.122)	(.123)	(.131)
Well-known coeff.:	Mean	1.62	1.71	1.74
		(.0865)	(.100)	(.0927)
	St. dev.	1.05	1.28	1.12
		(.0849)	(.0940)	(.0910)
TOD coeff.:	Mean	−9.28	−10.0	−9.94
		(.314)	(.315)	(.337)
	St. dev.	2.00	2.51	2.14
		(.147)	(.193)	(.157)
Seasonal coeff.:	Mean	−9.50	−10.2	−10.2
		(.312)	(.310)	(.333)
	St. dev.	1.24	1.66	1.33
		(.188)	(.182)	(.201)

[a] Standard errors in parentheses.

iterations of the Gibbs sampling were performed. The first 10,000 iterations were considered burn-in, and every tenth draw was retained after convergence, for a total of 1000 draws from the posterior. The mean and standard deviation of these draws constitutes the estimates and standard errors. For MSL, the mixed logit probability was simulated with 200 Halton draws for each observation.

The two procedures provide similar results in this application. The scale of the estimates from the Bayesian procedure is somewhat larger than that for MSL. This difference indicates that the posterior is skewed, with the mean exceeding the mode. When the MSL estimates are scaled to have the same estimated mean for the price coefficient, the two sets of estimates are remarkably close, in standard errors as well as point estimates. The run time was essentially the same for each approach.

In other applications, e.g., Ainslie *et al.* (2001), the MSL and SMP estimates have differed. In general, the magnitude of differences depends on the number of observations relative to the number of parameters, as well as the amount of variation that is contained in the observations. When the two sets of estimates differ, it means that the asymptotics are not yet operating completely (i.e., the sample size is insufficient for the asymptotic properties to be fully exhibited). The researcher might want to apply a Bayesian perspective in this case (if she is not already doing so) in order to utilize the Bayesian approach to small-sample inference. The posterior distribution contains the relevant information for Bayesian analysis with any sample size, whereas the classical perspective requires the researcher to rely on asymptotic formulas for the sampling distribution that need not be meaningful with small samples. Allenby and Rossi (1999) provide examples of the differences and the value of the Bayesian approaches and perspective.

We reestimated the model under a variety of other distributional assumptions. In the following sections, we describe how each method is implemented under these alternative assumptions. For reasons that are inherent in the methodologies, the Bayesian procedures are easier and faster for some specifications, while the classical procedures are easier and faster for others. Understanding these realms of relative convenience can assist the researcher in deciding which method to use for a particular model.

12.7.2. Multivariate Normal Coefficients

We now allow the coefficients to be correlated. That is, W is full rather than diagonal. The classical procedure is the same except that drawing from $\phi(\beta_n \mid b, W)$ for the simulation of the mixed logit probability requires creating correlation among independent draws from a random number generator. The model is parameterized in terms of the Choleski factor of W, labeled L. The draws are calculated as $\tilde{\beta}_n = b + L\eta$, where η is a draw of a K-dimensional vector of independent standard normal deviates. In terms of computation time for MSL, the main difference is that the model has far more parameters with full W than when W is diagonal: $K + K(K+1)/2$ rather than the $2K$ parameters for independent coefficients. In our case with $K = 6$, the number of parameters rises from 12 to 27. The gradient with respect to each of the new parameters takes time to calculate, and the model requires more iterations to locate the maximum over the larger-dimensioned log-likelihood function. As shown in the second line of Table 12.2, the run time nearly triples for the model with correlated coefficients, relative to independent coefficients.

With the Bayesian procedure, correlated coefficients are no harder to handle than uncorrelated ones. For full W, the inverted gamma

Table 12.2. *Run times*

Specification	Run time (min)	
	MSL	SMP
All normal, no correlations	48	53
All normal, full covariance	139	55
1 fixed, others normal, no corr.	42	112
3 lognormal, 3 normal, no corr.	69	54
All triangular, no corr.	56	206

distribution is replaced with its multivariate generalization, the inverted Wishart. Draws are obtained by the procedure in Section 12.5.2. The only extra computer time relative to independent coefficients arises in the calculation of the covariance matrix of the β_n's and its Choleski factor, rather than the standard deviations of the β_n's. This difference is trivial for typical numbers of parameters. As shown in Table 12.2, the run time for the model with full covariance among the random coefficients was essentially the same as with independent coefficients.

12.7.3. Fixed Coefficients for Some Variables

There are various reasons that the researcher might choose to specify some of the coefficients as fixed.

1. Ruud (1996) argues that a mixed logit with all random co-efficients is nearly unidentified empirically, since only ratios of coefficients are economically meaningful. He recommends holding at least one coefficient fixed, particularly when the data contain only one choice situation for each decision maker.
2. In a model with alternative-specific constants, the final iid extreme value terms constitute the random portion of these constants. Allowing the coefficients of the alternative-specific dummies to be random in addition to having the final iid extreme value terms is equivalent to assuming that the constants follow a distribution that is a mixture of extreme value and whatever distribution is assumed for these coefficients. If the two distributions are similar, such as a normal and extreme value, the mixture can be unidentifiable empirically. In this case, the analyst might choose to keep the coefficients of the alternative-specific constants fixed.
3. The goal of the analysis might be to forecast substitution patterns correctly rather than to understand the distribution of

coefficients. In this case, error components can be specified that capture the correct substitution patterns while holding the coefficients of the original explanatory variables fixed (as in Brownstone and Train, 1999).

4. The willingness to pay (wtp) for an attribute is the ratio of the attribute's coefficient to the price coefficient. If the price coefficient is held fixed, the distribution of wtp is simply the scaled distribution of the attribute's coefficient. The distribution of wtp is more complex when the price coefficient varies also. Furthermore, if the usual distributions are used for the price coefficient, such as normal or lognormal, the issue arises of how to handle positive price coefficients, price coefficients that are close to zero so that the implied wtp is extremely high, and price coefficients that are extremely negative. The first of these issues is avoided with lognormals, but not the other two. The analyst might choose to hold the price coefficient fixed to avoid these problems.

In the classical approach, holding one or more coefficients fixed is very easy. The corresponding elements of W and L are simply set to zero, rather than treated as parameters. The run time is reduced, since there are fewer parameters. As indicated in the third line of Table 12.2, the run time decreased by about 12 percent with one fixed coefficient and the rest independent normal, relative to all independent normals. With correlated normals, a larger percentage reduction would occur, since the number of parameters drops more than proportionately.

In the Bayesian procedure, allowing for fixed coefficients requires the addition of a new layer of Gibbs sampling. The fixed coefficient cannot be drawn as part of the MH algorithm for the random coefficients for each person. Recall that under MH, trial draws are accepted or rejected in each iteration. If a trial draw which contains a new value of a fixed coefficient along with new values of the random coefficients is accepted for one person, but the trial draw for another person is not accepted, then the two people will have different values of the fixed coefficient, which contradicts the fact that it is fixed. Instead, the random coefficients, and the population parameters of these coefficients, must be drawn conditional on a value of the fixed coefficients; and then the fixed coefficients are drawn conditional on the values of the random coefficients. Drawing from the conditional posterior for the fixed coefficients requires an MH algorithm, in addition to the one that is used to draw the random coefficients.

To be explicit, rewrite the utility function as

$$(12.6) \quad U_{njt} = \alpha' z_{njt} + \beta_n' x_{njt} + \varepsilon_{njt},$$

where α is a vector of fixed coefficients and β_n is random as before with mean b and variance W. The probability of the person's choice sequence given α and β_n is

$$(12.7) \quad L(y_n \mid \alpha, \beta_n) = \prod_t \frac{e^{\alpha' z_{ny_nt t} + \beta_n' x_{ny_nt t}}}{\sum_j e^{\alpha' z_{njt} + \beta_n' x_{njt}}}.$$

The conditional posteriors for Gibbs sampling are:

1. $K(\beta_n \mid \alpha, b, W) \propto L(y_n \mid \alpha, \beta_n) \phi(\beta_n \mid b, W)$. MH is used for these draws in the same way as with all normals, except that now $\alpha' z_{njt}$ is included in the logit formulas.
2. $K(b \mid W, \beta_n \,\forall n)$ is $N(\Sigma_n \beta_n / N, W/N)$. Note that α does not enter this posterior; its effect is incorporated into the draws of β_n from layer 1.
3. $K(W \mid b, \beta_n \,\forall n)$ is $\text{IW}(K + N, (KI + N\bar{S})/(K + N))$, where $\bar{S} = \Sigma_n (\beta_n - b)(\beta_n - b)'/N$. Again, α does not enter directly.
4. $K(\alpha \mid \beta_n) \propto \Pi_n L(y_n \mid \alpha, \beta_n)$, if the prior on α is essentially flat (e.g., normal with sufficiently large variance). Draws are obtained with MH on the pooled data.

Layer 4 takes as much time as layer 1, since each involves calculation of a logit formula for each observation. The Bayesian procedure with fixed and normal coefficients can therefore be expected to take about twice as much time as with all normal coefficients. As indicated in the third line of Table 12.2, this expectation is confirmed in our application.

12.7.4. Lognormals

Lognormal distributions are often specified when the analyst wants to assure that the coefficient takes the same sign for all people. There is little change in either procedure when some or all of the coefficients are distributed lognormal instead of normal. Normally distributed coefficients are drawn, and then the ones that are lognormally distributed are exponentiated when they enter utility. With all lognormals, utility is specified as

$$(12.8) \quad U_{njt} = (e^{\beta_n})' x_{njt} + \varepsilon_{njt},$$

with β_n distributed normal as before with mean b and variance W. The probability of the person's choice sequence given β_n is

$$(12.9) \quad L(y_n \mid \alpha, \beta_n) = \prod_t \frac{e^{(e^{\beta_n})' x_{ny_nt t}}}{\sum_j e^{(e^{\beta_n})' x_{njt}}}.$$

With this one change, the rest of the steps are the same with both procedures. In the classical approach, however, locating the maximum of the likelihood function is considerably more difficult with lognormal coefficients than with normal ones. Often the numerical maximization procedures fail to find an increase after a number of iterations. Or a "maximum" is found and yet the Hessian is singular at that point. It is often necessary to specify starting values that are close to the maximum. And the fact that the iterations can fail at most starting values makes it difficult to determine whether a maximum is local or global. The Bayesian procedure does not encounter these difficulties, since it does not search for the maximum. The Gibbs sampling seems to converge a bit more slowly, but not appreciably so. As indicated in Table 12.2, the run time for the classical approach rose nearly 50 percent with lognormal relative to normals (due to more iterations being needed), while the Bayesian procedure took about the same amount of time with each. This comparison is generous to the classical approach, since convergence at a maximum was achieved in this application, while in many other applications we have not been able to obtain convergence with lognormals or have done so only after considerable time was spent finding successful starting values.

12.7.5. Triangulars

Normal and lognormal distributions allow coefficients of unlimited magnitude. In some situations, the analyst might want to assure that the coefficients for all people remain within a reasonable range. This goal is accomplished by specifying distributions that have bounded support, such as uniform, truncated normal, and triangular distributions. In the classical approach, these distributions are easy to handle. The only change occurs in the line of code that creates the random draws from the distributions. For example, the density of a triangular distribution with mean b and spread s is zero beyond the range $(b - s, b + s)$, rises linearly from $b - s$ to b, and drops linearly to $b + s$. A draw is created as $\beta_n = b + s(\sqrt{2\mu} - 1)$ if $\mu < 0.5$ and $= b + s(1 - \sqrt{2(1 - \mu)})$ otherwise, where μ is a draw from a standard uniform. Given draws of β_n, the calculation of the simulated probability and the maximization of the likelihood function are the same as with draws from a normal. Experience indicates that estimation of the parameters of uniform, truncated normal, and triangular distributions takes about the same number of iterations as for normals. The last line of Table 12.2 reflects this experience.

With the Bayesian approach, the change to nonnormal distributions is far more complicated. With normally distributed coefficients, the conditional posteriors for the population moments are very convenient:

normal for the mean and inverted Wishart for the variance. Most other distributions do not give such convenient posteriors. Usually, an MH algorithm is needed for the population parameters, in addition to the MH algorithm for the customer-level β_n's. This addition adds considerably to computation time. The issue is exacerbated for distributions with bounded support, since, as we see in the following, the MH algorithm can be expected to converge slowly for these distributions.

With independent triangular distributions for all coefficients with mean and spread vectors b and s, and flat priors on each, the conditional posteriors are:

1. $K(\beta_n \mid b, s) \propto L(y_n \mid \beta_n)h(\beta_n \mid b, s)$, where h is the triangular density. Draws are obtained through MH, separately for each person. This step is the same as with independent normals except that the density for β_n is changed.
2. $K(b, s \mid \beta_n) \propto \prod_n h(\beta_n \mid b, s)$ when the priors on b and s are essentially flat. Draws are obtained through MH on the β_n's for all people.

Because of the bounded support of the distribution, the algorithm is exceedingly slow to converge. Consider, for example, the spread of the distribution. In the first layer, draws of β_n that are outside the range $(b - s, b + s)$ from the second layer are necessarily rejected. And in the second layer, draws of b and s that create a range $(b - s, b + s)$ that does not cover all the β_n's from the first layer are necessarily rejected. It is therefore difficult for the range to grow narrower from one iteration to the next. For example, if the range is 2 to 4 in one iteration of the first layer, then the next iteration will result in values of β_n between 2 and 4 and will usually cover most of the range if the sample size is sufficiently large. In the next draw of b and s, any draw that does not cover the range of the β_n's (which is nearly 2 to 4) will be rejected. There is indeed some room for play, since the β_n's will not cover the entire range from 2 to 4. The algorithm converges, but in our application we found that far more iterations were needed to achieve a semblance of convergence, compared with normal distributions. The run time rose by a factor of four as a result.

12.7.6. Summary of Results

For normal distributions with full covariance matrices, and for transformations of normals that can be expressed in the utility function, such as exponentiating to represent lognormal distributions, the Bayesian approach seems to be very attractive computationally. Fixed coefficients add a layer of conditioning to the Bayesian approach that doubles its run time. In contrast, the classical approach becomes faster for each coefficient that is fixed instead of random, because there are fewer parameters to estimate. For distributions with bounded support, like triangulars, the Bayesian approach is very slow, while the classical approach handles these distributions as quickly as normals.

These comparisons relate to mixed logits only. Other behavioral models can be expected to have different relative run times for the two approaches. The comparison with mixed logit elucidates the issues that arise in implementing each method. Understanding these issues assists the researcher in specifying the model and method that are most appropriate and convenient for the choice situation.

12.8   Bayesian Procedures for Probit Models

Bayesian procedures can be applied to probit models. In fact, the methods are even faster for probit models than for mixed logits. The procedure is described by Albert and Chib (1993), McCulloch and Rossi (1994), Allenby and Rossi (1999), and McCulloch and Rossi (2000). The method differs in a critical way from the procedure for mixed logits. In particular, for a probit model, the probability of each person's choices conditional on the coefficients of the variables, which is the analog to $L(y_n \mid \beta_n)$ for logit, is not a closed form. Procedures that utilize this probability, as in the first layer of Gibbs sampling for mixed logit, cannot be readily applied to probit. Instead, Gibbs sampling for probits is accomplished by considering the utilities of the alternatives, U_{njt}, to be parameters themselves. The conditional posterior for each U_{njt} is truncated normal, which is easy to draw from. The layers for the Gibbs sampling are as follows:

1. Draw b conditional on W and β_n $\forall n$.
2. Draw W conditional on b and β_n $\forall n$. These two layers are the same as for mixed logit.
3. For each n, draw β_n conditional on U_{njt} $\forall j, t$. These draws are obtained by recognizing that, given the value of utility, the function $U_{njt} = \beta_n x_{njt} + \varepsilon_{njt}$ is a regression of x_{njt} on U_{njt}. Bayesian posteriors for regression coefficients and normally distributed errors have been derived (similar to our results A and B) and are easy to draw from.
4. For each n, i, t, draw U_{nit} conditional on β_n and the value of U_{njt} for each $j \neq i$. As stated earlier, the conditional posterior for each U_{nit} is a univariate truncated normal, which is easy to draw from with the procedure given in Section 9.2.4.

Details are provided in the cited articles.

Bolduc *et al.* (1997) compared the Bayesian method with MSL and found the Bayesian procedure to require about half as much computer time as MSL with random draws. If Halton draws had been used, it seems that MSL would have been faster for the same level of accuracy, since fewer than half as many draws would be needed. The Bayesian procedure for probit relies on all random terms being normally distributed. However, the concept of treating the utilities as parameters can be generalized for other distributions, giving a Bayesian procedure for mixed probits.

Bayesian procedures can be developed in some form or another for essentially any behavioral model. In many cases, they provide large computational advantages over classical procedures. Examples include the dynamic discrete choice models of Imai *et al.* (2001), the joint models of the timing and quantity of purchases due to Boatwright *et al.* (2001), and Brownstone's (2001) mixtures of distinct discrete choice models. The power of these procedures, and especially the potential for cross-fertilization with classical methods, create a bright outlook for the field.

Bibliography

Adamowicz, W. (1994), 'Habit formation and variety seeking in a discrete choice model of recreation demand', *Journal of Agricultural and Resource Economics* **19**, 19–31.

Ainslie, A., R. Andrews, and I. Currim (2001), 'An empirical comparison of logit choice models with discrete vs. continuous representation of heterogeneity', Working Paper, Department of Business Administration, University of Delaware.

Albert, J. and S. Chib (1993), 'Bayesian analysis of binary and polychotomous response data', *Journal of the American Statistical Association* **88**, 669–679.

Allenby, G. (1997), 'An introduction to hierarchical Bayesian modeling', Tutorial Notes, Advanced Research Techniques Forum, American Marketing Association.

Allenby, G. and P. Lenk (1994), 'Modeling household purchase behavior with logistic normal regression', *Journal of the American Statistical Association* **89**, 1218–1231.

Allenby, G. and P. Rossi (1999), 'Marketing models of consumer heterogeneity', *Journal of Econometrics* **89**, 57–78.

Amemiya, T. (1978), 'On two-step estimation of multivariate logit models', *Journal of Econometrics* **8**, 13–21.

Arora, N., G. Allenby, and J. Ginter (1998), 'A hierachical Bayes model of primary and secondary demand', *Marketing Science* **17**, 29–44.

Beggs, S., S. Cardell, and J. Hausman (1981), 'Assessing the potential demand for electric cars', *Journal of Econometrics* **16**, 1–19.

Bellman, R. (1957), *Dynamic Programming*, Princeton University Press, Princeton, NJ.

Ben-Akiva, M. (1973), 'The structure of travel demand models', PhD Thesis, MIT.

Ben-Akiva, M. and M. Bierlaire (1999), 'Discrete choice methods and their applications in short term travel decisions', in R. Hall, ed., *The Handbook of Transportation Science*, Kluwer, Dordrecht, The Netherlands, pp. 5–33.

Ben-Akiva, M. and D. Bolduc (1996), 'Multinomial probit with a logit kernel and a general parametric specification of the covariance structure', Working Paper, Department of Civil Engineering, MIT.

Ben-Akiva, M. and B. Francois (1983), 'Mu-homogenous generalized extreme value model', Working Paper, Department of Civil Engineering, MIT.

Ben-Akiva, M. and S. Lerman (1985), *Discrete Choice Analysis: Theory and Application to Travel Demand*, MIT Press, Cambridge, MA.

Ben-Akiva, M. and T. Morikawa (1990), 'Estimation of switching models from revealed preferences and stated intentions', *Transportation Research A* **24**, 485–495.

Ben-Akiva, M., D. Bolduc, and M. Bradley (1993), 'Estimation of travel model choice models with randomly distributed values of time', *Transportation Research Record* **1413**, 88–97.

Ben-Akiva, M., D. Bolduc, and J. Walker (2001), 'Specification, estimation and identification of the logit kernel (or continuous mixed logit) model', Working Paper, Department of Civil Engineering, MIT.

Berkovec, J. and S. Stern (1991), 'Job exit behavior of older men', *Econometrica* **59**, 189–210.

Berndt, E., B. Hall, R. Hall, and J. Hausman (1974), 'Estimation and inference in nonlinear structural models', *Annals of Economic and Social Measurement* **3/4**, 653–665.

Bernstein, S. (1917), *Calcul des probabilités*.

Berry, S. (1994), 'Estimating discrete choice models of product differentiation', *RAND Journal of Economics* **25**, 242–262.

Berry, S., J. Levinsohn, and A. Pakes (1995), 'Automobile prices in market equilibrium', *Econometrica* **63**, 841–889.

Bhat, C. (1995), 'A heteroscedastic extreme value model of intercity mode choice', *Transportation Research B* **29**, 471–483.

Bhat, C. (1997), 'Covariance heterogeneity in nested logit models: Econometric structure and application to intercity travel', *Transportation Research B* **31**, 11–21.

Bhat, C. (1998a), 'Accommodating variations in responsiveness to level-of-service variables in travel mode choice models', *Transportation Research A* **32**, 455–507.

Bhat, C. (1998b), 'An analysis of travel mode and departure time choice for urban shopping trips', *Transportation Research B* **32**, 361–371.

Bhat, C. (1999), 'An analysis of evening commute stop-making behavior using repeated choice observation from a multi-day survey', *Transportation Research B* **33**, 495–510.

Bhat, C. (2000), 'Incorporating observed and unobserved heterogeneity in urban work mode choice modeling', *Transportation Science* **34**, 228–238.

Bhat, C. (2001), 'Quasi-random maximum simulated likelihood estimation of the mixed multinomial logit model', *Transportation Research B* **35**, 677–693.

Bhat, C. (forthcoming), 'Simulation estimation of mixed discrete choice models using randomized and scrambled Halton sequences', *Transportation Research*.

Bhat, C. and S. Castelar (2002), 'A unified mixed logit framework for modeling revealed and stated preferences: Formulation and application to congestion pricing analysis in the San Francisco Bay area', *Transportation Research* **36**, 577–669.

Bickel, P. and K. Doksum (2000), *Mathematical Statistics: Basic Ideas and Selected Topics*, Vol. 1, Prentice Hall, Upper Saddle River, NJ.

Bierlaire, M. (1998), Discrete choice models, in M. Labbe, G. Laporte, K. Tanczos, and P. Toint, eds., *Operations Research and Decision Aid Methodologies in Traffic and Transportation Management*, Springer-Verlag, Heidelberg, Germany, pp. 203–227.

Boatwright, P., S. Borle, and J. Kadane (2001), 'A model of the joint distribution of purchase quantity and timing', Conference Presentation, Bayesian Applications and Methods in Marketing Conference, Ohio State University, and Working Paper, Graduate School of Industrial Administration, Carnegie Mellon University.

Bolduc, D. (1992), 'Generalized autoregressive errors: The multinomial probit model', *Transportation Research B* **26**, 155–170.

Bolduc, D. (1993), 'Maximum simulated likelihood estimation of MNP models using the GHK probability simulation with analytic derivatives', Working Paper, Département d'Economique, Université Laval, Quebec.

Bolduc, D. (1999), 'A practical technique to estimate multinomial probit models in transportation', *Transportation Research B* **33**, 63–79.

Bolduc, D., B. Fortin, and M. Fournier (1996), 'The impact of incentive policies on the practice location of doctors: A multinomial probit analysis', *Journal of Labor Economics* **14**, 703–732.

Bolduc, D., B. Fortin, and S. Gordon (1997), 'Multinomial probit estimation of spatially interdependent choices: An empirical comparison of two new techniques', *International Regional Science Review* **20**, 77–101.

Borsch-Supan, A. and V. Hajivassiliou (1993), 'Smooth unbiased multivariate probability simulation for maximum likelihood estimation of limited dependent variable models', *Journal of Econometrics* **58**, 347–368.

Borsch-Supan, A., V. Hajivassiliou, L. Kotlikoff, and J. Morris (1991), 'Health, children, and elderly living arrangements: A multiperiod multinomial probit model with unobserved heterogeneity and autocorrelated errors', in D. Wise, ed., *Topics in the Economics of Aging*, University of Chicago Press, Chicago.

Boyd, J. and J. Mellman (1980), 'The effect of fuel economy standards on the U.S. automotive market: A hedonic demand analysis', *Transportation Research A* **14**, 367–378.

Braatan, E. and G. Weller (1979), 'An improved low-discrepancy sequence for multi-dimensional quasi-Monte Carlo integration', *Journal of Computational Physics* **33**, 249–258.

Bradley, M. and A. Daly (1994), 'Use of the logit scaling approach to test for rank-order and fatigue effects in stated preference data', *Transportation* **21**, 167–184.

Bradlow, E. and P. Fader (2001), 'A Bayesian lifetime model for the "hot 100" billboard songs', Working Paper, The Wharton School, University of Pennsylvania.

Brownstone, D. (2001), 'Discrete choice modeling for transportation', in D. Hensher, ed., *Travel Behavior Research: The Leading Edge*, Elsevier, Oxford, UK, pp. 97–124.

Brownstone, D. and K. Small (1989), 'Efficient estimation of nested logit model', *Journal of Business and Economic Statistics* **7**, 67–74.

Brownstone, D. and K. Train (1999), 'Forecasting new product penetration with flexible substitution patterns', *Journal of Econometrics* **89**, 109–129.

Brownstone, D., D. Bunch, and K. Train (2000), 'Joint mixed logit models of stated and revealed preferences for alternative-fuel vehicles', *Transportation Research B* **34**, 315–338.

Bunch, D. (1991), 'Estimability in the multinomial probit model', *Transportation Research B* **25**, 1–12.

Bunch, D. and R. Kitamura (1989), 'Multinomial probit estimation revisited: Testing new algorithms and evaluation of alternative model specification of household car ownership', Transportation Research Group Report UCD-TRG-RR-4, University of California, Davis.

Butler, J. and R. Moffitt (1982), 'A computationally efficient quadrature procedure for the one factor multinomial probit model', *Econometrica* **50**, 761–764.

Cai, Y., I. Deilami, and K. Train (1998), 'Customer retention in a competitive power market: Analysis of a "double-bounded plus follow-ups" questionnaire', *The Energy Journal* **19**, 191–215.

Cameron, T. (1988), 'A new paradigm for valuing non-market goods using referendum data: Maximum likelihood estimation by censored logistic regression', *Journal of Environmental Economics and Management* **15**, 355–379.

Cameron, T. and M. James (1987), 'Efficient estimation methods for closed-ended contingent valuation survey data', *Review of Economics and Statistics* **69**, 269–276.

Cameron, T. and J. Quiggin (1994), 'Estimation using contingent valuation data from a "dichotomous choice with follow-up" questionnaire', *Journal of Environmental Economics and Management* **27**, 218–234.

Cardell, S. and F. Dunbar (1980), 'Measuring the societal impacts of automobile downsizing', *Tranportation Research A* **14**, 423–434.

Carneiro, P., J. Heckman, and E. Vytlacil (2001), 'Estimating the return to education when it varies among individuals', Working Paper, Department of Economics, University of Chicago.

Casella, G. and E. George (1992), 'Explaining the Gibbs sampler', *American Statistician* **46**, 167–174.

Chapman, R. and R. Staelin (1982), 'Exploiting rank ordered choice set data within the stochastic utility model', *Journal of Marketing Research* **14**, 288–301.

Chesher, A. and J. Santos-Silva (2002), 'Taste variation in discrete choice models', *Review of Economic Studies* **69**, 62–78.

Chiang, J., S. Chib, and C. Narasimhan (1999), 'Markov chain Monte Carlo and models of consideration set and parameter heterogeneity', *Journal of Econometrics* **89**, 223–248.

Chib, S. and E. Greenberg (1995), 'Understanding the Metropolis–Hastings algorithm', *American Statistician* **49**, 327–335.

Chib, S. and E. Greenberg (1996), 'Markov chain Monte Carlo simulation methods in econometrics', *Econometric Theory* **12**, 409–431.

Chib, S. and E. Greenberg (1998), 'Analysis of multivariate probit models', *Biometrika* **85**, 347–361.

Chintagunta, P., D. Jain, and N. Vilcassim (1991), 'Investigating heterogeneity in brand preference in logit models for panel data', *Journal of Marketing Research* **28**, 417–428.

Chipman, J. (1960), 'The foundations of utility', *Econometrica* **28**, 193–224.

Chu, C. (1981), 'Structural issues and sources of bias in residential location and travel choice models', PhD Thesis, Northwestern University.

Chu, C. (1989), 'A paired combinational logit model for travel demand analysis', *Proceedings of Fifth World Conference on Transportation Research* **4**, 295–309.

Clark, C. (1961), 'The greatest of a finite set of random variables', *Operations Research* **9**, 145–162.

Cosslett, S. (1981), 'Efficient estimation of discrete choice models', in C. Manski and D. McFadden, eds., *Structural Analysis of Discrete Data with Econometric Applications*, MIT Press, Cambridge, MA.

Cowles, M. and B. Carlin (1996), 'Markov chain Monte Carlo convergence diagnostics: A comparative review', *Journal of the American Statistical Association* **91**, 883–904.

Daganzo, C. (1979), *Multinomial Probit: The Theory and Its Application to Demand Forecasting*, Academic Press, New York.

Daganzo, C., F. Bouthelier, and Y. Sheffi (1977), 'Multinomial probit and qualitative choice: A computationally efficient algorithm', *Transportation Science* **11**, 338–358.

Dagsvik, J. (1994), 'Discrete and continuous choice max-stable processes and independence from irrelevant alternatives', *Econometrica* **62**, 1179–1205.

Daly, A. (1987), 'Estimating "tree" logit models', *Transportation Research B* **21**, 251–267.

Daly, A. and S. Zachary (1978), Improved multiple choice models, in D. Hensher and M. Dalvi, eds., *Determinants of Travel Choice*, Saxon House, Sussex.

Debreu, G. (1960), 'Review of R.D. Luce individual choice behavior', *American Economic Review* **50**, 186–188.

DeSarbo, W., V. Ramaswamy, and S. Cohen (1995), 'Market segmentation with choice-based conjoint analysis', *Marketing Letters* **6**, 137–147.

Desvousges, W., S. Waters, and K. Train (1996), 'Potential economic losses associated with recreational services in the Upper Clark Fork River basin', Report, Triangle Economic Research, Durham, NC.

Dubin, J. and D. McFadden (1984), 'An econometric analysis of residential electric appliance holdings and consumption', *Econometrica* **52**, 345–362.

Eckstein, Z. and K. Wolpin (1989), 'The specification and estimation of dynamic stochastic discrete choice models: A survey', *Journal of Human Resources* **24**, 562–598.

Elrod, T. and M. Keane (1995), 'A factor analytic probit model for representing the market structure in panel data', *Journal of Marketing Research* **32**, 1–16.

Erdem, T. (1996), 'A dynamic analysis of market structure based on panel data', *Marketing Science* **15**, 359–378.

Forinash, C. and F. Koppelman (1993), 'Application and interpretation of nested logit models of intercity mode choice', *Transportation Research Record* **1413**, 98–106.

Gelman, A. (1992), 'Iterative and non-iterative simulation algorithms', *Computing Science and Statistics (Interface Proceedings)* **24**, 433–438.

Gelman, A. and D. Rubin (1992), 'Inference from iterative simulation using multiple sequences', *Statistical Sciences* **7**, 457–511.

Gelman, A., J. Carlin, H. Stern, and D. Rubin (1995), *Bayesian Data Analysis*, Chapman and Hall, Suffolk.

Geman, S. and D. Geman (1984), 'Stochastic relaxation Gibbs distributions and the Bayesian restoration of images', *IEEE Transactions on Pattern Analysis and Machine Intelligence* **6**, 721–741.

Geweke, J. (1988), 'Antithetic acceleration of Monte Carlo integration in Bayesian inference', *Journal of Econometrics* **38**, 73–89.

Geweke, J. (1989), 'Bayesian inference in econometric models using Monte Carlo integration', *Econometrica* **57**, 1317–1339.

Geweke, J. (1991), 'Efficient simulation from the multivariate normal and Student-t distributions subject to linear constraints', in E. M. Keramidas, ed., *Computer Science and Statistics: Proceedings of the Twenty-Third Symposium on the Interface*, pp. 571–578. Fairfax: Interface Foundation of North America, Inc.

Geweke, J. (1992), 'Evaluating the accuracy of sampling-based approaches to the calculation of posterior moments', in J. Bernardo, J. Berger, A. Dawid, and F. Smith, eds., *Bayesian Statistics*, Oxford University Press, New York, pp. 169–193.

Geweke, J. (1996), 'Monte Carlo simulation and numerical integration', in D. Kendrick and J. Rust, eds., *Handbook of Computational Economics*, Elsevier Science, Amsterdam, pp. 731–800.

Geweke, J. (1997), 'Posterior simulators in econometrics', in D. Kreps and K. Wallis, eds., *Advance Economics and Econometric Theory and Applications*, Cambridge University Press, New York.

Geweke, J., M. Keane, and D. Runkle (1994), 'Alternative computational approaches to inference in the multinomial probit model', *Review of Economics and Statistics* **76**, 609–632.

Goett, A. (1998), 'Estimating Customer Preferences for New Pricing Products', Electric Power Research Institute Report TR-111483, Palo Alto.

Gourieroux, C. and A. Monfort (1993), 'Simulation-based inference: A survey with special reference to panel data models', *Journal of Econometrics* **59**, 5–33.

Greene, W. (2000), *Econometric Analysis*, 4th edn, Prentice Hall, Upper Saddle River, NJ.

Greene, W. (2001), 'Fixed and random effects in nonlinear models', Working Paper, Stern School of Business, New York University.

Griffiths, W. (1972), 'Estimation of actual response coefficients in the Hildreth–Horck random coefficient model', *Journal of the American Statistical Association* **67**, 663–635.

Guilkey, D. and J. Murphy (1993), 'Estimation and testing in the random effects probit model', *Journal of Econometrics* **59**, 301–317.

Haaijer, M., M. Wedel, M. Vriens, and T. Wansbeek (1998), 'Utility covariances and context effects in conjoint MNP models', *Marketing Science* **17**, 236–252.

Hajivassiliou, V. and D. McFadden (1998), 'The method of simulated scores for the estimation of LDV models', *Econometrica* **66**, 863–896.

Hajivassiliou, V. and P. Ruud (1994), 'Classical estimation methods for LDV models using simulation', in R. Engle and D. McFadden, eds., *Handbook of Econometrics*, North-Holland, Amsterdam, pp. 2383–2441.

Hajivassiliou, V., D. McFadden, and P. Ruud (1996), 'Simulation of multivariate normal rectangle probabilities and their derivatives: Theoretical and computational results', *Journal of Econometrics* **72**, 85–134.

Halton, J. (1960), 'On the efficiency of evaluating certain quasi-random sequences of points in evaluating multi-dimensional integrals', *Numerische Mathematik* **2**, 84–90.

Hamilton, J. (1996), 'Specification testing in Markov-switching time-series models', *Journal of Econometrics* **70**, 127–157.

Hamilton, J. and R. Susmel (1994), 'Autoregressive conditional heteroskedasticity and changes in regime', *Journal of Econometrics* **64**, 307–333.

Hammersley, J. and K. Morton (1956), 'A new Monte Carlo technique: Antithetic variates', *Proceedings of the Cambridge Philosophical Society* **52**, 449–474.

Hanemann, M., J. Loomis, and B. Kanninen (1991), 'Statistical efficiency of double-bounded dichotomous choice contingent valuation', *American Journal of Agricultural Economics* **73**, 1255–1263.

Hastings, W. (1970), 'Monte Carlo sampling methods using Markov chains and their applications', *Biometrika* **57**, 97–109.

Hausman, J., ed. (1993), *Contingent Valuation: A Critical Assessment*, North-Holland, New York.

Hausman, J. and D. McFadden (1984), 'Specification tests for the multinomial logit model', *Econometrica* **52**, 1219–1240.

Hausman, J. and P. Ruud (1987), 'Specifying and testing econometric models for rank-ordered data', *Journal of Econometrics* **34**, 83–103.

Hausman, J. and D. Wise (1978), 'A conditional probit model for qualitative choice: Discrete decisions recognizing interdependence and heterogeneous preferences', *Econometrica* **48**, 403–429.

Heckman, J. (1978), 'Dummy endogenous variables in a simultaneous equation system', *Econometrica* **46**, 931–959.

Heckman, J. (1979), 'Sample selection bias as a specification error', *Econometrica* **47**, 153–162.

Heckman, J. (1981a), 'The incidental parameters problem and the problem of initial condition in estimating a discrete time–discrete data stochastic process', in C. Manski and D. McFadden, eds., *Structural Analysis of Discrete Data with Econometric Applications*, MIT Press, Cambridge, MA, pp. 179–185.

Heckman, J. (1981b), 'Statistical models for the analysis of discrete panel data', in C. Manski and D. McFadden, eds., *Structural Analysis of Discrete Data with Econometric Applications*, MIT Press, Cambridge, MA, pp. 114–178.

Heckman, J. and B. Singer (1986), 'Econometric analysis of longitudinal data', in Z. Griliches and M. Intriligator, eds., *Handbook of Econometrics*, North-Holland, Amsterdam, pp. 1689–1763.

Heiss, F. (2002), 'Structural choice analysis with nested logit models', Working Paper, University of Mannheim.

Hensher, D. (2001), 'The valuation of commuter travel time savings for car drivers in New Zealand: Evaluating alternative model specifications', *Transportation* **28**, 101–118.

Hensher, D. and M. Bradley (1993), 'Using stated response data to enrich revealed preference discrete choice models', *Marketing Letters* **4**, 39–152.

Hensher, D. and W. Greene (2001), 'The mixed logit model: The state of practice and warnings for the unwary', Working Paper, School of Business, The University of Sydney.

Hensher, D. and W. Greene (2002), 'Specification and estimation of nested logit model', *Transportation Research B*, **36**, 1–17.

Hensher, D., J. Louviere, and J. Swait (1999), 'Combining sources of preference data', *Journal of Econometrics* **89**, 197–221.

Herriges, J. and C. Kling (1996), 'Testing the consistency of nested logit models with utility maximization', *Economic Letters* **50**, 33–39.

Horowitz, J. (1991), 'Reconsidering the multinomial probit model', *Transportation Research B* **25**, 433–438.

Horowitz, J., J. Sparmann, and C. Daganzo (1982), 'An investigation of the accuracy of the Clark approximation for the multinomial probit model', *Transportation Science* **16**, 382–401.

Hotz, V. and R. Miller (1993), 'Conditional choice probabilities and the estimation of dynamic models', *Review of Economic Studies* **60**, 497–529.

Hotz, V., R. Miller, S. Sanders, and J. Smith (1993), 'A simulation estimator for dynamic models of discrete choice', *Review of Economic Studies* **61**, 265–289.

Huber, J. and K. Train (2001), 'On the similarity of classical and Bayesian estimates of individual mean partworths', *Marketing Letters* **12**, 259–269.

Imai, S., N. Jain, and A. Ching (2001), 'Bayesian estimation of dynamics discrete choice models', paper presented at Bayesian Applications and Methods in Marketing Conference, Ohio State University; and Working Paper, Department of Economics, Pennsylvania State University.

Joe, S. and I. Sloan (1993), 'Implementation of a lattice method for numerical multiple integration', *ACM Transactions in Mathematical Software* **19**, 523–545.

Johannesson, M. and D. Lundin (2000), 'The impact of physical preferences and patient habits on the diffusion of new drugs', Working Paper, Department of Economics, Stockholm School of Economics.

Johnson, N., S. Kotz, and N. Balakrishnan (1994), *Continuous Multivariate Distributions*, 2nd edn, John Wiley and Sons, New York.

Judge, G., R. Hill, W. Griffiths, and T. Lee (1985), *The Theory and Practice of Econometrics*, 2nd edn, John Wiley and Sons, New York.

Judge, G., R. Hill, W. Griffiths, H. Lutkepohl, and T. Lee (1988), *Introduction to the Theory and Practice Econometrics*, 2nd edn, John Wiley and Sons, New York.

Kamakura, W. A. and G. Russell (1989), 'A probabilistic choice model for market segmentation and elasticity structure', *Journal of Marketing Research* **26**, 379–390.

Karlstrom, A. (2000), 'Non-linear value functions in random utility econometrics', Conference Presentation, 9th IATBR Travel Behavior Conference, Australia; and Working Paper, Infrastructure and Planning, Royal Institute of Technology, Stockholm, Sweden.

Karlstrom, A. (2001), 'Developing generalized extreme value models using the Piekands representation theorem', Working Paper, Infrastructure and Planning, Royal Institute of Technology, Stockholm, Sweden.

Kass, R., B. Carlin, A. Gelman, and R. Neal (1998), 'Markov chain Monte Carlo in practice: A roundtable discussion', *American Statistician* **52**, 93–100.

Keane, M. (1990), 'Four essays in empirical macro and labor economics', PhD Thesis, Brown University.

Keane, M. (1994), 'A computationally practical simulation estimator for panel data', *Econometrica* **62**, 95–116.

Keane, M. and K. Wolpin (1994), 'The solutions and estimation of discrete choice dynamic programming models by simulation and interpretation: Monte Carlo evidence', *Review of Economics and Statistics* **76**, 648–672.

Kling, C. and J. Herriges (1995), 'An empirical investigation of the consistency of nested logit models with utility maximization', *American Journal of Agricultural Economics* **77**, 875–884.

Koppelman, F. and C. Wen (1998), 'Alternative nested logit models: Structure, properties and estimation', *Transportation Research B* **32**, 289–298.

Koppelman, F. and C. Wen (2000), 'The paired combination logit model: Properties, estimation and application', *Transportation Research B* **34**, 75–89.

Laplace, P. (1820), *Théorie Analytique des Probabilités*, 3rd ed., Paris.

Le Cam, L. and G. Yang (1990), *Asymptotics in Statistics*, Springer-Verlag, New York.

Lee, B. (1999), 'Calling patterns and usage of residential toll service under self-selecting tariffs', *Journal of Regulatory Economics* **16**, 45–82.

Lee, L. (1992), 'On the efficiency of methods of simulated moments and simulated likelihood estimation of discrete choice models', *Econometric Theory* **8**, 518–552.

Lee, L. (1995), 'Asymptotic bias in simulated maximum likelihood estimation of discrete choice models', *Econometric Theory* **11**, 437–483.

Lehmann, E. and G. Casella (1998), *Theory of Point Estimation*, 2nd edn, Springer, New York.

Levy, A. (2001), 'A simple consistent non-parametric estimator of the regression function in truncated samples', Working Paper, Department of Economics, North Carolina State University.

Lewbel, A. and O. Linton (2002), 'Nonparametric censored and truncated regression', *Econometrica* **70**, 765–779.

Liu, Y. and H. Mahmassani (2000), 'Global maximum likelihood estimation procedures for multinomial probit (MND) model parameters', *Transportation Research B* **34**, 419–444.

Louviere, J., D. Hensher, and J. Swait (2000), *Stated Choice Methods: Analysis and Applications*, Cambridge University Press, New York.

Luce, D. (1959), *Individual Choice Behavior*, John Wiley and Sons, New York.

Luce, D. and P. Suppes (1965), 'Preferences, utility and subjective probability', in R. Luce, R. Bush, and E. Galanter, eds., *Handbook of Mathematical Psychology*, John Wiley and Sons, New York, pp. 249–410.

Manski, C. and S. Lerman (1977), 'The estimation of choice probabilities from choice based samples', *Econometrica* **45**, 1977–1988.

Manski, C. and S. Lerman (1981), 'On the use of simulated frequencies to approximate choice probabilities', in C. Manski and D. McFadden, eds., *Structural Analysis of Discrete Data with Econometric Applications*, MIT Press, Cambridge, MA, pp. 305–319.

Manski, C. and D. McFadden (1981), 'Alternative estimators and sample designs for discrete choice analysis', in C. Manski and D. McFadden, eds., *Structural Analysis of Discrete Data with Econometric Applications*, MIT Press, Cambridge, MA, pp. 2–50.

Marschak, J. (1960), 'Binary choice constraints on random utility indications', in K. Arrow, ed., *Stanford Symposium on Mathematical Methods in the Social Sciences*, Stanford University Press, Stanford, CA, pp. 312–329.

McCulloch, R. and P. Rossi (1994), 'An exact likelihood analysis of the multinomial probit model', *Journal of Econometrics* **64**, 207–240.

McCulloch, R. and P. Rossi (2000), 'Bayesian analysis of the multinomial probit model', in R. Mariano, T. Schuermann, and M. Weeks, eds., *Simulation-Based Inference in Econometrics*, Cambridge University Press, New York.

McFadden, D. (1974), 'Conditional logit analysis of qualitative choice behavior', in P. Zarembka, ed., *Frontiers in Econometrics*, Academic Press, New York, pp. 105–142.

McFadden, D. (1978), 'Modeling the choice of residential location', in A. Karlqvist, L. Lundqvist, F. Snickars, and J. Weibull, eds., *Spatial Interaction Theory and Planning Models*, North-Holland, Amsterdam, pp. 75–96.

McFadden, D. (1987), 'Regression-based specification tests for the multinomial logit model', *Journal of Econometrics* **34**, 63–82.

McFadden, D. (1989), 'A method of simulated moments for estimation of discrete response models without numerical integration', *Econometrica* **57**, 995–1026.

McFadden, D. (1996), 'Lectures on simulation-assisted statistical inference', Conference Presentation, EC-squared Conference, Florence, Italy; and Working Paper, Department of Economics, University of California, Berkeley.

McFadden, D. (1999), 'Computing willingness-to-pay in random utility models', in J. Moore, R. Riezman, and J. Melvin, eds., *Trade, Theory and Econometrics: Essays in Honour of John S. Chipman*, Routledge, London, pp. 253–274.

McFadden, D. (2001), 'Economic choices', *American Economic Review* **91**, 351–378.

McFadden, D. and K. Train (1996), 'Consumers' evaluation of new products: Learning from self and others', *Journal of Political Economy* **104**, 683–703.

McFadden, D. and K. Train (2000), 'Mixed MNL models of discrete response', *Journal of Applied Econometrics* **15**, 447–470.

McFadden, D., A. Talvitie, S. Cosslett, I. Hasan, M. Johnson, F. Reid, and K. Train (1977), 'Demand model estimation and validation', Final Report, Volume V, Urban Travel Demand Forecasting Project, Institute of Transportation Studies, University of California, Berkeley.

McFadden, D., K. Train, and W. Tye (1978), 'An application of diagnostic tests for the independence from irrelevant alternatives property of the multinomial logit model', *Transportation Research Record* **637**, 39–46.

McGrath, E. (1970), *Fundamentals of Operations Research*, West Coast University Press, San Francisco.

Mehndiratta, S. (1996), 'Time-of-day effects in inter-city business travel', PhD Thesis, University of California, Berkeley.

Metropolis, N., A. Rosenbluth, M. Rosenbluth, A. Teller, and E. Teller (1953), 'Equations of state calculations by fast computing machines', *Journal of Chemical Physics* **21**, 1087–1092.

Morokoff, W. and R. Caflisch (1995), 'Quasi-Monte Carlo integration', *Journal of Computational Physics* **122**, 218–230.

Munizaga, M. and R. Alvarez-Daziano (2001), 'Mixed logit versus nested logit and probit', Working Paper, Departmento de Ingeniera Civil, Universidad de Chile.

Nevo, A. (2001), 'Measuring market power in the ready-to-eat cereal industry', *Econometrica* **69**, 307–342.

Niederreiter, H. (1978), 'Quasi-Monte Carlo methods and pseudo-random numbers', *Bulletin of the American Mathematical Society* **84**, 957–1041.

Niederreiter, H. (1988), 'Low-discrepancy and low dispersion sequences', *Journal of Number Theory* **30**, 51–70.

O'Donoghue, T. and M. Rabin (1999), 'Doing it now or later', *American Economic Review* **89**, 103–124.

Ortuzar, J. (1983), 'Nested logit models for mixed-mode travel in urban corridors', *Transportation Research A* **17**, 283–299.

Pakes, A. (1986), 'Patents as options: Some estimates of the value of holding European patent stocks', *Econometrica* **54**, 755–785.

Pakes, A. and D. Pollard (1989), 'Simulation and asymptotics of optimization estimators', *Econometrica* **57**, 1027–1057.

Papatla, P. and L. Krishnamurthi (1992), 'A probit model of choice dynamics', *Marketing Science* **11**, 189–206.

Petrin, A. and K. Train (2002), 'Omitted product attributes in discrete choice models', Working Paper, Department of Economics, University of California, Berkeley.

Rao, B. (1987), *Asymptotic Theory of Statistical Inference*, John Wiley and Sons, New York.

Recker, W. (1995), 'Discrete choice with an oddball alternative', *Transportation Research B* **29**, 207–211.

Research Triangle Institute (1997), 'Predicting retail customer choices among electricity pricing alternatives', Electric Power Research Institute Report, Palo Alto.

Revelt, D. (1999), 'Three discrete choice random coefficients papers and one police crime study', PhD Thesis, University of California, Berkeley.

Revelt, D. and K. Train (1998), 'Mixed logit with repeated choices', *Review of Economics and Statistics* **80**, 647–657.

Revelt, D. and K. Train (2000), 'Specific taste parameters and mixed logit', Working Paper No. E00-274, Department of Economics, University of California, Berkeley.

Rossi, P., R. McCulloch, and G. Allenby (1996), 'The value of household information in target marketing', *Marketing Science* **15**, 321–340.

Rust, J. (1987), 'Optimal replacement of GMC bus engines: An empirical model of Harold Zurchner', *Econometrica* **55**, 993–1033.

Rust, J. (1994), 'Estimation of dynamic structural models, problems and prospects: Discrete decision processes', in C. Sims, ed., *Advances in Econometrics: Sixth World Congress*, Vol. II, Cambridge University Press, New York, pp. 5–33.

Rust, J. (1997), 'Using randomization to break the curse of dimensionality', *Econometrica* **65**, 487–516.

Ruud, P. (1996), 'Simulation of the multinomial probit model: An analysis of covariance matrix estimation', Working Paper, Department of Economics, University of California, Berkeley.

Ruud, P. (2000), *An Introduction to Classical Econometric Theory*, Oxford University Press, New York.

Sándor, Z. and P. András (2001), 'Alternative sampling methods for estimating multivariate normal probabilities', Working Paper, Department of Economics, University of Groningen, The Netherlands.

Sándor, Z. and K. Train (2002), 'Quasi-random simulation of discrete choice models', Working Paper, Department of Economics, University of California, Berkeley.

SawtoothSoftware (1999), 'The CBC/HB module for hierarchical Bayes', at www.sawtoothsoftware.com.

Schechter, L. (2001), 'The apple and your eye: Visual and taste rankordered probit analysis', Working Paper, Department of Agricultural and Resource Economics, University of California, Berkeley.

Siikamaki, J. (2001), 'Discrete choice experiments valuing biodiversity conservation in Finland', PhD Thesis, University of California, Davis.

Siikamaki, J. and D. Layton (2001), 'Pooled models for contingent valuation and contingent ranking data: Valuing benefits from biodiversity conservation', Working Paper, Department of Agricultural and Resource Economics, University of California, Davis.

Sloan, I. and H. Wozniakowski (1998), 'When are quasi-Monte Carlo algorithms efficient for high dimensional integrals?', *Journal of Complexity* **14**, 1–33.

Small, K. (1987), 'A discrete choice model for ordered alternatives', *Econometrica* **55**, 409–424.

Small, K. (1994), 'Approximate generalized extreme value models of discrete choice', *Journal of Econometrics* **62**, 351–382.

Small, K. and H. Rosen (1981), 'Applied welfare economics of discrete choice models', *Econometrica* **49**, 105–130.

Spanier, J. and E. Maize (1991), 'Quasi-random methods for estimating integrals using relatively small samples', *SIAM Review* **36**, 18–44.

Srinivasan, K. and H. Mahmassani (2000), 'Dynamic kernel logit model for the analysis of longtitude discrete choice data: Properties and computational assessment', Working Paper, Department of Civil Engineering, University of Texas, Austin.

Steckel, J. and W. Vanhonacker (1988), 'A heterogeneous conditional logit model of choice', *Journal of Business and Economic Statistics* **6**, 391–398.

Swait, J. and J. Louviere (1993), 'The role of the scale parameter in the estimation and use of multinomial logit models', *Journal of Marketing Research* **30**, 305–314.

Talvitie, A. (1976), 'Disaggregate travel demand models with disaggregate data, not aggregate data, and why', Working Paper No. 7615, Urban Travel Demand Forecasting Project, Institute of Transportation Studies, University of California, Berkeley.

Theil, H. (1971), *Principles of Econometrics*, John Wiley and Sons, New York.

Thurstone, L. (1927), 'A law of comparative judgement', *Psychological Review* **34**, 273–286.

Train, K. (1978), 'A validation test of a diaggregate mode choice model', *Transportation Research* **12**, 167–174.

Train, K. (1986), *Qualitative Choice Analysis*, MIT Press, Cambridge, MA.

Train, K. (1995), 'Simulation methods for probit and related models based on convenient error partitioning', Working Paper No. 95-237, Department of Economics, University of California, Berkeley.

Train, K. (1998), 'Recreation demand models with taste variation', *Land Economics* **74**, 230–239.

Train, K. (1999), 'Mixed logit models for recreation demand', in J. Herriges and C. Kling, eds., *Valuing Recreation and the Environment*, Edward Elgar, Northampton, MA.

Train, K. (2000), 'Halton sequences for mixed logit', Working Paper No. E00-278, Department of Economics, University of California, Berkeley.

Train, K. (2001), 'A comparison of hierarchical Bayes and maximum simulated likelihood for mixed logit', Working Paper, Department of Economics, University of California, Berkeley.

Train, K. and D. McFadden (1978), 'The goods–leisure tradeoff and disaggregate work trip mode choice models', *Transportation Research* **12**, 349–353.

Train, K., D. McFadden, and M. Ben-Akiva (1987a), 'The demand for local telephone service: A fully discrete model of residential calling patterns and service choice', *Rand Journal of Economics* **18**, 109–123.

Train, K., D. McFadden, and A. Goett (1987b), 'Consumer attitudes and voluntary rate schedules for public utilities', *Review of Economics and Statistics* **LXIX**, 383–391.

Train, K., M. Ben-Akiva, and T. Atherton (1989), 'Consumption patterns and self-selecting tariffs', *Review of Economics and Statistics* **71**, 62–73.

Tuffin, B. (1996), 'On the use of low-discrepancy sequences in Monte Carlo methods', *Monte Carlo Methods and Applications* **2**, 295–320.

Tversky, A. (1972), 'Elimination by aspects: A theory of choice', *Psychological Review* **79**, 281–299.

Vijverberg, W. (1997), 'Monte Carlo evaluation of multivariate normal probabilities', *Journal of Econometrics* **76**, 281–307.

von Mises, R. (1931), *Wahrscheinlichkeitsrechnung*, Springer-Verlag, Berlin.

Vovsha, P. (1997), 'The cross-nested logit model: Application to mode choice in the Tel Aviv metropolitan area', Conference Presentation, 76th Transportation Research Board Meetings, Washington, DC.

Wang, X., E. Bradlow, and H. Wainer (2001), 'A general Bayesian model for testlets: Theory and application', Working Paper, Department of Statistics, University of North Carolina, Chapel Hill.

Wedel, M. and W. Kamakura (2000), *Market Segmentation: Conceptual and Methodological Foundations*, 2nd edn, Kluwer Academic Publishers, Boston.

Wen, C.-H. and F. Koppelman (2001), 'The generalized nested logit model', *Transportation Research B* **35**, 627–641.

Wen, D. and M. Levy (2001), 'An application of Bayes estimation under bounded asymmetric blinex loss: Direct mail decision problem', Conference Presentation, Bayesian Application and Methods in Marketing Conference, Ohio State University.

Williams, H. (1977), 'On the formation of travel demand models and economic evaluation measures of user benefits', *Environment and Planning A* **9**, 285–344.

Wolpin, K. (1984), 'An estimable dynamic stochastic model of fertility and child mortality', *Journal of Political Economy* **92**, 852–874.

Wolpin, K. (1987), 'Estimating a structural search model: The transition from school to work', *Econometrica* **55**, 801–818.

Yai, T., S. Iwakura, and S. Morichi (1997), 'Multinomial probit with structured covariance for route choice behavior', *Transporation Research B* **31**, 195–207.

Zavoina, R. and W. McKelvey (1975), 'A statistical model for the analysis of ordinal level dependent variables', *Journal of Mathematical Sociology* Summer, 103–120.

Zellner, A. (1971), *An Introduction to Bayesian Inference in Econometrics*, John Wiley and Sons, New York.

Index